From Tennessee to Oz

Look for the rainbows -
Michelle Russell

Books by Michelle Russell

The Deppe and Ganser Families (1790–1987)

Musical Memories: Songs the Gumm Family Sang

The Gumm Family Souvenir Song Book

Sabrina: The Autobiography of a Cat

Lily: Through the Eyes of a Child

From Tennessee to Oz, Part I

Look for the sequels –
Michelle Russell

From Tennessee to Oz

The Amazing Saga
of
Judy Garland's
Family History

Part II

By
Michelle Russell

Catsong Publishing
White Haven, Pennsylvania

Visit: http://www.catsongpublishing.com

First Printing 2011
ADVANCE COPY

Published by
Catsong Publishing
HC 1 Box 23Z-31
White Haven, PA 18661
570-443-8275

Russell, Michelle
From Tennessee to Oz, Part II
Includes bibliographical references, appendix and index
ISBN 978-0-9800642-3-0
Library of Congress Control Number: TBA

Cover design: Michelle Russell
Interior design: Marny K. Parkin

Printed in the United States of America

For Judy Garland's family and friends
who have contributed so generously to this work

Contents

Young Frank Gumm

Those Gumm Girls

Acknowledgements

RESEARCHING THIS BOOK HAS BROUGHT ME MANY NEW AND WONDERful friends who generously shared their memories and their photos. Unfortunately, with the passage of time, many of the people who knew Judy and her family passed away before I could complete this book. Posthumously, my deep gratitude to Wilma Hendriks Casper, who lived with and took care of Baby Gumm, and who became my very dear friend. Another wonderful friend was Dorothy Walsh Morrison, who took me with her-through her memories-to meet the Gumm family in a way that few people could do. Dorothy was a very lively ninety-something when I first "met" her over the phone. During the next years, we spent countless hours laughing over Ethel and the Gumm girls' antics. Another outstanding person was Glen Settle of Lancaster, California, a man who knew the family and had an exceptional memory. Although blind when I met him, he was able to give me accurate directions while riding in the car with me. He also generously shared his photos. Other generous persons who shared their early memories of the Gumms: Grace Pinkus, Dorothy Mumaw Darling, Dick and Bettie White, Bob Herbert, Walt Primmer, Ron Carter, Barbara Webb Ralphs, Bonnie Stone, June O'Clock, Eleanor Downing, Bernie Morris, Zella and Jonne McGugan. Sadly, I missed meeting Judy's best friend "Muggsie," who past away a shortly before I found the family. Her brother Will Lundy, and his son were of great help.

Another great debt is owed to the descendants of Nannie Gum Rion, beginning with Nancy Lee Dismukes, who invited me to her home and was the first member of the family to share her photos, Claire Webber, who came to my house in Murfreesboro and shared her archives and memories, Joy Rion Nelson, who searched tirelessly through her belongings for information on Mary Gumm, Wanda Rion Goodknight, who shared her photos, and Lee Covington who took time to talk with me. Bettie Gum Fox's family were also wonderful beginning with Aaron Todd, Henry Lee Fox (whom I enjoyed so much and who has since passed on), Leeann Harry, Bettie Nicholson, Mary Cole; and Larry Hannah, descendant of J.L. Baugh.

Many thanks to Ralph Puckett, as well, who has become a good friend and shared his historic letters and photos. Ralph took me to the old Gum/Fulks homeplace. And in Murfreesboro, thanks to Mrs. Patterson.

As for Frank Gumm's siblings descendants, I could not have done this without them. Many thanks for the kindness, generosity and friendship of Frank's brothers' grandsons: Bill Gibb who opened the family archives to me, James and Joyce Gumm who also shared their photos and time with me, and Richard Gumm. Geri Gumm, the wife of Judy's cousin, Richard, who invited me to her home and revealed the surprising information that Robert Gumm had another child, Mildred. Many thanks for the generosity of David Richardson, and Bettejane Kirschner. Thanks as well to Stephanie Johnson and Dennis Havens for their help and friendship.

Although I never expected to speak with the Gilmore family, research led me to them and I want to express thanks to all, including Bill and Joanie Gilmore, Jack Gilmore and the Ruth Gilmore's granddaughter for sharing their memories and the family reunion photo.

Addition thanks to the wonderful research institutions and the people who work there: the Tennessee State Library and Archives in Nashville, the Linebaugh Library in Murfreesboro, John Lodl of the Rutherford County Archives and Susan Daniel of the Rutherford County Historical Society, the librarians of Superior Public Library, Cloquet Public Library, and the Carlton Historical Society (One person actually went through the newspaper microfilm by hand, finding news items previously not known), and Leila Crowe of the Itasca County Historical Society. Special thanks to John Kelsch of the Judy Garland Birthplace for his help and support over the years. Additional thanks goes to Carrie G. Dorrance of the U.S.Forest Service for taking the time to look up the weather and snowfall history of Grand Rapids during the time the Gumms lived there!

In short, the very existence of this book is owed to the generosity of the descendents of the Baugh, Gumm, and Marable families, their friends and the historians of Murfreesboro; Grand Rapids, and Lancaster.

Since my first book was published, C.B. Arnette, the man who opened so many doors for me in Murfreesboro, passed away. C.B. often pushed me to finish quicker than I could, but continued to inspire and support me with his interest in this project. My deepest thanks to him, and to Curry Wolfe, without whom I would have half the book (or less) than I have. Thank you, Curry, for sharing this journey with me, and for making it fun and rewarding. I can never say thank you enough!

Finally, to my interior designer, Marny K. Parkin, many thanks for her patience and taking on the stupendous job of putting this material together and making it look beautiful.

Preface

As a child I was in awe of Judy Garland in her role as Dorothy in *The Wizard of Oz*, and equally fascinated by the woman my mother and I watched weekly on *The Judy Garland Show*. Later, the young Judy transfixed my view of what was possible when she sang to Clark Gable, and Judy and Mickey Rooney became my ideal friends. Ultimately, Judy inspired me to sing.

Despite the years of fascination, however, I really didn't want to write a book about Judy. That had been done already, many times. Nevertheless, I continued to be especially interested in her childhood and her father, two areas of her life which seemed to bear more research.

On my first trip to Grand Rapids, Minnesota to visit the Judy Garland Birthplace, I bridged the gap from legend to reality when I was introduced to a little lady, so bent by osteoarthritis, she could barely stand straight. Wilma Hendriks Casper had taken care of the child known as Baby Gumm, a real little girl who ran around, sang, giggled and got in trouble. Wilma and I became good friends, and as I prepared to create a living history program for the Judy Garland Festival in 1997, Wilma shared her memories with me. I guess you could say that was the beginning of this book.

In the ensuing years, my work to create a musical recording of the songs the Gumm family sang in vaudeville, took me further down the road toward this book as I met the people who had witnessed the Gumm family onstage. I asked them questions I thought had not been asked: *What did Frank and Ethel's voices sound like? What did they do on stage?*

Finally, as I attempted to discover more about Judy Garland's beloved father, Frank Gumm, I met Curry Wolfe, whose great grandfather, Jack Baugh, was the brother of Clemmie Gum, Judy's grandmother. Although I found it impossible to completely clear Frank Gumm's name, what is true is that there was a great deal more to Frank Gumm than has been previously told.

In time, I went to live in Murfreesboro, the Gum's hometown for five generations. My first day at the Rutherford County Courthouse had told me this was not going to be an easy road, but Curry and I, with the vast amount of information we found and the fact that I was living in a town that in some ways had changed very little over the last 150 years, enabled me to follow the trail. I must admit that new technology also enabled me to connect many of the dots, because although I traveled to many states, it would not have been possible to dig through all the records Curry and I searched and found online.

Finally, we are none of us just ourselves. We were formed in part by those who came before us. The reader looking here for Judy Garland will have to follow the trail as I did, with no preconceived notions, and see where it leads them.

Meanwhile, I must say that I have come to love all the people in this book. I wanted to know their joys and sorrows. Their stories deserve to be told. There have been times when I've thought no one would believe the stories on these pages, but I assure you they are all true. So now, onward to the journey; there are tragedies, scandals, kindness, success, love and, finally, laughter. I hope you enjoy it!

Will and Clemmie

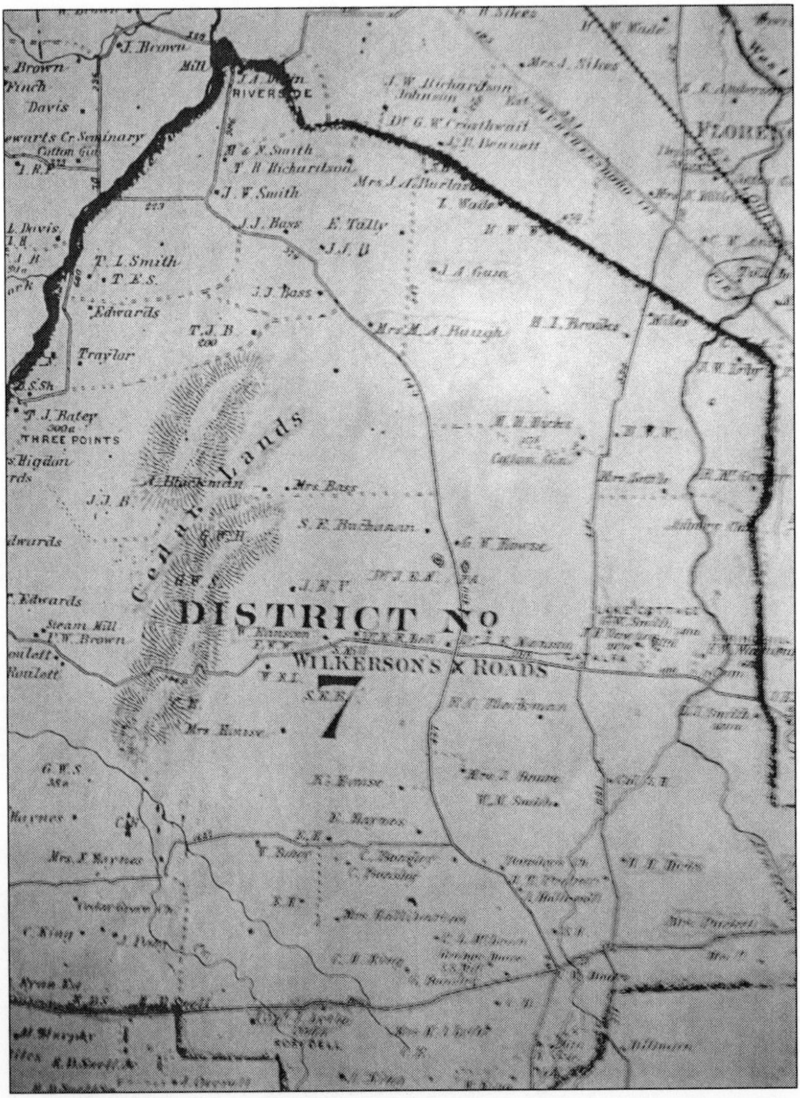

MAP of RUTHERFORD COUNTY, TENNESSEE
D.G. Beers & Co., Philadelphia, 1878

Chapter 1

New Beginnings

SOME TIME AFTER JOHN BAUGH'S DEATH IN 1870, MARY ANN CLIMBED into a horse-drawn carriage with daughter, Clemmie, and grandson, Rollie Howland, for a trip out Wilkerson Pike to the old Marable home-place. Leaving the house on East Main, the family traveled through the Murfreesboro town square, over the railroad tracks and beyond, where farm fields edged with cedar woods, stretched as far as the eye could see.

Less than a decade earlier these fields had been strewn with the bodies of the more than 20,000 severely wounded, dead, and dying men. After the Battle of Murfreesboro, the barren, winter fields had echoed the anguished cries of soldiers, punctuated by the deafening sounds of gun-shot and cannon. But as Mary Ann, Clemmie and Rollie traveled along the road that spring, the only sounds they heard were those of the horses' hooves on the hard-packed road, and the brilliant song of birds searching for insects in the grass. For the young people the past was gone, but for Mary Ann the painful wounds of wartime were ever with her.

After an hour's journey, the travelers reached the crossroads of Manson Pike and Blackman Road. Here, they could not miss the charred remains of Raiford Blackman's grand mansion on the left. It rose from the green fields, like a blackened ghost, testifying to the fact that the Yankees had indeed been here. Raiford was the son of Alfred Blackman, founder of the Blackman Community, and had vowed that he would not rebuild his home. Instead, he and his family were living in a former slave cabin

Old smokehouse near the old Marable property.

where, true to his word, he would spend the rest of his life.[1]

Turning north on Blackman Road, the carriage passed the old store, post office and blacksmith shop. As they headed north, Mary Ann felt the same sad apprehension she experienced on her first visit following the war. After the battle, her father, Benjamin Marable, had died a needless death and she had not been there to help him.

When the war was over, Benjamin Marable's possessions and livestock that survived the war had been sold at auction. J. Rowlett bought most of the livestock. Mary Ann bought a few items including a wardrobe, clock, table, a set of tablespoons, saddlebags, and a jar of honey. She also bought some of the bedding and books, one of which was Scot's *Napoleon*. The money from the sale had, of course, been divided between her and her sister's children.[2]

The carriage moved onward to a curve in the road. Just above this was Marable land—the place Mary Ann's parents called home for over fifty years. The house the Baughs were to stay in was not the Marable mansion house. That was likely inhabited by some of Mary Ann's deceased older sister, Elizabeth Marable Hick's children, or had been sold.

Mary Ann's house was a smaller and simpler abode; possibly the very cabin she had lived in during the early years of her marriage. As shown on the 1876 G.D. Beers Map, the home sat on the northeast side of Blackman Road, just where the road turns and travels west.[3] Some long-time residents recall that an old log cabin once sat on this spot.

Now in her mid-sixties, Mary Ann had finally come home to the land of her youth. She needed to heal from the chaos and sorrow of the last years; to make peace with the past, and this was the best place for her to do so. There had been no time before. During the war years, every ounce of strength had been taken in keeping the family alive. She had carried on through the battles and skirmishes surrounding her home, the lack of food, the tragic death of her daughter, Mattie, and the terrible circumstances of her father's passing. Then, just when it seemed she could feel safe and happy again, her husband, John Baugh, had died. In the months following John's passing, all the sorrows of the last years had overtaken her. As Matty Dillhunty, a resident of Old Jefferson wrote after the war, "I am tired out after a life of sorrow."[4]

The fact that Mary Ann could once again walk on the land where she had known happiness and serenity, must have brought some comfort to her. It was beautiful on Marable land. It was the place she had met John and fallen in love. On hot summer afternoons she could sit on the front porch and gaze across the green fields to the softly curving hills of the cedar lands. These protective and peaceful hills were a rare view in Rutherford County, and some of this was Marable land as well.

In the Blackman Community there were many dear, familiar faces. Besides the white families whom she had known since girlhood, a good portion of the area's black folks were still living nearby. Some had taken their former master's names, and as a result, there were many black Marables, Howses and Hickses, among others. Some had shacks on their former master's land, while others had moved to an area between the farmland and the hills where they built homes, a church and a school. They called their community Little Hope. The land was good here. The one disadvantage was the rattlesnake population, which came down from the hills in warm weather. Yet, somehow, the people made do and prospered.[5]

~

Despite Mary Ann Baugh's desire to find peace, she could not spend all her time in leisure. Since her husband's death, she had become a business woman. John Aldridge Baugh left behind a good number of properties and it was Mary Ann's responsibility to handle them. Her sons had businesses and families of their own to care for, though some of her sons-in-law, like Dallas Jacobs and Bob White, gave her advice.

Nowadays, Mary Ann was kept busy signing legal papers, negotiating sales, and collecting rents. These activities required frequent visits to town. The Baugh residence on Main Street was an extremely busy place when Mrs. Baugh was home, with a constant stream of merchants, renters, businessmen, family members and friends coming to call.

Public records have left some indication of the business Mary Ann Baugh transacted during these years:

- **May 20, 1870**—Sold to Isaac Miller, land adjoining the Christiana depot on the Nashville and Chattanooga Railway, received $350[6] (= $5,940 in 2009*).
- **December 2, 1870**—Sold to Benjamin Baugh, land on both sides of Old Stone Ft. Road, 75 acres bordered by John Pruett on the south, $2,741.66 (= $46,500 in 2009*).[7]
- **January 16, 1871**—Sold to John Pruett (son-in-law), land on both sides of Old Stone Ft. Road, bordering B.M. Baugh and Mrs. E. Childress, $3,080 (= $55,800 in 2009*).[8]
- **February 1, 1871**—Sold to M.T. Cooper, SE corner lot in Christiana, $150 & $50. $300 due (= $2,720, $906 and $5,440 in 2009*).[9]
- **1871**—Land returned to Mary A. Baugh by D.J. Tally[10]—The old Marable land near Shelbyville Road.†
- **November 13, 1871**—Sold to John M. Baugh, on Old Stone Fort Road, west line with Mathias Fox, $2,450.00 (= $44,400 in 2009*).[11]
- **November 10, 1871**—Sold to Jo Daniel, a lot in Christiana, in line with Cooper, property previously sold.[12]
- **November 20, 1874**—Sold to Nelson Wagner, a "colored" man, property in Christiana, south line of the Cooper property, $150 (= $2,910.00 in 2009*).[13]

Because it was not seemly for a woman of this period to travel or handle business by herself, Mary Ann Baugh often took her young grandson, Rollie Howland, along on these outings. Between the ages of thirteen and seventeen, Rollie frequently accompanied "Mammie," as the children called her, and helped with her business transactions. Mary Ann

* All monies are approximate based on CPI using www.measuringworth.com

† This would have been the land north of where Mary Ann and children were staying, possibly included it.

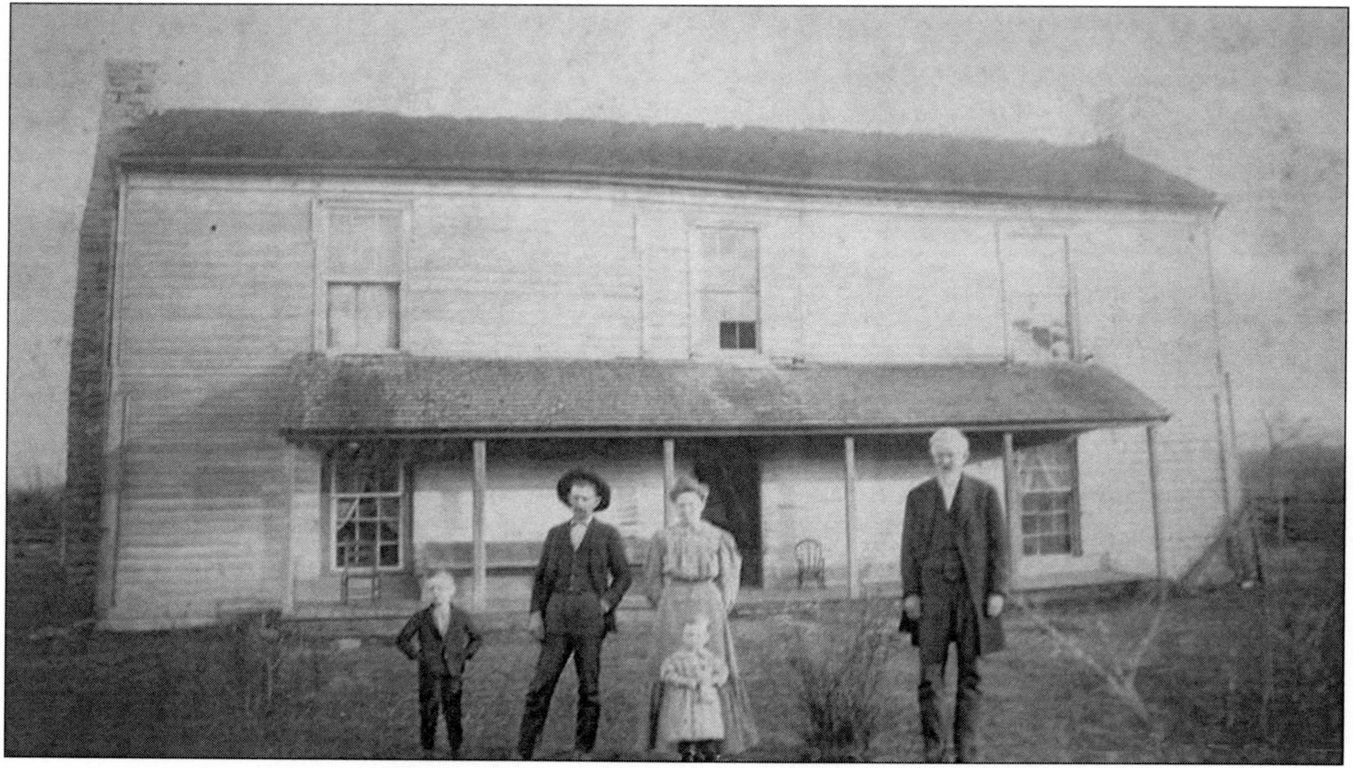

Robert and Bettie White's home in Old Millersburg, circa 1903. l. to r. Bob S. White, Burrell G. White, Lizzie White, Frank G. White and Robert White (Bettie Baugh's husband).
(Courtesy Sheri Thomas)

took great pride in young Rollie's ability, telling her friends, "He's the smartest and best boy I ever saw." Clemmie couldn't help feeling jealous when her mother spoke of Rollie in this way, but, of course, she wasn't a boy.

Some of Mary Ann Baugh's income came from renting rooms in her home on East Main Street. The majority of these boarders were relatives or friends of the family who were coming to town for a short period of time. During the year 1876, Fletcher Jacobs and his wife, Bettie, boarded with her for about a year.[14] Fletcher was the brother of her son-in-law, Dallas Jacobs.

The three-room brick office building next door to the big house, added to the rental income along with the small cabins at the back of the property. The cabins were usually rented by low-income people who could not always afford to pay the rent. According to a family member, Mrs. Baugh complained that these rentals sometimes meant more of a financial loss for her than gain.

~

In September of 1873, Mary Ann's youngest son, Charlie Richard Baugh, who was now twenty-two, married seventeen year-old Lizzie Miller. Lizzie was the daughter of Rollie Miller and Cassie Howland Miller. Lizzie's mother, Cassie, was the sister of Robert M. Howland, Rollie Howland's father. Growing up in the small community of Old Millersburg, Charlie and Lizzie had known one another since childhood, and were considered a fine match.

After their wedding, the couple moved to a house that sat on the curve of the road between Old Millersburg and Hoovers Gap, not far from brother Ben Baugh and his family. Living nearby were Bob and Bettie Baugh White. The Whites had lost their little son, who was born after the war. Since that time, Bettie had give birth to three more sons, John in 1867, Burrell in 1870 and Robert in 1875.

Living on the White's property were some of the Baugh's former slaves. There were Mammy Ran's two sons, Willis and Gilbert, and another black Baugh named Harrice. Willis was married to Harriet Howland, and the couple had four children: Harry, Mary, Hettie and Robert. Gilbert, 26, was also married and had a little girl, Anna, and a baby, Nancy. Also living in Gilbert's home was a former Baugh slave named Clementina Baugh. Interestingly, Clemintina had been born before John and Mary Ann's daughter, Clemmie.[15]

On the U.S. Census of 1870, the next house listed was that of Jack Baugh and his wife, Maria, with their three children, Thomas, 10, Mary, 5, and John, Jr., 1. Jack Baugh was listed as a farmer.

In the years after the war, many former slaves remained in the area, working on farms, either for housing and a share of the crops, or, if the owner could afford it, for money. Willis, a Civil War Veteran, and his brother, Gilbert, worked as farm hands, while their wives were able to stay home and keep house. Within the next few years, however, the lay of the land in Millersburg would change greatly. Many former slaves left the area. Willis and Gilbert moved south to Coffee County, where they both took jobs working for the railroad.[16]

~

In 1874, sorrow returned to the Baugh family when Fredonia and Dallas lost their two and a half year-old son, Johnny. The following year, at the

Old Millersburg home said to have been Ben or Charlie Baugh's home.

The Baugh Family

John Aldridge Baugh m. **Mary Ann Marable**

Joseph (Anna)	John M. (Maria)	Bettie (RM White)	Mattie (RL Howland)	Benjamin (Lethia)	Fredonia (DP Jacobs)	Mollie (RL Howland)	Eliza (J Pruitt)	Charles (Cassie H)	Clemmie (WT Gum)
Ashton (1857) Henry (1861) Ida (1867) Emma (1869)	Thomas (1861) Mary L. (1866) Lucy* (1868) John A. (1869) William H. (1872) Richard B. (1874) Murphey G. (1877) Benjamin M. (1879) Josephine "Betty" (1882) Robert W. (1884)	Mollie* (1861) William* (1865) John B. (1867) Burrell G. (1870) Robert M. (1875) Mattie (1878)	Rollie M. (1860) Mary B.* (1862)	Benjamin*(?) Mattie A. (1868) Edwin C. (1871) Bettie P. (1873) Owen W. (1875)	John C.* (1871) Ida (1873)	Robert L. (1867) Benjamin** (1869) Charles** (1873) John H. (1876) Peter A. (1879)	Mary S. (1868) Clemmie (1871) William (1874) John (1879) Ashton (1886) Rollie (1887)	Mary Ann (1870) Joe L. (1872) Rawley M. (1878) William G. (1881) Sammie L. (1883) Charles (1886) Bessie (1888) Cassie (1890) Johnnie B.** (1892) James D. (1894)	Baby Girl* (1879) Mary B. (1880) Robert E. (1883) Frank A. (1886) Will W. (1889) Alle R. (1892)

* Died in infancy. ** Possibly died in infancy or childhood.

age of twenty-nine, Fredonia died of an unknown illness. Left behind was the couple's only surviving child, two year-old Ida Jacobs. After Fredonia's passing, Dallas' mother and sister moved in with him to help take care of the little girl.

By the mid-1870s, Mary Ann Baugh began to worry about her middle son, Ben. He had always been a fine, young man, possibly Mary Ann's favorite child, but now, increasingly, there were signs that he was deeply troubled. Outwardly, Ben seemed successful. Besides farming, which was mostly done by the black folks, Ben worked as an accountant. In 1872, he was elected the Sheriff of Millersburg, and as veteran of the war and a member of the Free Masons, Ben Baugh was looked on with respect.[17] Privately, his four years at war, and the wound to his head, had taken their toll.

As the 1870s progressed, Benjamin Baugh began to divest of his property. In 1872, he sold a portion of his land to his brother, Charlie Baugh.[18] This property lay on both sides of the old Stone Fort Road, an old buffalo road that went down to Manchester. On the other side, it bordered on Robert White's land.[19]

Then, on March 8th of 1875, Ben Baugh transferred most of his property to his wife, Lethie M. Baugh, stating, "For the love and respect I bear my wife I transfer this deed to her."[20] The deed included two tracts of land on the Stones River; one north and one south of Old Stones Fort Road, and totaled 11 acres. Ben Baugh, a young man in his thirties, was letting go of the thing that had once been most important—land.

During this same time, Mary Ann Baugh sold a good deal of land to her son, Jack Baugh. The first property, near the Childress home and Hoover's Gap, was sold for $3,080 (= $55,800). Along with the landmark cedar trees which Rutherford County was known for, the deed noted a cherry tree.[21] The second property, bought in November of 1871, appears to have been next to the prior acquisition. For this acreage, Jack paid $2,450 (= $44,400). This land, which had a sugar tree, was next to Benjamin Baugh's property.[22]

With his eldest brother, Joe Baugh, living in Winchester, Jack Baugh seems to have taken on the roll of oldest son. Although Jack lived approximately fourteen miles from Murfreesboro, he visited his mother frequently, and saw to it that his children visited her as well. In addition, Mary Ann, who was quite social during these years, often enjoyed taking carriage rides out to Jack and Maria's farm.

Meanwhile, at home, Mary Ann's youngest child, Clemmie, dealt with the spinal problem she had been plagued with since birth. Like most parents of children with disabilities, Mary Ann must have felt some guilt about her daughter's condition. The exact details regarding Clemmie's birth defect are not known. Though it is possible she spent time in a wheel chair, what seems most likely is that she walked with difficulty, and could not stand straight or stay on her feet for any length of time. She had never been able to run and play as the other children did. This disability made for a fighting spirit in her; an unwillingness to be left out, and in a family of eleven children, you had to make your voice heard.

In 1877, Mary Ann Baugh was sixty-four years old, the same age John Baugh had been when he passed away. Not knowing how long she would live, Mary Ann often spoke to her children about Clemmie. She wanted to make sure, just as her husband had requested, that Clemmie would be provided for after her death. Clemmie's siblings all understood that. Considering her physical state, no one expected she would ever marry. Most men would not choose a woman with an affliction like hers.

~

Springtime on the land of the Marable, Batey, Bass and Howse farms was unbelievably beautiful. The emerald green fields stretched for miles, broken only by ancient cedar trees that had graced the land for a hundred years or more. Once again, the deer and rabbits roamed without fear, and in the clear skies, blue birds sang joyful songs. In this glory, one could forget the terrible war. Soon, the fields would be white with cotton and the black men and women, now free, would sing as they worked.

On warm, sunny afternoons, Mary Ann Baugh could sit in the old rocker on the porch and gaze out at the cedar lands in the distance, then close her eyes and feel the comfort of home, on the land she had known as a child. Perhaps during this time, she shared tales of her parents and early life with Clemmie and Rollie.

Mary Ann Baugh's neighbors included her nieces and nephews, the children of her sister, Betsey Hicks. When Betsy died in 1860, she left behind her husband, Jack Hicks and nine children. By now, the Hicks children were grown, but most of them still lived on the land they had inherited from their grandfather. This land was across Blackman Road,

just southeast of Mary Ann's land. Henry Hartwell Hicks, affectionately known to the family as "Cousin Hart," had a home and a cotton gin there. He visited the family frequently both in Blackman and Murfreesboro.

In the late 1860s, some respected citizens from other districts in Rutherford County bought land in the Blackman Community, including Dr. George Crosthwait and T.H. Richardson. By the mid-1870s, some of the Hicks family decided to sell their share of Marable land. Two men bought this land. One was Alexander Tassey, who was married to Robert E. Gum's daughter, Sara Elizabeth. The other was John Alexander Gum.

Chapter 2

The Gums after the War

BEFORE THE WAR BETWEEN THE STATES ENDED, ALEXANDER GUM WAS already looking to the future. Following The Battle of Murfreesboro in 1863, the Union troops moved permanently into Rutherford County, and Alexander's life as a Confederate Scout became far more treacherous. Many of his comrades were killed. By the end of that year, Alexander returned home and took the Oath of Allegiance to the United States.*

On his return to Jefferson, Alexander found that it was no longer the place it had been two years earlier. Many of the buildings had been burnt by the Yankees or were in a state of decay. Without the slaves to work the Ridley and Keeble plantations, their farmland was growing wild with weeds.[23] In addition, there were constant raids and threats by the Union soldiers. People were suffering and property values had decreased.

On January 21st, 1864, John Alexander Gum paid J.W. Jarratt and J.L. Barber $100 (= $1,410) for a one-acre lot in Jefferson. The lot, originally owned by R. McGregor, who had lost it in a sheriff's sale, was bounded by H. Robertson on the west, John Shacklett on the north, R. McGregor on the East, and Jefferson Pike, a road leading to Nashville, on the south.[24] Though it was unusual for a citizen of the South to have much cash at this time, it seems Alexander had been able to save money either from his Confederate Scout earnings or even via some war booty

* Although no record of an "Oath of Allegiance" has been found for Mr. Gum, had he not taken it, he could not have transacted any of the business in the 1860s.

that he had captured. His profession, still listed as "plasterer," may also have given him some income.

Nine months after the war ended, Alexander bought two additional lots. These properties included a quarter-acre on the west corner of the Old Jefferson Square and another lot directly across the road on the east corner.[25] The latter property was known as the "warehouse lot." The owner, T.J. Odeneal, sold these two lots to Alexander Gum on November 4th, 1865 for $100.[26] The prices Alexander paid for his properties show the devastating effect of the war. Property values in Jefferson had nearly descended to what they were sixty years earlier when the town was a tiny hamlet in the midst of the wilderness.

By now, Alexander Gum's family was growing. His sons, Willie and John, Jr., were now ten and seven. In addition, Alexander and his wife, Martha, had two little girls. There was Laura, now four, and Lucy, a year and a half. On March 2nd, 1865, only weeks before the war ended, Martha gave birth to their fifth child. The baby, a girl, was a sweet little thing with blue eyes and black hair. The couple named her Mollie.

Martha's mother, Nancy Wade, had survived the war, and now in her mid-50s, was living three houses away from the Gums, with Martha's younger sister, Elizabeth Jones. In 1854, Elizabeth had married William E. Jones, a well-established merchant seventeen years her senior. The couple had five daughters: Dorn, Mattie, Nanny, Emma and Lucy.

The Jones family seems to have survived the war without too many difficulties. However, most people were hurting for money. This may have been true for Nancy Wade's other children because on August 3rd, 1866, she sold thirty acres of land to L.H. Martin for $378.00.[27] This property had most likely been part of the estate belonging to Mrs. Wade's husband.

Although the identity of Nancy Wade's husband has yet to be discovered, many of the Wades were quite wealthy and highly respected citizens. The Wade family had originated in Warwickshire, England, and immigrated to Maryland in the 1600s. John Wade, Sr. fought in the Revolutionary War. In fact, Washington, D.C., now stands on some of the land his family donated.[28]

In the 1820s, several Wade families moved from Maryland to Rutherford County. Some of them settled just outside Old Jefferson, in the community later known as Bethel-Leanna. This area includes the land where Reverend Ebenezer MacGowan settled in 1816 and built his Bethel Church. Some of the Wades belonged to this church. [29] (*See* Part 1.)

As was proper for the period, the deed for the land Mrs. Wade sold contains the names of all her living children. The names of her married daughters' spouses were also included. Women at this time, if married, were never listed on a property deed without their husbands, even if the deed was for land from a parent. The names listed on the Wade deed were: B.T. Wade, Wm. E. Jones, Elizabeth Jones, John A. Gum, Martha Gum, James McClain, (husband of Lucy Wade) and G.R. Wade. The deed also states that the property being sold bordered Old Jefferson Road and B.L. Ridley's land.

Nancy Wade's son, Benjamin T. Wade and his wife, Susan Robertson were now living just outside of Old Jefferson, in District 9. They had three children of their own, James, 8, Willie, 5, and a baby, Lucy. The census taker of 1870 also listed two additional children, Betsy, 12, and Mary, 9, who may have been relatives in need of a home, or orphaned

Ben and Susan Wade's family at home in Old Jefferson sometime in the 1800s or early 1900s. Likely, the older woman is Susan Wade's mother, Susan Robertson. (Courtesy Lucy May Lenoir)

by the war. Also living in the home were two black children, Anthony Edmondson, 4, and John Edmonson, 1. Although it cannot be said why these children were there, in some cases, following the war, white families took in the children of poor black families and raised them. This was often considered another form of slavery because the children were sometimes used as servants and not allowed any education. While the situation in Ben Wade's home is unknown, he did have a very full house.

Across the river from Old Jefferson in a place known as Walter Hill, Ben Wade had a store. The Walter Hill property contained a "dwelling house" and store building set on two acres of land. For a while, Ben and his father-in-law, George K. Robertson, shared the ownership of this property. Then, in the late 1860s, Ben made a trade, exchanging ten acres of cedar land near Old Jefferson and ten acres of land with a house near the Gum family for entire ownership of the two acre parcel in Walter Hill.[30]

Meanwhile, one year after purchasing the "Ware House Lot," Alexander Gum sold it to W.S. Bone, a blacksmith in the area. Although his plan for a business there may have failed, his ownership of the property ended favorably. On last day of 1866, Alexander received twice the amount he had originally paid for the land.[31] At this same time, something new occurred with Alexander—for the first time he began to use his full name. Property records and legal documents would now refer to him as John Alexander Gum or J.A. Gum.

~

John Alexander Gum's cousin, John Gum, (the son of Robert E. Gum) had survived his service in the war without apparent injury. After the war, he returned to his farm in the southern part of Rutherford County. By the late 1860s, John was a fairly successful man. In 1867, he was elected Justice of the Peace for his district—a position he held until 1869. That year, he was appointed County Surveyor. Today, John Gum's name and surveying work are preserved in many of Rutherford County's property record books. It is said that the area known as "Gum" was named in his honor.

During the years 1810–1870, the children and grandchildren of pioneer settler Norton Gum had gone their separate ways. While most of the Gums were still in Tennessee, shortly before the war, Norton Gum's youngest son, Hinchey Petway Gum (the uncle of Alexander and John), moved his large family from Kentucky to Franklin County in northern Missouri. Though it seems the Gum cousins were well-aware of one another, how closely they remained in contact had been a mystery until an old letter came to light.

In 1866, Hinchey Petway, who now went by H.P. or "Petie" Gum, wrote several letters to his nephew, John. The letters reveals a fairly literate man, who had great affection for his family. It should be noted that without the existence of this document, the relation between Norton Gum and his descendants would be largely supposition. In addition, H.P.'s letters reveal some of the hardships of post-war life, and Mr. Gum is not without his bitterness.

Mt. Hope, MO, December 30th, 1866

My Dear Nephew:

This very cold December night in this cold dreary county, I am seated by a comfortable fire and can think of nothing at which I could be better employed than in writing to my dear relatives for it seems that there is at the present time no other chance to have a conversation, only in silent language of the pen, or in this case it is the pencil for I have no ink nor do I suppose that there is any ink in this county—for our ink is all froze out.

Well, John, how are you getting along? What has the war done for you? Where is your brothers Wilson and William? What has become of A. Tassey? Where is Alexander Gum? I received a letter from him some weeks ago which I answered immediately but in his letter he did not tell me where to direct my answer and the Post Office mark was so dim I could not tell his Post Office, therefore I sent my letter to Old Jefferson. Please find out his Post Office and write to me immediately, on the reception of this.*

Tell me all the news. Where is Col. Gowen? What became of J.C. Spence?† Is he a radical? What has the war done for him? What

---

* Alexander Tassey was married to Sara Elizabeth Gum, John Gum's sister. Tassey, who lived near his brother-in-law in 'Gum, bought the Blackman property next to Alexander Gum, showing that the Gum cousins did indeed keep in touch.

† J.C Spence mentioned is the same man, author of Annals *of Rutherford County* which the author quoted from generously in Part 1.

are you all, Rebs, Feds or something else? Tell me all about it. Now I imagine I hear you say, "Uncle Pete, you are the oldest and should tell your whereabouts first," so here goes.

Well, in the first place I was for Bell and Everette, but when Mr. Lincoln was constitutionally elected president I was a Lincoln man. Well, I took him for my guide in all national matters. He began to twist and turn, first one way, then the other, and then straight ahead, so I soon found out I was like David Crockett's Bay that was ordered to run to a certain Red Cow when he went to lay off a land in his plowing. Well, he fixed his eye on the cow in order to run a straight furrow and at the same time the cow was feeding off in a different direction, so you know that the furrow was not very straight.*

So it was with me, I got twisted about until I could not tell how to get back to the place where I started—in fact, I could not trace my steps back, but had to turn up over at several places. So you see that Mr. Lincoln and his party left me before I found out that a N----- was better than a white man.† Now I had not found out that a N----- was more competent to exercise the Right of Sufferidge—then a white man. These things were kept a secret from me until I had got so far behind that there was no chance for me to catch up. So I backed in the (unreadable) and would not pull one pound and here I am today disfranchised, whipped, kicked, cuffed and a big wad to pay by. Well, this is pretty bad, but I would not swap "Jolancy" (word not clear) with some I am acquainted with in Missouri who exercise all their rights.

Like many Southerners, H.P. Gum was angry that the white former Confederates had lost their right to vote and hold public office, while the black former slaves were able to do both.

---

* John Bell, Representative from Tennessee who ran for President with Edward Everitt for VP in 1860 on the Constitutional Union ticket. The party was formed in 1860 with former conservative Whigs who wanted to avoid having the Union break up over the issue of slavery. The idea was to stand for no political principle other than the U.S. Constitution.

† We have left evidence of this unfortunate reference which historically shows the anger of those unable to deal with the war's outcome and which uses an unfortunate word, used of persons of African American ancestry.

The new Governor of Tennessee, William Gannaway Brownlow, who was elected in May of 1865, issued a decree stating that those who had sided with the rebellion had "forfeited all rights to citizenship, and to life itself."[32] Naturally, this intensely angered the majority of Tennesseans, who were forced to pay taxes on their land, income and bank accounts without the right to vote. Having little cash (many had put their money in Confederate bonds, which were now worthless) or servants to help farm the land, people all over the south were loosing their property.

To further add to the trouble, white Northerners, or "Carpetbaggers," came to the Southern states in droves, attempting to influence the new black voters. They procured land for next to nothing and bought their way into the government with graft and bribes. Out of this situation, an intense anger was born and the Klu Klux Klan took hold. On the positive side, that July 2nd of 1866, Tennessee became the first Confederate state to be readmitted to the Union.[33]

Several days after completing the first part of his letter, Uncle Petie took up his pencil and continued.

January 2nd, 1867

Well, John, I have been very plain not knowing who I am writing to but I cannot help it. I am a Southern man and one of the characteristics of a Southern man is to tell the truth when he tells anything, so you must excuse plain talk and be sure in your reply to be equally plain. Tell me your whereabouts, tell me how you like Brownlow, tell me how you will swap him for our Dear Little Tommy Fletcher, Governor of MO. Tell me all the news generally.*

I had 3 sons and one son-in-law in the Rebel Army. All got home safe, none of them got wounded, 2 of my sons are at home, one is in Texas.

Since the war came up I have corresponded with but few but I am anxious to know how you are getting along. Let us open up a correspondence. Let's hear from you. Tell all your brothers and sisters, brother-in-laws, all to write to their Uncle Pete.

---

* Thomas Clement Fletcher was as Governor of Missouri at the same time Brownlow served in Tennessee. He issued a proclamation abolishing slavery, and dealt with key issues, including amnesty for former Confederates and free education for children.

Well, I will say this is the coldest country I ever saw in all my travels. Your coldest winter day would be called pleasant in this country. You may guess its pretty cold when ice will form in the corner of your eyes, but it's too true to make a joke of. But it's a great country, after all times in this county are very dull. Stock has gone down which makes money very scarce.

Since I have been in this state I have lost two children by death. My youngest son, Samuel T., and one of my daughters, Ann W. She was married to a Mr. Martin. She left us 3 little children to care for, two girls and one boy. She has been dead near three years. Sallie our oldest daughter is married to a Mr. W.B. Couchman and lives in St. Charles County in this state.

If your grandmother is still living, give her my respects. My respects to Col. A.P. Gowen John, be sure to find out Alexander's Post Office. If you see him, tell him I answered his letter, directed it to Old Jefferson and not knowing any nearer Post Office I will send this to Murfreesboro.*

When you write tell me if you have a more convenient Post Office. Now John, I have written a good deal of stuff, though I hope nothing has been written of an offensive character.

Give my love to all who may ask after me. All my family joins me in love to you and family. All your brothers and sisters and their families. Write very soon. Tell all to write. Direct your letters to Chapel Hill, Lafayette County, Missouri.

As your old friend and relative,

H.P. Gum

P.S. Give my respects to J.C. Spence. Tell him to write to me if he feels like doing so—him or any of his family. HPG.[34]

~

In was now fourteen years since John Alexander Gum's brother, William "Billy" Norton Gum, and his wife, Margaret, had left Rutherford

---

* A.P. Gowan (1795–after 1860) was a County Representative in 1832 and a longtime resident of Rutherford County.

County. Remaining in Tennessee, they moved to Gibson County, Weakley County, and finally, Obion County.[35] Naturally, during these years, Billy and his brother, Alexander, kept in touch. In 1864, when Billy and Margaret's seventh child was born, they named the baby "John Alexander Gum" in his honor.

Prior to the war, Billy Gum was quite successful financially, and had purchased a number of slaves to help run his farm. While the slaves worked the land, Billy spent time in his favorite occupation, hunting. He would later boast that he had killed more than 1,000 deer and scores of bears and panthers during his lifetime.[36]

After the war, Billy Gum continued his work as a stone and brick mason, carefully saving his money. In 1869, the family decided move to Missouri. Billy, Margaret and their nine children settled in the southern part of the state, Dunklin County, approximately 172 miles from his Uncle Petie.

By the summer of 1870, Billy Gum owned a 240 acre farm in Freeborn, Missouri. In time, he would buy an additional 154 acres on Horse Island, where *Goodspeed's History of Missouri* reported, he had "a fine farm." He also owned several "smaller tracts" of land.[37]

Billy Norton Gum was an interesting man whose qualities may reveal many of the Gum family attributes. Besides being a farmer, a stonemason and a hunter, Billy Gum was an avid reader and a good conversationalist. He was also religious, faithfully attending the Methodist church. And he was also thrifty with his money. It is said that he built his fortune from the original $500 he earned, cutting stone for the Tennessee State Capitol.

Billy Gum was a man of high energy. He did not believe in hitching a horse to a wagon when he could walk. He often walked from his farm in Freeborn to his farm on Horse Island, a journey of 34 miles. He was also known to walk all the way from his home by the "pole road" in Freeborn to the Mississippi River, where he crossed over into Tennessee. This was a journey of nearly 100 miles. Later in life, Billy learned to ride a bicycle, which, in old age, he found a preferable means of travel to walking.

~

By the late 1860s, John Alexander Gum was the last Gum remaining in Old Jefferson. Battling the continued ill effects of the war, Mr. Gum worked hard to make a success of his ventures and support his growing family. Around 1867, J.A. Gum purchased an additional one and a half acre property on the west side of the Jefferson Square. The lot included a "dwelling house," outhouses, a store house and "all appurtenances." For this property, Mr. Gum paid Mr. G.A. Huddleston the sizeable amount of $600.[38] (= $8,980)

That March, Martha's youngest sister, Lucy McLane died at the age of twenty-four. Lucy was buried in the Ward Cemetery, next to Ben and Susie Wade's three little children who died during the war. Although it was not unusual for young people to die, the war had taken its toll. There were many strong men and women, who, weakened in body and spirit, died within a few years of the war's end.

In 1869, only two years after the passing of Rebecca Crosthwait Ridley, the residents of Old Jefferson would learn of Bromfield Ridley's sad passing. The Ridley-Crosthwait plantation, "Fairmont," remained deserted, little more than a pile of burnt rubble. Even that had been picked over for wood, and anything else that might be of use to those who were suffering in poverty. In his will, Ridley gave expression to what many in the area felt when he wrote:

> *My fortune has been crippled and exhausted almost by the burnings and desolation and stealing of the Yankees and I am reduced to my wallet and staff.*[39]

In April of 1867, John and Martha welcomed another baby girl into their midst. They named her after her grandmother, Nancy Wade Gum, though she would always be known as "Nannie."

When little Nannie Gum was four years old, her grandmother, Nancy, transacted a bit of strange business. At this time, Mrs. Wade owned a piece of property that seems to have been in a strategic position, being bounded by Bromfield Ridley's estate on the north, Walter Keeble's estate on the east, G.R. Waller on the west, and L.H. Martin on the south. On March 23rd, 1871, Nancy Wade sold this property consisting of forty acres of cedar land in exchange for "... the consideration of five hundred dollars to me paid in shoes and hats."[40] Nancy's son, Ben T. Wade, witnessed the transaction.

It seems that Mrs. Wade sold this land in order to help her son, Ben, with his business. In any case, Nancy Wade's transaction must have supplied the Wades with shoes and hats for a long, long time!

In April of 1872, Nancy Wade sold the four lots she bought in the 1850s from Billy Norton Gum: Lots 125, 126, 127 and 128 to her son, Ben Wade (*See* Book 1).[41] The price for these four lots was $500 (= $9,060). Nancy, who was now in her 60s, was slowly but surely divesting herself of all her property.

The same day Mrs. Wade sold the above named property to her son, Ben, he sold the lots to Paul Saunders for $500, along with a tract of land containing 4 acres bordering Shelbyville Road.[42] For the latter parcel, Mr. Wade retained a lien of $600 to be paid within two years. Ben would continue to be busy with property the following year when he bought a ten acre plot along the edge of the Stones River in Old Jefferson. (The acreage included land to the center of the river.) Although he paid William B. Owens $936 for this property, Ben may later have found that this purchase was a mistake.[43] Increasingly, property along Stones River flooded during the rainy season, leaving only the crest of the hill in Jefferson above water.

Meanwhile, John Alexander Gum was not doing as well in business as he had hoped. In fact, he was falling deeper into debt. Attempting to rectify the problem, Mr. Gum sold some of the property he had acquired over the last twenty years. He began by selling his half-acre lot on the west corner of the Jefferson town square to T.W. Wright in 1870 for two hundred dollars.[44] Shortly after this, J.A. Gum sold another property in town to J.W. Baker for $175.[45] Although his actions suggest he was attempting to pay off his debts, it appears that he had another plan as well.

In 1873, Mr. Gum conducted a transaction which property owners sometimes used to confirm ownership of a property if the deed was missing. He sold the lot his family had been living on since 1867 to F.C. Ward, and, then, bought it back the same day.[46] Apparently, he had improved the property greatly over the last six years. As a result, it was now valued at $5,000 (= $84,800). The deed was registered by the court on January 2nd, 1874.

A few weeks later, John Alexander Gum went through the same procedure for eighty acres of land in District 7. This property line began in the "the center of the Jefferson & Shelbyville road near the gate of the late Benjamin Ward's resident," passed F.C. Ward's residence "to the center of Overall Creek" and then traveled south along the Creek "to the line of

Charles Moore (formerly James M. King)" and back to the Jefferson and Shelbyville Road.[47] The property also included twenty acres of cedar land in District 9. With all these property transactions completed, J.A. Gum was ready to make his most important purchase.

On April 12th, 1875, John Alexander Gum exchanged properties with Mary E. Prater, the daughter of Elizabeth Marable Hicks, and niece of Mary Ann Baugh. The land Mary E. Prater received from J.A. Gum was the same land in District 7, standing at the interchange of the Jefferson and Shelbyville Roads, for which he had confirmed ownership the previous year.

It is interesting to note that the deed for John A. and Martha Gum's property was made out to Mary E. Prater alone. However, the land John A. Gum received was deeded to him from H.T. Prater and wife. It is interesting to note that in addition to being Mary Hicks' husband, Mr. Prater was also the census taker for Old Jefferson.

In exchange for his property, John A. Gum received 56 acres in the Blackman Community. Both properties were valued at $2,000 (= $40,300), making it an even exchange. The land John Alexander Gum procured was described as follows in the deed:

> *. . . situated in the Civil District No. 7 . . . Beginning at a stake in a lane, corner of the Burleson land, running with Burlason's line N5East 49 poles, thence continuing with Burleson's line N 88½, W. 67 poles to a stake, thence S 2½ W. 61 poles to a stake in Mrs. Baugh's line, then East 14 poles to a stake [in] Mrs. Baugh's corner, then S1W with her line 76 poles to a stake . . . containing forty-nine acres. . . .*[48]

In addition, there were two small lots of cedar land; one consisting of 3 acres and the other totaling 4¾ acres. These also bordered on Mrs. M.A. Baugh's cedar land. The deed further described the land as part of "the Hicks interest in the land owned by the late Benjamin Marable."[49]

Despite John Alexander Gum's hope to succeed financially in his new venture, all was not free and clear. The deed also states that there was a lien on Mr. Gum's property due to the fact that a "levy of an execution in favor of Yarbre & Reid," a store in Murfreesboro, had been rendered against him in court.[50] The amount owed was "One hundred and Twenty dollars" (= $2,430). Also, there was an additional lien by the same company for $265 (= $5,340).

While the particulars of this case are unknown, the information in the deed shows that Alexander Gum's financial situation was not as good as it seemed. Yet, rather than lose his capital by paying his debt in full, J. A. Gum was determined to invest his money in a fine property which could earn him more money. He was also moving his family to a better area, and, possibly, to a finer home.

~

A short time after the above transaction, an event occurred in Rutherford County which touched the heart of every member of the Gum clan. That May, one hundred year-old Elizabeth Fulks, the mother-in-law of Robert E. Gum, passed away. She had known Alexander's father, William, and, likely, his grandfather, Norton Gum. She had seen the beginnings of Rutherford County, and lived through the devastating war, which tore it apart. The local newspaper reported her passing as follows:

> Mrs. Elizabeth Fulks, probably the oldest lady in our county, died on the 28th day of May, 1875. She was born the 15th day of January 1775, being 100 years, 4 months and 13 days old.
>
> She was born in Pennsylvania, fifty miles from Philadelphia and emigrated with her husband, John Fulks to Rutherford county in the fall of 1804, and settled where the county poor house is now located in the year 1806. They removed to Cripple Creek where she continued to live until 1870, when she went to live with her grandson, John Gum, Esq. and remained there until her death.
>
> She was accompanied to her grave by her grandchildren, great grandchildren and great-great grandchildren. Probably there has never been many such occurrences in Rutherford County. She never had but one child, and that was Esquire Gum's mother, who died some thirty-three years ago. Her husband John Fulks died several years ago. She had always been a very industrious, stirring woman.[51]

Elizabeth Fulks was buried in the Gum graveyard. Her grave is not marked. Mary Ann and Robert E. Gum are said to be buried just outside the graveyard.

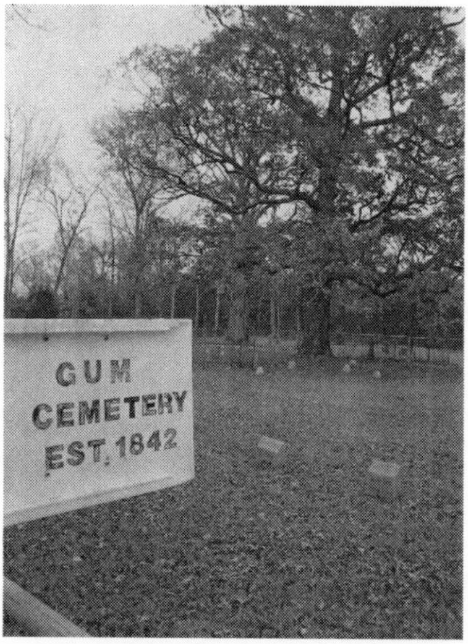

~

By 1875, J.A. Gum's little family had doubled in size. The household now consisted of 48 year-old John Alexander, 40 year-old Martha and eight children: Will T., 22, John A. Jr., 20, and six girls: Laura, 16, Lucy, 12, Mollie, 11, Nannie, 9, Bettie, 4, and Susie, 2. The older brothers must have felt quite overcome with all the little girls in the house. The Gums were a lively bunch! And now they were the neighbors of Mary Ann Baugh.

While John Alexander Gum continued his profession as "plasterer," like many people at that time, he planned to go into a second line of business. With his two sons, he would open a produce business. The land in the Blackman Community was considered some of the finest farmland in middle Tennessee. "Jere," as he was now called, would use the land to grow vegetables. Will and John, Jr. could sell the produce to stores. Jere purchased a horse and wagon to facilitate this. Among their duties, Jere's sons would be given the job of driving the goods ten or more miles to Nashville.[52] Jere's half brother, Anderson Crosthwait, and his mother, Malinda, were now living in Nashville and may even have given him some advice on this.

Once the Gums moved to the Blackman Community, it did not take long for the neighbors to become acquainted with this lively and attractive family. Mary Ann Baugh probably paid them a visit to welcome them The Gum girls would be good company for Clemmie, who, by now, was eighteen. Fifteen year-old Rollie would not have minded the company of so many pretty girls either.

In Rutherford County society, the Baugh and Gum families were of two different classes. The Baughs had been slaveholders and the owners of hundreds of acres of land. The Gums had neither of these. But slavery was gone, and the playing field for many had been leveled.

As the granddaughter of Reverend Henry Hartwell Marable, from her early years, Mary Ann Baugh had mingled with every class of people. Because of this, it is not surprising that in the months that followed, she and her family spent time with Mr. and Mrs. Gum and their family. During their visits, Will Gum and Clemmie Baugh became acquainted.

Mrs. Baugh must have been surprised when Will Gum asked if he might call upon Clemmie. It was not that Clemmie was unattractive or without charm, but her "affliction," as they called it, was something that kept most eligible bachelors at a distance. But Mrs. Baugh gave her consent for Will to call. At the very least, she was happy her daughter would have some social interaction with people her own age.

Chapter 3

Love and Marriage

CLEMMIE WAS A PERSON OF SPIRIT. IF YOU COULD SAY ANYTHING ABOUT her, you could say that. She had never let anyone push her around, and had always stood up for what she felt was her share.[53] Clemmie must have liked Will from the day she met him. So, in late 1876, or early 1877, Will Gum came to call.

If Will looked anything like his brother, or his eldest son, he was of middle height and weight with light brown hair and blue eyes. He had handsome features, a pleasant smile and a great deal of charm. As with most of the Gums, people found him very likeable.

Both Will and Clemmie had experienced the terrors and deprivations of the war, but while they shared this past, Will had another attribute Clemmie liked; he knew how to make her laugh. During his visits, Will likely entertained Clemmie with tales of his young life. There were stories about old Grannie Wade in Jefferson, Uncle Ben, who ran a store near Walter Hill, and his Wade cousins, Hootie and Dinkie. Aunt Sue and Uncle Ben had eight "young uns" at home. The youngest Wade, Martha, born in the autumn of 1876, had been named for Will's mother.

Meanwhile, Will's brother, John, Jr., had a sweetheart of his own. Uncle Ben Wade and G.R. Waller had sold some land "fronting the Jefferson & Milton Turnpike" to John and N.J. Trigg, for $500, with a note for $150.[54] The Trigg family was of Norwegian descent, a line said to come from royalty. Mr. and Mrs. Trigg had a son and three beautiful daughters. It did not take long for John, Jr. to be smitten with pretty, young Lucy Trigg.

As shown on the D.G. Beers and Co. map, the Trigg farm lay northeast of Blackman, just south of the railroad. Whether the couple met as a result of the land transaction or the Gum brothers' travels is not known. The brothers were certainly busy during this time. The 1877 tax records for Rutherford County show that Will, and his brother, John, each paid $1 in poll tax.

John and Lucy's courtship was swift. They were married at the Rutherford County Courthouse by Rev. Wm. Robison on the 17th of January 1877. Although Lucy stood to inherit property in the future, at the time of their marriage, she and John, Jr. had little money. Nevertheless, they seemed quite happy.

Throughout the spring of 1877, Will Gum continued to court Clemmie Baugh. We can picture him coming to call, hat in hand, eager to see her. Though no photos of Clemmie are known to exist, she must have been a pretty girl. How her eyes must have sparkled as she listened to Will speak, her dark hair accentuating the fairness of her skin. Apparently, her disability did not bother him, for Will came to call again and again.

Somewhere along the way, Will and Clemmie formed an attachment. Will had big dreams, but he had not been one to go out and make them happen. Now, he and Clemmie began to dream together.

During their months of courtship, Mary Ann was no doubt charmed by Will. He seemed to have a good head on his shoulders. When Will Gum came to ask for Clemmie's hand, whatever reservations Mary Ann may have had, she put them aside. Above all else, she could not extinguish the light in Clemmie's eyes.

Along with Mrs. Baugh's desire for her daughter to have a happy life, was the knowledge that if she withheld her consent to the marriage, she would not have had an easy time. Clemmie was not one to say "no" to. Once she made up her mind about something, there was no changing her. And if Clemmie wanted to marry Will, Mary Ann wanted her to be happy.

Meanwhile, at sixty-four, Mary Ann was beginning to feel her age. She had grown quite attached to her youngest child, and had always expected that Clemmie would be there, to care for her in her old age. She realized now that Will's not having money or a home to offer Clemmie did not have to be a detriment. It would work just as well for Will to move into the big house on Main. There was plenty of room, with four large bedrooms upstairs and two small side rooms downstairs. At the same time,

Mrs. Baugh would be able to see that Clemmie was well cared for, having servants that Will could not afford. Clemmie, in turn, could look after her.

When the news reached the Baugh siblings that their sister was getting married, they were both surprised and delighted. The Gums seemed to be a very pleasant, respectable family, even if they were not wealthy.

~

With marriage ahead of them, Will and Clemmie began to plan for the future. One of the decisions to be made concerned the line of work Will would take up. He had spoken so often about the stores his father and Uncle Ben Wade owned that a store seemed the logical choice. Clemmie's mother had a good deal of land at East Main and Maney Avenue, which would be would be an excellent spot for a store.

Maney Avenue led to the Manchester Highway, otherwise known as "Dixie Highway" because it went all the way south. Maney and Main were the main arteries between Tullahoma and Nashville. A store situated there would have plenty of traffic, both customers and suppliers. Although there were quite a few stores in Murfreesboro, the town was growing and could certainly use another store. In this location, Will Gum was certain he could make an excellent living.

The first problem, however, was that Will Gum had no money of his own. They could use Mrs. Baugh's land, but a store would have to be built and goods bought to fill it. Clemmie decided to ask for the thousand dollar inheritance her father had promised each of his children. ($1,000 = $20,200) She had never received hers. In this way, Will could set up his store, and they could be married. Clemmie had never dared to dream that she would have a life like her sisters, but now she would. She wanted to marry Will, and she had the means to make it happen.

When Clemmie asked her mother to give her the inheritance money for Will's store, Mary Ann Baugh may have balked but Clemmie was persuasive. A prudent business woman, Mary Ann did not give her daughter the entire amount. Instead, she gave her half, $500, to buy goods and get the store started. With these plans in place, the question of marriage was solved and the wedding date set. Will T. Gum felt he was the happiest and the wealthiest man in the world.

~

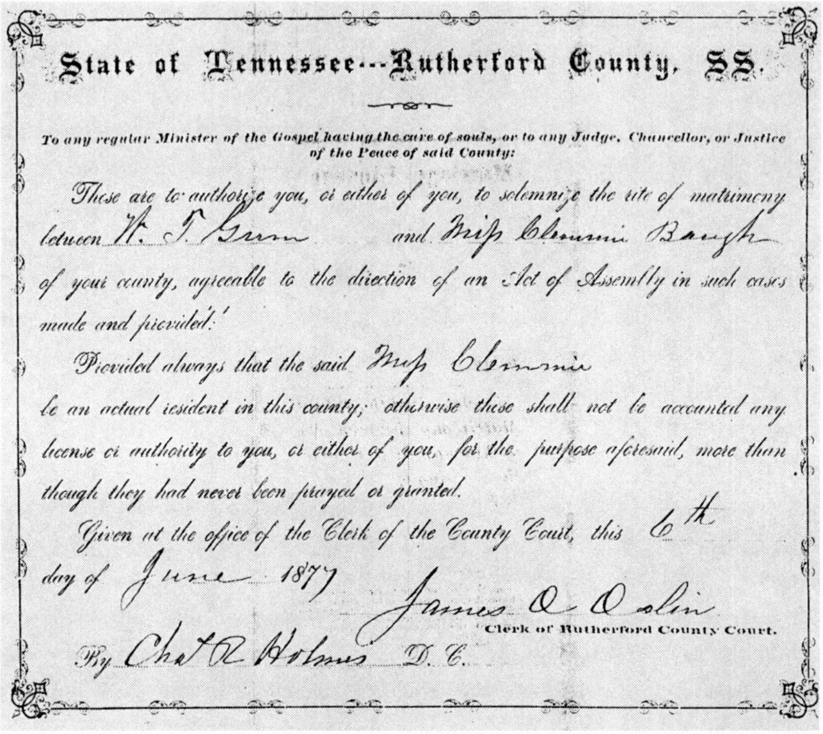

State of Tennessee---Rutherford County, SS.

To any regular Minister of the Gospel having the care of souls, or to any Judge, Chancellor, or Justice of the Peace of said County:

These are to authorize you, or either of you, to solemnize the rite of matrimony between W. T. Gum and Miss Clemmie Baugh of your county, agreeable to the direction of an Act of Assembly in such cases made and provided.

Provided always that the said Miss Clemmie be an actual resident in this county; otherwise these shall not be accounted any license or authority to you, or either of you, for the purpose aforesaid, more than though they had never been prayed or granted.

Given at the office of the Clerk of the County Court, this 6th day of June 1877

James O. Oslin
Clerk of Rutherford County Court.

By Chas R. Holmes D. C.

Courtesy Rutherford County Archives

On Tuesday, June 6th, 1877, Will T. Gum and Clemmie W. Baugh went down to the Rutherford County Courthouse with the husband of Clemmie's cousin, Henry T. Prater, the same man who sold John Alexander Gum the land in Blackman. In keeping with tradition, the court clerk asked for a $1,200 bond to ensure that the groom went through with the marriage. One percent of the bond amount had to be paid when the marriage license was taken out.

Eleven days later, on Sunday, June 17, 1877, Will T. Gum and Clemmie W. Baugh were married. Where they were married or by whom is uncertain. Possibly, the wedding took place in the Baugh home on East Main Street. With the huge sliders between the large front parlor and dining room opened, there would have been space for a large crowd.

If Clemmie wished to follow in her parent's footsteps, the wedding may have taken place at the old Marable homeplace or even in the Gum home. In early summer, roses and wildflowers, delicate, fragrant and full of color would be used to decorate the wedding.

There were so many relatives who would have attended! First, there were Clemmie's seven brothers and sisters and their husbands and wives. Brother Joseph Baugh, in Winchester, brought his family to Murfreesboro on the train. There were also Mary Ann's twenty-nine grandchildren; children would have been everywhere.

Along with Clemmie's family was Will's family; his parents, six sisters and brother, John, with his new wife, Lucy. In addition, Mrs. Gum had just given birth to a baby boy one month prior to the wedding. They had named him John H. Gum. Along with family members, there were also friends who would have attended the wedding, such as Mr. and Mrs. Thomas Jarratt, Mr. and Mrs. James E. Richardson and Mr. W.D. Robison.

Mammy Ran and other black servants would have been called in to help, and may have brought some of their children along, who would have peeked in wide-eyed at the proceedings.

That evening, musicians playing fiddles, banjos and even a pianoforte livened the evening air. Despite Clemmie's disability, there could not be a wedding without music and dancing. It was a new day, a joyous day after the dark shadow of war and death which had hung over their lives for so long. Clemmie had found her dream man; handsome, sweet, and so in love with her. Clemmie was not a person to keep her feelings to herself and on this day she must have over-flowed with expressions of joy. At last she was a full-person; a married lady like her sisters. She was Mrs. W.T. Gum!

~

After the wedding, Will Gum moved into the Main Street home with Clemmie. The house was certainly big enough for all of them. With the possible exception of the Ridley mansion, "Fairmont," the Baugh home was probably the grandest residence Will Gum had visited. Now, he would be living there. With his marriage, he had entered a new level of society.

In the weeks that followed, Will oversaw the building of the store, perhaps doing some of the work himself. The building was erected at the corner of East Main and Maney Avenue, with the entrance facing Maney. It was a fairly good-sized building, measuring 100 x 80 feet. He had decided to call it, *W. T. Gum & Company*. It would contain all manner of foods, such as chicken, eggs and butter, as well as flour, corn and dry goods.

Courtesy Curry Wolfe

Although Will brought his family experience to the creation of the store, Clemmie seems to have contributed as well. If nothing else, she was certainly the driving force behind it. Clemmie was in love with Will, and she wanted to make her husband happy. If his dream was to have a store, then she wanted that dream to come true.

After months of work and preparation, Will began stocking the store, but he soon realized that Clemmie's money would not be enough to complete the job. Rather than give Will Gum more of Clemmie's inheritance, Mrs. Baugh decided that she would loan her new son-in-law the necessary money with a note. Although Will was not required to pay his wife back, he would be required to pay her; either in cash, or in goods. With this contract, Mary Ann Baugh showed herself to be something of a prudent business woman.

~

In the weeks and months following Will and Clemmie's marriage, Rollie Howland, who was still living with his grandmother, watched to see how things progressed. Home did not feel the same. Clemmie had always been somewhat jealous of Rollie and not willing to share her place as the baby of the house. Now, with her marriage, Clemmie seemed to take on something of a proprietary air about the house. Rollie was never one to look for trouble, but he sensed it was in the offing.

Chapter 4

Home Life

One day in 1877, shortly after Clemmie's marriage to Will, seventeen year-old Rollie Howland came back from a day out on his own.[55] He had been to an auction on the Murfreesboro Square and bought a few things with some money he had saved. As he walked back to the house, he was feeling quite happy, with that sense of pride and independence a young person feels as they begin to enter the world on their own.

Hearing Rollie in the front hall, Clemmie came out to see him and glimpsing the little package of brown paper under his arm, called,

"Oh. Buddy, what did you get? I know you got something! Lemmie see!"

"Buddy" was the name Clemmie and others in the family used for him. Rollie did not want to show Clemmie what he had. He knew how spoiled she could be; always insisting on getting her way, but she begged him over and over until finally he gave in.

"I bought them for Aunt Mollie, so, don't touch them," he said as he prepared to open the presents he had bought for his stepmother, who was Clemmie's sister and the sister of his deceased mother.

"I won't, Buddy. Why do you act like such a goose!"

Rollie carefully untied the string and unfolded the paper to reveal some small, but pretty items he had chosen with care.

"Oh! Oh, look at those lovely, little things. Let me have them!" cried Clemmie.

"No, Clemmie, I told you they were for Aunt Mollie," said Rollie.

"You can buy some others for Sister Mollie. I want these."

"No, Clemmie."

"I'll pay you a dollar!" ($1.00 = $21)

"No."

"A whole dollar. Please!"

"No, Clemmie! I told you, I'm taking them home to give to Aunt Mollie."[56] And with that, Rollie turned his back on Clemmie and went upstairs.

The next few days following this event, Clemmie pouted and sulked, refusing even to speak to Rollie. You would have thought he had done something truly terrible. Will Gum's looks in his direction coupled with Clemmie's anger, made Rollie feel increasingly uncomfortable living in the house.

Poor Rollie. He was a young man without a true home. Grandmother Mary Ann had always treated him as if he were her son. Nevertheless, he was aware that after his mother's death, she had "taken him in"; Grandmother Baugh's home was not his.

At his father, Robert Howland's home, Rollie felt he belonged in a different way, but Robert and Aunt Mollie had their own family, and that was not entirely his home either. In any event, Rollie was a smart young man and he knew that he would soon be an adult with a life of his own.

~

Shortly after the disagreement with Clemmie, Rollie went to visit his father and Aunt Mollie down in Beech Grove.[57] Living in their home were Rollie's half-brothers, Robert, 10, Benjamin, 8, Charles, 4, John, 1, and a new baby, Peter. The Howlands also had a boarder who may have paid rent or helped with the farm.

Robert Howland, seeing his son's unhappiness, questioned him. He was concerned. Living with Mrs. Baugh had been fine up to now, but Rollie was a young man and it was time for him to prepare for his future.

It so happened that around this time, a letter arrived from Rollie's Uncle Joe down in Winchester. Since his return to Tennessee, Joseph Baugh had been quite successful with his dry goods store on the Winchester town square. In addition, he had recently been appointed Treasurer on the Board of Trustees for the Carrick Academy, soon to be considered one of the finest schools in Tennessee.[58]

After speaking with his son, Robert Howland contacted Joseph Baugh who responded by offering to arrange Rollie's admittance to the Carrick Academy. Joseph wrote that he and his family would be happy to have his nephew live with them while he attended school. Thus, in a short time, a new life was arranged for Rollie Howland.

Mary Ann Baugh must have been quite surprised when she was informed that instead of returning to the East Main Street home, Rollie would be going away to school in Winchester. Since the age of three, he had seemed almost like a son to her. She took a great deal of pride in him and, in recent years, had come to depend on him a great deal.

After reading Robert Howland's letter, Mary Ann Baugh sat down and wrote her son-in-law, offering to pay for part of Rollie's education. In the envelope, she included a receipt against all claims of expense for the years Rollie had lived with her.[59] As much as she would miss him, she knew that he was an extremely intelligent boy, and should take advantage of Joseph's offer.[60]

~

By the mid-1870s, Joseph Baugh and his father-in-law, Ashton Butterworth, were respected members of the Winchester community. After the war, Mr. Butterworth rebuilt his "Town Creek Mills" bigger and finer than the previous ones. The mills, which sat on Lynchburg Road in Owl Hollow—the Harmony area—about 5 miles west of town, were powered by the extensive waters which flowed from the Tennessee River into Tims Ford Lake. Mr. Butterworth's factories included a cotton mill, "woolen mill with twelve looms, a carding-mill," and "a large grist and flouring mill" for grinding grains like wheat and corn.[61]

During the Civil War, Winchester had been a hot bed of strong abolitionists and bushwhackers, so when the Union soldiers came to town they hit the area hard. As a result, many businesses were destroyed. In the 1870s, evidence of burnt-out buildings still existed. The Yankees had spared nothing, including The Episcopal Trinity Church, of which the Butterworths were members.

Around 1872, Mr. Butterworth took the profits from his business and paid for Trinity Church to be rebuilt. Mr. Butterworth's son, John,

who also worked at the mills, donated a tract of land near Owl Hollow Creek for the Bethel Methodist Church.[62]

The Trinity Episcopal Church was of Gothic design and at the present time is said to be the oldest, unaltered building in Winchester. The building was consecrated in 1876 by Bishop Charles Quintard. In the post-war years of hardship, Trinity Church's parishioners had great respect for, and gratitude to Mr. Butterworth for rebuilding the church.

Sadly, the rebuilding of the church had just been completed when Mr. Butterworth's factory mills caught fire and burnt to the ground. Financially destroyed, Ashton Butterworth returned to England to raise the capital to rebuild his mills. His wife and daughter would never see him again. A short time after arriving in England, sometime between 1873 and 1874, Mr. Butterworth died. His wife, Eliza, who was already living with Joseph and Anna, would remain with them for the rest of her life.

The Baugh family lived in a nice two-story house, with a garden and barn approximately two blocks from the square.[63] The Carrick Academy was also a short distance from the family residence. On nice days, the children were able to walk to school.*

The Baugh store, operating under the name, J.L. Baugh, was located on the town square in a good-sized, two-story building. Considered a dry goods store, the advertisements suggest that a good deal of business came from purchases by students attending the local academy. Mr. Baugh sold men's suits, hats, shoes and other items such as ties and spectacles.[64] Living in Winchester, it appears that Joseph Baugh found greater prosperity than many of his relatives in Murfreesboro.

---

* Neither the store nor the family home is still in existence.

Joseph L. Baugh's store in Winchester, TN. The building no longer stands. (Courtesy Lawrence Hannah)

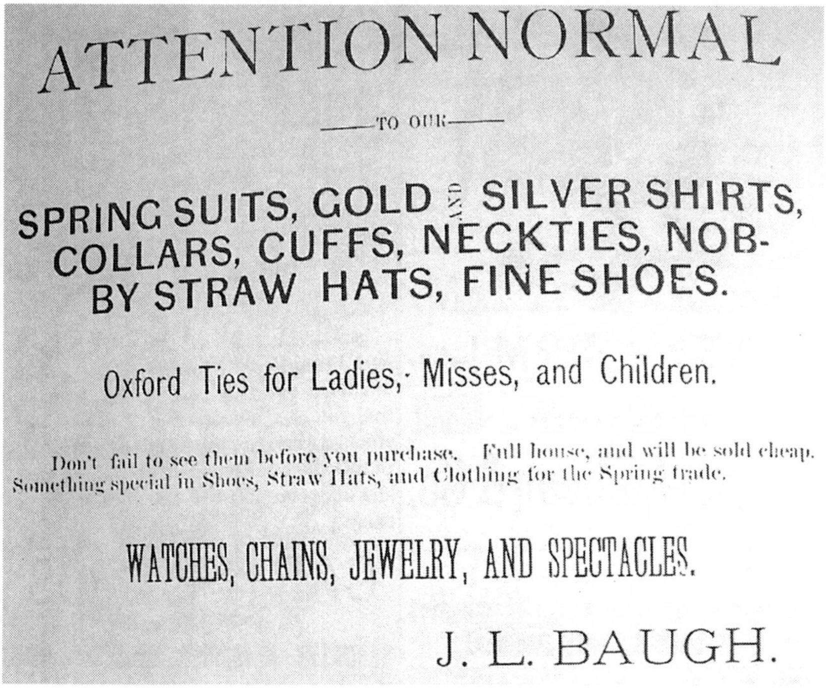

Historically, Winchester was an area of excellent education. The first large school in town had been the Carrick Academy, named for Samuel Carrick, the early Presbyterian preacher in Knoxville, who founded Blount College. During the Civil War, Carrick Academy had been used as a hospital for soldiers arriving from the Battle of Murfreesboro. After the war, the building remained abandoned for many years because the trustees had no money to re-open it. Then, in 1872, a young teacher, Rufus Anthony Clark, arrived in town and impressed the trustees with his ideas. He told them that he would be willing to accept the "tuition fees expected from an estimated seventy-five pupils" as his salary for the first year.[65]

The year the school opened there were only eight students. Mr. Clark was soon joined by his brother and J.M. Bledsoe. Together, the three men worked to improve the school and build the student body. By 1877, when Rollie Howland arrived, the school had seventy-one students, which included young men from Texas, Alabama and Mississippi. Around this time, the three teachers decided to include girls in the early grades and in this way increase their student numbers. By the beginning of 1878, the school had been renamed Winchester Normal, and, by the fall, 220 students were enrolled.[66]

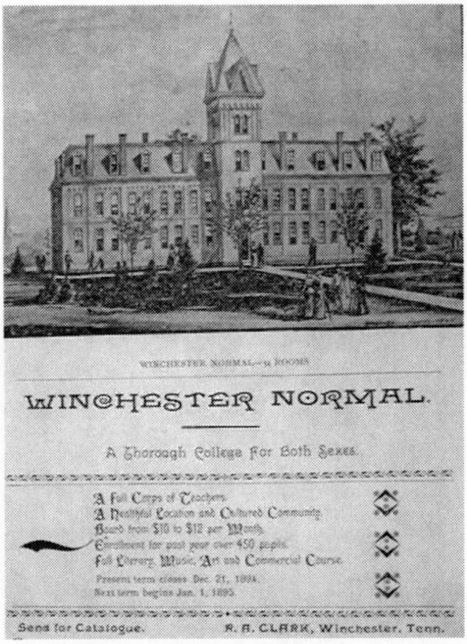

When seventeen year-old Rollie Howland arrived in Winchester, Joseph Baugh's family was living quite nicely. Rollie found the Baugh family residence to be a lively, but well-disciplined and orderly home. Along with his Aunt Anna, Uncle Joe, and Anna's British mother, Eliza Butterworth, were his four cousins: Ashton, 20, Henry, 17, Ida, 11, and Emma, 8. Cousin Henry attended school with Rollie.

Courtesy Larry Hannah

Henry, who was a brilliant scholar and studied continuously, would graduate one year early.[67]

Rollie Howland appears to have enjoyed living with Joseph Baugh's family. It was a family to which he belonged. His Uncle Joe was born five years before to his mother, had many memories of her. Uncle Joe's wife, Mrs. Anna Baugh, was a proper English-Southern wife and mother, who insisted that her daughters call each other, "Sister Ida" and "Sister Emma." Full of fun, the girls called each other "Stick" and "Stem" for short.[68]

Joseph Baugh's family was also very talented musically. In the evening, there was often musical entertainment in their home. Cousin Ida played the pianoforte and guitar. It is said that Ida, a brilliant musician, could "make the guitar talk." Eventually, she would teach music at Mary Sharp College in Winchester. Other members of the family, like Cousin Ashton Baugh, had strong, musical voices, whether singing in the Baptist church, which Uncle Joe had joined, or around the pianoforte on musical evenings.

One year after entering school, Rollie went home to visit his father on school break. While he was there, he fell in love with a young girl named Daisy Slattery. Whether Daisy was someone Rollie had known previously or just met is unknown. In any case, Rollie decided he was in love and asked Daisy's parents for her hand in marriage. The wedding date was set for September 8, 1878, but that day while the family waited at the church for the groom to arrive, Rollie had other things on his mind.

That morning, Rollie's dog had run off and gotten lost. Distracted and upset, Rollie went to look for his dog and never showed up at the church. Needless to say, the wedding was called off. Whether the dog was ever found is unknown, but Uncle Jack made a note of this unusual situation in the family Bible.[69]

Rollie returned to school that September. The Winchester Normal school provided the finest education and teaching methods with subjects in English, Latin, mathematics, science and moral philosophy; which today would be civics and political science.[70] Rollie was a bright student and excelled. He graduated from the Literary School in 1881, one year after his cousin, Henry Baugh.[71]

~

Great things are not created overnight. It took until the end of 1877 for W.T. Gum & Company to be ready to open its doors to the public. Will planned for the Grand Opening to take place on New Years Day of 1878. To announce the big event, he took out an ad in Murfreesboro's Daily News Journal.

New Year! New House! New Goods! New Prices!

W.T. Gum & Co.

W.T. Gum desires to inform his friends and the public generally that he has opened a new and complete store of staple and fancy groceries on the corner of Main Street and Maney's Avenue. I mean business and intend to have it if quick sales and short profits will bring it.

My goods have been bought for cash and will be sold accordingly. All I ask is a small profit but remember, I am **"not closing out at and below cost."**

As well you know how it is yourself. Remember the Grocery Store on the corner. Try me and be convinced that I sell for a shorter profit than any house in the city.

The HIGHEST MARKET PRICE PAID FOR COUNTRY PRODUCE to cash or barter.

Goods delivered to any part of the city free of charge. A call is requested and satisfaction guaranteed. Jan 3

The day the announcement appeared in the paper, there must have been a great deal of excitement in the East Main Street house, at least for Will and Clemmie. With the Murfreesboro store opened, Will felt an immense sense of importance. His advertisement shows that he had grand plans for the future. He was confident that he would soon be a successful merchant.

Will's Uncle Ben Wade had been able to support a wife and seven children with his store. Certainly, he could do even better in the heart of Murfreesboro. Will felt his ads and idea about selling cheap to start would get his name out there and quickly return his and Clemmie's investment.

In addition to the store goods, Will purchased a horse and wagon. He would also need to hire a man to deliver groceries because no self-respecting person in Murfreesboro would carry their own purchases home.[72]

Meanwhile, unbeknownst to most people, perhaps even Clemmie, it had taken more than the $650 (= $13,700) Clemmie gave Will to set up the store. On December 28th, 1877, a few days before the grand opening, he borrowed some additional money from his new mother-in-law. That day, Will T. Gum and Mary Ann Baugh went down to the County Clerk's office, where Will signed a Deed of Trust. In part, the deed read:

> *"I, W.T. Gum of the County of Rutherford & State of Tennessee, for and consideration of Eight hundred and fifty dollars ($850) (= $18,000) to me in hand paid by Mrs. M.A. Baugh of the town of Murfreesboro, … do sell and convey to the said Mary A. Baugh, my entire stock of groceries, supposed to be between nine hundred & fifty & ten hundred ($950 & $1000) dollars (= $21,100 and $22,200) … upon condition that if the said W.T. Gum pay to the said Mary A. Baugh eight hundred & fifty ($850) dollars with interest in one year … this shall be void."*[73]

The store on the corner of Maney Avenue and East Main Street was now fully stocked and ready for business, but in a short time, Will would find that this corner had one disadvantage; the ground here was lower than the street and needed to be built up. When it rained, the corner outside the store formed a huge puddle. In the winter, it formed an ice pond that Will and his customers had to skate across to enter the store. Perhaps, Will scattered straw or dirt across the ice so that neither he nor his patrons fell!

Nevertheless, success was in the offing for Will Gum. With his charm and energetic personality, it didn't take long for people to know who he was. Soon, he was doing a good amount of business. Will's success may have surprised everyone but Clemmie. Will meant the world to her, and she had complete faith in him. As far as she was concerned, the six hundred and fifty dollars of her inheritance had been well spent.

It was 1879 and a new year had begun. Clemmie was going to have a baby! It was amazing. Clemmie who was crippled and had struggled her entire life, unable to do the things that others could do, was with child. She must have been overjoyed but her happiness was short-lived. The child, a little girl born on March 14, 1879, lived only a few hours.

At the Baugh and Gum plots in Evergreen Cemetery there are several unmarked graves. Likely, the baby was buried there. No name was listed for her in the family Bible.[74]

Clemmie was heartbroken, and Mary Ann, the loving mother of eleven children, comforted her youngest daughter, assuring her that she would have more children.

It was not long before Clemmie was with child again. Less than a year after the loss of her first child, another baby arrived. Born on February 15th, 1880, the little girl arrived healthy and full of life. They named her Mary Baugh Gum, after her grandmother. It was a token of affection, respect, and gratitude.

An old store on Maney Avenue not far from where W.T. Gum & Co. stood.

Chapter 5

Life in Murfreesboro

On March 13, 1877, Will T. Gum's father, John Alexander Gum, sold what seems to have been his last parcel of land in District 9 near Old Jefferson. The property was bought by J.J. Ward and consisted of twenty acres bordered by the Creech, Henderson, Miles and Butler families. For the sale, John received $110 (= $2,330).[75]

That same year, the Gum's 49 acres of Marable land in the Blackman Community was valued at $740, far less than Mr. Gum had paid for it. The family paid $3.33 ($73.90) in state, county and school taxes. The following year, 1878, John and Martha Gum exchanged their forty-nine acres in Blackman for a double lot on Maney Avenue, only blocks from Will's store.

The men who exchanged their town lot for the Marable land were William and James Ransom. The lot was bounded by the Buchanan's on the north, Hancock Street on the south and backed up against the City Cemetery on the west. There were two houses on the property; a log cabin which stands today and a larger house which the Gum family chose to live in. Although the property was not large, there was room for a vegetable garden, chickens and a horse or cow, which many of the town locals kept on their lots. Living in Murfreesboro would certainly make life easier for Jere and Martha. Maney Avenue, although not far from the town center, was still very countrified.

It appears that Jere Gum could no long sustain the produce business without the help of his sons, nor did he want to. He was now fifty and like many people of his generation, likely feeling his age.

John Gum, Jr. and wife, Lucy Trigg, moved to Murfreesboro shortly after their marriage. In December of 1878, Lucy gave birth to their baby girl, Annie.

John, Jr. owned a store just off the town square, which sold baked goods and confectionary, or sweets, but by late 1879, he was having financial problems. To protect himself and keep his store open, on January 1, 1880, J.A., Jr., arranged for the official transfer of all his store goods to his wife, Lucy E. Gum, in exchange for $1. The document, referred to as a "mortgage," stated that the property was located in No. 1 Masonic Temple. It read in part:

> *I am indebted to the said Lucy E. Gum by a note bearing the date May 14th, 1880 and falling due on January 1, 1882 for money advanced to me in the amount of Four hundred dollars ... [Should] I fail to pay the said note ... the said Lucy E Gum is hereby authorized to ... sell the same after giving lawful notice of time and place...*[76]

Recently, Lucy's mother, Mrs. N.J. Trigg, had passed away. Although Lucy was entitled to a portion of her mother's land, John, Jr. had to go to court in order for her to receive it. Once the case was settled and Lucy received her share of the land, John promptly sold it. He did not want to be a farmer, and they needed the money. By the time the U.S. Census taker came to call in 1880, John, Lucy and baby Annie had moved in with Jere and Martha Gum on Maney Avenue.

The following year, John, Jr. moved his family into their own home, a short distance away. On August 31st of 1881, Lucy gave birth to their first son, Trigg Alonzo Gum.

By January of 1882, John, Jr. went out of business, selling his entire stock to his brother, Will, for the token payment of $1.00.[77] The Deed of Trust read as follows:

> *... my entire stock of goods, wares, merchandise, notes, accounts & all other evidences of indebtedness and fixtures situated in the stone house & baking establishment thereto attached now occupied by me as a confectionary and Bakery and which is on the East side of the Public Square in the Town of Murfreesboro, County & state Aforesaid.*

The stock included:

> *... candies, tobacco, cigars, canned fruits, pickles, cakes, toys & such other articles as are usually left in a confectionary, also the implements and utensils used in my Bakery as well as all the fixtures of every kind and description belonging to & used in said business.*

There was a condition for this transfer required that Will Gum sell the goods and pay his creditors:

> *I am indebted to the following named persons in the sums set out at specific as follows to wit: To Barton & Ridley $200.00 for house rent; to William T. Gum $195.70* due by account; to Burgreen & Co. of Louisville, KY $102.00 due by account, Geo. Wissel & Co of Nashville, Tenn. $108.00 by account; Northern Lake Ice Company, $100.00 due by account; Cowan & Co. $100.00 due by account, B.F. Moore & Co., $35.00 by account; Spire & Duff $50.00 by account, J.T. Warren $34.00; J.W. Thomas & Co $ Lipscomb & Co $20.00; J.B. Ward $20.00; Spurlock & Co. $40.00; Thomas Kerr $4.00; Albert Jetton $8.00.*[78]

John, Jr. listed two other creditors to whom he owed money Fite & James and B.S. Rhea & Sons, both of Nashville, Tenn., who he promised to pay once he "authenticated" the bills.

This Deed of Trust was an added responsibility for Will Gum, but he wanted to help his brother. Since he was also one of the creditors, in the long run, he would also benefit. Will was in the best position to speedily dispose of the goods and pay off his brother's debts, possibly leaving some profit for himself. Shortly after disposing of their store, John, Lucy and their two babies left Tennessee.

~

Beginning in 1878, Mary Ann Baugh conducted several property sales. In February of that year, she sold property in Old Millersburg to her son-in-law, Robert L. Howland, for the sum of $5,377.60 (= $119,000). The total amount was divided into quarters, to be paid over a period of three years, concluding in 1880.[79]

---

* This means Will Gum had given his brother $195.70 (= $3,590) in goods that he had yet to paid for.

In October, Mary Ann sold Leah Sharp the lot in Christiana next to the lot she had sold several years earlier. For this, she received $150.[80] The following year, on January 6th, she sold Catherine Jamison some land lying between Millersburg and Christiana for $650. The amount of $325 was paid in cash with $325 was due in twelve months.[81] Then, in December of 1879, she sold a lot in Christiana to Jane White, a "colored" woman for $150.[82] Whether Jane was a former Baugh slave or not is unknown. Certainly, she was from the area.

The money earned from these sales appears to have been money Mary Ann Baugh used to support herself. No further property sales were made until December 8, 1881, when she sold land in District 7 to S.W. Peebles. The price paid for this land was $575, with $287.50 down and another payment of that amount due in August of 1882.[83] This property was known as the "Old Searcy tract" bordered Dr. and Mrs. R.W. Richardson's property, just north of where the family had been staying in Blackman.

There was plenty of activity in the house on East Main Street, but for the most part Will and Clemmie Gum seem to have kept to themselves. As a good mother-in-law, Mary Ann let them be. Besides, she had her own business and friends to keep her busy.

During these years, Mary Ann Baugh was a very social woman, and she often walked down East Main Street to visit her neighbors, the Richardsons. She had known Dr. John W. Richardson and his wife, Augusta Mary Starnes when they lived in the Blackman area. Dr. Richardson passed away in 1872, at which point his wife, Augusta, moved in with their son, James D. Mary Ann enjoyed visiting the Richardson home, but it was with Augusta's daughter-in-law, Mrs. A.R. Richardson, that the truest bond of friendship was formed.

Mrs. A.R. Richardson was a woman approximately thirty years younger than Mary Ann Baugh, but the two women felt a kinship and soon became very good friends, visiting one another several times a week. Born Alabama Rebecca Pippen in Greene County, Alabama in 1843, Alabama and James D. Richardson, an adjutant General, met and fell in love during the Civil War. The couple married in 1865 and settled in Murfreesboro. Mrs. Richardson and Mrs. Baugh became acquainted shortly after the Richardsons moved into the house on the western corner of the Baugh's block, around 1867.

By 1880, Alabama was the mother was five children; three girls: Anna (1865), Ida (1867), Alle (1869) and two boys, John W. (1872–1873) and James D., Jr. (1875). Mr. Richardson, an attorney, following in his father's footsteps, was elected to the Tennessee House of Representatives in 1871. He was twenty-eight at the time and, remarkably, on his first day was elected Speaker of the House.[84] After serving as a State Representative for two years, James Richardson was elected to the Tennessee Senate (1873–1875).

John E. Richardson, James Richardson's younger brother and a memeber of his household, having graduated from Princeton University in 1877, had begun to practice law in Murfreesboro as a junior member of the firm, Ridley & Richardson in 1878. The Richardsons were quite an illustrious and charming family and Mary Ann Baugh was glad to know them. Since James E. Richardson was away a great deal of the time, and the family had servants to help with the house and children, Mrs. A.R. Richardson often came to visit with Mrs. Baugh. She enjoyed learning about her long and interesting life.

At this time, Mrs. Baugh had three boarders living in her home.[85] There was sixty year-old widow Sarah Hicks (it is not known if she was related to Mary Ann's sister's family), a seventy-eight year-old single gentleman, Charles Webb, and Fannie Rushing, a thirty-six year-old widowed seamstress. In the U.S. Census of 1880, Mary Baugh and Clemmie Gum were both listed as "keeping house." Will Gum was listed as a "merchant."

Clemmie was happy now and Mary Ann was thankful she did not have to worry about her youngest daughter. Yet, as she sat before the fire, knitting in the winter of 1880, her thoughts turned to worries about her other children, especially her son Benjamin, whose life had become increasingly troubled.

In the last year, Ben's wife, Lethie had come to her about the situation at home. Mary Ann had tried to encourage her to stay in the marriage. To facilitate this, she had even written an agreement with her daughter-in-law stating that if she stayed in the marriage, she would receive a gift of land.

It appears Lethie left Ben for a time, but returned in an effort to keep the marriage going. Their youngest child, Owen White Baugh was born in 1875, the same year Lethie's father passed away. By 1880, Lethie took the children and moved down the road to her mother's house.[86] At this point, Mattie was 12, Edwin, 10, Bettie, 7, and Owen, 5.

Although it is uncertain what Benjamin Baugh's symptoms were, it seems apparent that he was suffering some form of post-traumatic stress syndrome. As a result of his four years at war, there were likely nightmares, lost wanderings, and even times when he thought he was still in battle. Lethie may have feared for her safety and the safety and well-being of the children. As a result, she did something rare for this time period; she filed for divorce, and it was granted.

Documents show that sometime between 1880 and 1882, Benjamin's condition deteriorated to the point that he was committed to the County Asylum. Though it is uncertain where he was sent, one asylum in the area was the Tennessee Hospital for the Insane on Murfreesboro Pike, just south of Nashville. It had been in existence since the 1830s. In 1847, Dorthea Dix, champion of prison and insane inmates, visited the place. With her help and that of the people working there, some improvements were made; however, conditions were still deplorable.[87] In most of these asylums, care of the patients was not good and disease was rampant.

Before Ben was taken to the asylum, knowing that his life would not be long, he gave Mary Ann his gold Mason ring. She wore the ring in memory of him until her death. It was one of her most cherished possessions.

Benjamin Marable Baugh died on September 10th, 1882. He was thirty-nine years old. Of all the children Mary Ann lost, Ben's death was the one that touched her most deeply.

Four years later, in 1886, Mary Ann willed a good portion of land to Lethie Baugh, "for love and affection of my daughter-in-law ... so long as she remains unmarried."[88] At her death the property was to go to the children. Lethie Baugh, who passed away before 1893, never remarried.

During this time, Mary Ann's son, Jack Baugh, and his family moved to the Salem community, and settled on the old homestead, "May Place," with Jack's mother-in-law.

Although Jack does not appear to have suffered the same emotional trauma as his brother Benjamin, he lived with his memories of the war and knowledge of the terrible slaughter many of his brave comrades had suffered. It had been a shock to learn that one of the finest men he fought under, Irish born General Patrick Cleburne, had been shot dead through the heart only miles from Murfreesboro. Following one of the bloodiest battles at the end of the war, the Battle of Franklin, Cleburne's body, along with the bodies of four other Confederate Generals, had been laid out on the porch of Carton Plantation.[89]

Of course, Jack carried another constant reminder of the war; his left arm, which hung helpless by his side. For a while, former slaves in need of work had helped to farm the land in exchange for some of the crops. As Jack's sons grew older, they also helped with the farm, but there was not much money to be made in farming these days and none of the boys seemed inclined to continue in the profession. To bring some income into the family, Jack took a job as a school teacher in the Salem Community. The family got along on the combined income of his teaching salary and the money from the farm, but they were hardly rich.

~

One person who visited the Baugh home on East Main Street quite often was Mary Ann's son-in-law, Dallas Polk Jacobs. Dallas was someone Mary Ann admired, both for his business practices and personal life. Although Dallas Jacobs had married again after Fredonia's death (to Anna Bell Mankins about 1881), he continued to visit Mrs. Baugh and often brought his daughter, Ida Jacobs, to see her grandma. Ida had frequent asthma attacks and was considered "frail," causing Mary Ann to worry that the little girl would not live long. However, now that Ida was nearly a young lady, Dallas, whose successful merchant business had made him fairly well-off, planned to send her to a good boarding school.

So, life progressed for the Baugh and Gum families in Murfreesboro. Although life had its sorrows, for the most part, it was good.

Chapter 6

W.T. Gum & Co.

BY 1883, BUSINESS AT W.T. GUM & COMPANY WAS PROCEEDING AT A steady pace and Will had every reason to be proud. Each morning he rose and headed happily down East Main Street to the corner of Maney. On his way, he passed the "brick office," a small one-story building consisting of three single rooms with outside entrances.

From the brick office building to the corner was a stretch of vacant land through which Mary Ann's flower and vegetable gardens could be seen. At the corner, approximately thirty-five yards from the brick office building, was Will's store.

If Will was not too busy at noon, he could easily take a mid-day dinner break to visit Clemmie and Baby Mary. At present, Will had hired Mrs. Baugh's boarder, eighty-one year-old Mr. Newman as his clerk.

Turning right onto Maney Avenue and walking to the next corner at Vine Street was the small cottage Mary Ann had given her former slave, the faithful Mirandy Miller.

A small cottage near Vine, likely similar to Mammy Ran's.

The cottage was known to all, simply, as "Mammy Ran's house." Mirandy, who was only a couple of years younger than Mrs. Baugh, still came most days to cook for the family.

The extra rooms in the main house were usually rented to family members or friends in need of a place to stay. The back of the house had a long veranda, as was customary for many Southern plantation homes. The outdoor stairs to the veranda allowed the boarders, servants and children to enter the upstairs area without going through the kitchen, or the front entrance, which was reserved for family and special guests.

Although Will T. Gum's store was doing quite well, it appears he had not saved any money. Of course, there had been Mrs. Baugh's loan to repay, but he and Clemmie lived under Mrs. Baugh's roof and received their food free of charge. Six years after their marriage, Will had little to show for all his success.

Mary Ann liked having Clemmie nearby. Increasingly, as she grew older, she felt the need for her presence, but Will could not help feeling that because they were under Mary Ann's roof, Clemmie's family looked down on him. These feelings helped put a chip on his shoulder. He thought Clemmie's siblings could not possibly know what it was like to live in his place, nor could they imagine all he and Clemmie did for Mary Ann. In the six years since their marriage, Mary Ann Baugh had aged and Clemmie felt a growing responsibility toward her mother's care.

The Gum family seem to have welcomed Clemmie into their midst, though there is no record of how much mingling took place between the Baughs and the Gums. Although Will's parents lived only a few blocks away, some of their children were still quite young, and this kept them very busy. In 1882, Jere and Martha Gum had seven children at home: Laura, 22, Lucy, 20, Mollie, 17, Nannie, 15, Bettie, 10, Susie, 8, and Johnny, 5.

On March 13, 1883, Will and Clemmie Gum became the proud parents of their first son, Robert Emmett Gum. The baby was a sturdy little boy, and his sister, Mary, now three, was quite pleased with his arrival. In the future, family members would call him by his middle name, Emmett, but as he grew from infant to toddler, he was known simply as Totsey, a nickname passed down in the family for the little ones tottering about.[90]

~

On July 16th, 1883, Mary Ann Baugh agreed to a new business venture. That day, she signed an agreement to lease space on her property to the Murfreesboro Roller Skating Assembly and Gymnasium Club. The lease for the property read in part:

> *a lot of ground on Main Street ... beginning at a point just 10 feet west of the northwest corner of the store room occupied by W.T. Gum as a produce store; running thence west 50 feet along Main Street, thence South 100 feet; thence East 50 feet, thence North 100 feet to the beginning ... Said property is leased for the purpose of placing immediately thereon a building to be used as a skating rink & Gymnasium Club and each other purpose the said company may decide; not unlawful in itself or immoral. But it is understood no spirituous liquor shall be sold thereon, nor shall there be sold thereon any groceries including cigars, tobacco or any other merchandise, unless otherwise agreed.*[91]

The rental of the property was to be for a minimum of 5 years, garnering Mrs. Baugh $50 (= $1,100) a year, which could be paid in quarterly payments. The lease was an opportunity for Mrs. Baugh to bring in a bit more money, at the very least, enough to cover her property taxes.

Although his feelings on the matter are not known, he may have reasoned that he might benefit from the skating rink's traffic. There are no records as to how well this venture went. Certainly, it would be interesting to picture a skating rink in this area of town, with young people and adults coming to skate and have fun. Perhaps there were even live musicians in a gazebo, playing classical and popular songs for the added pleasure of the skaters.

All was well with this venture, or so it seemed. Then it happened; FIRE! Fires occurred so often during these years, they were common news events. When and how the fire occurred has not been documented. Likely, it started with a kerosene lamp or candle; a spark in the night slowly burning without notice until suddenly, it turned into a conflagration that no one could stop. The calls and bells for the fire wagon, only a few blocks away at South Vine and West Church Streets, were too late. The fire spread to the store. The rink and store were both completely destroyed.

In 1884, after all of Will Gum's success, his livelihood was gone. He had some insurance on the store, but not enough to cover the full cost of the structure and the goods inside. Clemmie's inheritance was gone, and despite the store's earnings, Will was now penniless.[92]

After the fire, Will hung around the house, bored and unhappy. One day, after many months of this, Mrs. Baugh asked, "Will, what do you intend to do for your future?" Will said he didn't know. "Will, you must find some work," said Mrs. Baugh.[93] At this point, the pair had a long conversation. Will told his mother-in-law that if he had more money, he would rebuild the store and go back into business. Finally, she agreed to provide whatever funds were needed. This time, Mary Ann Baugh signed herself on as a partner in the business. The amount of money she lent Will Gum was $530 (= $12,220). Although it is not clear from the legal papers left behind, it appears that Mrs. Baugh took out a loan for this money. She and Will co-signed* the Deed of Trust.

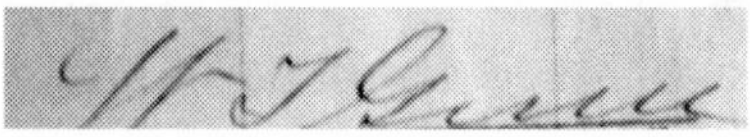

With the borrowed money, Will Gum not only built a new store, he added a "confectionary" next to the store. This was a business he felt certain would be quite profitable.

~

Now, at the age of seventy-two, Mary Ann Baugh was thinking about the end of her life, and what she would leave her children when she was gone. Recently, she had begun to worry about her financial affairs. It seemed her money was going out faster than it was coming in. Her husband, John Baugh, had planned what he wished to leave, but Mary Ann realized that if things continued as they were, not only would she be unable to fulfill her husband's wishes; she would have nothing at all left to give. So, on December 10th, of 1884, Mrs. Baugh deeded some of the former Marable land in the 7th District, to Lizzie Miller, her son Charlie's wife.

Charlie Baugh had been on good terms with his mother and sister, Clemmie, until recently. In fact, in 1880, he and Lizzie named their new baby, Will T. Gum Baugh in honor of Clemmie's husband. Of late,

* Signature Courtesy Rutherford County Archives

however, Charlie had done something that greatly displeased his mother. Dallas Jacobs would later recall that when Charlie was in trouble, he, Dallas, had approached Mrs. Baugh on Charlie's behalf, asking her to help her son. But Mrs. Baugh was stubborn. She had made up her mind about Charlie. In response to Dallas Jacob's request, she said, "I would not help him if he was as naked as the day he was born."[94] In time, with coaxing, Mr. Jacobs convinced her to change her mind. Still, Mrs. Baugh was not a person you wanted to make angry.

By the mid-1880s Charlie and Lizzie Baugh had five children: Mary Ann, 15, Joe, 13, Rawley Miller, 7, William G., 4, and Sammie L., 2. Over the next ten years, the couple would have four more children. Theirs was not an easy life.

The deed Mary Ann Baugh had drawn up for the land was written to insure that her grandchildren eventually inherited the property. The deed also stated that Mrs. Baugh was to be paid $1,000 for the property. Although the land may have been worth more than that, it is questionable whether she ever received money from Charlie or his wife. What seems more likely is that she gave the family this land in lieu of the inheritance Charlie's father had promised him.[95]

One year later, in 1886, Mary Ann deeded the Millersburg property previously mentioned, to her daughter-in-law, Lethie Baugh, and her four grandchildren. The property, in the 25th District, was bounded by the land of R.M. White (Bettie Baugh), and John Pruitt (Eliza Baugh).[96] This appears to be the same land Jack Baugh lived on prior to the war. He had given it to Charlie Baugh, who returned it to Mary Ann, possibly in exchange for the land up north in Blackman.

By now, Mrs. Baugh had a total of thirty-eight grandchildren, and though she did not see them all the time, they were certainly in her mind. Joe had 4 children, Jack had 8, Bettie had 4, Mattie, 1, Ben, 4, Fredonia, 1, Mollie, 5, Eliza, 4, Charles, 5, and Clemmie, 2.

In 1885, Larry and Ellen Maynor, old friends of the family, came to stay with Mrs. Baugh for nine months as boarders. They would return again a couple of years later. During their first stay, the couple visited with Mary Ann Baugh in her room, which was downstairs behind the front staircase. There was a small parlor room directly in front of Mrs. Baugh's which may have been Clemmie and Will's room. With Clemmie's disability, she likely was unable to get up and down stairs without help.

When the Maynors visited Mrs. Baugh, she often spoke of Clemmie, and of her desire to build her daughter a house. She wanted to build it down by the store on Maney Avenue but she said she was worried because the land lay so low there. Mary Ann also told Clemmie of her idea about the house, saying, "I want to give you Mammy Ran's house, so that you can have a woman to cook and wash for you." Obviously, Clemmie was unable to do these things herself.[97]

During this time, Mary Ann Baugh certainly had more on her mind than the Gums, but increasingly she was feeling unhappy with Will Gum. For over forty years, Mrs. Baugh had been married to a devout man with a strong work ethic. It was true they lived on her father's land early in their marriage, but John Aldridge Baugh worked hard to get ahead and make a life for his family. Now, along with certain things Mrs. Baugh had witnessed regarding Will Gum, there were rumors around town about him. These things only served to confirm her doubts and suspicions about her son-in-law.

Chapter 7

Whiskey and Fire

Seven years after his marriage to Clemmie, Will Gum was restless. He had married Clemmie at the age of twenty-three. Now, he was father of two children, with his own business, yet he was still living in his mother-in-law's home. Although it was a large, lovely home near the square, it was not the same as having his own domain. Even Will's store was partially owned by his mother-in-law. Considering the difficulties of the time, many men would have been happy to be in Will's place, but he was not. Will was bored and soon found himself seeking other entertainment.

Murfreesboro was a rather conservative town, but it did have its areas of abandon and sin. There were places men could go to do whatever they wanted. One of these areas was known as Mink Slide. This part of town was just down the hill from the Murfreesboro Square (now Broad Street). Mink Slide was full of narrow, winding streets and shacks, inhabited by poor whites and blacks. In the rainy season, Mink Slide's streets were flooded as waters rushed from the Stones River, overflowing the connecting waterways like Lytle Creek, which ran right through Mink Slide.

Down the hill from the town square, there was drinking, gambling and women; about anything you wanted. Even some of the city leaders and respected citizens visited Mink Slide for one reason or another. It could also be dangerous. At night, there were fights, knifings and murders. Mink Slide had its own excitement and appeal, and likely Will Gum found himself down there after work when he didn't feel like sitting in the parlor with Clemmie and his mother-in-law.

One day someone saw Will Gum in Pig Alley, a place not far from East Main where black people lived. Will was there gambling. He knew the places to go where the law didn't prevail, but word got around and people in the Baugh family heard about it. It seems that everyone heard about it but Clemmie. Even if the rumors reached her, she would not have believed them. She had full faith in her husband.

One evening, Bettie Baugh's husband, Robert White, came to visit. Mr. White sometimes helped Mary Ann with her business affairs, but this evening's visit was purely social. As they ate supper before the fireplace in her room, Mr. White asked,

"Where is Bill Gum?"

Mary Ann responded that Will had gone to Nashville.

"He's pretending to try to get into business, but I don't believe that's so," she said.

Robert White was rather surprised at her response and seeming bitterness. Prior to that moment, he had had no idea she felt any differently about Will than any of her other son-in-laws.[98]

Clemmie never complained about her husband, nor would she say a bad word against him. But Mrs. Baugh had begun to suspect there was a lot more trouble behind Will's affairs than he let on. It was her opinion that her son-in-law was not serious about his business or the support of his wife and children.[99]

～

Will Gum conducted his business in a manner that many storekeepers living near a farm area like Murfreesboro followed. Farmers would bring him so many eggs, so much butter and so many chickens, and Will would either sell them in his store or take a quick trip up to Nashville. In the city, he could sell the farm goods to a store owner or exchange them for items not plentiful in Murfreesboro such as shoes, hats, fabric, or even tools and dishes.

W. T. Gum,
GROCER AND
General Produce Dealer,
Having increased my facilities for buying and shipping I am now enabled to pay the highest market price IN CASH for all kinds of Tennessee Produce.
Butter, Chickens and Eggs
SPECIALTIES.
As I am always in the market, NEVER OVERSTOCKED, and
Willing to Pay Fair Prices,
It will be to the interest of every one selling in this market to give me a call. I also carry a choice fresh
Stock of Family Groceries
Which I will sell or exchange for Produce, at prices that defy competition. Try me and be convinced.
Respectfully,
W. T. GUM,
Corner Main Street and Maney's Avenue, Murfreesboro, Tenn.

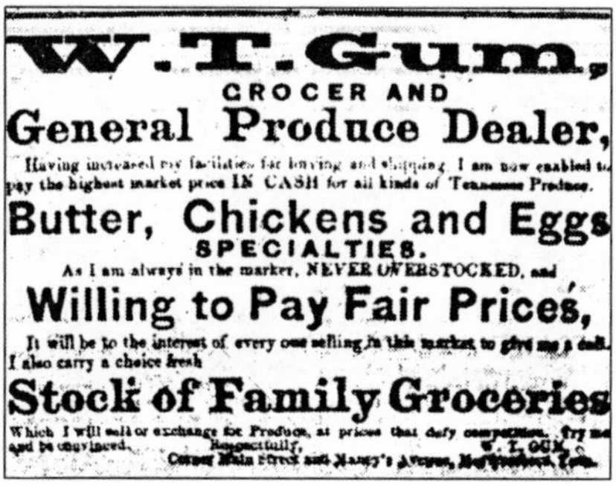

Murfreesboro Free Press, October 1881.

Will probably visited Nashville fairly often. Besides, he had other reasons to visit the city. His father's half brothers, the Crosthwaits, Uncle Anderson and Uncle Henry, lived in the heart of Nashville. Henry Davis Crosthwait was a paper hanger and boarded at 321 S. Market Street.[100] Brother Anderson Lemuel Crosthwait lived with his wife, Helen, and their 5 children at 415 South College Street. As listed on the 1880 Federal Census, also residing in the home were Ellen, 18, George D., 13, Charles A., 12, John H., 10, Thomas L., an infant of two months and Will's grandmother, Malinda Gum Crosthwait, 79.* At that time, Anderson was the keeper of a saloon, which, as listed in the Nashville City Directory, was under the roof of the Linick Hotel.[101]

During the Civil War years, Malinda lived in the Gum home, where she remained until 1870. It is said that sometime after the war, Malinda and her husband, William Crosthwait, went to live "in Indian Territory." Where the "Indian Territory" was, and what happened to William Crosthwait, is unknown. Possibly, the couple lived for a time in Missouri or Oklahoma.

When Malinda returned to live with her son, Anderson, in Nashville, John Alexander Gum must have taken the family to visit her. In any case, Will was well-acquainted with the Crosthwaits and likely happy to visit his old grandma.

In 1881, Anderson Crosthwait and family moved to Humphreys and South Cherry Streets, where Malinda was listed in the City Directory as a boarder. At this point, Anderson held the position of Deputy Sheriff at the Nashville Courthouse, and soon opened his own Cigar and Tobacco Store on the corner of Cherry near the Maxwell House Hotel.

Malinda Crosthwait passed away on November 11, 1883 at the age of 83. At the time of her death, the family bought at plot in Nashville's historic City Cemetery. Although her grave is without a marker, Malinda is buried alongside the other Crosthwait family members there.

In the summer of 1885, Will Gum made at least one business trip up to Nashville.[102] While he was there, something unusual occurred; all the bars in town shut down. In 1885 there were ninety saloons to the sixty-five churches serving Nashville's 40,000 residents. What could be the cause of this outrageous occurrence?

---

* The census lists Malinda Crosthwait as 82, but she was born in 1800.

It would not have taken Will Gum or any other person in town long to find out. A Methodist preacher with a growing reputation named Sam P. Jones had pitched his tent in Nashville. Reverend Jones was a former lawyer who had become a hard drinker and gambler. After turning his life over to Christ, he reformed and was now on the warpath against these evils.

Will decided he would go and see what this Mr. Jones had to say. He was not alone. Among the others curious or miffed that the bars had closed was Captain Tom Ryman, a riverboat magnate. Ryman's riverboats sold whiskey and had gambling. Upset about the possible loss of business, as well as the slur to his reputation, Captain Ryman took a few of his friends to the meeting with a plan to heckle this renowned preacher.

Sam Jones was a rather slight man, with a long mustache and an intense manner. There was something about him that drew people. Shortly before coming to Nashville, Rev. Jones had gone to Memphis. After boasting about the size of the crowd he would attract, many people there laughed, but his appearance at the corner of Eighth and Broadway in downtown Memphis drew ten thousand people.

On his arrival in Nashville, Rev. Jones preached in a tent pitched for the occasion. He began his intense sermon by quoting from the Bible:

> *"Because sentence against an evil work is not executed speedily, therefore the heart of the sons of men is fully set in them to do evil."*
>
> *Ecclesiastes 8:11*
>
> *The question which I now propound plainly stated is this: "Why will you continue in sin?"*

Jones did not waste time launching into his subject:

> *You let me go into a bar room and take a drink of whisky, and it is wired all over the country, and read in every newspaper at the breakfast table tomorrow morning. You go in and take a drink every morning and nobody notices you. This is the difference between a gentleman*

and a vagabond ... You can swear every day. Nobody expects any better of you for it. That is the difference between a gentleman and a vagabond. I thank God, I have lived to see the day in my State when nobody will swear or drink whisky but vagabonds.

You don't like that? Do you? I don't blame you. I would not either. Fifteen years ago I would have felt very much insulted if I had heard a Preacher say that."

Jones was famous for his outburst and cutting to the quick. Ryman, Will Gum, and a host of others were surprised by this and held in suspense. Reverend Jones continued,

Ignorant of the nature of sin! Will you say you don't know your life is wrong? ... I heard a Minister say once, "That Science is going to demonstrate that there is no hell." Said I, "When the delegation comes back I want to be on hand ... Science knows as little about hell, and what is in hell, as science knows about the birth place of God. The biggest fool I know is the fool who gets into the biggest, broadest way to hell, and stops by the way and tries to persuade men there is no hell. The biggest fool is the man who spends his probationary existence in arguing that there is no hell, and then lies down in hell forever, realizing there is one."

Then Sam Jones turned to his own experience, something that would have touched Will in a particular way,

... Thank God, no man was ever satisfied with himself as a sinner.... And when those innocent children throw their lovely arms around your neck and look up into your face, in all the innocence of their nature, you say, "Of all the women [men] that God ever gave children to, I am least calculated to lead them to God and everlasting life."

Many in the crowd began to cry, thinking of their children. One can imagine Will thinking of his own children at home and, perhaps, sobbing over how he had let them down.

There was music that night as well. Reverend Sam Jones understood the important relation of religion and music. He had been working with Edwin Othello Excell on songs. The two would continue to work together creating songs like "Count Your Blessings" and "Since I Have Been Redeemed."

Sam Jones brought home to people the immediacy of what he was telling them.

> *You have got to surrender to God this evening. The hell spirit is here and you have got to expel this spirit out of your heart. If that drunken man knew that in his next drunken dream God would send him to hell ... they would not drink ... any more. ... Don't put it off any longer. Choose this day whom you will serve."*

That night, Captain Thomas Ryman gave his heart to Christ. He would follow the preaching of Sam Jones for the rest of his life and support temperance. He built the Union Gospel Tabernacle to give Reverend Jones a place to preach in Nashville and to encourage the growth of religion. After his death in 1906, Sam Jones preached at his funeral and said that the Tabernacle should be called Ryman's Auditorium instead. In the coming years, Ryman's would become the home of the Grand Ole Opry.[103]

Will T. Gum left Nashville with something new in his heart. On July 12th of that year, W.T. Gum joined the Cumberland Presbyterian Church, the same church where his parents were members. Records state that he joined by profession of faith.[104] He was determined to turn his life around. Some years later, on April 18th, 1890, Will's sister, Susie Gum, would also join the Cumberland Presbyterian Church.

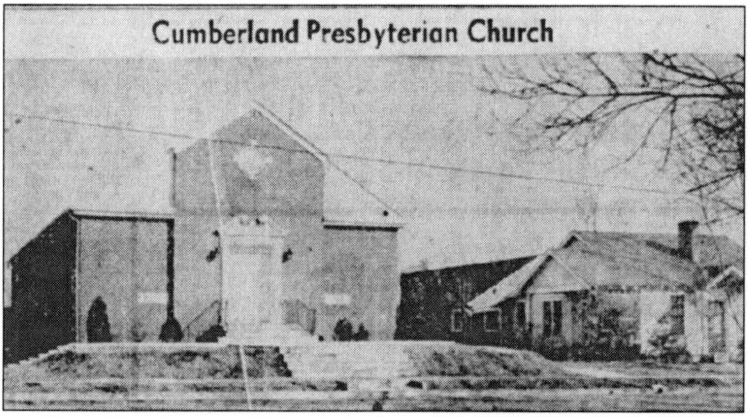

A short time after the event in Nashville, Reverend Jones came to Murfreesboro and pitched his tent in the square. That night, the tent was full and the people inside were shouting and crying. George Howse, a young man, who was passing by, looked in to see people down in the straw, moaning about what sinners they were. As recalled by his daughter, Elizabeth Howse, in her book, *Falling Stars*, George felt "disgusted" and was about to leave, when Rev. Jones raised his hand and in a huge voice said,

> *"Go back to your seats and be still. I want to preach."*

People obeyed him, and the crowd grew completely silent. Then, Rev. Jones delivered such a powerful sermon against sin, that people scarcely know what had happened to them. George Howse later told his daughter, "I can't tell you what Sam said, but before long . . . I found myself shaking his hand and saying I wished to join a church."[105]

One of the things Rev. Jones told his listeners was,

> *". . . Brother, if you don't pray in your family, go home and begin tonight."*

We have to wonder what Will Gum told Clemmie when he came home. Did he start praying with his wife and children? It was not easy for Will because living with his mother-in-law, he did not feel he was the master of his own home, and he needed that for his own sense of accomplishment and self-respect.

~

On March 20th, 1886, approximately nine months after Rev. Jones came to Nashville, the Gums had another blessed event with the birth of their second son. They named him Frank Avent Gum. Frank Avent was a lawyer in town, perhaps a friend of the family. The exact reason the baby was given this name has been lost to time. Clemmie recovered well from the birth and Frank was a healthy, happy, little baby. So, for a time, life was peaceful on East Main.

Frank was not the only grandchild Jere and Martha Gum welcomed into their family during these years. On September 11th, 1884, their twenty-two year-old daughter, Lucy, married Charles Dillard McKnight, a native of Rutherford County. The couple settled in Murfreesboro and over the next six years had four boys: Roy Alexander, born on July 11, 1886, Clair Dixon, born on May 9, 1888, Charles Herschel, on November 11, 1891 and Harry Neil on October 5, 1893.

~

On the 29th of August, 1886, Will T. Gum was urgently summoned to his parent's home. It was a hot day, the air thick with humidity. Will jumped in his delivery wagon, flicked the horse's reigns and rode quickly down the three blocks to his parent's home.

On his arrival, Will found his mother, father and five siblings—Laura, Nannie, Bettie, Susie and eleven year-old Johnny, in a state of despair. A tragedy had occurred; Will's twenty-one year-old sister, Mollie Gum, was dead. She had been such a lively and stylish girl; a joy to everyone who knew her. No one in the family could imagine that she had died so suddenly. The cause of her death is not known.

Jere and Martha bought a family plot next to the Baughs' plot at Evergreen Cemetery. For Mollie's grave, they hired a stone cutter to carve an elaborate stone with a likeness symbolizing Christ, and the words of a popular hymn, "Fell Asleep in Jesus." The funeral was a terrible and heartbreaking affair, considering how young and full of life Mollie had been.

Will's parents were in shock and, for a long time, the entire family remained in a deep state of sadness over Mollie's passing. Some time later, Jere and Martha commissioned an artist to paint their daughter's portrait from a photograph she had taken a short time before she died. The result was a large painting, so beautiful and life-like; it seemed as if Mollie was still there in the house, smiling down on them. This portrait was a great comfort to her parents.

With the stress and sorrow of his sister's death, some time during the next few months Will Gum backslide into his old ways. One night, another fire occurred, and once again the store was completely destroyed. This time, at least, the store was insured.

~

On May 20, 1887, Mary Ann Baugh rode down to the Rutherford County Courthouse and had a deed drawn up of a different kind. It read in part:

Mollie Gum.
(Courtesy Nancy Lee Dismukes)

For and in consideration of the love and affection that I have for my daughter Clemmy (sp) W. Gum, wife of W.T. Gum, I this day bargained and sold and hereby transfer and deliver unto the said Clemmy W. Gum all my right, title and interest in … the entire and a absolute ownership thereof a stock … consisting of family Groceries, Confectionaries, Produce, Tobacco, Cigars and all other Merchandise together with the store furniture of which is contained in a one story frame storehouse situated on the corner of Main Street and Maney Avenue, and heretofore occupied by W.T. Gum & Co. The above mentioned property I convey to my said daughter Clemmy W. Gum to her sole and separate use and estate. I covenant with the said Clemmy W. Gum that the above property is mine absolutely and that I have good right to convey it—This May 19th, 1887. 106

Mary A. Baugh

Will was drinking and gambling again. Sometimes, late at night when Clemmie was asleep, Will came in from wherever he had been, asking Mary Ann for money. His manner was frightening. She was growing tired in her old age, and feeling unwell from the stress of her living situation. Whatever happened, she wanted to make sure that Clemmie was protected. Now, she hoped and prayed that Will would not bother her anymore.

Chapter 8

Money

By early 1888, W.T. Gum & Company was back up and running, seemingly as good as ever. Once again, Will placed ads in the paper. Apparently, he was able to get some fairly large orders, possibly from businesses in the Nashville because along with his store advertisements, he had ads requesting 10,000 spring chickens and 1,000 pounds of butter. With his success, everyone was happy. Clemmie was expecting again, and soon Will would have even more responsibility.

Around this time, Mary Ann Baugh's twenty-eight year-old grandson, Thomas Saunders Baugh, the son Jack and Maria Baugh, became one of her boarders. Thomas had been hired by M. Hirsch & Company, a dry goods store on the Murfreesboro Square, and he needed a place in town to live.

Mary Ann was happy to have another member of the family under her roof. Not only could she use the money, but she missed having a large family around her. Most of her children, Bettie White, Eliza Pruett, Mollie Howland, Joseph Baugh and Charlie Baugh, from whom she was estranged, seldom, if ever, visited. Rollie Howland, since his marriage the previous year, rarely came to see her, either, and Rollie was someone she missed greatly.

Thomas Baugh was a nice young man with the handsome features of the Baughs—the long nose, deep-set eyes, and wavy blond hair. Perhaps he reminded Mary Ann of her husband. She found him to be a responsible, polite young man, and enjoyed talking with him.

John A. Baugh, Jr. No photo exists of his brother Thomas, but the two had similar features. (Courtesy Curry Wolfe)

For his part, Thomas was surprised by how warmly his grandmother welcomed him into her home. She treated him almost like a son. On many occasions, he was invited to visit with her in her room, where she shared her worries and business woes with him. In time, on returning home from work, Thomas could expect his grandmother to request that he take supper with her. During these visits, the conversations often turned to Rollie Howland.

"You know, Rollie Howland, your cousin, lived with me since he was a baby. I do miss him. He was the best boy I ever had. When I die, I intend that he and Ida Jacobs should have their mother's share. That is how I want it."

"Yes, Grandmammie."

"As to Will T. Gum, I intend to drive him off from here."

Thomas felt rather surprised hearing this statement one spring evening. Earlier that afternoon, his grandmother and Will had seemed friendly enough.

"Do you know why I am telling you this, Thomas?"

"No, Grandmammie, I thought all was fine.'

"No, Thomas, it is not fine," she said, with an intensity that seemed to spark in her eyes, "I am very afraid he means to do me some harm."

Thomas sat silently, watching the fire crackle in the grate, unsure of what to say. Then, Mrs. Baugh said something that shocked him with its intensity.

"I would as soon see the Devil come through that door there as see Will Gum!"

Thomas went to bed that night wondering. His grandmother had her moods, but she had always seemed sensible. What had happened to make her speak this way? He could not imagine.

Early one morning, following one of her worst confrontations with Will Gum, Mary Ann Baugh asked one of the hired black boys at the stable to hitch up her two-seat buggy and drive her out to May Place.

In was late in May of 1888, and the fields outside Murfreesboro were a lush green. Though Mary Ann had serious troubles on her mind, the four-mile ride along Salem Pike refreshed her spirits. Laborers were busy tending the fields, and here and there cattle grazed in open pastures. The trees had risen once again out of the rich Tennessee soil, and stretching their leafy branches over the winding country lanes, made a canopy of green for travelers to pass under. It seemed at last the deep scars of war had begun to fade. Fences, barns and houses had been rebuilt. Everything was coming to life. The beauty of Tennessee on this spring morning was as near to heaven as you could get. If only she could be rid of the awful fear and worry in her life. The terrible stress was taking its toll.

As Maria Baugh looked out the front window that day, she was surprised to see her mother-in-law, Mary Ann Baugh, arriving in a two-seat buggy with a Negro boy at the reigns. By the time the young boy had helped Mary Ann down from the buggy, the entire family at May Place, including Jack and Maria, Jack's mother-in-law, Louisa Jarratt, and Maria's sister, Josephine Blake, who was visiting from her farm next door, were at the door to greet her.

At this time, Jack Baugh's family was staying with his mother-in-law, Louisa Jarratt, at the homeplace known as May Place. Mr. Jarratt had passed away back in 1877, but Louisa had continued on by herself, seeing that the land was farmed. Louisa and Mary Ann were close in age, possibly friends from their youth, and always enjoyed visiting together.

After greetings all around, Jack questioned his mother as to what they owed the pleasure of her unexpected visit. It was a business visit, she told him. "I need to borrow some money."

Meanwhile, there was time to visit with the grandchildren before they discussed this business. It was always a pleasure to see her lovely young granddaughter, Mary, who had been named for her. While some of John and Maria's nine living children were already grown, there were still some at home: Richard Batts, 14, Murphey George, 12, Benjamin Marable, who had been named for his uncle, 9, as well as the littlest ones, Josephine Elizabeth, 6, and Robert White Baugh, 4.

John M. Baugh Family about 1883, l. to r. (Back) Delia Blake, Mary, John A., Jr., Will H., (Front) Dick, Murphey George, John M., Maria, (baby) Josephine "Betty" Elizabeth, Ben M. (Courtesy Susan Robling)

When the family sat down for a meal, the table was quite full. Josephine's daughter, twelve year-old Delia Blake, who was also living with the Baugh family, joined them. After the short repast, the adults went out to the porch and sat in the shade of the large, old trees.

After a few moments, Louisa turned to Mary Ann, eager to share the most recent events of her life. Louisa, who had always been a handsome woman, with dark hair and smooth features was still beautiful, but of late had aged and grown a bit frailer.

"Mary, I have recently had my will made and, I tell you, it has been a great relief to me that all has been taken care of. Have you thought of making yours?"

"Well, no, Louisa, I have not."

"You really should."

"Well, I have thought of making one, but whenever I am about to do it, Will Gum will do something that makes me mad. And now, I don't reckon that I ever will make it."

Jack Baugh's eyes widened at bit at these words. He had always known his mother to be changeable in her ways. If she heard something she didn't like about a person, she would easily change her opinion of them. Since Clemmie's marriage, it seemed to him that his mother had become less sensible than ever. Now it was difficult for him to contain himself.

"Why, for goodness sakes, Mammie, won't you write your will?"

"Because I'm afraid," said Mary Ann.

At this point, Maria and Josephine who were sitting nearby turned their full attention on Mrs. Baugh.

"Why would you be afraid to write your will, Mammie?

"Because John," said Mary Ann, looking at him intensely and speaking in an almost a hushed voice, "I am afraid that if I don't make the will to suit Will Gum, he will burn my house down over my head."[107]

"Mammie, why don't you get rid of him? Put him out."

"I can't, John. I fear what he may do. That is why I came today. I paid $2,000 of debts for Will Gum." (= $46,500)

John and Maria were shocked by this news. Two thousand dollars was a huge amount for her to be paying out. Jack was used to Mary Ann's outbursts. Possibly, he thought she was being dramatic. Yet, if things kept on as they were, Jack had no doubt his mother would run out of money. To his mind, she was an old woman, who was obviously being taken advantage of.

"I want to give Clemmie the advantage of having property when I am gone, but having to pay all this money for Gum makes me not care whether she gets it or not. That is why I came to visit. I need to borrow some money to pay debts."

What Jack Baugh replied is not known. He and Maria were living "comfortably" but they certainly did not have a great deal of money. In addition, they had a lot of people to support.[108]

Jack, Maria and Josephine would never forget this visit. Was Mrs. Baugh simply an old woman imaging things or was Will truly threatening her?

The one verifiable matter was that Mary Ann's money was quickly disappearing. Her words stunned everyone present, but knowing her to be a strong-willed and opinionated woman, Jack realized there was nothing he could do.

Two years after this lovely spring picnic, Louisa Jarratt died. She was buried on the Jarratt property alongside her husband, behind the barn. There were no markers; the family just knew where they were.

Chapter 9
An Accident

ROLLIE HOWLAND'S WHEREABOUTS AFTER GRADUATING FROM THE Winchester Normal School are unknown. It seems likely he returned to his father's home in Beech Grove and attempted find work. Around this time, he met a young woman six years his junior, Ellen Townsend, who was attending school in the area.

Miss Ellen Townsend was the only child of Daniel C. Townsend of Marshall County, which lies just west of Rutherford County. Ellen's mother, Elizabeth Ellen Lowe, passed away when Ellen was eleven years old, leaving her the heiress to quite a bit of land.

Rollie and Ellen were married in Rutherford County on September 8, 1887.[109] Following the marriage, they moved into the Townsend family mansion near Chapel Hill with Ellen's widowed father and three black servants. There was Mr. Townsend's personal servant, his wife, the cook, and their daughter, who served as a housemaid. The mansion sat on Ellen's inherited property, a 250 acre farm, which they were able to managed to plant with the help of some of the young black men and boys who lived in the area.[110]

At the start of their marriage, Rollie was ambitious and made plans on how he would grow his wife's wealth. Working with his fifty-five year-old father-in-law, they hired several additional young men from families living on the outskirts of the farm. While the "day laborers" farmed the land, Rollie and D.C. Townsend tried to repair the barn and the rotted fence railings around the property. Some of the property had not been cared for in a long time.[111]

Though the year dates do not match with their marriage, it is said that Rollie and Ellen had a daughter, born on November 16. The little girl was named Mary R. Howland, but like many children of the time she did not live more than a few years.[112]

Rollie kept in touch with his grandmother during this time, but life in Marshall County kept him busy. As a result, he visited his grandmother less and less frequently.

Then, in late 1888, Rollie had an accident. The exact cause of the accident has yet to be discovered, but it can be assumed that something occurred while he was farming. Possibly, he had fallen from his horse or a wagon tipped over and fell on him. Because of the severity of the accident, Rollie was unable to leave his bed for many months. He had severe pain in his back and central organs. During this time, he asked Ellen to write a letter to his grandmother for him, expressing regret that he was unable to visit her, but he hoped all was well.

~

In January of 1889, Will and Clemmie took a short trip to Mt. Pleasant, Tennessee, a small town south of Murfreesboro. Recently, due to the discovery of phosphate, a mineral used in fertilizer, the town had experienced a large growth spurt. The Gums' visit may have been for business, combined with a short vacation, but while they were there, Clemmie suddenly went into labor. On January 3, 1889, Will and Clemmie's 4th child, a big, healthy boy was born. A few days later, they bundled the new baby up and returned to Murfreesboro.

On their return, Mary Ann was delighted to see Will and Clemmie in such good spirits and especially surprised to see that the baby had already arrived. Clemmie had her hands full, but Mary who was now nine, helped her mother a great deal. Emmett, five, and Frank, almost three, were excited to find that they had another brother. The couple had not decided on a name for the little boy, so they called him "Baby." They had decided to take their time in naming him.

Despite the celebration over the new arrival, Will Gum was not the man he had been. His behavior seemed more and more erratic. He was restless and nervous, coming and going at all hours. In addition, Will had no money and was unable to pay his bills. This time, Mary Ann Baugh could not help him.[113]

On February 2nd, 1889 Mrs. Baugh was forced to sell more of her father's land in order to come up with some cash. Luckily, she had a buyer in her sister's son, Henry Hartwell Hicks, "Cousin Hart." For the 104 acres of former Marable land, Mary Ann received a sizeable amount of "cash in hand" totaling $1,184 (= $28,500). One year after the sale, she was to receive an additional $500 (= $12,000), and in two more years, another $500.[114] This money was needed to pay off certain debts, as well as the property taxes.

~

It was a chilly afternoon in February of 1889 that Mr. R.N. Ransom came to Mrs. Baugh's home in order to inquire about the now vacant store on the corner. After all the fires and restorations, W.T. Gum & Company was out of business.

Mary Ann Baugh welcomed Mr. Ransom in the front parlor. After a few moments of pleasantries, Mr. Ransom stated that he understood Mrs. Baugh to be the owner of this store and that he was interested in renting it. A discussion followed, and a monthly rental amount was agreed upon. Mr. Ransom's arrival on the scene was a blessing. In addition to renting the shop, he agreed to buy the remaining supplies left by W.T. Gum & Company.

~

In Montgomery County, Rollie Howland was still laid up from his severe accident. Having very little money of his own, Rollie pondered his situation. Recently, he had learned that a neighbor of theirs, Mr. Hicks (not related to the Rutherford County Hicks), was selling a large piece of land which bordered on Ellen's property. Rollie, who was eager to have his own income, reasoned that if he was able to purchase this land, which was excellent farmland, he would do quite well. He decided to write his grandmother about his inheritance.

When Mary Ann Baugh received Rollie's letter, she was overjoyed. Her life with Will T. had become a trial and she was feeling very low. Since her eyesight was not good, she asked Clemmie to read the letter.

Rollie had written to his grandmother about his health, stating that it would be some time before he would be well enough to visit her. Then, his letter turned to money and his thoughts about his inheritance. As Clemmie continued to read Rollie's letter, Mary Ann became increasingly agitated. She had expected an expression of love and affection, but instead, just like Will Gum, Rollie appeared to be interested only in getting her money. It was too much for her to bear.

Clemmie could see that her mother was not pleased. By the time she finished the letter, which concluded with best wishes for "Sister Clemmie's new baby," and a suggestion that the baby might be named after him, Mary Ann was fuming. She and her husband had worked very hard for what they had. Now Rollie Howland, whose wife had more money than any of her children, was asking her for money. One thing she could never stand was having others telling her what she should to do.

Mary Ann asked Clemmie to get paper and pen and write a letter to Rollie for her immediately. Although Clemmie had her own feelings of resentment toward Rollie, she refused.

"No, Mammie, I won't do it! If I write that letter for you, Rollie will think that I am the one who has caused you to be angry with him. I won't do it!"

"Very well, then," said Mary Ann. Clemmie was like her. Once she made up her mind about something, you couldn't budge her.

The next day, Miss Maggie Muirhead came to visit. Maggie was Mrs. A.R. Richardson's granddaughter. Maggie's grandfather, James D. Richardson, had been elected to the U.S. House of Representatives five years earlier, in 1884, a position he would serve in until 1904. During his time in Washington, DC, James D. Richardson compiled two historical works of value to scholars: *Messages and Papers of the Presidents* and *Messages and Papers of the Confederacy*.

Mrs. Baugh enjoyed her visit with Maggie. After their usual pleasantries and conversation about the latest events at home, Mrs. Baugh asked Maggie if she would write a letter for her.[115] Miss Muirhead gladly agreed. Later, when Clemmie came into the room, Mary Ann told her very pleasantly that the letter had been written and sent.

Some days after this, as Rollie was adjusting himself in bed, trying to lie in a way that would ease the pain, Ellen came in with the mail which a neighbor had kindly delivered from the post office in town.

Rollie was excited to see the neat little envelope addressed to him from Murfreesboro. Opening the envelope, he read:

Murfreesboro, Feb 21st, 1889

Dear Rollie:

Your letter of the 18th was just received and I was pained to hear that you had received a hurt and trust that it may not prove serious. Your letter finds all of us well except myself.

Clemmie is up and has a large splendid looking little boy. As yet he has not been named. Certainly you offer strong inducements to have him named for yourself. Don't know what Clemmie will decide on in the way of a name.

I have been in a great deal of trouble for the past three or four weeks, and have been greatly depressed. It seems that misfortune after misfortune has come upon me in the way of money matters."

It is true that I have sold the land. Cousin Hart paid $1184 cash for the land, and gave me notes for the remaining $1,000. It is furthermore true that I have already paid out the $1,184 and am not through paying yet. And I have been greatly troubled over these debts that have come against me. $400 went to pay for debts for which I had contracted the remainder of debts coming against Mr. Will Gum for which I was bound for and could not get out of paying, by his getting me into the firm as Gum & Co.

I have given you the facts and have gone into detail in order that you may see how utterly impossible it is for me to comply with your request. When I made you the promise that I would give you a $1000 I saw nothing at that time that I thought would prevent my complying with the promise, and was sincere and honest for it.

Regret that it is not in my power to hand over to you that amount, but the trouble Mr. Gum has involved me in makes it impossible. The remaining note on Cousin Hart for the one thousand dollars I will have to keep to pay my insurance and taxes with, these two things have to be met.

You knew too of the little income I have for the rent of the houses on the place. After loosing rent by Negroes and other renters I have barely enough to keep up current expenses and would not by any means pay my taxes and insurance from the rents I get.

Neither am I out of debt yet. I have still another note to meet bearing interest. I wish it were otherwise. But I do not feel that you will have to wait long for your mother's interest in my estate.

My days could not be many at best, and coupled with the trouble I have already seen and do see I feel that I shall not be here much longer. Have a little patience and you will have your rights. Remember all of us to your wife and family, and come and see us.

With much love,

Mary A. Baugh

PS: Will Gum has been closed out. He has nothing to do with the store now. Mr. Rob Ransom owns the stock and rents the store.[116]

So that was that. Rollie would not get the money he desired. He must have wondered what further troubles Will Gum had brought upon Mary Ann. His grandmother had always had money, but he had seen the beginnings of this trouble in Clemmie's marriage to Will when he left the house in 1877. It was a terrible shame.

Rollie, who had always known love from his grandmother, did not see the full extent of her anger over his request for the inheritance she had always promised. He was in too much pain of his own and he sympathized with hers.

In the months that followed, Mary Ann waited but she heard little from Rollie, nor did he visit her. She may have thought he was upset, and really cared little for anything but her money. The truth was that, Rollie was laid up in bed for 10 months. When he finally was able to leave his bed, he was required to wear a back brace that was extremely uncomfortable, and which sent him back to bed a short time after getting up. He tired easily and would have to loosen the brace in order to lie down. Rollie would not be able to ride a horse for many more months due to the injury to his back.

Will and Clemmie decided to name their baby boy, William Wade Gum; William for his father and being a name handed down in the Gum family. The Wade, of course, was in honor of Will's mother.

Chapter 10

In the Darkness of Night

As 1889 progressed, Mary Ann's grandson, Thomas, began to question the wisdom of staying at the Baugh home. Increasingly, he felt uncomfortable with some of the treatment his grandmother received at the hands of Will and Clemmie. One night toward the end of the month, Mary Ann seemed more anxious than usual to talk to him.

When he came into her room to pay the rent, she lifted her finger to her lips and said,

"Shhsh. Come in and close the door."

Even with the walls more than a foot thick, it was obvious his grandmother was afraid of being heard.

"Now, promise me this, don't ever say that you have given me money or paid rent in Will Gum's presence, and don't ever tell him that if he asks."

"No ma'am."

"If you do, he will worry me to death until he gets it."

Thomas promised that he would not say anything.

"That old Devil will make me give it to him if he knows I have it,"[117] she repeated.

To Thomas, the air in the house seemed thicker with tension each day. Now that Clemmie was up and about, she sometimes came in and asked what they had been talking about. She seemed to be very sweet to her mother, always inquiring what she needed and if she was comfortable. However, when Mrs. Baugh was not feeling well, Clemmie often grew impatient.

Once, Thomas witnessed something that rather shocked him. Mrs. Baugh had been sick to her stomach and was feeling a bit dazed and confused. Clemmie, who was helping her, suddenly got angry and cried out,

"You old fool! You are too much trouble!"[118]

This upset Mrs. Baugh, who already embarrassed at her condition and it upset Thomas to see his grandmother spoken to in this way.

~

On March 20th, the family celebrated little Frank's third birthday. Only days later, on a cold and windy night, the alarm went up again. The store on the corner was in flames! Built completely of wood, the building went up like a tinderbox. This time, there had been insurance on the building, though not enough to cover the cost of the structure and its contents. Mary Ann had lost her investment once again, and Mr. Ransom had lost his as well.

During this period, Mary Ann Baugh lent Will and Clemmie more money, signing notes of $500 and $300 (= $12,000 and $7,200). One night, she sat at the dining room table, angrily questioning Will and Clemmie about some notes they said were due. She thought she had already paid them. Clemmie said she had renewed the notes without her mother's knowledge. Mary Ann was upset, but she had no choice. She had to pay them.

The stress for an old woman was too much. She told Thomas about Will Gum's late night visits; asking for money; threatening her with what he would do if she did not give it. She trembled at the memory of these visits, and at the thought that he might be waiting in the darkness to hurt her.

Strangely, on the mornings following these encounters Will Gum came to breakfast, as pleasant as could be; only complaining of a headache. Mary Ann Marable Baugh, a well-respected woman of the community, watched helplessly as her money disappeared bit by bit, and in some cases, chunk by chunk. Clemmie, crippled from birth, now blessed with a marriage and children, defended her husband. She believed he was a victim of bad luck. But Mary Ann knew better, Clemmie had a bad husband.

One day, after listening to his grandmother speak about Will Gum, Thomas asked her,

"Grandma, why don't you just make him leave?"

"Oh, Thomas," Mary Ann replied, "I would like to get rid of Will Gum, but I am so afraid ... Besides," she added with a sigh, "I cannot stand to think of the disgrace it would be for the poor little children, Mary, Emmett, Frank and the innocent Babe."[119]

~

That June, seeing that her money was low, Mary Ann sold the cedar timber off her Marable tract to Benjamin Blackman for $310 (= $7,460). The note stated that Blackman was to remove all the timber on the 1st day of April, 1892. [120]

One night, Will and Clemmie forced Mary Ann to sign over $1,000 note. Will told Mary Ann that he must have the money. He had done a fellow a favor and gotten into trouble. He was desperate. Likely, Will had gotten into trouble over a gambling debt, and feared for his life. There were areas of Rutherford County where citizens would think nothing of putting a bullet in someone's back. In desperation, Will told Mrs. Baugh to sell her land.

"I have," she said, "and it does not cover the cost of these debts. Soon, there will be nothing left."

With Will on one side, pushing her to sign, and Clemmie, on the other side, crying and begging, Mary Ann finally gave in, and signed the note.

That autumn, Thomas began to feel that the Gums resented his presence. Clemmie, in particular, seemed suspicious of the time he spent talking with Mary Ann. Perhaps she suspected her mother was speaking badly about her and Will.

It seemed to Thomas that it might be better if he left. He hated to tell Granny because he knew she enjoyed his company, but in a short time he found a good job in Nashville, and the deal was cinched. Once he was gone, he truly hoped that Will and Clemmie would be kinder to his grandmother.

~

It the late autumn of 1889, Rollie Howland finally felt up to riding down to Murfreesboro to visit Grandmother Baugh. As he entered her room, he was surprised to see how much his grandmother had aged. She seemed small and frail, and did not get up from her chair to greet him.

As usual, they spoke of many things; of relatives, the rentals, money and the old times when Grandfather Baugh was alive, and the entire family lived in Old Millersburg. Just before he left, Mary Ann Baugh turned to her grandson and said,

"Now Rollie, when I die, you are to get your mother's share. You will get the $1,000 your grandfather left for each of the children in my will. I know you were hoping to get some of the money sooner, but I have just not been able to part with the cash. When I am gone and the property is divided, you will get it."[121]

This statement was something Rollie had heard over and over. Even though the money was not available now, he was sure his grandmother would be true to her promise. That promise represented her love for him as much as financial gain.

At the close of 1889, Mrs. Baugh's granddaughter, Ida Jacobs, came for visit. Ida was attending a boarding school, but had returned home for Christmas. Mary Ann told her that day, "My memory is not what it was, dear Ida. I am getting old."

~

At the end of 1890, Thomas' eighteen year-old brother, William Baugh, came to stay in Will Gum's store building, which had now been rebuilt.

William H. Baugh later in life. (Courtesy Curry Wolfe)

Will Baugh had been hired by J.D. Cramer to sell tobacco. His job included driving large wagonloads of tobacco leaves to various destinations, both in and outside of Rutherford County. Because of this, William would not always be in town.

When he was in town, William came back to the house for his noon-time meal. It was then, or sometimes before retiring, that Mary Ann often asked her grandson to come and visit with her. It seemed to him that she was always troubled these days. He was surprised to see the amount of fear she had toward Will Gum.[122] She told him, "It is terrible to have things and be afraid to ask for them. If I do ask for them, Clemmie will 'snap them up.'"

These days, more and more, Mary Ann stayed at home. With the exception of Mrs. Richardson, who visited regularly, Will and Clemmie were the only people who saw her most of the time.

~

In 1891, Will Gum was back in business, this time in a partnership with J.W. Perry, though the store remained under the name, *W.T. Gum & Co.* The two men rented a store building from James W. Avent, on the corner of the Public Square and Church Street, where they sold staples like coffee, tea, cigars, tobacco and "fancy groceries." Will was paid a salary of $30 a week plus a percentage of the profits (= $730). Though the partnership seemed hopeful, the new store soon failed, and by June of 1891, was closed.

That August 6th, Mary Ann Baugh turned seventy-nine. By now, even Clemmie was aware of how much her mother had aged. One day, she asked old Aunt Ran, as the family sometimes called Mirandy, if she would ask her mother to make her will and give her whatever she was going to give her while she was able to make her wishes known. Clemmie dared not make the suggestion herself.

Ran, who still came each day to cook the family's meals, was quick to observe what was going on. She was now about seventy-four years old, and had known Mary Ann Baugh most of her life. She could see that Mrs. Baugh was failing and would not be around much longer. So, one day, while in Mary Ann's room, Ran asked her,

"Why don't you make a will and give Miss Clemmie what you are 'gwine' to give her, while you're on your feet?"[123]

Mrs. Baugh got the old determined look on her face, and turning to Aunt Ran said, "I'm not gwine to do it."

She was angry about something Clemmie had done that day; having her sign deeds that she thought were paid. Ran would later say, "She was in a passion…" So, it was no use.

Toward the end of the year, Eliza's husband, John Pruitt, came up to Murfreesboro on some business and after he was finished, stopped by to have dinner with his mother-in-law. That night, she told him, "I am going to disinherit some of my children."

Chapter 11

Christmas 1891

On Christmas Eve, Rollie and Ellen Howland drove into Murfreesboro on their way to a reception for one of Ellen's relatives in Old Millersburg. They intended to visit Rollie's grandmother and wish her a happy Christmas, but before that they needed to do a bit of shopping.

Mr. Bell. (Courtesy Bell Jewelers)

As Rollie pulled the horse up in front of Mr. Bell's jewelry store on the northeast side of the square, he saw Will Gum walking by. Rollie and Will greeted one another, and Rollie explained that they were going to buy a wedding gift, but once they were finished, they would visit Grandmother Baugh.

Will seemed pleasant enough, and said he would see them soon. Then, Mr. and Mrs. Howland hurried inside, intent on finding the perfect gift. Mr. Bell's store contained not only jewelry and spectacles, but silverware and silver items. After purchasing a gift, the couple left the store with parcel in hand.

As Rollie clicked the horse's reigns and turned the wagon toward Main Street, the sun was getting low in the afternoon winter sky. Just then, some young boys ran from the square down East Main yelling,

Dr. Lyon's home in Old Millersburg

throwing firecrackers into the street and firing "Christmas guns." The sound made Rollie's new horse skittish, and it broke into a run. Luckily, Rollie, with his bad back, was able to slow the horse down.

Rather than risk another incident, Rollie turned the buggy down a side street toward Vine. Meanwhile, Will Gum, who had been talking to friends on the square, saw Rollie and Ellen, and came over to the buggy. Hopping on the carriage step, he rode with them "round to Vine Street, where Mr. Allen's horse stalls were."[124]

By the time they reached Mr. Allen's stalls, Ellen said she was not feeling well. It was a cold winter's day, and being unable to park directly in front of the Baugh home, they would have to walk several blocks to the Baugh house. Rollie decided they should head out to Old Millersburg instead. Dr. Lyon, with whom they would be staying, had a grand home, where Ellen would be well-cared for.

Rollie asked Will Gum to please send Mrs. Baugh their apologies and let her know that instead of visiting today, he and Ellen would come for a visit on their way home. He hoped she would understand. Then, he dashed a short note off to Grandmother Baugh, which he handed to Will, who promised to pass it on. As Will set off on his way home, Rollie flicked the reigns, and the Howland buggy moved swiftly down the road in the direction of the Manchester Highway and Old Millersburg.

~

That afternoon, Mary Ann sat quietly by the window, waiting for her grandson and his wife arrive. Clemmie, who sat near by, knew how much her mother was looking forward to this visit. A short time later, Will Gum entered the room with a small piece of paper in his hand. He said it was from Rollie, whom he had seen shopping in the square. Rollie would not be visiting that day.

What Will told his mother-in-law is uncertain. He could have had his own reasons for allowing Mary Ann to be displeased with Rollie. In any case, Mrs. Baugh found it difficult to accept the fact that Rollie, who had only been three blocks away, had failed to visit her for Christmas. It cut her to the heart.

Clemmie couldn't help feeling a little smug. Her mother had always set such store in Rollie, and, now, look at what he had done. He was selfish; just as she had always thought. Will told Mary Ann that Rollie would visit in a week, but after Mary Ann received the message, she turned her face away and said nothing for most of the evening.

Between Christmas and New Years, Mary Ann's friend, Mrs. Alabama Richardson came to visit. The two ladies chatted about this and that; the weather, the neighborhood and family. Then, Mrs. Richardson asked,

"Mary, did your family visit over Christmas?"

Mrs. Baugh did want to talk about her Christmas. Instead, she said,

"You know, Alabama, I always intended on building Clemmie a house on Maney's or even on East Main Street, but I no longer have enough money to build it."

Mrs. Richardson tried to compliment Mrs. Baugh on how lucky Clemmie was to live with her, Mrs. Baugh replied,

"I know but I always intended for Clemmie to have her own home."

"And how is Rollie Howland?"

"Rollie Howland," replied Mrs. Baugh, with a bit of annoyance in her tone. "I have given him all I ever intend to give. I don't intend to give him more. He has married a lady who has a-plenty. He has no need for more money, like some of my children."[125]

Yet, even with her annoyance at Rollie Howland, Mary Ann Baugh still loved him. When Will or Clemmie said anything against him, she pursed her lips and would not say a word.[126]

~

One week after Christmas, Rollie and Ellen came back through town on their way home. This time, Rollie parked the horse and carriage in front of the house and came in. Mary Ann Baugh was in her room when they arrived.

Rollie M. Howland, circa 1907.
(Courtesy Tennessee State Library and Archives)

"Hello Grandma," Rollie called, waking her from a doze before the fire. "Ellen and I are here."

Grandmother Baugh's face lit up with a smile, like sunshine breaking through clouds.

"Come and sit with me, Rollie, and tell me how you have been."

Rollie recounted the story of Christmas Eve and the reason he and Ellen had not come that day. Indeed, Ellen had been quite ill and, when they arrived at Dr. Lyons' home, had taken to her bed for several days.

Grandmother Baugh seemed quite cheery with Rollie and Ellen, and they had a wonderful visit. Mary Ann did tell him that she had been feeling much older of late and had missed seeing him for such a long while.

While Rollie and Ellen were there, Clemmie and Will came in and visited with them. Later, Clemmie took Ellen to see the children who were in another part of the house. With Ellen out of the room, Rollie's grandmother took the opportunity to fill him in on the details she had mentioned in her letter regarding Will Gum and the notes she had been forced to sign.

"Will has taken to drink and gambling, and has got into a lot of trouble. Sometimes, he comes in late at night and says the most terrible things to me."

"Grandma," said Rollie, feeling disgust for the treatment Mary Ann had received, "I would not stand for this in my own home. If I were you, I would put them out."

"I won't do it," said Mary Ann, showing some of her old strength.

"I just meant, Grandma, that you should not be treated like that in your own home."

His Grandmother was thirsty, so Rollie went out to the kitchen and found Clemmie. Together they prepared a pot of tea and biscuits, which they brought back to Mary Ann's room. They visited pleasantly the rest of the afternoon. Will Gum had gone out, and Rollie did not bring his name up. He was happy the dark shadow cast by Will Gum would not be delved into further.

That day, when Rollie kissed his grandmother goodbye, he did not know it would be the last time.

Chapter 12

Stricken

The Christmas season of 1891 had come and gone. Then, two days after New Years, Mary Ann was stricken suddenly and became unable to speak or move the right side of her body.

Will Gum went for Dr. Bilbro, who lived several blocks down East Main Street, and was considered a well-respected doctor. After a short examination, Dr. Bilbro told the family that Mary Ann Baugh had suffered a stroke. It was difficult for her to talk or swallow. Because she could not talk or fully show expression on her face, no one was certain as to how keen her mind was.

Word was sent to family members in Salem, Winchester, Old Millersburg and Beech Grove of Mrs. Baugh's illness. Daughters, Bettie White and Eliza Pruitt, rushed to be by their mother's side. Jack and his children in Salem came as well.

Clemmie was unable to help her mother much. In addition to her disability, she was once again with child. The baby was expected to arrive sometime in June, and already she was having trouble maneuvering around the room.

As Jack Baugh drove the wagon into town with his wife, Maria, and daughter, Mary, he could not help but remember his last conversation with his mother shortly after Christmas. She had said to him, "I'm not going to make a will. I want you and Joe to wind up my estate." Had she felt her time was coming?

Jack left Maria at his mother's home for several days, where she helped her sister-in-laws with the "round the clock" care Mary Ann required. Daughter, Mary, would stay longer. William Baugh, who was still boarding with his grandmother, stopped by between trips delivering tobacco.

"Hello Grandmammie. How are you? It's Will Baugh."

Although Mary Ann was sitting up in bed, she only looked at him, but showed no sign of recognition.

"Grandma," said Mary, "It's Will. Will! You know him."

Grandma Baugh reached toward him as if to kiss him and tried to speak but only a string of sounds came out

"Uhmmm_iyah_ahhh_ta."

It was difficult to take. Will understood nothing.

A few days later, Will Baugh stopped by again. This time Mary Ann, who was again sitting up in bed, appeared pale and ill. She looked so much older than the strong woman he had always known. He said "hello" and kissed her, but she showed no response. "She's failing," he thought to himself, but tried to be cheerful.

"How do you feel, Grandma?"

Mrs. Baugh waved her hand and tried to mumble something he did not understand. Shortly after that, he left.

Mary Ann Baugh's friend, Mrs. Richardson came to visit her daily. Her steady, cheerful personality brought some light to the home, as well as a sense of normalcy for Mary Ann.

The house was once again bustling with activity and family members, just as it had in the old days. People came and went, each doing their share to show concern and make things run smoothly. Even Mammy Ran, who had not worked as much of late, made some home-cooked broth that she thought Mary Ann might be able to swallow more easily.

One day, while coming through the dining room, Ran noticed Will and Clemmie were seated at the table talking and heard Will say to Clemmie, "Has she said anything yet?" to which Clemmie replied, "No." Ran knew the couple was talking about Mary Ann making a will. It seemed too late now.

While Clemmie's sister, Bettie, was visiting, she noticed that each day Clemmie brought two of the children in to see her mother. One day,

Mary and Emmett, the oldest two, had the measles and since Mary Ann had never had measles, the other family members stopped Clemmie from bringing them into the room. A short time later, Clemmie returned with five year-old Frank and two year-old Will, whom Clemmie called "Totsy." Clemmie took the children up to Mary Ann's bed and asked,

"Which one do you love best, Totsy or Frank?"

Mary Ann did not answer, but put her hand affectionately on little Will's head.[127]

The family was worried about Mary Ann's condition, and unable to understand what was going on with her, they called Dr. J.B. Murfree in to give a second opinion.

James Brickell Murfree was the grandson of Hardee Murfree, for whom the town was named. After studying medicine at Johnson College in Philadelphia, Dr. Murfree had set up his practice in Murfreesboro. In 1889, when the state legislature of Tennessee voted to establish a state board of medical examiners, Dr. Murfree was appointed president of that board.[128] Dr. Murfree was the best physician the family could have called to treat Mary Ann Baugh.

Meanwhile, at Jack Baugh's urging, Will Gum said he would write Rollie Howland to let him know about his grandmother. It would take a while for the message to arrive, so there was no sense in waiting.

So, the family gathered around, cooking, cleaning, and caring for the mother who had bore all of them, and who for sixty years had been the light of the family. It was almost impossible to think that soon life was going to change and she would no longer be among them. There was one thing on everyone's mind these early days of January, and someone had to see that it was taken care of.

Chapter 13

The Will

[*Note:* The existence of a court case from 1893 has given us a window into the past that otherwise would have been impossible. This chapter presents the events of one day in novel form, but they are the facts as recorded by those who were there.]

IT HAD BEEN COLD THE PAST FEW DAYS OF JANUARY, BUT NOT NEARLY SO cold as it might have been. Still, family members hardly noticed. They were thinking of Mary Ann Baugh lying ill in her bed, unable to move after such a long and active life.

To the friends and business associates who visited her in the days following her stroke she seemed hardly sensible. Sometimes, in answer to a question, she would nod her head for both "yes" and "no." But, to those who took care of her, like Clemmie and granddaughter Mary Baugh, she seemed entirely sensible. She was only caught in a body which would no longer do her bidding. It was the family's job to try to understand her wishes and carry them out.

The morning of Friday, January 26th, Eliza Pruett arrived from Old Millersburg in a horse and buggy. Her mother's appearance was a shock to Eliza, but Mammie was nearly eighty years old now and in a life this long she supposed it was to be expected. Eliza, now forty-two, was already feeling the aches and pains of age.

Eliza watched sister Clemmie, disabled though she was, bustling around, taking charge of the big house and her mother's care. Eliza was glad she could help, but most of all, she wanted to be near Mammie.

The following Monday morning at nine o'clock Sister Bettie White arrived from Old Millersburg. For Bettie, it was strange to enter the family home, and know her mother would not greet her in her usual way.

As Bettie entered her mother's room through the door behind the stairs, a painful sight met her eyes. Mary Ann was sitting up in bed, bent over a bowl, throwing up repeatedly. Next to her stood Eliza, who was trying to help her. For a moment Mammie's blue-gray eyes met Bettie's, but it seemed the soul that looked out of those eyes was gone for she showed no recognition of her. Then, Mary Ann sighed, and crying out in a deep voice, heaved again. As she lay back against the pillows, Eliza gently wiped her face with the soft cloth she had dipped in the washbowl sitting on the dresser. Once Mary Ann was somewhat settled, Eliza looked up at Bettie and said,

"There Mammie, there's Bettie, come to see you. You know her, don't you?"

Mary Ann simply lay with her head against the pillows, her face almost as pale as they, while Eliza pulled the counterpane up to keep her warm. When her mother did not respond, Bettie thought sadly to herself, "Mammie doesn't know me anymore." She wished she had visited her mother more often in recent years. Now she knew her mother would not be there much longer. It was a realization that cut her to the heart.

Since Mammie needed to rest, Eliza suggested they go back to the dining room for some tea and refreshments. It had been a long, cold journey from Old Millersburg by horse and buggy, and Bettie would like something warm. Clemmie joined them and the three sisters spoke quietly about their mother and life in general. The house seemed to be bustling with people coming in and out all day, yet it had that lonely feel when the one who has made a place home for so many years is about to leave its walls forever.

A short while later the three sisters settled themselves before Mammie's bedroom fire. After a while, Bettie saw Mary Ann's eyelids flutter open and asked her if she was not feeling better. After a moment, Mary Ann responded with soft difficult syllables formed on one side of her mouth, "Yes, I am."

"Did you know me, Mammie, earlier when I came in?" asked Bettie, unable to restrain herself. "I wasn't sure you did."

"Yes, I did. I was just so sick."

"What is my name?" Bettie asked, still uncertain her mother knew her.

"Bettie," Mary Ann responded.

Hearing her mother say this brought some small comfort to her. Mammie looked pale, but seemed comfortable. There was always some hope.

Visitors continued to come and go throughout the morning. Brother Jack's eldest son, Thomas, stopped to visit. He only stayed a few minutes. Will Gum's mother, Martha Wade Gum, also came to help.

Around three o'clock that afternoon, the bell rang once again and the women learned that Dr. J.B. Murfree had come to check on their mother.

As Dr. Murfree entered the room, the women rose to greet him. Six feet tall, with broad shoulders, a gray goatee and piercing dark eyes, Dr. Murfree's dignified presence filled the room. As a physician, he had become legendary in Murfreesboro. His knowledge as a doctor was unparalleled and his loving care as an intense believer in the word of Christ was a comfort to all he treated. Dr. Murfree believed that he was simply the middleman for God's healing power. He treated the rich who could pay him and the poor, who could not, with the same care.

Dr. J.B. Murfree.
(Courtesy Mrs. C.B. Huggins, III)

After greeting Eliza and Bettie, as well as Martha Gum, Dr. Murfree turned to Mary Ann, and in a soft, kindly voice said, "Good afternoon, Mrs. Baugh. How are you today?"

Placing his large black bag on the table near Mary Ann's bed, he opened it slowly and deliberately. It did not take him more than a few moments of observing Mary Ann and checking her pulse to sum up the situation.

"Mrs. Pruett, I wonder if you might do me a favor?" he said, "Would you be so kind as to bring some water to wash your mother's mouth out?" Then turning to Bettie he said, "And Mrs. White, would you bring me a clean rag?"

Eliza Pruett and Bettie White hurried out of the room to do the doctor's bidding. Bettie was the first to return and on reaching the door of her mother's room she was very surprised to find the door closed and Mrs. Martha Gum standing in front of it.

"Oh, you can't go in, Mrs. Pruett," said Mrs. Gum. "Dr. Murfree doesn't want anyone to come in."

"Dr. Murfree just sent us to get a rag and water for Mrs. Baugh," said Bettie, speaking in the formal manner of the day. To her, Mrs. Gum was an outsider.

"He only did that to get you out of the room. He has sent everyone out so as to speak with Mrs. Baugh alone," explained Mrs. Gum in a commanding tone.

Just then Eliza arrived from the kitchen with a pitcher of water and a glass. The two women did not quite like this, but there was no arguing with Dr. Murfree, or Mrs. Gum for that matter. The sisters moved away from the door, taking the items they had brought and leaving Mrs. Gum standing there.

Inside the room, Dr. Murfree carefully examined Mrs. Baugh, listening to her pulse, looking into her eyes and attempting to move the paralyzed parts of her body. Then, as was his custom, Dr. Murfree knelt by the side of the bed and began to pray. He understood there was more than just a body that needed healing. There was a soul to be taken care of. The words that passed in that room between the good doctor and Mrs. Baugh will never be known. He did not speak of them in later years, even in court, but his visit no doubt precipitated actions that filled the next hours.

Before he left, Dr. Murfree met Eliza Pruett in the hall and informed her of what he knew to be true about her mother's condition. The words were not hopeful for this world.

After Dr. Murfree left, Eliza remained in the front hall with tears streaming from her eyes as she realized Mammie was dying. Her grief was soon interrupted by the clop of horse hooves and the creak of a wagon as it stopped before the house. Looking out the side windows by the door, Eliza observed her nephew, Will Baugh, pulling up in front of the house. As she came out on the porch to greet him, he jumped down from a tightly packed wagon and bounded up the steps, leaving the horse untied. Will had a load of tobacco on the wagon, which he was transporting for J.D. Cromer & B.F. Christopher. Today his route would take him south, down Manchester Highway, and he wanted to visit his grandmother before he left.

"Good morning, Aunt Eliza," he said, removing his hat to reveal his fair wavy hair and light blue eyes. Eliza couldn't help noticing that Will Baugh had the features of the Marables in his fair face, along with the Baugh's long, aquiline nose.

Eliza Pruitt's milking pail and red & white tablecloth. (Courtesy Lurlene Rushing)

"Your grandmammie is not too well today. She had a terrible bout this morning and Dr. Murfree has just been here to check on her."

When Will entered the back room, he saw that Grandmammie appeared pale and weak and did not seem to recognize him at all. For about an hour, Will sat by her bed, holding her hand. Now and then he spoke to her, but he got no response. As he came from the back parlor into the front hallway, Aunt Eliza met him at the door.

"Where are you off to, Will?"

"Well, I'm heading to Beech Grove with this wagon of tobacco, Ma'am."

Aunt Eliza's face was pale, and Will noticed a trace of tears in her eyes.

"Will, Dr. Murfree says your Grandmother is liable to die at any minute. If you can go to your Aunt Mary Howland's house in Beech Grove along the way, please tell her to come at once if she expects to see her Ma alive."[129]

Courtesy Curry Wolfe

"Yes, Ma'am, I will," said Will, hastily. Then, he climbed up onto the wagon, and clicking the reigns, headed down East Main.

That afternoon as Bettie and Eliza sat next to their mother's bed. Mary Ann suddenly stirred and extending her hand to Eliza, who was closest to the bed, indicated that she wanted her to take off the plain, gold wedding band on her finger.

"Mammie, what do you want me to do with this?"

"You and Bettie," Mary Ann mumbled.

"Mammie, do you want me to give this to Sister Bettie?"

"Yes."

Eliza took the ring off the pale, aged hand of her mother, and handed it to her sister, Bettie.

Mary Ann then indicated that she wished her other ring taken as well—the treasured free Mason ring of their brother Ben.

Bettie took the plain gold ring Eliza had handed her and looked inside. Engraved there were the letters M.A.M.B, standing for Mary Ann Marable Baugh.

It felt odd to have this ring on her finger. Before the day was over; both rings were back on Mary Ann's fingers. Although she knew they stood for her mother's love, Bettie felt they should remain with Mammie as long as she was alive.

A short while later, the three sisters, Bettie, Eliza and Clemmie sat near the foot of Mammy's bed, close to the fire. Even in serious illness, one always hopes for recovery, but Dr. Murfree's words had brought home the fact that they would not have their mother much longer.

Mary Ann stirred in the bed. "Wull," she struggled to say with a side of her face that would not move. "Wull! Wull!"

"You want Will?" asked Clemmie pulling herself up and bending over her mother. Mary Ann nodded her head and Clemmie limped out the door going into the back hall, which led to the kitchen.

When Clemmie returned with Will, Eliza was standing by the bed, next to the parlor door on the other side of the room. She had gotten up to see how Mary Ann was. Looking up from her mother, she saw what was to her, Will's sour and anxious expression.

Mary Ann looked at Will intently and said, "Go for Johnny Richardson and Frank White."[130] She spoke haltingly, taking a breath between every two syllables, "I want … to write … my will."

"Yes, ma'm, but I don't think you are sick enough to write your will," said Will Gum, trying to be reassuring.

Mary Ann looked at him with the wide, intense eyes of one who has seen much more pain and fear than anyone would wish to know. "Yes, Willie," she said. "I am sicker than you think. I'm go-in' to die."

The sisters looked on in silence, keeping close to the fire to ward off the January chill. Will turned and hurried out the door.

Walking swiftly down the brick sidewalk of Main Street, Will Gum crossed the street just before reaching the square and went into a two-story brick building where the offices of McLemore & Richardson were located. The office was empty, so Will went next door to Frank White's office and told him that Mrs. Baugh wanted to see him. Frank White, a relative of Bettie's husband, said he could not go to Mrs. Baugh's now and he had no idea where Mr. Richardson was.

Will, feeling perturbed that he could not find help when it was most urgently needed, hurried over to another attorney, Mr. Burns' office, where he found Burns and Judge McLemore playing draughts.* Judge McLemore told Will Gum that Mr. Richardson had gone up to Nashville and would not be back until the following day; however, he had another suggestion. Will thanked him and hurried back home to Mrs. Baugh.

Back in Mrs. Baugh's room, Will informed her of the situation, and quickly asked:

"Would Horace Palmer do?"

Mrs. Baugh agreed that he would, and asked Will bring him to the house along with Court Clerk Frank White. Will didn't tell her that Frank couldn't come, but hurried quickly out the door.

This time, Will Gum turned east and headed toward Maney Avenue. It was nearly dark on this winter afternoon and he shivered as he walked the two blocks down to the Palmer home.

Palmer House.
(Courtesy Barry Lamb)

* Draught, pronounced "drafts" is an English-American checker board game.

The Palmer home was a beautiful brick house built by General Joseph Palmer as a gift for his wife shortly after his return from the war. Joseph Palmer had passed away less than two years earlier, in 1890. The home was now owned by his son, Horace Palmer, who had lived there with his father.

Will rang the front bell of the large, red brick mansion and was let in by a servant. The entrance to the Palmer home was spacious and beautiful with a small parlor to the right, and a large parlor to the left. But there was not much time to notice the home now. It was essential that Horace Palmer return to Mrs. Baugh's house immediately, before it was too late.

Will stood anxiously, hat in hand, waiting to explain the urgency of the matter. In the past he had complained about Mrs. Baugh, but since he and Clemmie had been married he had always had a lovely home to live in and food on the table for his family. It must have been a great shock to realize that soon this could be gone. It was no secret to him that Clemmie's siblings did not like him.

Mr. Palmer, a handsome gentleman of medium height with dark hair and a large mustache, was approximately thirty-seven years old. He met Will Gum in the hall and, after listening to Will's explanation of the situation, agreed with great kindness and concern to come back to Mrs. Baugh's home immediately and take down her will. Mr. Palmer took a long pad of paper and pen. Then, putting on his topcoat, warm muffler and hat, he followed Will out the door and down two blocks to the Baugh home.

When Horace Palmer entered Mary Ann's room all three sisters looked up sadly and hopefully. Now, they would hear their mother's final wishes. Mr. Gum introduced Attorney Palmer to Mrs. Baugh's daughters, Mrs. White and Mrs. Pruitt. Then, Mr. Palmer approached the bed where Mary Ann Baugh lay.

"Good afternoon, Mrs. Baugh, It is good to see you."

Horace Palmer could not help but see how frail she was; a woman who had not long to live. Nevertheless, Mrs. Baugh extended her left hand to him.

"Please, take a chair," she said.

The right side of Mrs. Baugh's face seemed to droop. Unable to move her lips and tongue on that side, prevented her from articulating clearly.

"Do you know me?" he asked.

"Yes, it's Horace Palmer."

Horace Palmer.
(Courtesy Mary Palmer Thompson)

Mrs. Baugh pronounced his name, "Harse," rather than "Hor-ace" as she would ordinarily have done. Yet even now, Mr. Palmer was surprised at her thoughtfulness. She was just as kind and polite as she had always been.

"How are you Harse?"

"I'm mighty fine, Mrs. Baugh."

"And how are your two little boys?"

Mr. Palmer's two little sons had contracted typhoid fever in September. One of his sons had been extremely ill, and they had not been sure he would survive. As ill as she was, Mrs. Baugh continued to show her southern manners, and concern in asking about his family.

"Is your little boy better? Has he completely recovered his strength? Ah, that is good to know," she said after Mr. Palmer had replied in the affirmative.

"I remember your father well. You must miss him. Have you a partner now?"

"Yes, Ma'am, I do."

"What is his name?"

"Mr. Ridley."

At this point Mr. Palmer excused himself, got up and walked to the fireplace where Bettie, Eliza and Clemmie were seated.

"I have been passing Mrs. Baugh's house, now, every day for over 20 years, but I have not seen her since she was stricken. What do you think of your mother's mental condition?"

"Why," replied Eliza Pruitt with her usual forthrightness, "Mammie can't talk much, but she's got as much sense as she ever had."

"It is truly a pity and very unfortunate that your mother did not make her will when she could talk better."

After this short conversation, Mr. Palmer returned to Mrs. Baugh's bedside.

"Mr. Gum has told me that you want me to attend to some business for you."

"Yes, I want you to write my will."

Placing his pad of paper down, Mr. Palmer removed a pen from his coat. Holding it elegantly, he waited for Mrs. Baugh to make her first statement. His first business was to find out what she wanted to do with the house.

"Do you want to give Clemmie the house?"

Mrs. Baugh shook her head. "The lot east my house, Clemmie," she said with difficulty.

Mr. Palmer was not entirely sure what she meant. Will Gum, who was sitting on the bed next to Mrs. Baugh's feet, said hopefully,

"Maybe she means she wants to give Clemmie this house. You can ask her."

Mr. Palmer did not ask. Uncertain of Mary Ann Baugh's mental condition, there was a danger of putting words in her mouth. The statements must come from her.

"No, Mr. Palmer," Eliza piped up, "Mammie don't mean that! She has other children besides Clemmie."

"Well, Mammie ought to provide a home for Clemmie," replied Sister Bettie, "she has been a slave to her for fifteen years."

At this point, everyone in the room began to speak at once; each trying to state their opinion: "She wants this." "I heard her say that." They were all speaking at once, raising their voices above one another, while Mrs. Baugh, in her weakened state, tried to be heard above them.[131] Through it all, Horace Palmer remained calm.

About this time, Will Gum got up to leave. Just before exiting the door, he turned to Horace Palmer and said,

"Mr. Palmer, my wife has heard her mother say how she wants her will written. Clemmie knows what Mrs. Baugh wants done with her property. Mrs. Baugh has told her."

"I am writing her mother's will," replied Mr. Palmer, "Not hers."

Everyone in the room grew silent. What Clemmie's siblings thought of Will Gum was another matter, but it was now clear that Mr. Palmer was in charge.

A few moments later, Clemmie went out into the hall to find Will. Someone was at the door, and she opened it. It was one of Mrs. Baugh's tenants, a "Chinaman," who had a laundry business in one of the brick offices. He wanted to pay the rent, so Clemmie let him in.

Meanwhile, eighty-nine year-old Charlie Webb, who had been boarding with Mary Ann Baugh for over ten years, came in. He had just learned that Mr. Palmer was there to take down Mrs. Baugh's will. He was concerned about her condition.

Just then, Will Gum came into the hall and, seeing Clemmie speaking with the "Chinaman," interrupted her saying, "You had better go in with your mother. That is where you are needed. You're out here trying to collect seventy-five cents while you loose a thousand by not being in your mother's room."

Clemmie returned to her mother's room.

Meanwhile, Horace Palmer had been trying to decipher what Mary Ann Baugh wanted. Her words were not clear, but with her left hand she was making signs to clarify her wishes.

"You mean you want to give the lot and residence to your daughter, Mrs. Gum?' Mr. Palmer asked patiently.

"No, I do not." Mrs. Baugh was definite.

"Mrs. Baugh, I did not understand what you told me. Please repeat what it is you wish to give to Clemmie, your daughter, Mrs. Gum."

With great effort, Mary Ann Baugh pointed toward the window, and then down the block in the direction of the brick offices and the store.

"Lot and store for Clemmie." Then, after a pause she added, "I want Clemmie to have the lot down there. I want the balance sold."

Mr. Palmer repeated her words as he thought she intended them, and asked if this was what she wanted. She nodded. In this way, the writing of the will proceeded. Clemmie must be provided for, but at the same time, she must have enough for her other children.

Following this, Mr. Palmer named each child. In this way he was able to discover which children would be included in the will and which ones would not.

When Mr. Palmer had a clear idea what Mrs. Baugh wanted, he asked for the use of a table on which to write the will. Mrs. Baugh told him to go home and have supper. He could write the will there and "return that night." It was now after 6 o'clock. Considering the state of Mrs. Baugh's health, Mr. Palmer had no time to waste.

~

Around 9 o'clock that night, Horace Palmer returned. By now, the family had eaten supper, and the lamps were lit and glowing in the windows. Eliza brought a lamp to the table by Mrs. Baugh's bed, while Mr. Palmer carefully took out two long pieces of paper from his bag and laid them on the table.

"Now, Mrs. Baugh, here is your will, do you understand?"

Mary Ann, who was lying quietly against the pillows, looked at him intently, and nodded her head.

"I am going to read this and for each point you should let me know, "yes" or "no"—whether it is what you want or not. Do you understand?"

Again, Mary Ann nodded her head.

A rather large crowd gathered in Mary Ann's small room that night. Mrs. A.R. Richardson was there along with Mrs. White, Mrs. Pruett, Mr. and Mrs. Gum and several other people.

Mr. Palmer read the will, stopping after each section to ask Mrs. Baugh if the previous statement was what she intended. Each time, she nodded her head. Included in the will was a description of how the property was to be divided. Clemmie was to receive her share in her own name, separate from her husband. It was enough land to live on, and to earn an income from rentals. With this, they should be set to raise their five children.

During the reading of the will, Eliza Pruitt wondered about the division of land. She wasn't sure that Mr. Palmer had written it correctly, but she was so caught up in the grief of the moment that she said nothing.

"Will you be able to sign the will?" asked Horace Palmer.

Pointing to her right hand, Mrs. Baugh asked Mr. Palmer to sign it for her. Mr. Palmer asked for Mrs. Baugh's middle initial, and Clemmie replied, "Marable," so he wrote "Mary M. Baugh." Recalling the moment, Horace Palmer said,

> *. . . Mrs. Richardson was standing between Mrs. Baugh and me holding a lamp when I asked what her middle name was . . . I had signed her name to the will and she touched the pen with her left hand and made her mark ("x.")**

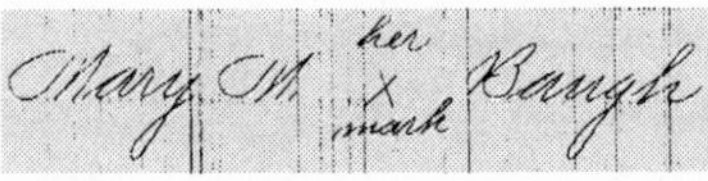

The will of Mary Ann Baugh was now complete.

~

After Mr. Palmer left, the lights in the Baugh home were dimmed, and everyone prepared to retire. There was a strange feeling of finality in the air. All the talk and suppositions were done. The will had been written. It was decided.

During the days that followed, many more family members came to visit. John Baugh, Jr. arrived from Texas and stayed with his aunt,

---

* Permission Rutherford County Archives.

Mrs. Butler. Dick Baugh also came to visit. As he sat by her bed, Mary Ann asked that he be given dinner.

The will had been written on Monday, and with each succeeding day Mrs. Baugh grew weaker. In a short time, she stopped talking, and, by Thursday, she had drifted off into a deep sleep from which she would never awaken.

Chapter 14
Death

Mary Ann lay pale and white on the bed where she had suffered too long. The cold, white light of January, which shown through the eastern window, was dimmed as Eliza pulled the curtains together. Now, the fire was growing dim as well, but the women in the room paid little attention.

Eliza was silently and lovingly bathing her mother's face one last time. While Bettie combed Mary Ann's hair, Clemmie sat at the foot of the bed and wept.

Mary Ann was dead. Her suffering, fears and disabilities were finally over. But so was life on East Main Street, a home where all felt welcome; where local vendors and neighbors alike paid daily visits, and where anyone looking for a room to rent, might find a safe haven. It was all gone forever.

Eliza bit her lip to stop the bitter words which wanted to come out, but she could not help thinking of the difficulties Will and Clemmie had brought upon their Mammie. Still, everyone had to die some day and Mary Ann had lived a good, long life.

Bettie, the older, wiser and more motherly of the sisters took matters in stride. As the eldest living sister, she had the most memories of her mother. She remembered a much younger mother. Her own sufferings, including the loss of children and the indignities of war, had helped her understand her mother better; all these things shown in her dark eyes and the wrinkles which now creased her face.

Oh, the regrets of death that nothing can take away. The words spoken, wished erased; the words from the heart that were never spoken, for which it is too late. The sisters grieved for a loving, good mother who had taken care of her eleven children the best she could. They respected their mother for her devout ways, her strength and for taking care of business during the more than twenty years following their father's death.

When the women finished with the last act of kindness they could pay their mother, they and sat talking quietly and weeping. Bettie, who had been in her mother's room for most of the week since she arrived, now realized how very tired she was. As the hours passed, more family members began to arrive: Mary Howland, Jack Baugh and Joe Baugh, among others.

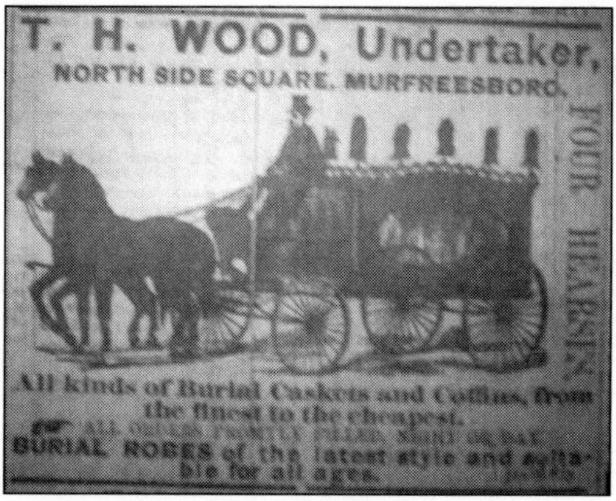

By mid-morning, the undertaker, T.H. Wood, arrived to embalm the body. Then, they would place her in a fine wood box and lay her in the front parlor. Later, those who had known Mrs. Baugh would come to pay their respects, bringing elaborate wreaths of flowers. But these hours were for family members only.

One of the black servant ladies sat upstairs with the Gum children. Mary Gum was nearly twelve now. She would remember her grandmother the best. The others were still children: Emmett was eight, Frank, almost six, and Will was two.

That night, the house was full of family members. Will Gum slept in the attic with Will Baugh so that Clemmie could share their bed with her sisters. As the men lay in the dark, Will Baugh was thinking of his grandmother, the comforter of his childhood and a light to them all. In the midst of these thoughts, Will Gum began to speak.

"Well, the old lady has made a will and she certainly did nicely by Clemmie. Don't say anything, but if the rest of the family lets it stand, I am going to try to be a different man and a better husband for Clemmie."

Will Baugh felt distaste hearing his grandmother referred to as "the old lady," and at the fact that Will was talking about money, while his grandmother lay dead in the front parlor. He was sure Will and Clemmie must be scared after depending on his grandmother all these years. Still, the statement showed something of his character. Suddenly, a question occurred to him.

"Did she include Rollie Howland in her will?" he asked.

"I don't want to talk about it," said Will Gum, and with that, he turned over and the room fell silent.

The next day, family members stayed upstairs while the people of Murfreesboro, who had long known Mrs. Baugh, came to pay their last respects.

The following day was filled with guests, tears and food. Even with the flow of traffic, the house seemed strangely still without Mary Ann's warm presence, her laugh, her greetings and concerned inquiries.

The coffin was sealed and loaded into T.H. Wood's black hearse with glass windows. The men followed in buggies, while the women stayed in the residence. The trip to Evergreen Cemetery was only half a mile, through corn and cotton fields, now barren in the midst of winter. At Evergreen, Mary Ann Marable Baugh was laid to rest beside her beloved husband, John Aldridge Baugh.

After a repast at the East Main Street home and an evening of music—as custom dictated—family members would return to their homes and some semblance of normality. But for Clemmie and Will, nothing would ever be the same again.

~

For the first time in her life, Clemmie was without her mother. She had complained about Mary Ann and been weary with taking care of her, but her mother's absence must have touched the core of her being. Clemmie had never in her thirty-five years of life been separated from her mother. It was a terrible shock to know that Mary Ann was gone forever.

The house was lonely; lonelier than Clemmie could ever have imagined. Sometimes she felt that Mammie was still there in her room, or in the parlor, but the silence of the house told the truth.

Out of respect for Mrs. Baugh, some of Mary Ann's old friends and business acquaintances came to call on the Gums. But Mrs. Alabama

Richardson and her family were the ones who continued to call and show care and concern for the little family. Others stayed away as they did not like Will Gum.

During the months that followed, Clemmie felt the weight of life on her shoulders. Now, there was no one to turn to for help, but Will. If Clemmie had not accepted the fact before, now she had to realize she could not fully depend on him. The real healing and comfort came from the children, whose cheerful and energetic antics overcame all the dark moments. There was also the new life she carried inside her.

Meanwhile, Clemmie's siblings went ahead with all of the official business of implementing the will. Only days after Mary Ann's funeral, the County Clerk came to the big house on East Main Street, and took inventory of Mary Ann Baugh's belongings. Registered on February 2nd, 1892, beginning with her bedroom, some of the items listed were as follows:

> 1 bureau, 1 bedstead, 1 feather bed, 1 bed spring, quilt, blanket, 2 sheets, 2 pillows, 2 cases, 1 wash stand, 3 bed stand pitchers, 3 lamps, 4 carpets, 1 small trunk, 1 large mirror, paper holders, 1 window shade, 2 bronze waiters, 5 pictures, 3 gilt frame pictures, 2 rocking chairs, 1 looking glass, 2 slop cans (used for toilet at night when one didn't want to run out to the out house), 1 curtain, 1 waiter, 1 satchel, 1 chalk box, 2 pokers, … 7 pictures, 2 trunks, … 2 tin lock boxes, 3 vases, … 1 card basket, 1 pitcher, 1 steps carpet, 1 cedar chest, 4 paint cans, 9 bowls, 2 steak dishes, 2 butter dishes, 17 goblets, 2 safes, dining table, 1 side table…[132]

Profits from the sale of these goods would go to Clemmie's brothers and sisters. Though nearly half of the land on East Main was Clemmie's, the Gum family would not have to move to smaller quarters until the house was sold. She and Will would decide later if they would be able to build a home, as Mary Ann's will directed. Life would be simpler, and their home would belong to them, but there would no longer be an unlimited pool of money to dip into as needed.

~

Rollie Howland had received one postal note from Will Gum on Saturday, January 30th. It stated that Mrs. Baugh had had a stroke and was partially paralyzed. Dated January 26th, Rollie thought his grandmother sounded ill, but Will stated she was holding her own. Rollie decided he would go to see her on Monday.

On Sunday, Rollie received another "postal" stating that Mrs. Baugh was much worse, and he should come immediately. Rollie wasted no time. Hitching his horse to the buggy, he set off for Murfreesboro. Along the way, he decided to stop at his Uncle Jack Baugh's home, which was more than halfway to town.

It was about 4 o'clock when Rollie arrived at Uncle Jack's. Just as he rode up to the house, he saw his Uncle Jack and his family riding into the front yard in their buggy. As they descended one by one from the old buggy, Rollie felt his heart sink. Every member of the family was dressed in black.

Rollie descended from his buggy, and Cousin Mary approached him.

"Dear Cousin Rollie. I am so sorry. Grandmammie is gone. We have just returned from her funeral," she said extending her arms to him.

Grandmother was gone, and no one had told him. He had not even been able to attend her funeral!

During the weeks that followed, Rollie struggled with his feelings. He was in shock. His first loyalty was to his wife, but Mary Ann had raised him as her son. Then came the final blow; Rollie had been left out of his grandmother's will. All these years she had told him he would receive his mother's share. It was the very last thing she had said to him on his visit only weeks earlier. What had happened?

Speaking to Uncle Jack and other members of the family, Rollie began to put the pieces together. As he learned more, he began to suspect foul play. Rollie was not the only one left out of the will; Ida Jacobs had been left out as well. Dallas Jacobs agreed that, although his daughter did not need the money, it was the principle of the thing. By the fall of 1892, Rollie and Ida had decided they were going to contest the will.

~

That June, Clemmie gave birth to her sixth child. The baby was a beautiful, strapping boy, with dark hair and blue eyes. They named him Allie Richardson Gum, in honor of Mrs. Alabama Richardson's daughter, who had been of great help and support to Clemmie and the children. It had not been an easy time for her. For the first time now, Mammie was not there to coo over the new baby. Nevertheless, little Allie was a sweet comfort to her.[133]

True to his promise, Will Gum was trying to be a better husband. He stayed away from the taverns and the Mink Slide area. Each day he walked to his part-time job on the Square. He was not paid much, but at least it was something. As long as they had the rents from the store, the brick office building and the small tenement house where Mammy Ran lived, they would be able to get along.

When the news reached them that Rollie and Ida were contesting the will, the Gums were shocked. Rollie had more than enough money with his wealthy wife. The possibility that the property Mary Ann had left them might be taken away, or further divided, was a frightening thought. Their very existence depended on everything Clemmie's mother had given her. With their future once again uncertain, the only thing they could do now was wait.

Chapter 15

To Court, 1893

THE RUTHERFORD COUNTY COURTHOUSE HAD STOOD ON THE SQUARE since 1859 when the Masonic Fraternity laid the corner stone."[134] The red brick building with its tall, white cupola rose with dignity over the town, a symbol of pride to the people of Rutherford County. Now, in 1893, it would be the place where the Baugh and Gum families revealed their darkest secrets.

Rollie Howland and Ida Jacobs had chosen John E. Richardson, Esq. to represent their case. As a member of the law firm *McLemore and Richardson*, he was a well-respected attorney. Mr. Richardson, the brother-in-law of Mrs. Baugh's good friend, Alabama Richardson, was the attorney Mrs. Baugh had wanted to write her will. Rollie and Ida's choice must have stirred some feelings in the family. They all knew John Richardson quite well, but then, in a small town like Murfreesboro, almost everyone was connected in some way.

As Mary Ann had wanted, J. L. and J. M. Baugh were named the executors of her will. They hired the attorney they considered the best; a man of great integrity, one who knew the most about Mary Ann's condition when she wrote her will, Horace Palmer. Mr. Palmer would be able to fight any allegations that Mary Ann Baugh had been incapable of writing her will.

Horace Palmer, a member of the law firm, *Palmer and Ridley*, had been practicing law for sixteen years. He was not only well-known as an attorney and the son of the much loved Joseph Palmer, he also had served as

Murfreesboro's mayor (1885–1887) and Rutherford County's representative to the Tennessee State Assembly. Mr. Palmer was considered one of the best attorneys in town.[135]

The attorneys' preparation for the case was a long and arduous. The first subpoenas were not sent out until October of 1892.

~

February 28, 1893 was the first day of the trial and the Rutherford County Courtroom was packed. The courtroom and new upstairs gallery buzzed with energy and excitement as onlookers chattered, eager for the trial to begin.

Whenever there was a large case in the Rutherford County Courthouse, especially one with well-known personalities, people traveled long distances to attend. For the residents of this farming community, court trials were a combination of news and soap opera. Candy and cigarettes were sold to visitors inside the building. Outside, there was a cart with popcorn for people to eat during the trials.[136]

Attorney John E. Richardson, a young man of twenty-six with thick, dark hair and an equally thick mustache, was seated to one side on the courtroom. Next to him was his client, Rollie Howland, looking pale and serious. Although the case was titled, *J.L. & J.M. Baugh vs. Rollie Howland and Ida Jacobs*, Rollie Howland and Ida Jacobs had brought the suit to trial. The court would later state that the case had been improperly docketed.

As the moment grew closer for the trial to begin, the court stenographer entered, seated himself and laid out his paper, pens and pencils for transcribing the testimony. Shortly after that, a jury of twelve "good and lawful men" filed into the courtroom and took their seats. The twelve men had been chosen from Rutherford County's twenty-four districts. When Mr. Lenoir of Old Jefferson, did not show up that day, he was replaced. The jurors were:

J.M. Witherspoon, J.F. Hood, Z.T. Dismukes, J.L. Brandon, Sam P. McKnight, T.E. Alsup, S.H. Marlin, John W. Boyd, J.G. Cromer, C.A. Robertson, W.T. Sanders, and W.L. Rowlett.

The courtroom was lit by a row of windows behind the judge's seat and the huge, flickering gaslights hanging from the ceiling. The area where the crowd sat was somewhat dark. Perhaps that was why no one realized that lingering in the back of the room was Will Gum.

Precisely on the hour, the court clerk called in a loud voice, "Presenting the Honorable Judge Robert Cantrell." The noisy courtroom grew hushed as the elderly Judge entered in his black robes and took his seat.

Attorney Horace Palmer was called to make the opening statement. Looking dignified and thoughtful, he walked to the center of the courtroom, where he cleared his throat and began.

> Mrs. Mary A. Baugh is dead. She died in Rutherford County the latter part of January, 1892. I wrote her will. It was written on Monday, January 25th, about half past 4 o'clock in the afternoon...[137]

Mr. Palmer then recounted the story of how W.T. Gum had come to his home, and the events that followed, the afternoon he wrote Mrs. Baugh's will. When he was finished, Mrs. A.R. Richardson was called to the stand as a witness to the signing of the will.

Mrs. Alabama Richardson, at thirty-nine, was still a beautiful woman with golden hair, flawless skin and blue eyes. As she approached the witness stand, the crowd expressed appreciation of her beauty and dignity. Asked to state her name and relationship to Mrs. Baugh, she said:

> I am the wife of James D. Richardson. I had known Mrs. Baugh about twenty-five years. She lived a short distance from my home and I knew her well.

Mrs. Richardson then told the court of her visit to Mrs. Baugh's home the night the will was read.

> I heard the will read to Mrs. Baugh by Mr. Palmer. She undoubtedly understood it. She made her mark to the will and at her request Mr. Palmer and I witnessed it as her last will and testament . . . she was of sound mind and . . . competent to make her will . . .

As Mrs. Richardson left the stand, Attorney Horace Palmer requested that Mrs. Mary Baugh's will be read to the court, and Judge Cantrell gave permission for him "to do so." (*See* Appendix A.)

After the reading of the will, John E. Richardson rose to make the Opening Statement for his clients, Rollie M. Howland and Ida Jacobs. It was their contention, he stated, that the will presented in court was *not* Mrs. Baugh's true will. To begin with, it was signed incorrectly with the name, "Mary M. Baugh." Her name was Mary A. Baugh.

Further, Richardson informed the court, it was the Defendants' goal to prove Mrs. Mary A. Baugh was incapable of writing a will at the time it was written, and had been influenced by those around her to leave out the grandchildren she loved and to whom she had always promised a share of their deceased mothers' inheritance. By the time Mr. Richardson finished his statement, the air in the courtroom was tense. Now, the first witness was called: Rollie M. Howland.

Tall and thin, his sandy hair falling over his forehead, Rollie Howland walked to the stand and took the oath. He answered the questions put to him with a solemnity that showed everyone present his sorrow over what had occurred.

> Q: What was your relationship to Mrs. Mary A. Baugh?
>
> A: Mrs. Mary A. Baugh was my grandmother. My mother is dead. My father's present wife is also a daughter of Mrs. Baugh. I lived with my grandmother a long time. I left there when I was about 16 to go to school. My grandmother claimed nothing for my having lived with her and gave my father a receipt against all claims. When I

John E. Richardson.
(Courtesy John R. Rucker, Jr.)

lived with her I attended to matters for her and helped her generally about the place.

Q: Did your grandmother, Mrs. Baugh, give you your mother's share, the $1000 your grandfather willed to all his children?

A: I never got my mother's share or interest, either in my grandfather's or grandmother's estate. My grandmother never paid me the $1000 which she promised to pay me as going to my mother's share.

Rollie then recalled the events of Christmas 1891.

A: I did not ... see any change whatever in her feeling for me. Everything was just as pleasant, and she was just as affectionate as ever.

Q: Did you receive any letters from the family, stating that your grandmother was ill? If you did, please state when.

A: I did not see my grandmother ... during her illness. I did not receive any news of her condition from Mr. Gum until the last week of her illness. I got two postals ...

It was Horace Palmer's turn to cross-examine Rollie as to whether his grandmother might have changed her mind about her will due to the fact that his wife had money.

A: My grandmother did not know what I possessed so far as I know. She did not learn it from me.

Q: Was your grandmother, Mrs. Baugh, easily influenced?

A: My grandmother's disposition was such that she was easily influenced. She was very easily flattered. One child could easily influence her against or in favor of another.

Mr. Richardson now re-examined Rollie.

Q: Please state what you know about Mrs. Baugh's financial situation in regards to Mr. Gum.

A: ... She said she had become involved in business with Gum who had asked the use of her name, said she had paid drafts and checks, and promised to advance him $1000 as soon as she sold some land.

Following this, Rollie Howland was dismissed.

Dallas P. Jacobs, as "next friend" of his daughter, Ida, was called to the stand. His examination was extremely brief. After speaking of his relationship with Mrs. Baugh, Horace Palmer asked,

Q: Isn't it true that both you and Rollie Howland are in good financial condition?

A: Rollie Howland is in good financial condition. I am in comfortable financial condition.

"Objection, your Honor," called John Richardson rising from his chair.

"Overruled," said Judge Cantrell. "The proof may show that for said reasons R.M. Howland and Ida Jacobs are disinherited."

When pressed to say more about Mrs. Baugh's state of mind, Mr. Jacobs replied,

A: Mrs. Baugh was a woman of good sense, but she was getting very feeble in body and mind. I saw her also during her last illness, several times .... If she had a sound mind, I couldn't perceive it. She didn't look intelligent out of her eyes.

"No further questions, your Honor," said Horace Palmer.

After finding that several witnesses were not present, Mrs. Baugh's son, J.M. Baugh was called to the stand. Jack Baugh, a thin man of medium height, with a dark beard grown down to his chest, took the oath and was seated. Strongly opinionated, Jack had no hesitation in voicing his views about his mother.

John D. Richardson asked, "How many times did you see your mother during her final illness and what was her state of mind during this time?'"

> A: I saw [my mother] after she was stricken with paralysis . . . and every day or two during her sickness. At one time she did not recognize the room she was in. She kept pointing around the room and I said, "You do not know where you are." She shook her head. . . . From what I saw and knew of her, I do not think that she was of sound mind or capable of making a will . . .

Q: Was Mrs. Mary A. Baugh a woman easily influenced?

Jack Baugh agreed to the affirmative, and began to tell of her visit in May of 1888 to his home, May Place.

Q: Was she afraid of Gum?

Courtesy Curry Wolfe, Permission Rutherford County Courthouse

A: She ... said she hated him. In that conversation, she said she was afraid to make a will that didn't please Mr. Gum ... I asked her why she didn't get rid of him; she said she was afraid he'd burn her house and her in it ... She told me this in '89, '90 and '91.

Jack Baugh also recalled that his mother had stated repeatedly that Rollie Howland and Ida Jacobs should have their mother's share. She intended for "Sister Clemmie" to have the advantage, "*but she said since she had had to pay that money for* Mr. Gum, *she didn't care*."

After a lengthy questioning by Mr. Richardson, Mr. Palmer rose for the cross-examination, during which Jack Baugh showed a great deal of anger and disgust over his mother's treatment by Mr. Gum and her handling of things.

Q: Are you saying that you do not think your mother was capable to make a will?

A: I don't think my mother was competent for five (5) years. She might have been if it hadn't been for certain circumstances—the effect of Mr. Gum's conduct.

Mr. Palmer then questioned Mr. Baugh about a statement he made in John E. Richardson's office in front of Will Gum and his brother, Joe, shortly after his mother's death.

A: I said things that morning that I was hardly responsible for. I myself would not have been competent that morning to write a will.... My mother told me she was not competent to make a will.... I accepted what she said about that as being veritably true ... She might have been if it hadn't been for ... the effect of Mr. Gum's conduct.

After Jack Baugh's lengthy questioning, Robert M. White, the husband of Bettie Baugh, Ida Jacobs, a pretty, yet pale and delicate girl of twenty wearing fine clothes, Mary Baugh, her cousin, and Mary's aunt, Mrs. Josephine Blake, all testified.

Judge Cantrell then called for a recess. While the courtroom emptied, John E. Richardson took a moment to jot down the names of the people who should still be called as witnesses. It had been a long morning.

That afternoon, Horace Palmer made a full statement and also was questioned as a witness. Mr. Richardson cross-examined Mr. Palmer briefly as to how long Mrs. Baugh had been paralyzed when the will was written. Mr. Palmer stated that she had been paralyzed for about a month.

Mrs. Richardson was also back called to the stand again and questioned about the conversations she had in the last years with Mrs. Baugh.

> A: She told me she intended to build Clemmie a house on Maney's Avenue or Main Street, but that she did not then have money enough to build it . . .
>
> She told me sometime near Christmas before she was taken sick that she had given Rollie Howland . . . all she ever expected to give him and did not intend to give him any more . . .

As John E. Richardson rose to cross-examine the witness, the tension in the courtroom heightened. The crowd had suddenly realized Mrs. Richardson was about to be questioned by her own brother-in-law.

> Q: Did you not hear Mr. or Mrs. Gum try to get Mrs. Baugh to sign a check for $700 after the will was signed that night?
>
> A: I heard nothing of the kind.

The gentle southern lady had suddenly become defensive. Then, as if defending Clemmie, she said,

> Mrs. Gum is afflicted. She has some spinal disease, and has had from childhood.
>
> Q: Was Mrs. Baugh a woman easily influenced?
>
> A: Mrs. Baugh was not easily influenced. She was firm and a woman of good business sense.

"Your honor," Horace Palmer said, as Mrs. Richardson left the stand. "The court would like to call Dr. James Brickell Murfree."

The crowd, whispering among themselves, strained to see the six foot tall Dr. Murfree as he entered the courtroom. Many in the room had been treated by the doctor, and were eager to hear what he had to say.

> Q: For the court, please state your name, occupation and how you knew Mrs. Mary Ann Baugh?
>
> A: I waited on Mrs. Baugh during her last sickness. I graduated in medicine in 1859 and have been practicing since. I have known Mrs. Baugh for many years. She was a discreet, careful, prudent, business woman.

Q: Were you present when the will was written or signed? In your opinion, was Mrs. Baugh capable of writing a will?

A: I was present when Mr. Palmer was at Mrs. Baugh's the night the will was signed. I had an engagement and did not stay until it was read and signed. She could talk well enough to be understood. At the time Palmer was there and before, I could understand what she said. Her mind was not so much affected as her body.

Q: Please tell the court what her physical and mental state were at that time?

A: She had paralysis. It affected the right side of her body, destroyed ... the voluntary use of the right side of the body. The effect was not worse than that. Paralysis did not kill her.... She died of inanition—want of nourishment.... She had a lesion on the left side of the brain and most probably it was the bursting of a blood vessel, the same cause that produced the paralysis, caused her death ultimately .... But in my opinion, she had capacity on the day the will was written sufficient to understand and make a will...

Following Dr. Murfrees' revelation of what he knew, Mrs. A.R. Richardson's teenage granddaughter, Miss Maggie Muirhead, was called to the stand. Maggie had written the letter to Rollie Howland for Mrs. Baugh.

Q: How well did you know Mrs. Baugh?

A: I knew Mrs. Baugh well. She and my grandmother were intimate friends.

Maggie said she visited Mrs. Baugh daily during her illness and sat with her "while the family dined" the night the will was written. Miss Muirhead described Clemmie and her mother as "mutually dependant" on one another.

Q: Did you ever hear her say anything about Mrs. Clemmie Gum? If you did, did she speak kindly or not about her and what would she say?

A: I have heard her say a hundred times that she wanted and intended to provide a home for Mrs. Gum and her children and give her money besides ... She said this to me in the fall before her death. She was not easily influenced. She was positive and firm in character.

R.W. Ransom, the renter of W.T. Gum's corner store testified that Mrs. Baugh had been in his store shortly before she became ill. He told the court,

> She was at the store and said that some of her children were a little jealous of what she was doing for Mrs. Gum, but she intended to provide for her. I thought her mind was good.

Mr. Ransom added that while he was visiting Mrs. Baugh during her final illness, she was able to "indicate to members of the family something she wanted done and they seemed to understand her and did what she wanted."

Richard Brand, a lawyer and insurance agent, testified as to Mrs. Baugh's positive character. Several persons subpoenaed that day did not appear including Clemmie's brother, Charlie Baugh, and Clemmie's sisters, Mrs. Robert White and Mrs. John Pruitt. The court was now adjourned. Between February and June, John S. Hicks and his uncle Henry Hartwell Hicks were the only witnesses to testify.

~

In late June of 1893, the trial resumed. By now, the intense southern summer heat was upon them. The air was sweltering, and visitors in the gallery sat fanning themselves. The courtroom schedule for Tuesday, June 27th was brief. Two witnesses appeared: Fletcher P. Jacobs and his wife, Bettie.

Bettie Jacobs took the stand first. When asked how she knew Mrs. Baugh, Mrs. Jacobs stated that she and her husband had boarded with Mrs. Baugh in 1876 before Will and Clemmie were married. Mrs. Jacobs said,

> I went to see [Mrs. Baugh] every time I came to town. I was at her house ... when Rollie Howland was hurt. Mrs. Baugh told me that Mrs. Clemmie Gum, her daughter was mad at Rollie and would not write to [him] for her ... Said she ... didn't have any means of helping him then because Mr. Gum had ruined her, but that she expected for Rollie to get his mother's part of the estate [and] that she loved him.

Fletcher Jacobs stated,

> I am the brother and business partner of D. P. Jacobs ... On the Monday before she died, I saw Mrs. Baugh at her house ... She was

> in the little room at the left end of the hall. She was lying there in bed. I stayed almost an hour. Saw her try to talk. She did not say anything . . . that I could understand . . .
>
> Mrs. Clemmie Gum asked me if her mother knew me. I said no and she told me that morning that her mother had not recognized anyone for a day or two. Dr. Murfree came in while I was there. I saw one of the postals that Mr. Gum wrote Rollie Howland when she [Mrs. Baugh] first got sick."

It seems Will Gum had written Rollie Howland, but he waited for nearly a month, until the will was written and Mrs. Baugh was dying, to mail it. By then, it was too late.

~

In the ensuing months, Clemmie waited patiently at home for news of the trial. She could only hope that the land her mother had willed her was safe. Once again, Will Gum was unemployed. Most days he was out looking for work. When the trial was on, Will spent his days at court, returning home later to tell her what people had said about them.

During these difficult months, Clemmie may have found some help from her mother-in-law, Martha, and sisters-in-law, Nannie and Susie, who loved their Gum niece and nephews. Clemmie's pregnancy at the age of thirty-five, especially for one who had suffered a spinal deformity, had not been easy.

Daughter Mary, a sweet girl who loved to sing around the house, brightened her day. Mary was always cheerful and happy to help. The boys, Emmett, nine, Frank, six, and two and a half year-old Willie, were full of energy, running and playing in the large yard between the big house and the store. Emmett and Frank enjoyed coming up with creative ideas of things to do. Frank was something of a clown, always with a smile on his face and a tune on his lips. Together, he and Duxie, as Clemmie called Emmett, made their mother laugh. Even with other worries, the children made life wonderful.

~

On Wednesday, June 28th, 1893, Will and Clemmie went down to the courthouse to file some papers. Family members, who were party to the case, had been ordered to pay for the trial's expenses. The Gums' declaration stated:

> *W.T. Gum and wife Clemmie Gum, do solemnly swear, that owing to their poverty, they are not able to bear the expense of the action...*

In response, Rollie Howland and Dallas Jacobs immediately "made an oath that the allegation of poverty made this day by W.T. Gum and wife ... is probably not true and therefore move the Court to dismiss the action." The Gums were thereby ordered to give security for the costs or "justify their action." The result of this order is not known.

That same day was a busy one for the case, *J.L. & J.M. Baugh vs. Rollie Howland and Ida Jacobs*. Several depositions from witnesses who could not be present in court were read that day before the judge and jury.

The first deposition was a simple statement from Joseph Frank, a former Murfreesboro merchant who had recently moved to Nashville. After that, the deposition of Thomas S. Baugh was read.

Thomas, now thirty-one, was working as a traveling salesman. His testimony, answering questions previously submitted, had been sworn before a notary public.

Q13: Do you know anything of the relations that existed between Mr. W.T. Gum and Mrs. Baugh?

A: Mr. W.T. Gum was her son-in-law. I have heard her say that she would drive him off. She always treated him friendly when he was about but did not like him. She was afraid he would burn her house or do her some harm.

Q14: Was she afraid of Gum? If you ever heard her say anything on the subject state when and where it was and what she said.

A: Yes, she was afraid of him. I heard her state this when I was there in the year 1888 and often since ... She would say that she would as soon see the Devil come in as see him.

Q15: State whether or not Mrs. Baugh made a claim or statement to you relative to Mr. and Mrs. Gum compelling her to do anything?

A: She told me that Mr. and Mrs. Gum made her sign some notes, which made her very mad and that she could not help herself, as she was afraid Mr. Gum would kill her.

At these words, shock waves ran through the courtroom causing Judge Cantrell to bang his gavel and call for order. Meanwhile, in the shadows of the courtroom, Will Gum sat silently, taking in every word.

The clerk continued reading Thomas Baugh's answers.

Q16: Did you or not ever hear Mrs. Clemmie Gum say anything to Mrs. Baugh relative to giving R.M. Howland or Ida Jacobs anything?

A: I heard Mrs. Clemmie Gum say to Mrs. Baugh I would not give Rolly (sp) and Ida anything as they did not need it and Mrs. Baugh said to her she would do as she pleased. "I want them to have their share."

Q: Did you ever hear Mrs. Baugh, your grandmother speak about Rollie M. Howland. Did you or not ever hear Mrs. Baugh say anything about how she wanted her property to be divided with regards to him?

A: She would always speak of R.M. Howland as her child. She missed him and felt as near to him as any of her children. She said she wanted him to have his mother's part of the property.

William H. Baugh's statement was read next. William, now twenty-one, was living in Louisville, Kentucky. His answers were written on 3″ x 5″ note paper, causing the reader to turn many pages. He stated that during his grandmother's illness, he had seen her twice.

A: I heard Mrs. Mary A. Baugh say several different times while I was staying in her house she wanted Rollie Howland and Ida Jacobs to have their mother's part … I have heard Mrs. Mary A Baugh say that Rollie Howland was like a son to her.

Q: Did you ever hear Mrs. Gumm speak about Rollie M. Howland and Ida Jacobs. If so, how did she speak of them?

A: I have heard Mrs. Clemmie Gum say that Rollie Howland had done her a wrong and for that she had no more use for him … I have heard Miss Clemmie Gum say this of Rollie in the presence of her mother, Mrs. Mary A. Baugh, but she never opened her mouth. She always turned her head.

Q: Was she afraid of Gum?

A: Mrs. Mary A. Baugh always spoke with fear toward Mr. Gum. She … has not only said in my presence that she was afraid of Mr. Gum, she has said many times while I was staying with her ... that she would make Mr. Gum leave but she was afraid he would burn her house and her in it. I never heard her speak of Mr. Gum—only in fear.

These statements by two of Mrs. Baugh's grandsons were the most damaging to the Plaintiff's case. It almost seemed as if, far from Murfreesboro, they felt safe to speak.

With Thomas and William Baugh's testimony completed, Horace Palmer now called one of his key witnesses, a party to the suit, Clemmie Gum.

Q: Please state your name, age and relationship to Mrs. Mary A. Baugh.

A: I am the wife of W.T. Gum. We have five children. The oldest is thirteen years old and youngest is six months old. Mrs. Baugh was my mother. I always lived with her. Neither my husband nor I have any property except what is given me and my children in the will.

Q: Did you at any time try to influence your mother, Mrs. Baugh as to Rollie Howland?

A: I never at any time tried to prevent Mammie from doing anything for her children or grandchildren. I never tried to influence her against any of her children or grandchildren. I didn't try to get her to make a will. She often told me she was going to give me that lot which is given me in the will ... She said she was going to give me the offices, the store and Aunt Ran's house ...

As Clemmie spoke, she seemed to know what many of the witnesses had said, and what some who had yet to testify were going to say. Now, her tone grew heated and defensive.

A: I did not talk against Rollie in the presence of W.H. Baugh or anyone else. I never threatened Mammie nor did anything to try to make her afraid. Will did not either. She wasn't afraid of anybody. Will did not ask me while she was sick if "Mrs. Baugh had said anything yet" and I said "no." Neither of us ever tried to compel her to sign any notes or to do anything else.

This last statement was made to oppose Ran Miller's statement, though Ran, who was subpoenaed by the court, had yet to appear. Being a person of color, who had lived most of her life with the Baughs, it is doubtful Ran would lie.

About her mother's name, Clemmie explained,

A: She signed her named Mary A. Baugh but ... she was especially proud of the Marable name. She had the letters M.A.M.B. on her trunk.

Q: Was there reason for your mother to leave Rollie Howland out of her will?

A: She told me of two conversations Rollie had with her which offended her. The first was before he married and the last, after his marriage. In the last one, she said he told her if he was in her place, he would kick me and Will and my children out of doors in the street.

John Richardson then cross-examined Clemmie with regards to money matters.

Q: Was your husband, Mr. Gum, in business with Mrs. Baugh? If so, please state the amounts of money which she lent him.

A: She paid for Will at one time $530 and at another $300. That was all. She and Will were in business; their firm was W.T. Gum & Co. They borrowed money to go into business on and I signed her name to the notes. She authorized me to do so. The notes were renewed several times. I signed her name to the renewal notes. When she learned that I had signed her name to them she was displeased because she thought the notes she had authorized me to sign were paid ... I have been married sixteen years and Will has been out of business about four years. The store was burned twice...

~

At this time, Horace Palmer made the decision to call Will T. Gum to testify. Prior to this time Will may not have been included on the list of witnesses, but recent depositions made his testimony necessary. When Mr. Palmer announced his intention in court, John E. Richardson stood up.

"Your Honor, I object!"

"On what basis?" asked Judge Cantrell. It seemed to him Will Gum was an important witness.

"You Honor, Mr. Gum has been present during the entire trial. He was listening through the rule as to how the witnesses spoke."

"The rule" was known to all in the legal profession, and had stood forever. It was understood that a witness should not listen to testimony prior to giving their own as it might influence what they would say. Will Gum had broken that rule.

Horace Palmer responded, "Your Honor, I ask for an exception to the rule. The party is with the suit and the rule doesn't apply. . . ."

"Exception taken," said Judge Cantrell.

Will Gum would be the 14th witness on behalf of the Plaintiffs. Horace Palmer began by questioning him with regards to the day Mrs. Baugh wrote her will. It was not long, however, before Will Gum felt impelled to defend himself against all prior testimony.

A: I never in my life said to Mrs. Baugh, don't you want to give Clemmie another $1,000 … I never said to Mrs. Baugh or anyone anything about burning her house down … Such a thing never occurred to me.

Will Gum then returned to the subject of the will:

A: I remember having a conversation with T.S. Baugh. He slept with me the night she (Mrs. Baugh) was a corpse.

Although this statement may seem offensive now, in 1892, the word "corpse" was commonly used for the remains of one who had passed on.

A: He wanted to know about the will, what it contained. He asked me if Rollie Howland was given anything. I did not tell him she had done nicely by Clemmie and that if the rest of the children treated me right I would let the will stand. I told him I didn't want to discuss the matter and turned over and went to sleep.

Q: Mr. Gum, please describe your relation with Mrs. Baugh. Were you in business with her?

A: After I married, I first went into business by myself and so continued until 1884. The house burnt and the insurance did not cover my loss. In 1885, Mrs. Baugh said I must have something to do … I told her I could not do business without money. She said she had or would have the money. We went into partnership. We borrowed money to go into business on. She signed the notes, I bought the confectionary. When [the notes] became due, they were renewed. I would sign them myself and bring them to the house for Mrs. Baugh's signature.

Will's story sounded accurate and, perhaps, he believed it himself. Yet too many people testified otherwise about him. If the court reviewed the records for deeds and loans, they would have found that Mrs. Baugh had lent Will Gum a lot more money than he or Clemmie claimed.

When John E. Richardson stood for the cross-examination, Will must have felt a little nervous.

Q: Did you threaten Mrs. Mary A. Baugh? Was she afraid of you?

A: I never in my life threatened her. She never was afraid of me. Mrs. Baugh did not say anything about taking it all ... I did not say Mr. Palmer my wife knows what her mother wants. Mrs. Baugh paid for me $830.00.

Finally, when he was questioned about the Christmas of 1891, Will said,

A: Rollie looked out of the window and said if he thought the next day would be worse than today, then they would go home that day. Mrs. Baugh ... said ... "The weather would be worse tomorrow than it is today."

Will meant to show that Mrs. Baugh really did not care for Rollie and his wife to stay. Clemmie had told the same story, but Rollie said that Will was not there that day at all.

Q: Did you write to R.M. Howland regarding his grandmother's illness?

A: Jack Baugh told me to write members of the family of Mrs. Baugh's sickness. She objected to my doing so, but I did write two postal cards to Rollie Howland.

This concluded Will Gum's testimony.

~

By October, the case of *J.L. & J.M Baugh, Extrs. vs. Rollie Howland and Ida Jacobs* had been in court for nearly a year. Still, Palmer and Richardson pressed on for one last testimony that might turn the decision of the trial. John E. Richardson subpoenaed Ran Miller and her daughter Jane Hoover once more, this time, making sure they appeared in court. He also sent a clerk out to Salem to take down the testimony of Mrs. J.M. Baugh.

On the Plaintiff's side, the Maynors, Larry and Ella, who were former boarders of Mrs. Baugh also testified on this day. Their testimony brought nothing new other than to confirm what had been said previously, that Mrs. Mary A. Baugh had planned to provide well for her daughter, Clemmie, and had changed her mind about leaving Rollie Howland anything.

The depositions of Professor John White, and that of his mother, Bettie White, also were read on this day. Each showed clearly that Mrs. Baugh, though very ill, still had possession of her right mind and was capable of making a will. Mrs. White's testimony was taken by Knox Ridley. When asked to state what her mother suffered from, Bettie replied,

> *A:* Mr. I can't say that word. My teeth are out and them's a heap of cares.... It's paralysis.

Bettie was able to bring some clarity to the questions of both attorneys, in particular Mr. Richardson. The one thing Bettie White questioned was how the property was drawn in the will.

> *Q61:* ...I further ask you if the reason you didn't' then make objection to the will was because there had already been, in your opinion, too much squabbling over the matter...?
>
> *A:* ...I didn't think I had any right to say anything. I hadn't heard any squabbles...
>
> *Q65:* Didn't Mr. Gum ask Mrs. Baugh after the will was written ... if she didn't want to give his wife another $1000?
>
> *A:* I think he did.
>
> *Q66:* When was it he asked her that?
>
> *A:* That was before the will was written.

Bettie was then reexamined and the person questioning her stated that Mr. Palmer and Mr. Gum had both been at Mrs. White's house the prior Saturday. During that conversation, she mentioned that in the last days of her mother's life, she'd had a conversation with her regarding the fact that she'd changed her mind about Rollie Howland and didn't plan to give him anything.

> *A:* I said she had changed. I didn't say I thought she didn't intend to give Rollie anything. If I said that, I made a mistake... She didn't talk about Rollie as she used to. She thought he thought too much of Ellen's kin.

On October 24th, Mirandy Miller and her daughter, Jane Hoover, came to testify at the Rutherford County Courthouse. Jane Hoover testified that she was present when her mother asked Mrs. Baugh why she didn't make her will, adding,

> I heard her say of Rollie Howland and Ida Jacobs that they shim (should) have their portions or shares. Heard her say that the first or second year that I was here in town and I came to town five years ago. My mother and I lives in the house on the corner of Mrs. Baugh's lot.

The notice for their appearance in court had been sent to Courtland Street, a place where many black people lived. Twice, they had not responded to the subpoenas summoning them. Perhaps Ran and Jane feared retribution should they say the wrong thing about Will Gum or Clemmie.

Next on the stand that day was Tom Crocker, Mrs. Baugh's butcher, who had known her for ten years.

> That year before she died, I sold beef to her. In the fall, one day when I was selling her beef she said ... "I can't pay you now what I owe you. That son-in-law of mine, Will Gum, has failed and embarrassed me, but you continue to sell to me. I will pay you. I intend to have what I want as long as I live and when I am dead, I don't care what becomes of what is left.

The last person to testify in the courtroom was Mrs. Baugh's long-time boarder, Charlie Webb. He had been subpoenaed as a witness for both the plaintiff and the defense. Mr. Webb stated:

> A: I knew Mrs. Baugh well. I boarded a long time at the house. I checked for W.T. Gum & Co. in the store on the lot. I was in the house the day the will was written.

Mr. Webb proceeded to answer questions regarding the story of the Chinaman in the hall and the overheard conversation of Mr. and Mrs. Gum. Mr. Webb was now ninety years old, and two years had passed since the event. John Richardson, asked:

> Q: Did you not hear Mr. Gum say to his wife that she was trying to collect a dollar or less from the Chinaman and loose $1000 by not being in her mother's room.

> A: I do not remember that Mr. Gum said that.

Charlie Webb may have forgotten, or even, possibly, felt threatened by Mr. Gum. Obviously, Mr. Richardson was repeating something Mr. Webb told him earlier.

The trial stopped now as Horace Palmer claimed that Mr. Richardson was trying to "refresh the witness's recollection." Judge Cantrell declared, "Objection sustained," and the testimony was closed.

Next, Eliza Pruett's deposition was read. She was considered a witness for the defense because she felt the will had not been written as she had understood her mother meant it to be. Her confusion was mainly in how the lot had been cut; she felt that Clemmie got more than her mother had meant her to have. At the same time Eliza did not believe the will was written correctly, she also did not know the names of the streets or where the garden fence went.[138]

Eliza also was questioned about the situation in Mrs. Baugh's room the night the will was written. Her opinions, while similar to others, were a bit sharper.

Q32: Where was Mr. Gum while he was in the room?

A: He was sitting on the foot of the bed, I think.

Q33: How near to your mother's feet?

A: Right against them, I reckon.

Q34: Where was his wife?

A: She was sitting close to the foot of the bed.

Q53: Were you present just before your father died? If so, did you hear him make any request of your Mother?

A: Yes, Sir. I heard him say to remember Sister Clemmie and Rollie—Not to forget them ... My father wanted my sister Clemmie to have more than the balance because she was crippled...

Eliza Pruitt was questioned by both attorneys; once with Mr. Palmer present, and later for a re-examination on behalf of the defense.

The final testimony read for the case was that of Maria, Mrs. J.M. Baugh. Earlier in the year, she had been ill. It was not until October that the attorneys or their representatives went to the Baugh home and took down her testimony. Like her husband, Jack, Maria recalled the conversation at May Place.

A. [Mrs. Baugh] said she didn't reckon she ever would make her will... Said if she would make her will and didn't make it to suit Will, she was afraid he'd burn her house over her head. Mr. Gum I should have said, but she always called him "Will." Them's as near the words as I can tell it.

Q: If you knew her feeling towards Mr. Gum, please state it.

A: Well, she never liked him. She spoke of that often. She despised him. Hated him in her sight. But I hate to say these things. I don't want to say them!

Q: You say that Mrs. Baugh never liked her son-in-law, Mr. Gum ... Do you know how she regarded her daughter, Mr. Gum's wife, Clemmie?

A: She loved her like she did her other children. She would have been an unnatural mother if she hadn't.

~

By the end of the October 1893, all witnesses had been heard and cross-examinations completed. It was time for the summations. Attorney John E. Richardson rose to plead the Defendants' case. The courtroom was hushed as he began to speak. It had been an intense, even shocking trial. Now, Mr. Richardson hit each point of the trial clearly and succinctly: Mary Ann Baugh's name had not been signed correctly in the will; throughout her life she had stated that she wished to give Ida Jacobs and Rollie Howland their mother's share, especially Rollie, whom she had raised. There had been never been any ill will between them, nor any reason she would not include him in the will. Then, the most explosive point:

> Her feeling toward her son-in-law Gum, husband of chief devisee in the will ... shows that testatrix was constantly in fear of said son-in-law and had said that she was afraid to make a will that did not please him for fear he would burn her house down... Five witnesses testify to statements that she was afraid of ... Gum.
>
> Now, strange to say, during the very time that Mrs. Baugh was making declarations that she did not intend to give Howland and Miss Jacobs anything of her estate, she was making also statements to the contrary, and asserting that they should have their mother's respective shares ... Why was she making these conflicting statements? What changed her mind so often or changed her will?

Horace Palmer's summation was simple and to the point. Mary A. Baugh had originally intended to give Rollie Howland and Ida Jacobs their share, but she had changed her mind. Many persons, including the good doctor, James B. Murfree, had declared Mrs. Baugh, despite her illness, capable of writing a will.

Judge Robert Cantrell, Jr. made the final statement to the jury:

> It is necessary that I explain to you the amount of mind that is necessary to enable a party to make a will. It does not depend upon the strength of the body ... The question for you to settle in regards to her mind is did she have mind sufficient to comprehend or know the property she owned, did she know the relation she bore to the parties ... Gentlemen, take this case and give such verdict as you think right under the law.

~

By late October, the jury took the first vote. At that time, most of the jurors voted against the plaintiffs and the will. Then, as J.W. Boyd, one of the jurors, would later report, while in the jury room, another juror, Mr. Sanders, asked how many of the jurors had seen or experienced a case of paralysis. Some of the jurors stated that they had. One juror improperly brought up a man he had known, Mr. M. Pitts, who had his right side paralyzed but was able to talk and had been in his right mind until a day or two before his death. Altogether, the jurors knew of five cases with paralysis.

The foreman of the jury called out that according to the rule, they were not to discuss these things. Other cases had nothing to do with this trial. Again, the jurors took a vote, and although a decision was not reached, two or three jurors changed their vote.

By the end of October, the jury made a decision on the side of the plaintiffs, stating that Mrs. Baugh had been capable of writing her will and knew what she wanted without the influence of those around her.

The decision was announced, and immediately Rollie Howland and Ida Jacobs requested that Attorney John E. Richardson ask for an appeal. Shortly after that, Judge Cantrell responded:

> After consideration of said motions, the Court is pleased to overrule the same ... an appeal to the next term of the Supreme Court at Nashville, which was granted...

The appeal, titled: *R.M. Howland & Ida Jacobs, Plaintiffs in Error vs. J.L. & J.M. Baugh & W.T. Gum, Defendants in Error*, was filed in December. Witnesses would not have to travel or give testimony again. The original testimony would be transcribed into neat longhand and submitted to the Tennessee Supreme Court. The wait would not be long.

Early in 1894, two years after Mary Ann Baugh's death, the Tennessee Supreme Court ruled in favor of J.L. & J.M Baugh & W. T. Gum. The original ruling held. The Tennessee Supreme Court's decision quoted William Ransom's statement that Mrs. Baugh felt "some of her family members were a little jealous of what she was doing for Mrs. Gum." The Court's decision questioned the Baugh's testimony regarding Will Gum's threats. These threats, they said, had only been spoken of by five members of the family and no one else. Finally, there was no reason to believe that Mrs. Baugh's will had not been written according to her wishes. The will would hold.

There must have been great celebration in the Gum home that day. Not only had they won, Rollie Howland and Ida Jacobs would be required to cover all court costs, including the monies paid for witnesses. The court costs, not including attorneys, came to $170.08. (= $4,370)

It was not a good result, either monetarily or emotionally for Rollie Howland. The grandmother who had raised him and to whom he was never been able to say goodbye, had changed her mind and left him out of her will. At least, he was not alone; Cousin Ida had also been left out.

Although Jack Baugh's family treated Rollie kindly and certainly believed in his case, from here on, Rollie Howland would, for the most part, remain closer to his Howland relatives and the relatives of his wife.

Chapter 16

Sorrows

THE GUM FAMILY HAD BEEN ABLE TO STAY IN THE BIG HOUSE FOR MORE than a year following Mary Ann Baugh's passing, but now that the trial was over, it was time to move. Bit by bit, things had been sold and family members had come to take what they wanted. The home that had been the Baughs' for twenty-five years was no more.

During this time, Jack Baugh came to visit Clemmie to discuss the results of the trial and catch up on family matters. The little Gum boys, Emmett, Frank and Willie stared at their Uncle Jack with his long dark beard streaked with gray. Uncle Jack was so different from their father. His eyes were great, dark and sunken in. His arm clung to his side and did not move. The boys knew that Uncle Jack had fought in "The War" with General Forest. He was a hero to the South, and someone very important in their eyes.

When Uncle Jack Baugh visited again he brought one or two of his children along. Murphey George, although nine years older than Frank, later recalled playing with him and his brothers. Perhaps to give Will and Clemmie a break, Jack took the boys out to his farm in Salem, where they could play without encumbrance and help with the many farm chores, which would have been a novel experience for them. Jack Baugh, a school teacher, loved to tell his nephews stories of his youth and the war.

In later years, Uncle Jack's granddaughter, Betty Baugh would often repeat the statement that had been passed down in the family; that without slavery and the labor of the blacks, the farmers went broke. None of Uncle Jack and Aunt Maria's children would see a way to earn a living farming.

The sale of Mary Ann Baugh's house would bring some much needed cash for everyone. Will and Clemmie Gum were not the only ones in need of money. Jack Baugh was not having an easy time with his finances either. Two years after the sale of the Baugh home, on January 14th, 1896, Jack would transfer his farm property, including the farm animals and tools, along with his interest in Eagleville and Salem Turnpikes to his wife, Maria, likely to protect it from creditors.[139]

On December 5, 1894, the big house on East Main Street was sold to Ada J. Murfree, the wife of Dr. James Brickell Murfree. Ada and five of the Murfree children, all adults or near to it, moved into the home which Dr. Murfree's grandfather, Matthias Murfree, built in 1832. Dr. Murfree was in New York, studying the latest techniques in surgery. The Murfrees had intended to buy the house back from Mr. Osborne at the end of the war, but had been unable to afford it. Now, it was back in the family.

The Murfrees paid $4,510.00 (= $116,000) total for the house with an initial payment of $1,503.38 (= $38,700). In addition, the notes on the house for the following amounts were to be paid off within the next two years for $250.55, $501.00 and $751.86 (= $6,442, $12,900 and $19,300).[140] The Murfrees would own everything from the line of the brick office building, now occupied by the Gums, along the edge of Mrs. Baugh's garden fence and back to Vine Street. A spacious yard on the other side of the house toward the square was also part of the property.

For the younger Gum children, moving day may have been an adventurous game. By now, Emmett was eleven, Frank, eight, Willie, six, and Allie, two. But for Will, Clemmie and fourteen year-old Mary, it was a strange, sad day as they moved their few possessions and any furniture that would fit into the "brick tenement."

A tenement, as described by *The Concise Standard Dictionary of English Language* of 1913, was "a room or rooms for a family; usually of inferior grade." The three-room building had always been called the "brick office building" because it was built to be used for business. The Rutherford County court would later describe the building as "three, small, brick rooms with two small sheds behind..."* There was no kitchen and no bathroom. As with all houses in Murfreesboro for many years, the property included an outhouse or "privy" in the back yard.

A privy was a small wooden "shack" with a door that locked from the inside. A broad piece of wood with at least two holes of varying sizes was nailed like a low shelf across the back wall for use. An old ladle to scoop lime from a bucket to throw into the pit was kept nearby, as well as, a stack of newspapers, or corncobs.[141] Such were the conveniences of life at this time.

The Gums likely did not have any running water. There were several springs nearby, and perhaps a hand pump in the garden, where they could pump a bucket or pitcher of water for use in the house.

The friends of Mrs. Baugh who rented these rooms to live in had used the big house for meals and visiting. Considering this, the building hardly seemed suitable for a family of seven, but Will and Clemmie had little choice. At present, they were grateful to have a roof over their heads. Besides, they considered this a temporary situation.

Living in the office building, the family heard the whistles of over one hundred trains which passed through Murfreesboro day and night. The walls of the old house were thick, but in the small brick building, the long, deep call of the train whistles at night were so loud, it almost seemed as if the tracks were behind their house.

~

Will Gum was doing the best he could to take care of his family, but he had been unable to find gainful employment. His reputation around town had not been good to start, but after the trial, whatever shred of dignity he had been able to maintain earlier was now destroyed. Doubtless, every word spoken in the Rutherford County Courtroom had been repeated around town.

Once Will T. Gum had owned his own store and resided proudly in the Baugh home. Now, he had nothing. The land and the house belonged to Clemmie and the children. The years of drinking and gambling had

---

* Statement Palmer & Ridley, Solicitors, 1896. The "two small sheds"—crossed out."

taken their toll. Will Gum was now forty years old, with a wife and five children whom he could not support.

As the reality of the situation descended on him, it must have been difficult to keep his promise to be a better husband and father. The taverns on the square beckoned him, and not far from them, lady luck called. A roll of the dice or a card game might change his fortune, a voice said. But Will did not have money for that. In his present state, he needed every penny just to buy food and coal for his family.

In 1894, the former W.T. Gum & Company store was still rented to Mr. Ransom for $10.00 a month. (= $264) This rent, along with the rent from the cottage on Maney and Vine of $4.00 (= $105) was essential for the Gum family's survival.[142]

Meanwhile, Will Gum found a few odd jobs which earned him some income. He must have looked back on the days he had complained about with nostalgia.

~

In April of 1894, Will's parents, Jere and Martha, had their own drama to contend with. On the 26th day of the month, Martha Gum looked out the door of the Gum home to see some men removing the fences around her property! When questioned, she was informed that they were taking possession of a portion of her land for a street. In the process, the city would be cutting a ten-foot deep section off the side of the side yard and six feet off the front yard, leaving their home almost on the edge of the street. Mr. and Mrs. Gum were not pleased.

In order to prevent flooding problems during the rainy season, the officers told the Gums, they would also re-grade the land, cutting their yard down about 2½ feet in the front, and three feet on the south side. In this way, they would fill in the road's edge to prevent "the outflow of surface water;" which otherwise, would turn the area into a "pond or bog."[143]

Martha and Jere Gum immediately went down to the courthouse and placed a "stay" on the building of the street. At the same time, they opened a case against Mayor T.H. Woods and the City's Alderman. The case was titled: *J.A. Gum and wife, Martha Gum, Citizens of Rutherford County, Tennessee vs. The Mayor and Aldermen of the town of Murfreesboro, Tennessee and a Municipal Corporation of said County.* The Gum's daughter,

Laura, who was working for the dry goods store, Hirsch and Company, where Will Baugh worked a few years earlier, signed the papers for her parents, agreeing that she would "be surety for costs in this cause."

In court, Mr. and Mrs. Gum, without an attorney, stated that the land had been taken with no notice or offer of compensation. Meanwhile, the court produced a legal decree from 1860 stating that the town plat had been made without streets around 1812, but that certain lots were to be left open for the creation of these streets and access to the local spring for water. The area where the Gum property sat had been slated to have a street put in since the beginning. It had simply been up to the city as to when that would take place; it was a matter of need.

The Gums said that they had invested a great deal in their property since moving there. As a result, their property was now worth about $1,200 and contained a "substantial structure." Their lot was also enclosed by a "substantial fence," built on boundary lines according to the deed. It had been thus enclosed for the last 30 years and no official person had given them any notice or set claim to the land the city was now claiming. Their property was already quite narrow, and they had never been informed they would loose part of their land for a street when they bought the property.

The argument went back and forth. The Mayor and Aldermen insisted that it was understood some day a street would be put in when needed.

They were only taking the portion that belonged to the town. Martha Gum, whose name was on the deed, responded that they had never known anything about this until the men appeared in their yard. The land the city was taking had been included in her deed.

Martha Gum was irate. She worried about a bog forming as a result of the city's work. The city officials stated they had no intention of damaging the Gum's lot. There was already a natural sinkhole on her property. This meant that all the surface water would run into it without troubling the Gums. Meanwhile, the street was already partially opened and grated.

The town officers now produced a document showing that the Gums had been given notice of the new street. In fact, everyone else in the neighborhood on the same line had been given the same notice and each resident had followed the directives. Mrs. Gum was the only exception. Read it in court, the document, dated April 4th, 1894, stated:

> The Board of Mayor and Aldermen have ordered the extension of the street known as State or Castle Street, through the Old City Cemetery, the same to be the width of Forty-nine and one-half feet. You are hereby notified to remove your fense (sp) on the territory included in said extension … within ten days from the date of this notice, or same will be abated as a nuisance and removed by the City.
>
> Very Respectfully, N.C. Maney, City Marshall

At this point, Mr. and Mrs. Gum could no longer deny having received the notice. The city attorney, P.O. Mason, stated that Mrs. Gum had no right to "interfere with the exercise *of the rights of the defendants*," meaning the town.

The Gums said they wished to appeal the case, and take it before the Tennessee Supreme Court in Nashville, however, as the old saying goes, "you can't fight city hall." Jere and Martha Gum finally agreed to "dissolve their injunction" in exchange for which the city of Murfreesboro would pay all court costs. Everyone agreed and the case was closed.[144]

When the Gum boys, Emmett, Frank and Willie visited their grandparents during this time, they must have witnessed the Gum tempers flaring. However, as with most children, the boys watched the transformation of their grandparents' yard with great interest.

~

The beginning of January 1895, a partial settlement of the Estate of Mary A. Baugh was recorded in the Rutherford County Courthouse.[145] In February, family members received their first installment from sale of the house.[146] According to Mary Ann Baugh's will, Clemmie's proceeds were to be used to build a house, however, Will and Clemmie soon realized that it would take more than they had to build a home. Will was out of work, and they still owed taxes on the property. Sometimes, they barely had money for food.

Old Tennessee Cubby Corner and detail, circa late 1790s or early 1800s, said to have come from the Gum home.
(Courtesy Roy Newsom)

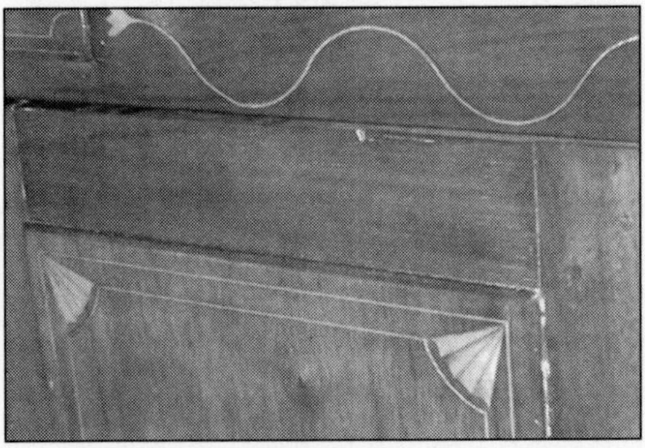

As they realized they were stuck living in the small brick cottage, the darkness of their unhappy situation sank in and began to wear on the couple. Three small rooms with five noisy children seemed even smaller with no end in sight.

From his auspicious beginnings, Will Gum had sunk into a deep hole that even Clemmie's inheritance could not relieve. His brother, John Gum, Jr., who had once been deep in debt himself, was now making a good living in Atlanta, Georgia. The move had been a good choice for John, but Will was stuck.

Although the brick office building had no kitchen to speak of, at the least there were either wood- or coal-burning stoves in each room. Mary Ann had once spoken of building an upstairs on the brick building, but after taking on Will's debts, she had run out of money. The decision about what to do—if there was one—was now completely in Clemmie's hands.

With the exception of little Will and Allie, all the Gum children were in school. Each day, Frank walked to the Murfreesboro Grammar School a few blocks away on Bell Street.[147] After school, he walked his friend, and distant cousin, Rebecca Jetton, down the hill from square to the little stone bridge that crossed Lytle Creek. Rebecca lived just outside the town center in a big house on Church Street and would long remember how, when they were only seven or eight years old, Frank carried her books each day after school. At the bridge, Frank would hand her the books. Then, they would each go their way, turning to wave to one another; Rebecca, as she walked down Church Street, and Frank, as he headed up the hill to East Main. Rebecca later said she knew Frank from the time he lived in the big house.[148]

~

In the wee hours of an 1895 March morning, fire struck once again in the lives of the Gum family. Fire was a frequent occurrence during these years, and the amount of fires in Murfreesboro, which mostly occurred at night, kept the fire department very busy.

As soon as someone in town was aware of a fire, an alarm was signaled. This alarm rang from the engine room of Christy and Huggins Ice Bottling Works on Manchester Pike, not far from Jere and Martha Gum's house. Sounded by a brass steam whistle, it could be heard throughout the town. Most buildings in Murfreesboro were wood, and there could be no time wasted in putting out a fire. In 1856, a fire on the square had destroyed an entire row of buildings, which were replaced by brick buildings for safety.

The steam whistle from Christy & Huggins was said to have an "eerie" and "ominous" quality, especially when it sounded late at night. The sleeping town came to life. Lanterns were lit and people came running to see if they could help. The fire engine, a heavy, old steam engine, was pulled as quickly as possible by a horse to the location in flames.

People used fireplaces and wood stoves to keep warm during this time, along with candles and kerosene lamps to light their homes. Although many objects in homes and stores were easily flammable, it does seem there were an unusual number of fires in the life of Will Gum. This fact, coupled with the statements by his mother-in-law that he had threatened to burn her home, leads to the question: was Will Gum at fault? Did he have a problem with fire and had he, in states of drunken anger, set fire to the store?

When people started buying insurance, and an insured building caught fire, some residents just stood and watched it burn, thinking of the money they would collect. This was certainly not the case with Will Gum. This time, the family had been too poor to pay for insurance and let the policy lapse.[149] The following week, *The Liberty Herald* reported:

> Last Saturday morning the store of R.N. Ransom, corner of Main street and Maney avenue, was discovered on fire. The building was owned by W.T. Gum.

The store burned to the ground, and the Gum family's main source of income was gone. Will and Clemmie attempted to get a loan to rebuild it, but having no income, they were unable to find a bank, or anyone for that matter, who would give them a loan. Officially, they were supposed to go before the court before making any decisions as to the property, but the court schedule was full and time was of the essence. Without the income from the store, they simply could not survive.

J.L. Baugh.
(Courtesy Lawrence Hannah)

In the past, Will Gum borrowed money from Dallas Jacobs, but that March 23rd, fifty year-old Dallas had died. When his record books came to light, it would be found that Will Gum still owed him $25. (= $659)

In desperation, Clemmie contacted the only person in the family who really had any money, her eldest brother, Joseph Baugh, and begged him for a loan.

Although Joseph Baugh was not living in Murfreesboro, as

one of the executors on his mother's will he was well aware of Will Gum's business history. Joseph agreed to lend Clemmie the money she needed, but his agreement followed along the lines of Mrs. Baugh's will. In part, the loan agreement read:

> This contract made between Mrs. Clemmie Gum of the first part and J.L. Baugh of the second part as follows: I, the undersigned Clemmie Gum, am the owner for life of my sole and separate use free from the control of my husband, under the last will of my late mother Mary A. Baugh, of a lot situated on the corner of East Main Street and Maneys Avenue ... The storehouse was recently destroyed by fire. I am anxious to have the storehouse rebuilt and have not the means with which to have it rebuilt.
>
> Now J.L. Baugh has agreed to furnish me with the money necessary for rebuilding the same—Two hundred & Eighty-five ($285.00) dollars. (= $7,510) J.L. Baugh is to have the control ... of said property, to manage and control it, collect rent, etc. He is to retain of the rents collected by him, $6.25 each month. The balance of cents he is to pay over to me ... (= $158)

The agreement further stated that the money was to be lent for four years. If more money was needed to complete the store, J.L. Baugh would furnish the additional amount. The agreement between Joe and Clemmie was signed on April 15th, 1895, with the stipulation that the building be insured.

During the summer, the buildings were completed and the store rented once again. In order to create additional income, Will used some of the money he had recently earned to build a meat shop.

It was a long, hot, sweltering summer in the brick office building. The children joined in to help Clemmie, with a good deal of the responsibility falling on the shoulders of fifteen year-old Mary. In another time and place, Mary might have been sitting on the porch in a pretty dress, greeting her beaus and attending parties. But there was no time for that now and no money for pretty dresses, unless perhaps, her Gum aunts gave her their cast-offs. In her grandmother's home, Mary lived like a lady. Now, her family was living like the lower class.

The one distraction and escape from their problems was music. The Gums all sang (and likely played at least one instrument) in their small rooms or on the front porch at night when it was too hot to stay inside. It has been said that all the children had good voices. Their parents must have had some musical ability as well. Music, in the little Gum house, brought some sunshine into all their lives.

With the coming of autumn, another development took place in the Gum home; Clemmie's health began to fail. Despite her disability, up to now she had seemed well enough. The move from the big house, and the conditions that accompanied this life in the brick tenement, likely helped destroy Clemmie's health.

In the late 1890s, there were no death certificates in Rutherford County. The whereabouts of the undertakers' records, which might have held answers, are unknown, and Dr. Murfree's records also have disappeared. While the cause of Clemmie's ill health has not been found, there were many forms of illness that took people's lives in Murfreesboro during the late 1800s: flu, consumption, pneumonia, and diseases of the stomach.

When Dr. Murfree was home, he likely spoke to the children and came to visit Clemmie. He would often ride out in the morning to see a patient in the country and, then, in the evening, drive his horse and buggy twenty or thirty miles back to check on them again. He never worried about whether his patients could pay him or not. If he was in town, Dr. Murfree would surely have tried to help Clemmie.

Although we cannot know what Clemmie's condition was, what is known is that on October 28th, 1895, Clemmie Baugh Gum departed this life, leaving behind her five children and a husband who was unable to support them. Clemmie was thirty-eight years old.

On a day with clear blue skies and leaves that had turned to gold, Clemmie Gum was laid to rest. How sad that day in the little home, as the simple funeral took place. Will's parents and siblings were there along with Clemmie's brothers and sisters. Mrs. Richardson and her family would have come as well. Clemmie's siblings must have paid for the burial. Will Gum could not afford to. Could Clemmie's brothers and sisters help but think how soon she had died after her mother? Could they help but wonder if Mary Ann were still alive, would Clemmie have died so young?

The carriage came and took the plain wooden casket with Clemmie's body away. How sad to see the faces of her young children as they bid their mother goodbye. The thought of that is heartbreaking.

From here on, Mary would be a substitute mother to the little ones, with the responsibility of keeping house fully on her shoulders. Emmett and Frank had lost the one, warm comfort in their lives. Will and Allie, little children, could barely realize all they had lost, but felt deserted by their Ma. The Gum aunts, Nannie and Bettie, though they had families of their own, lived nearby and would try to do what they could for their nieces and nephews. Will was sobered by Clemmie's death, but the pain also fueled his desire for the old medicine.

As was customary in Rutherford County, after the death of one parent, the other parent went to court to request custody of their children. On November 2, 1895, Will T. Gum appeared at the Rutherford County Courthouse and was officially appointed the guardianship of his five children.

Meanwhile, Will's situation was more complex than most. The property on which he lived now belonged to his children. From here on, Will Gum could not make a decision regarding his children, or their property without court approval. As a result, a legal trail of the family's comings and goings was preserved for posterity.

~

One of the first orders of business for the Rutherford County Court in January of 1896 was to assign the Gum children a guardian ad Litem, who would represent their interests in court in an unbiased fashion. For this job, Thomas B. Lytle, grandson of Murfreesboro's founder, and a well-known local attorney was chosen. On January 20th, Mr. Lytle signed the necessary papers accepting the position. Regarding this decision, the Court commented, "...said defendants being infants of tender years and their Guardian ad Litem not having any personal knowledge of the facts of case."

A few days later, the children were summoned to appear before the judge at the Rutherford County Courthouse. Mary was a few weeks shy of sixteen, Emmett, twelve, Frank, almost ten, Willie, six and Allie, three and a half. In their interest, the court reviewed all business regarding their inheritance and welfare.

The first matter held up for review was the loan agreement between Clemmie and her brother, Joe Baugh. After a thorough review, it was agreed that this contract was in the children's best interest. The only problem was that since Clemmie's death, Joe Baugh had not received any of the rents in repayment for his loan. The court noted that the total cost of rebuilding the storehouse had been $301.50. By the time Clemmie passed away, Joseph L. Baugh had received $37.50 in return. The amount of $7.50 had been paid out for insurance.

Will Gum agreed that Joseph Baugh should be paid, but asked that the remainder of the money from the store rents and Aunt Ran's old house be given to him for the support of the children, rather than going to the children's fund. When asked if he was able to support his children without using their rents, he replied, "No, Sir." Will was out of work, and his request was granted. The attorney handling the case was Horace Palmer. Mr. Palmer would continue to handle it up until the children reached adulthood.

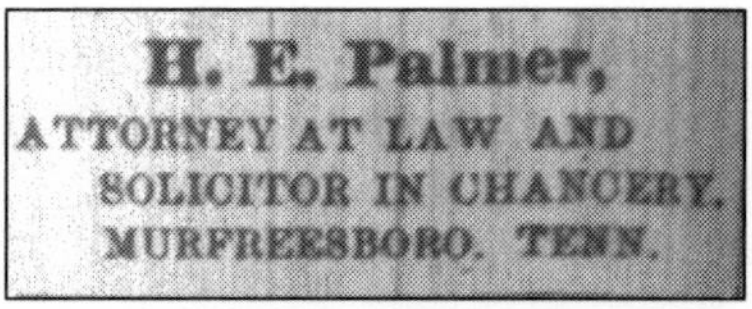

The funds held for the children from the sale of Mrs. Baugh's big house were in the amounts of $617.38 (= $12,572.17), $367.38 (= $7,409.49) being in cash and $250.00 (= $5,047) being in a note. There is no doubt Will Gum was hoping to obtain this money for the care of the children, but the court would have to weight in on it.

By 1896, Will began to show his sensible side and attempt to turn the tide. Going before the court, he expressed a desire to move his children out of the brick offices, a space, he said, that was far too small for the family. His request was denied.

Will Gum must have been in a state by now. Everything he had done in the past had brought him to this point. He had carried himself as a man who had bad luck, for which he deserved the greatest sympathy. But now, in his darkest hour, having hit bottom, Will pulled himself together and concentrated on taking care of himself and his children. Not allowing them to move out of the brick office building where Clemmie had died could endanger the children's health. Will felt the court was tying his hands.

A week later, it happened again. The brick office building caught fire. Late one night that January, Will Gum came home and somehow, some time in the night, a fire started and spread to the roof. Whatever the cause, the Murfreesboro Fire Department, though only 4–5 blocks away, was unable to get there in time. The family ran out, saving what little they could before the roof came crashing in. Many precious mementos were likely lost that night, including, possibly, photos of Mary Ann Baugh, Clemmie and Will.

The cause of this late-night fire was not passed down, but it did leave one mark. Twelve year-old Emmett Gum, in an effort to fight the fire or save one of his brothers, was burned. His little finger was burnt so badly that a draft card would note: "right hand deformed at little finger from burn."[150] As an adult, Robert Emmett Gum would always self-consciously hide his right hand when being photographed.

The Gum family was now without a home. Will found a place to rent nearby. The family would remain there while they waited for their next court appearance.

With all the fires on the block, one can imagine Dr. Murfree and wife, Ada, wondering about their neighbors. But the Gums were not the only ones in the neighborhood to have fires. In 1897, the Murfrees would have their own fire. As noted in the *Liberty Herald* of February 10th, 1897,

> A large range in the kitchen at the home of Dr. J.B. Murfree was blown up last Friday morning by steam from the boiler attached. The range was blown into bits and the kitchen was badly damaged, the glass in the window being broken out and the ceiling splintered. A negro woman standing near the stove at the time of the explosion and pieces of iron were driven into her body."[151]

~

In February 1896, W.T. Gum petitioned the court to sell the lot where the brick office building stood. The Murfrees were interested in buying it and willing to pay more than the land's value to expand the property around their home. The amount they agreed to pay was $600 (= $15,800). In turn, Will stated that he could sell the bricks from the office building and bring in additional money for the support of the children.

The court analyzed Will's idea. The court clerk, Hickman Weakley, stated that it would cost approximately $175 to remove the bricks, or approximately $152 in repairs to make the brick office building once again habitable. The court also reported that the taxes on the children's property in the amount of $28.65 (= $755) had not been paid.

Meanwhile, Will had found a new home for the family. One day while visiting his parents, Will learned that Mary W. and James T. Richardson, the owners of a nice home one block south of his parents, on the other side of Maney Avenue, were interested in selling. The home was fairly new, and solidly built with good-sized rooms, which would mean that Mary could have her own room and the boys theirs. In this house, the entire family could live rather nicely, especially compared to how they had been living. The price the Richardsons were asking was $825 (= $21,700). In order not to loose the house, Will went ahead and put a deposit down without asking the court.

Permission to sell the lot and buy the new home took a long time. The County brought in William Ransom, who appraised the value of the land and the various buildings that the Gum children owned, as well as the home that Will proposed to buy. Mr. Ransom agreed that the lot where the brick office building once stood was too small for anyone to buy and build on. This meant that its value to the Murfrees was greater, and what they were willing to pay, an excellent price. With Mr. Ransom's positive report, it appeared that all was settled. On March 1st, the Rutherford County Court agreed to the sale.

On July 22, 1896, Will T. Gum was once again called into court to answer to his handling of the children's money. It was stated that Mr. Gum was insolvent. Regarding the children's rental property at Main and Maney, Joseph L. Baugh, who had paid $15 insurance on the store buildings, was to receive half the rents until his loan to Clemmie was repaid. Will was ordered to use the balance of the rents for the support of his children. He was then questioned about the children's money which he had already spent.

Q: If you have put any building on the lot belonging to your children…, state when it was done and the kind of building it is.

A: Yes, Sir. I have put a building on it. It was in October 1896. It is a butcher shop—a frame building about 20′ x 30′.

Q: Is it or not completed [and] what did it cost?

A: Yes, Sir. The building, including the necessary fencing and pavement in front of it, cost $200.00.

Will said that the cost of construction had been paid for as well as the materials—glass and paint. He had also paid $5 to insure it. Mr. Weakley, the court clerk had taken the funds out of the case to pay. However, the materials had not been paid for. He had used $3.60 of his own money for the nails. (= $80) He proudly added that the place was now rented for $7.00 (= $184) a month, which would mean an additional $84 per year (= $2,240), and it was rented through 1898.

Q: Why did you build this house and expend this money without the order of the court?

A: Mr. Jones, who occupies the house, had to move from where he was in the fall … I knew if the house was not built for his fall trade, he would go some where else, and as he is a good tenant, and a reliable man and was willing to pay the rent above stated, I felt it was to the best interest of my children.

Will told the court that he had asked the guardian ad Litem, Mr. Lytle, and the council, and though they could not confirm that the court would agree, they thought it was a good idea.

Courtesy Mrs. C.B. Huggins, III

Seventy-four year-old C.B. Huggins was called to testify as to whether the new building added to the property's value or not. He believed that it did. John E. Richardson was also asked to testify, and agreed as well.

Asked what amount of the children's money he still held, Will replied, "$617.38, of this sum, $367.38 is in cash and $250 is in the note of Dr. Murfree and is not due until November 1896. This note is for part of the purchase money on the old Baugh residence."[152]

Will's idea for their new residence was reviewed thoroughly by the court, and it was finally agreed that the money from the lot where the brick "cottage" had stood could be invested in the Richardson house and lot.

Will was very happy with the Court's decision. At last, he had come up with a good plan and had succeeded in seeing it implemented. To his credit, when he wasn't drinking, he had something of a good business head on his shoulders. At last, the family would have a nice place to call home. The one sad thing was that Clemmie would not be there with them.

It had taken the court from April to July to approve the purchase of the Richardson home. Will, however, had placed a down payment on the house April 30th. The Richardson property was described as being part of the "old Murfree Estate," bordered by Castle, Prim and Maney Avenue. It was ¾ of an acre.

In the summer of 1896, the Gums settled happily in their small, white house on the corner of Maney and Castle Street, one block south of their Gum grandparents, and one block north of Manchester Highway.

Now, for once, good fortune seemed to smile on Will Gum. An old acquaintance of his, John J. Lee, a farmer from the Big Spring area, had recently been elected Murfreesboro Sheriff. J.J. Lee, as he was known, had a large family of eleven children and seems to have been a kind person. Knowing how desperately Will Gum needed a job, in August of 1896, Sheriff Lee requested Will as one of his deputies.[154] The court agreed that he was qualified and he was accepted.

J.J. Lee.
(Courtesy Rutherford County Sheriff)

The term for Sheriff was two years. If Will stayed out of trouble, he would be gainfully employed for that time. There are no known reports on Will Gum during this period, so we may assume that all was calm. Perhaps at last, he had found a job that suited him. His occupation was similar to that of his great grandfather, Norton Gum, years ago in Old Jefferson.

A sample of deputy crime reports in Murfreesboro exists for the year 1895. These reports include attempted rape, profane language, a woman driven from her home by the violence of her daughters and, on the humorous side, a man who had his pants stolen while visiting a house of ill repute. Will Gum must have found plenty of interesting situations to fill his days and nights.

~

In January, W.T. Gum was called to court to answer questions on the handling of his children's money:

Q: ...that you as guardian of your minor children, the defendants in this case, received as damage by fire to their brick office described in this case the sum of $124.81. (= $3,290) Now state whether you have this sum, and if not what became of it.

A: I haven't it now. I used $25.00 of it in paying for the Richardson lot which cost $825.00. The $800 was paid by Mr. Hickum Weakley, Rutherford County Court Clerk. The balance I paid in rents for a dwelling for my family to live in and improvements on the place I bought.

It had been necessary to do some work on the new house, including moving the outhouses and putting a ceiling on the kitchen and the porch.

Q: State whether or not ... you are now able to support your children, or is the rent received from their property necessary for that purpose?

A: The rents are necessary for that purpose. With the aid of the rents I take care of them. My oldest child, Mary, has finished the course in the public school and ought to be sent to a suitable school but I am not sending her for lack of means.[153]

Education was very important in Murfreesboro, particularly the education of women. In the late 1800s, there were several schools in town for women, most notably Soule College for Women founded in 1852. Obviously, Will Gum felt some sense of guilt about his situation.

At the conclusion of this court appearance, the court paid out money for the children's expenses. The monies totaled $1,217.38. The additional costs for taxes from 1895–1896 and repairs by W.T. Gum totaled $1,098.59, leaving a balance in the children's fund of $118.79. As of

January 18, 1897, after the costs for building the butcher shop were paid, the children were left with $12.19.

~

On June 28th, 1897, Will's mother, sixty-one year-old Martha Wade Gum passed away. Martha was laid to rest next to her daughter, Mollie, at Evergreen Cemetery. Still living at home during this time were thirty year-old Nannie, twenty-three year-old Susie and twenty year-old Johnny. Jere Gum must have been heartbroken. He was now seventy years old and had lived with Martha for forty-six years. Despite the empty space in his life, Jere Gum would live on for another seven years after his wife's death.

Chapter 17

Family Ties

On September 25th' 1888, a few weeks shy of her sixteenth birthday, Will's sister, Bettie, married the handsome, twenty-five year-old Henry Lee Fox. Henry, who worked for a bank in Nashville, was considered quite a good catch. He invested in a home on Academy Street and by 1892, in addition to his position with the bank, he and his brother, Walter D., were selling real estate in and around Murfreesboro. Henry Lee and Bettie had their first child, William Lee, in 1890. The following year, another son was born whom they named for Henry's brother, Walter, but little Walter only lived a few months. Three years later, on February 21, 1894, the Fox family would be blessed with a daughter whom they named Anna Lee.

In 1890, twenty-three year-old Nannie Gum married Edwin T. Rion, a native of Rutherford County. During the first years of their marriage, the couple lived in the log cabin next door to Nannie's parents.* Edwin, the twenty-eight year-old son of Thomas Rion, had been raised on a large plantation in the Lascassas area. He was tall, thin and good-looking with dark hair. It is said that the Rions were descendants of French royalty. In later years, there would be whispers that the family, who came to the United States from Canada, were descended from the Dauphin of France.

* Based on property records, it is uncertain whether this home was originally part of the Gum property or that of a neighbor's.

Courtesy Claire Rion Weber

Edwin Rion adored Nannie, and, after their marriage, took her on a trip to North Carolina where he had a miniature portrait of her painted on a pendant. Nannie was fair and looked more Scandinavian than many of the Gum family. During these years, Edwin Rion went into the insurance business and made a good deal of money.

In 1898, the battleship *USS Maine*, which was anchored in Havana Harbor, suddenly exploded and sank, killing three-quarters of the crew. For many years, there had been protests in the U.S. over Spain's rule in Cuba. When the *Maine* sank, people were ready to blame Spain. News articles and public opinion called for President McKinley to declare war.

On April 23rd, Congress declared that war with Spain had begun on April 21st, the day the *Maine* blew up.[155] Men, all over the country, began to sign up to go to war. In Tennessee, "the volunteer state," among the young men rushing to enlist were Murphey George Baugh, Henry Lee Fox and John H. Gum.

It was not an easy time for Murphey Baugh, who was mustered into the army as a private on June 15th. In July, he was tried for a violation and sentenced with a $100 fine. By August 1st, like many men in this war, he was sick. Finally, on the 11th he was placed in the line of duty.

E.V. Finlayson.
(Courtesy John von Rosen)

The Spanish–American War didn't last long. Spain lost and the United States gained control of Cuba, Puerto Rico, Guam and the Philippines. A little over a year after volunteering, the soldiers were coming home, many of them discharged at the port in San Francisco.[156]

That summer, while the U.S. was at war with Spain, the Gum siblings took a trip to North Carolina. During their visit, Susie Gum met Elias Vance Finlayson, a thirty-three year-old merchant. Susie, a gorgeous girl of twenty-four with black hair, creamy skin, and

Suzie Gum Finlayson.
(Courtesy John von Rosen)

the bluest of eyes captured Mr. Finlayson's heart. He followed Susie back to Murfreesboro where he asked for her hand in marriage. The couple was married in Rutherford County on September 12, 1898.

Susie and Elias settled in Charlotte, North Carolina where Mr. Finlayson had a dry goods store with his brother, David Burruss Finlayson. Sometime after Susie's marriage, her sister and brother-in-law, Lucy and Charles McKnight, decided to move to North Carolina as well, and settled down next door to the Finlaysons. Susie's older sister, Laura Gum, also moved to North Carolina around this same time. Laura never married, and later in life seems to have had some emotional problems.

~

During these years, most of Robert E. Gum's descendants continued to live in the Gum Community. Robert E.'s son, Wilson Alexander married Martha Benson sometime around the Civil War. The couple had seven children and lived on some of the land he inherited from his father, Robert E. and his grandfather, John Fulks. Wilson Alexander Gum, Sr., died without a will in 1896.

John Anderson Gum (1875–1955) and wife, Sallie Jernigan (1877–1969). (Courtesy Ralph Puckett)

It was thought that Wilson's wife, Martha Benson Gum was at least part Indian. She lived to be nearly 100 years old. In the early 1900s, Wilson Gum, Jr. moved to down to Texas. Like many other Tennesseans, he found Texas to be a place of greater opportunity and prosperity.

Wilson and Martha's son, John Anderson Gum, would eventually inherit most of the former Gum/Fulks homestead, and spend his life farming the land. He married Sallie Jernigan on December 15th, 1896.

In the early 1900s, John Anderson Gum tore down the old Fulks log cabin, and having bought additional land in the area, bought a Sears and Roebuck pre-fab home, which stands on this land today. The road to John Anderson Gum's home was a mile long, and at this time, is still lined with the limestone walls which John Gum placed there chink by chink.

John Gum's daughter, Mattie Gum, married her cousin, Gum Puckett. Mattie knew

her grandmother, Martha Benson Gum, well. The intersected lives of Elizabeth Fulks, Martha Benson Gum and Mattie Gum Puckett span 200 years.

Mattie Puckett, who lived into her late eighties, would later relate some of the family history to Robert Emmett Gum's daughter, Mildred, after her husband, Alton Durham, wrote a letter to Mattie Puckett in hopes of discovering more about her ancestry.

~

By the turn of the 19th century, much had changed in Old Jefferson. Martha Gum's brother, Ben, had passed away in 1872, and by 1880, their mother, Nancy Wade, was also gone. After Ben's passing, Susan Wade moved in with her widowed mother, Susan Robertson. The Wade children grew and married, and for a while there were many extended family members in the area. Although Ben Wade, Jr. did not live long, three of his sisters, whose nicknames were "Hootie," "Dinkie" and "Da," remained in Old Jefferson.

The Wade Family and friends in Old Jefferson.
(Courtesy Lucy May Lenoir)

"Dinkie," the youngest daughter, Martha, married Brutus Lenoir in 1901. Staying on in the old family home after everyone was gone were Darlene and Lucy. The two sisters never married, though an unusual story has been told about Darlene, one that no doubt reached her cousin Will Gum and all the family in Murfreesboro.

In 1891, fourteen year-old Darlene was being courted by a young man twenty-eight. Mack Clark was a very handsome man whose family came from outside the area of Old Jefferson, though it is believed that he served as Jefferson's postmaster for a time.

In 1891, Darlene Wade was a beautiful girl with a perfect Gibson girl figure and blonde curls framing her lovely face. Darlene and Mack fell in love and soon were engaged to be married.

One afternoon, Mack came to visit Darlene and by the time he left, it was dark outside. He bid Darlene goodbye at the door and went down the walk to the Wade's front gate. Just as he reached the gate, a shot rang out and Matt fell to the ground, dead. He had been shot through the heart.

The neighbors said they heard the sound of someone running across their porch, but no one seemed to know who had fired the fatal shot. Darlene, although heartbroken, was silent as well. A funeral card lists the date of R.M. Clarke's funeral as June 7th, 1891.

Some years later, a detective came to town to investigate the murder. He met the beautiful Darlene, and after courting her, she agreed to marry him. No marriage certificate has been found, but possibly the fear over what had happened to Mack caused her to leave town on the agreement that they would marry in another location.

The couple boarded a train for New York. En route, the young man began to question her.

"You must know something about Mack's death," he said. "Tell me. You must tell me who did it."

Darlene refused to say anything. She didn't want to talk about it, but her fiancé continued to question her. Finally, she said,

"The only reason you wanted to marry me was to find out about who killed Mack Clark. The marriage is over."

At the next train stop, Darlene got off and went home.

While no other facts have been found to verify this story, there are more than a few persons, both relatives and former residents of Old Jefferson, who have heard the story of this unsolved murder.

Ruth Dunn, a visitor to the Wade home as a young girl, recalls the last time she saw Miss Wade. Darlene and Lucy were packing their things to move in with the Lenoirs, when Miss Darlene showed Ruth the photo of a very handsome young man with a mustache. "This was the only man I ever loved," she said.

A short time later, Darlene Wade died.

~

Ida Jacobs remained closest to her father's side of the family in Beech Grove. In 1901, she married William T. Stephenson, a resident of the Millersburg area, and the son of a Confederate Veteran who had been a comrade of her Baugh grandfather in the Civil War. Ida and William had one child who died shortly after its birth in 1906. After suffering from ill health for many years, Ida passed away on March 28, 1914, at the age of 40. She is buried on the old Jacobs property near Millersburg.

Following the court trial of 1892, Rollie Howland continued to live with his wife, Ellen, and father-in-law, D.C. Townsend, much as he had before. How much contact he had with his Baugh relatives after 1893 is not known. He was probably somewhat heartbroken. In addition, the loss of the case cost him a good deal of money.

Rollie must have learned of Clemmie's passing with mixed emotions. Throughout his childhood, she had been his sister. He even called her "Sister" in his younger years. No doubt, he blamed Will Gum for Clemmie's early demise, as well as the fact that his grandmother had left him out of her will.

In 1901, Rollie Howland would have a sorrow of his own when, on July 14th, his wife, Mary Ellen, died at the age of thirty-five. Rollie continued to live with his father-in-law, D.C. Townsend, and together they worked to put the farm in better condition.

Around 1904, Rollie made the acquaintance of Mattie Beulah Williams, the granddaughter of Rev. James Williams, a Methodist minister who settled in the Chapel Hill area around 1812. The Williams family lived on Rev. William's plantation, Civil Order, which was about five miles from the Duck River where Rollie lived. On June 13, 1904, Rollie and Beulah were married in Franklin. Beulah moved into Rollie's home on Townsend land. In 1906, D.C. Townsend passed away.

That same year, Rollie Howland ran for the office of Tennessee State Representative. He was elected for one term and served from 1907–1908. His District in Marshall County was historically very conservative, which may be one reason Rollie only served for one year.

In 1908, Rollie and Beulah Howland moved to Redlands, California. At the time, California, then a state for fifty-eight years, was considered a paradise. With its mild climate year round, fruits rare to most of the United States could be easily grown. For twenty years, Rollie "cultivated" orange trees.[157] Around 1927, he and Ellen moved to Fullerton, in order to be near her sister's family.

Rollie and Beulah were living in California at the time Frank Gumm and his family moved there, but it is doubtful Frank was aware of this, or even knew his cousin Rollie.

Rollie M. Howland passed away on November 12, 1928. at the age of sixty-eight. With the funds that had been left for care of the Townsend graves, he was buried beside his first wife, Mary Ellen, and his father-in-law, D.C. Townsend, at Evergreen Cemetery in Murfreesboro. A large monument marks the spot.

Mattie Beulah Howland lived another twenty years in California, enjoying time with her sister's family and writing the Williams family history. She is buried in California. Beulah and Rollie never had any children.

By 1897, the nineteenth century was in the process of winding to a close. It had been a long hundred years; years that included war with the American Indians, turning the land from forest to farmland, and brothers killing brothers on these same fields. It was also a century when men and women of color were freed from slavery. In the ensuing years, there was a new civilization, one of peace and progress with tidy homes, city streets and schools.

The families of the Baughs, Gums, Crosthwaits and Wades had all grown and spread out. The old people, who remembered the past and the old ways, were dying. The young people were just beginning to know about life, and they were ready for a new century.

The Gum Family

John Alexander Gum m. **Martha Wade**

William T. (1854–1906) (Clemmie)	John A. (1857–1923) (Lucy T.)	Laura (1860–1928)	Lucy (1862–1942) (McKnight)	Mollie (1865–1886)	Nannie (1867–1946) (Rion)	Bettie (1872–1944) (Fox)	Susie (1874–1924) (Finlayson)	John H. (1877–1913)
Baby Girl* (1879)	Annie (1878)		Roy A. (1886)		Edwin, Jr. (1900)	William (1890)	Mildred (1899)	
Mary B. (1880)	Trigg A. (1881)		Clair D. (1888)		Virginia (1909)	Walter D.* (1891)	Suzanne (1910)	
Robert E. (1883)	James H. (1884)		Charles H. (1891)			Anna Lee (1894)		
Frank A. (1886)			Harry N. (1893)			Jack H. (1900)		
William W. (1889)						Martha (1904)		
Allie R. (1892)								

* Died in infancy.

Endnotes
Book 1—Will and Clemmie

1. *The History of the Blackman Community* by Robert Baskin, Sr., 1986, p. 134–135

2. Rutherford County Wills/Inventory, p. 332–334

3. There is no way to truly know, at this point, when Mrs. Baugh and family returned to the East Main Street home. We only know that it was bought in 1866, and then a wing added which doubled the size of the home. In the 1870s, Mary Ann was listed both in the tax collections list as living in District 7, as well as represented as such, near the Gum Farm, on the 1878 D.G. Beers map.

4. Matty Dillahunty, Mt. Pleasant, Titus County, TX to Annex Rucker, Smyrna, TN October 5, 1869, Ibid from the Thesis of Wm. Foster Fleming, p. 114

5. Interviews with Little Hope Community, Clarence Wallace of Lilliard Methodist Church, Lillian Howse, Sallie Mae Hicks—2007

6. Rutherford County Record Book No. 17, Rec. No. 214, p. 184

7. Ibid, Book 17, Rec. No. 288, p. 367

8. Ibid, Book 17, Rec. No. 348, p. 440

9. Ibid, Book 17, Rec. No. 389, p. 484

10. Ibid, Book 17, Rec. No. 65, p. 64

11. Ibid, Book 18, Rec. No. 217, p. 214

12. Ibid, Book 18, Rec. No. 507, p. 538

13. Ibid, Book 20, Rec. No. 226, p. 403

14. All information in this chapter which is not otherwise footnoted comes from the Rutherford County 1893 trial, J.L. & J.M Baugh et al vs. R.M. Howland & Ida Jacobs, Testimony F.L. Jacobs, 1893

15. U.S. Federal Census of 1870

16. U.S. Federal Census of 1880, notes from Mary Fox, Willis Baugh's granddaughter

17. Rutherford County Records, Book GG, 1872

18. Jimmy Fox on his tour of Old Millersburg, 2004

19. Rutherford County Property Records Book No. 18, p. 581

20. Rutherford County Property Records Book, 20, Rec. No. 398, p. 608

21. Ibid, Book No. 17, Rec. No. 348, p. 44

22. Ibid, Book No. 18 , Rec. No. 217, p. 214

23. The Keebles: A Half Century of Southern Family Life, Thesis Presented to the Faculty of the Graduate School of the University of Texas by Wm. Foster Fleming, B.A., Austin, TX, August, 1951, p. 108. Part 1—Keebles were the Wade's neighbors.

24. Rutherford County Property Records Book No. 15, Rec. No. 99, p. 89

25. Rutherford County Property Records Book No. 13, p. 355

26. This lot was bought by Mr. Odinneal at a Sheriff's sale in 1850 from the property of R. McGregor, Bk 4, p.675

27. Rutherford County Property Records Book No. 17, Rec. No. 278 p. 243–244

28. Ibid. P. 28 Note: National Daughters of American Colonists have erected a Monument on 15th St. between Constitution Avenue and East Street.

29. RCHS, Pub No. 8, Winter 1877, p. 26, See Part 1, *From Tennessee to Oz*

30. Rutherford County Court Record//// FILL IN

31. Rutherford County Property Records Book No. 14, Rec. No. 303, p. 240

32. Coulter, Brownlow, p. 262–263, The Keebles, Thesis for the University of Texas, Wm Foster Fleming, Austin, TX, 1951 p. 110–111

33. http://en.wikipedia.org/wiki/William_Gannaway_Brownlow

34. Courtesy of Ralph Puckett

35. Hoffman, Muriel, *Leaves of the Gum Tree*, Cornbelt Press, Fairbury, IL 1885, p. 548, Curry Wolfe research

36. *Goodspeed's History of Missouri*, After 1870

37. *Democrat*, August 21, 1908, Dunklin Co, Missouri—Obituary. The balance of information on Billy Gum comes from this article.

38. Rutherford County Record Book, No. 16, Rec. No. 679 p. 583, (Prior record No. 6, p. 175—Thomas Burk?)

39. Rutherford County Wills & Estates Book (1869) 23, p. 409

40. Rutherford Countary Property Record Book #17, p. 595

41. Rutherford County Record Book No. 24, Rec. No. 489, p. 550

42. Rutherford County Record Book No. ? Rec. No. 460, p. 308–309

43. Rutherford County Record Book, No. 19, Rec. No. 193, p. 218

44. Rutherford County Record Book No. 17, Rec. No. 255, p. 330

45. Ibid, Book No. 19, Rec. o. 427, p. 275

46. Rutherford County Record Book, No. 19, Rec. No. 644, p. 319–320

47. Rutherford County Record Book, 19, Rec. No. 619 & 620, p. 488–489

48. Rutherford County Record Book No. 21, Rec. No. 2, p. 2–3

49. Rutherford County Record Book 21, p. 4

50. We were unable to locate this judgment.

51. Clipping unmarked, a Murfreesboro paper, 1875 Courtesy Ralph Puckett

52. This reference exists, but has been misplaced.

53. Based on various court documents, testimony and other public records.

54. Rutherford County Property Record Book, No. ?. Rec. No. 370, p. 579

55. In her 1893 testimony, Clemmie claims this took place after her marriage, but before Rollie's marriage and was the only time she had real feelings "against" him. P. 19 my typed testimony

56. J.L & J.M. Baugh vs. Rollie Howland. This information comes from Clemmie's own testimony. In some cases the author has extended and dramatized the dialog, the facts are true.

57. Beech Grove, a post office in 1819, became a village. 1890s population: 250. History of Coffee County, 2004.

58. Winchester Historical Society source or School book

59. RU Cty, 1893, J.L. Baugh & J.M. Baugh vs. R.M. Howland & I. Jacobs, Rollie Howland Testimony

60. Court Case quote

61. *Franklin Historical Society Review*, Vol. XX, No. 2, 1989, p. 122. The origin of this information is Goodspeeds Franklin County, p. 789

62. *Franklin County Historical Review*, Vol., III, No. 1, p. 39

63. Ibid, Vol. No. 1, p. 5

64. *Franklin County Historical Review*, Vol. XVI, No. 1, 1985, p. 56

65. Ibid, p. 7

66. History of Winchester Normal by Mrs. Ethel Blanton Colston, 6/9/1954, Franklin County, Winchester Library history Archives

67. The US Census of 1880 shows that Rollie Howland living with his Uncle Joseph Baugh. His name was written RAWleigh which must show how it was pronounced. He was 19 and a student.

68. Mrs. Norma Hannah interview, 2004

69. Baugh Family Bible

70. Franklin County Historical Review, Vol Xvi, No 1, 1985, p. 29

71. Franklin County Historical Review, Vol XVI, No. 1, 1985, p. 85

72. Elizabeth House Ridley (WHICH BOOK)

73. Rutherford County, Deed of Trust Book, December 18, 1877, pg.

74. The original records for Evergreen Cemetery were burnt in the early part of the 20th Century. Persons went through the cemetery attempting to recreate the records, but obviously, those graves with no stones remain a mystery for us.

75. Rutherford County Record Book, No. 370

76. Rutherford County Record Book, CC, No. 206, p. 164

77. Rutherford County Trust Book No. CC, p. 465–466

78. Rutherford County Trust Book, CC, No. 635, p. 465

79. Rutherford County Record Book, No. 23, Rec. No. 288, p. 354

80. Ibid, Record Book No. 24, Rec. No. 37, p. 67

81. Ibid, Record Book No. 24, Rec. No. 148, p. 161

82. Ibid Record Book No. 24, Rec No. 548, p. 627

83. Ibid Book No. 26, Rec. No. 112, p. 79

84. Rutherford County Obituaries; http://genealogytrails.com/tenn/rutherford/obits.html

85. 1880 U.S. Federal Census, TN, Rutherford County,

86. E.T. Childress Dec'd Will recorded Sept 21, 1875, Record Book 25, p. 13

87. http://www.tngenweb.org/poor/

88. Rutherford County Record Book No. 28, Rec. No. 414, p. ?

89. See *Carnton Plantation*; http://www.carnton.org/cleburne_exhibit.htm

90. J.L. & J.M. Baugh vs. R.M. Howland, etc. Testimony OF

91. Rutherford County Property Record Book No. 28, p. 56–57

92. In the 1893 Court Case testimony, Will T. Gum claimed he was in business by himself until 1884.

93. J.L. & J.M. Baugh vs. R.M. Howland & Ida Jacobs; Will Gum's testimony

94. Dallas Jacobs Testimony, J.M & J.L Baugh Etrs v. R.M. Howland and Ida Jacobs, 1892

95. Rutherford County Property Record Book No. 21, p. 495

96. Rutherford County Property Record Book No. 28, p. 337

97. J.L. & J.M. Baugh vs. R.M. Howland & others, 1893, Clemmie Gum testimony

98. RU County Court Records, Baugh vs. Howland, 1893, R.M. White Testimony

99. Based on Mrs. Baugh's comments repeated in family testimony in the trial, *J.L & J.M. Baugh vs. R.M. Howland*, 1892

100. Nashville City Directory for years 1870–1880

101. U.S. Census, 1880, 8th Ward, Nashville, Davidson County, TN, p. 15, Dis No. 3, Enumerator Dist No. 48?

102. We are not certain that Will Gum saw Rev. Jones in Nashville, but we do know he went to Nashville at this time and that he did attend a meeting of Rev. Jones at some time, for certain in Murfreesboro.

103. www.sun-sentinel.cmo/travel/getaways/sfl-swick13colnov13.0.33344628.column?coll … 1/15/2006

104. Archives of the Cumberland Presbyterian Church, Murfreesboro Session Book 1899–1905 (copied into this book from another book.)

105. Falling Stars, Elizabeth O. Howse, 1960, p. 26

106. Rutherford County Record Book No. 29, No. 222, p. 267

107. Chancery Court Case J.L & J.M. Baugh vs. R.M. Howland & I. Jacobs, 1892, Testimony of J.M. Baugh, Mrs. J.M. Baugh & Mrs. Blake

108. "Comfortably" is a quote from Jack Baugh's Testimony in the above listed trial.

109. *Marshall County Historical Quarterly*, Vol. VII, Winter 1976–77, No. IV, p. 116

110. The U.S. Federal Censuses for 1880 and 1900 show that Mr. Townsend always had a minimum of 3 servants.

111. Some of this work was much later, as noted in the *Marshal County Historical Quarterly*, Vol. VII, Winter 1976–77. No. IV.

112. This date has been listed as 1882, but if Rollie and Ellen had a child, it would have to be 1888.

113. His erratic behavior is only a guess, but follows from the fact that Mary Ann Baugh said he never had any money and was constantly asking her for money, despite his having the store and all the money she invested in it.

114. Rutherford County Record Book No. 30, Rec. No. 417, p. 568

115. This story comes from Mrs. Anna Richardson and Maggie Muirhead's Testimony in the 1892 trial.

116. Taken from the above named RU County court testimony

117. Ibid. Almost an exact quote from Thomas Baugh's 1892 testimony.

118. Ibid Thomas Baugh testimony

119. Chancery Court Case: JL & JM Baugh vs. R. Howland & I. Jacobs by Thomas Howland.

120. Rutherford County Record Book No. 31, Rec. No. 259, p. 455

121. JL & JM Baugh vs. RM Howland & others 1893 Rutherford Country Chancery Court case. Rollie Howland's testimony.

122. Chancery Court Testimony by Wm. H. Baugh, June 8, 1893 from Louisville, KY (handwritten)

123. From Ran Miller's sworn testimony in the 1892 trial

124. Rollie Howland's testimony in J.L. & J.M. Baugh vs. Rollie M. Howland & others

125. Although Mrs. Baugh's statements are taken from Mrs. Richardson's testimony in the trial, Mrs. Richardson's statements are only assumed and not quotes.

126. Testimony of Will Baugh, A23

127. Baugh v. Howland, Bettie Baugh's testimony, p. 114 author's transcript.

128. A History of Rutherford County, Carlton C. Sims, Editor, Chapter VII by J.B. Black, p. 104

129. Testimony of Wm. H. Baugh, 1893, A12

130. Mrs. Mary Baugh's words as reported by Will Gum in court, 1893

131. Eliza Pruitt's Testimony

132. Rutherford County Record Book No. p.

133. We have no letters from this time and can only assume what a woman who had lived with her mother, a mother loved by all in the town who knew her, would feel.

134. Annals of Rutherford County, Volume 2, John C. Spence, RCHS, 1991, p. 139

135. Daily News Journal, Murfreesboro, TN, 1912 news obit clipping

136. Mr. Brandon, a resident of Murfreesboro who lived to be over 100 years old, recalled popcorn being sold outside the courthouse in 1910.

137. J.L. & J.M. Baugh vs. R. L. Howland & I. Jacobs, Rutherford Chancery Court Records, October 1893

138. See questions 23–27 and Cross-examination 22–25, June 26, 1893 depo

139. Curry Wolfe research of Rutherford County Property Records

140. Rutherford County Property Record Book No. 36, p. 134

141. Falling Leaves by Elizabeth O. Howse, 1970, p. 17

142. Rutherford County Court Files, J.L. Baugh & J.M. Baugh extrs. vs. Mary E Gum, Jan 3, 1895, p. 3

143. *J.A. Gum and wife, Martha Gum, Citizens of Rutherford County, Tennessee vs. The Mayor and Aldermen of the town of Murfreesboro, Tennessee*

144. Rutherford County Court Case: Jno A. Gum & wife, Martha Gum vs. Mayor & Alderman, April 27, 1894, No. 2829, Rutherford County Archives

145. Rutherford County Court Minute Book OO, p. 425 (1892–1895)

146. Rutherford County Court Files, J.L. Baugh & J.M. Baugh extrs. Vs. Mary E Gum, Jan 3, 1895, p. 3

147. From Mrs. Lurlene Rushing, who was friends with Rebecca Jetton and took notes when speaking with her about Frank Gum.

148. Taken from the notes and interview with Mrs. Rushing who knew Rebecca Jetton.

149. Rutherford County Court Files, J.L. Baugh & J.M. Baugh extrs. vs. Mary E Gum, Jan 3, 1895, p. 2

150. Indianapolis, Ind. Draft Board, No. 1345, 13-3-15, September 1915

151. http://www.tngenweb.irg/decalb/herald121.htm

152. RC Court Case, J.M & J.L Baugh extrs and others vs. Mary B. Gum & others, July 1896 Original and Supplemental Bills, RC Archives

153. RC Court Case, J.M. Baugh & J.L. Baugh, extrs and others vs. Mary B. Gum and others, January 1897, RC Archives

154. Rutherford County Minutes, 1878–1901, August 1896, Book PP, p. 223

155. http://en.wikipedia.org/wiki/Spanish-american_war

156. Army Records, Tennessee State Archives, Nashville, TN

157. Descendants of Robert L. Howland, Sr., Curry Wolfe, 2010

Young Frank Gumm

Chapter 18

The Darrows

At the end of the Civil War, there had been an influx of new residents in Murfreesboro. Some were persons from the North who wished to take advantage of the poverty and cheap land prices. Others were persons from different parts of the South who wished to relocate. Mrs. Elizabeth T. Swope, a wealthy widow from Memphis, was one of the latter. In 1884, she purchased the historic Oaklands Plantation for $8,505 (= $192,000).

Mrs. Swope, originally Elizabeth Tempe Hayley, was the widow of Jake Swope. Mr. Swope's ancestors were Royalists who left England in 1715, after King Charles I was beheaded at Whitehall (1649). The early Swopes settled in Pennsylvania. It was there, during the Revolutionary War, that George Washington gave Michael Swope command of the Continental Army for the last battle on the island of New York. After suffering greatly through the cold winter battles, Michael Swope moved his family south to Virginia.[1]

Jake and Elizabeth Swope, who were married in 1856, lived on a plantation in Lauderdale County, Alabama. Their son, Jacob, was born in 1857. During the Civil War, finding themselves in the area of battle, the Swopes moved to a plantation in Mississippi, where, in 1862, their daughter, Tempe was born.

Like most Southerners, Mr. Swope's finances were affected by the war; however, he was not deterred by this. Within a few years, through hard work and speculation, Jake Swope increased his holdings to $40,000

(= $543,000) in property and $1,000 (= $13,600) in personal effects.[2] Sadly, Jake did not live to enjoy the fruits of his labor. In 1870, at the age of thirty-eight; he died, reportedly, from drowning in a river. His wife and daughter were left with a fortune in plantations and cash.

In 1884, Mrs. Swope was quite happy with her purchase of the Oaklands Plantation. The purchase included the mansion house and two hundred acres of land. The home was well-situated, being less than half a mile from the Murfreesboro Square. As an added feature, a good portion of the mansion's furnishings, including the "Bishop's bed," where Jefferson Davis slept in on his 1862 visit, were a part of the sale.[3] Mrs. Swope's one misgiving about the property was its name. Thinking "Oaklands" did not sound elegant enough, she named the plantation "Oak Manor."

The land comprising Oak Manor was originally purchased by Colonel Hardee Murfree in 1798. Murfree's daughter, Sally, who was married to Dr. James Maney, inherited the land. Rather than the usual log cabin, the couple built a two-room brick house to live in. During the 1820s and '30s, they added a second story and additional rooms.[4]

In 1846, Sally and James Maney's son, Lewis, married Rachel Adeline Cannon, the daughter of Tennessee Governor Newton Cannon. Lewis and Rachel further enlarged the house, turning it into an elegant Italianate mansion. Among the additions were four high-ceilinged rooms, a circular staircase and an entire new front to the home, with an "L"-shaped portico. The Maneys also hired a Chicago decorator to fresco the entrance hall ceilings.

After the Civil War, the Maneys attempted to hold on to their estate by selling off small portions of land. The city bought a good amount of acreage from them for the creation of Evergreen Cemetery. Two years after her husband's death, Rachel Maney found it necessary to sell Oaklands and move to a smaller, but still elegant home. The home the Maneys built was on the lane leading up to the plantation, known as Maney Avenue. Mrs. Rachel Cannon Maney would reside there until her death on January 7, 1911.[5]

Shortly after Mrs. Swope moved to Oak Manor, daughter Tempe, now twenty-one years old, went to visit some of her wealthy relatives in

Memphis. Tempe loved the social life, and during this visit she was invited to many parties. As fate would have it, at one of these parties she met an unlikely mate in the form of the handsome and fascinating George M. Darrow.

Darrow, a native Virginian, was the son of Henry and Sarah Darrow. Henry Darrow had been born in Vermont around 1819, and as a young man moved to Charlottesville, Virginia where he worked as a Master Carpenter. The Darrows had three children: Richard, born in 1851, William, born in 1853, and George, the youngest, born in 1856.

By 1860, just before the start of the Civil War the Darrow family was living in a large residence (possibly a boarding house) with an overseer and seven carpenters between the ages of sixteen and thirty.[6] These men were probably apprentices, hired to work under Mr. Darrow.

Although not poor, the Darrows had far less than the Swopes. The 1860 census records Jake Swope with holdings of $65,000 (= $1,730,000) in real estate, and $75,000 (= $2,000,000) in personal assets. In contrast, Henry Darrow owned $6,700 (= $178,000) in real estate, and had $9,000 (= $240,000) in personal assets. Despite their monetary differences, the Darrows appear to have been well-educated and cultured people.

After the war, the Darrow family moved to Omaha, Nebraska. Later in life, George Darrow would speak of how the family's lack of money forced him to go to work at an early age.[7] By 1880, Darrow's older brother, Richard, was a physician, and George was working as a clerk in a drug store.

George Morris Darrow was a man of many interests; restless, and eager for new opportunities. In the early 1880s, George left home and traveled to the "wild west," looking for adventure. His experiences included humorous characters and hair-raising escapades. Later, he wrote a short story about these adventures.[8]

After his brave escapades in the "golden west," George Darrow traveled east and settled down in Memphis, Tennessee where he found a job as a clerk in a dry goods store. His job included delivering groceries on a bicycle to some of the finest homes in town.

George Darrow later told young Elizabeth Howse that he often worked until his legs and back ached. Yet, through it all, he dreamed that one day he would be invited to one of these mansions. "Ten years from the day I had my first job," "the courtly Mr. Darrow" told Elizabeth, "I was invited

George and Tempe Darrow on their honeymoon.
(Courtesy Tempe Thompson)

to a great party in one of the houses to which I had taken many a load of food stuff."[9] That night was the luckiest night of Darrow's life because it was the night he met Tempe Swope.

By now, George was twenty-eight, handsome, and a good conversationalist with enough adventures under his belt to draw a crowd. Apparently, he kept the lovely Miss Tempe Swope's attention, and she kept his. It did not take long, for the couple to realize that they were kindred spirits.

The courtship was brief, and apparently Mrs. Swope did not object to the match. George and Tempe were married in Memphis on November 11th, 1885. After the wedding, the newly married couple traveled northwest to Omaha, Nebraska so that George could introduce Tempe to his family. Following the visit, George and Tempe traveled to Wisconsin where they spent their honeymoon in the early winter snow. On their return to Murfreesboro, they settled at Oak Manor with Tempe's mother.

Murfreesboro had always been a very social town, and it did not take long for the Darrows to become part of that social life. In the coming years, Oak Manor would lend itself perfectly to the Darrows' parties and their many house guests.

Visitors to Oak Manor traveled down a long, tree-lined drive, exiting their carriages at the mansion's front steps. Two sets of double-doors brought the guests into a spacious hall with a gently curving stairway. To the left, was a large, high-ceilinged parlor, and beyond that, an equally spacious and grand dining room. To the right of the entrance was a study with long windows looking out to the veranda. It is believed Mr. Darrow used this room as his office. Behind this study, was a sitting room, where Tempe and her guests spent time talking and making music.

During their years at Oak Manor, the Darrows extensively remodeled the home, adding electricity, plumbing, new bathrooms and doorways. They also purchased cedar wood paneling from the Tennessee Centennial of 1897, and, in keeping with the style of the times, added it to the study walls for "the Boss," as Mr. Darrow was called.

In 1890, Tempe's mother, Elizabeth T. Swope, passed away. For a time, a portion of the plantation's ownership passed into the hands of Tempe's Uncle Hayley. Eventually, Tempe inherited this as well. For some legal reason, Mrs. Darrow was not allowed to give the property to her husband.

Instead, she rented it to him for $1.00 a year. In this way, Mr. Darrow was the provider, and through his efforts Tempe Swope Darrow's property made a great deal of money for both of them.[10]

~

The Darrows were ardent Episcopalians, yet in the 1880s Murfreesboro was still without an Episcopalian Church. By 1892, Episcopalian Sunday services were being held at the Odd Fellows Hall on Main Street.[11] Seeing that Murfreesboro had no prospects for the creation of an Episcopalian church, the Darrows decided to organize an effort to build one, and form an actual congregation. A handful of persons joined them in this effort: Miss Mary Knowles Murfree, (a local novelist known in literary circles as Charles Ebgert Craddock*), her sister, Miss Fanny Murfree, the Belchers, Frank Burgdorf, Mrs. Bernon Ordway, and William Howard Douglas.

In 1893, this small group of people raised over $2500 (= $66,700). A portion of the money ($900) was used to purchase a lot on the corner of Spring and College Streets, one block from East Main Street. The membership decided to name their new church St. Paul's. With the help of the Darrows and the Murfree sisters, the church came into being much more quickly than it might have. From 1897 to 1927, Mr. Darrow, who was always closely allied with the church, served as Treasurer of the Episcopalian Tennessee Diocese.

The new wood frame church was soon built, and in memory of her mother, Tempe Darrow donated money for the altar.† A dedication was engraved on the side of the wooden altar, which can still be seen today in the original church, now called St. Paul's Chapel.

On February 4th, 1893, St. Paul's was completed and Bishop Quintard came to Murfreesboro for the dedication. Wearing his finest vestments, he spoke to the new parishioners.

> "The little congregation at this place cannot be too highly commended for the earnestness, zeal and liberality which they have displayed in erecting this beautiful church."[12]

---

* At this time, women could not be respectably known or accepted as authors. Instead, to gain a following, they would adopt a male pen name.

† Later, the building was moved to East Main Street and covered with stone.

By the late 1890s, the Darrows had become an integral part of life in the little town. Along with their work for the church, the Darrows helped with the founding of many other beneficial projects, including Murfreesboro's hospital.

George and Tempe Darrow were good friends of Mr. and Mrs. Horace Palmer, with whom they enjoyed socializing. In summer, there were always games of croquet. Later, Mr. Darrow formed a gentlemen's literary group known as the "Beacon Club." Its purpose was to discuss the latest books and news.[13]

Mr. Darrow was often out and about, taking in what interested him, and keenly aware of what was going on around the town. In a small town like Murfreesboro, where everyone knew everyone and their business, it was difficult to keep good or bad news quiet. Thus, it is not surprising that Mr. Darrow was aware of the Gum family, and, in particular, Frank Avent Gum.

When and where Mr. Darrow first heard young Frank Gum sing is unknown. It could have been on a visit to the Murfreesboro Grammar School, or simply a sunny day as eleven year-old Frank walked down the street, singing. It is said that Frank was always singing. He was drawn to music, and had a beautiful voice. Wherever Mr. Darrow first heard young Frank, as a connoisseur of the arts, he was quick to recognize his talent.

Mr. Darrow asked Frank if he would like to join St. Paul's choir. Certainly, that would be a better outlet for him than singing on the streets, and the new choir needed voices. Apparently, Will Gum gave his consent, because Frank was soon a member of St. Paul's choir.

Sundays at St. Paul's, Frank was thrilled to lend his pure soprano tones to the choir, which consisted of approximately ten boys and girls. The brilliant red and white choir robes added to the pageantry. Frank, with light brown hair cut short and freckles across his face, took his job seriously. Other members of the church could not help but notice the fervor with which he sang hymns. At this time, St. Paul's was quite small with a congregation of 26 members. Their minister, Rev. Primitivo Abel Rodriguez, was a Castilian Spaniard from Mexico, who was much loved.

Frank was happy singing in the choir, and soon became the soloist. Other members of the family began attending services at St. Paul's just so they could hear him sing. The Baughs were Methodist, and the Gums, members of the Cumberland Presbyterian Church, but as one local writer noted, people in Murfreesboro changed churches fairly often.

~

Will Gum and his children were now happily ensconced in their new home. Although life was much more peaceful than it had once been, the family still lived with periods of financial difficulty.

Emmett and Frank were industrious boys, full of energy and ideas. Music had always been a part of their lives. In the future, it was something the locals would remember about Will and Clemmie's children. The Gum siblings sang for "the entertainment of friends, at concerts and local entertainment."[14]

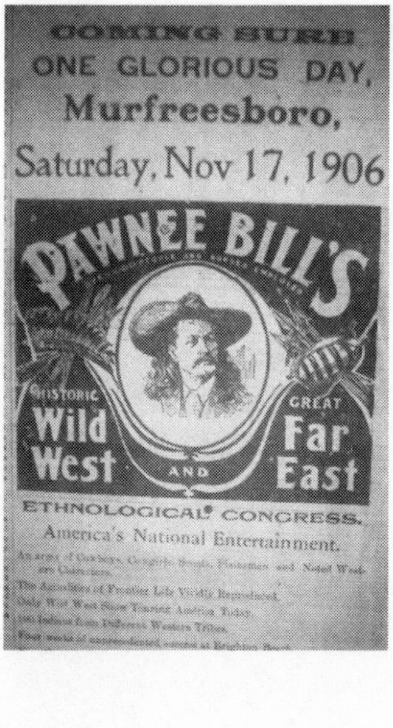

The Murfreesboro town square boasted a small theatre which was visited by various theatrical and vaudeville companies. Despite the fact that Murfreesboro was a small town, sometimes even world famous performers came to town, people like Sarah Bernhardt and Buffalo Bill.

In the summer, there was a Chautauqua. A large tent would be raised just outside the town and performers, lecturers and ministers would all come for a week or two of programs, which were both educational and entertaining.

With little or no supervision at home, the lively Gum boys were free to go where they pleased. Emmett and Frank missed very little of what went on around town. With their household greatly in need of cash, the two eldest Gum boys decided to fashion themselves after some of the performers they had witnessed and see if they could earn a little money.

Like the popular minstrel performers of the day, ten year-old Frank and thirteen year-old Emmett charcoaled their faces black and finished off their looks with vests, string ties and black hats. Together, the boys created a performance of song and dance. At the conclusion of their little show, they passed the hat for money. After enough performances, Frank was able to procure a ukulele, which he taught himself to play.[15]

Emmet soon found a regular job, so Frank teamed up with his younger brother, eight year-old Will. Now, anxious to make as much money as possible, Frank hatched a new plan. Singing on the street corner in a small town like Murfreesboro, they were bound to be recognized. That was probably not something their father would approve of. If caught, it could mean a whipping. Instead, Frank and Will boarded the train to Chattanooga and entertained passengers during the one to two hour journey. Riding the train not only meant money, it was a great adventure.[16]

The Gum brother's efforts probably brought in some much needed cash for food and necessities. If no one else was pleased, at least their sister, Mary, would have been happy. Their work may have helped to provide food and wood or coal for the stove. The money they earned would also have given them enough cash to attend performances at the local theater where they could learn the latest songs and dances for their next performances.

Despite these adventures, and Frank's seemingly happy-go-lucky attitude, unhappiness in the Gum home continued. For young Frank, it was apparently too much to bear. He dreamed of escaping to a life on the stage. When a minstrel troupe traveling through town offered him a job, twelve year-old Frank Gum packed his little bundle and left with them.[17]

Whether Frank returned home on his own, or because his father or Mr. Darrow brought him back is unknown. Nevertheless, he was soon back in Murfreesboro, but it would not be for long.

Chapter 19

Sewanee

George Darrow entered the elegant study at Oak Manor with a purposeful step. He had something of the utmost importance to take care of, and it could not wait. Through the long, nearly floor-to-ceiling windows, Mr. Darrow could see the beautifully cared for green lawn, and beyond, the light green shoots of corn stalks and cotton. They were growing quickly in the June heat.

Opening the elegant mahogany desk with carved angels on the lid, Mr. Darrow took out a pale blue sheet of stationary. At the top, in delicate, brown letters were the words, "Oak Manor, Murfreesboro, Tenn."

Dipping his pen carefully in the inkstand George Darrow wrote,

My Dear Mr. Wiggins:

Your kind letter regarding my young friend Frank Gum has given me great pleasure. I will bring the boy up Tuesday morning. I am sure neither you or any of those interested will ever have cause to regret helping this bright boy along. He knows that he is taken for his services in the choir, and that he must be ever anxious to render service to his benefactors.

With warmest regards,

Sincerely yours

G.M. Darrow

June 7 – 99.

Vice Chancellor Benjamin L. Wiggins and the letter from George Darrow which changed young Frank Gum's life. (Courtesy University of the South)

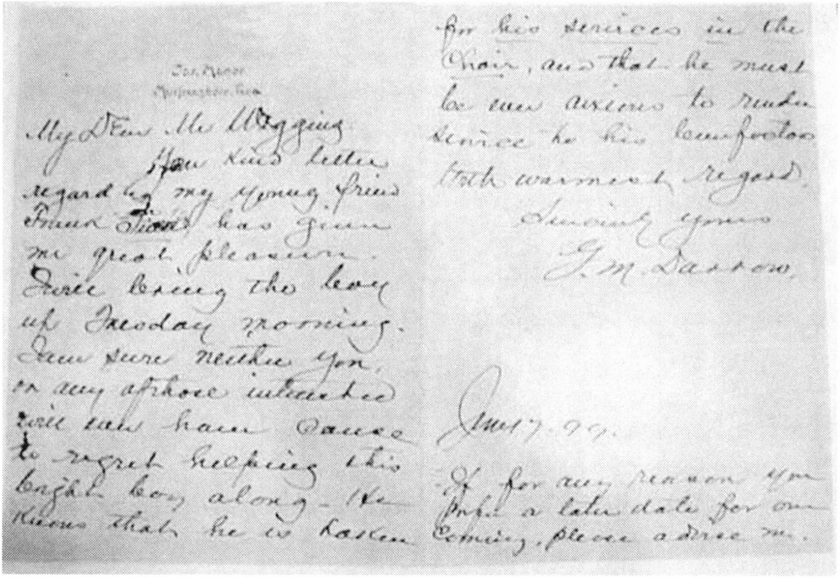

My Dear Mr Wiggins
Your kind letter regarding my young friend Frank Gum has given me great pleasure. Will bring the boy up Tuesday morning. I am sure neither you or any of those interested will ever have cause to regret helping this bright boy along. He knows that he is taken for his services in the Choir, and that he must be ever anxious to render service to his benefactor.
With warmest regards,
Sincerely yours
G. M. Darrow.

Jan 7. 99.

If for any reason you prefer a later date for our coming, please advise me.

If for any reason you prefer a later date for our coming, please advise me.

Placing the letter in a matching blue envelope, Mr. Darrow addressed the envelope, sealed it, and then pulled the tasseled ringer for his servant. A black gentleman appeared, and bowing said in a low, pleasant voice,

"Yes, Sir, Mr. Darrow (pronounced "Dare-rah" in Tennessee.)

"Please give John Murray this letter. He is to see that it is delivered to Sewanee."

"Yes, Suh," said the man as he turned and left the room.

Now with the letter completed and on its way, George Darrow turned to other business. The note he had written would indeed change one young man's life, and, in the long run, the future of a family and the world.

Mr. Darrow was determined that Frank Gum, with his rare musical gift, receive the proper vocal training.[18] There could be no better training for him than at Sewanee. Obviously, Mr. Darrow had spoken to Will Gum, who was agreeable to the idea.

George Darrow, who was often spoken of as Murfreesboro's first millionaire, was an impressive man. He and Tempe, as dedicated Episcopalians, took seriously the idea of serving their fellow men and doing good for others. In addition, they were benefactors of the school at Sewanee.

Though no records have been found confirming whether George Darrow paid for Frank Gum's education, it has been assumed that he did. Arthur Ben Chitty, Sewanee Historiographer, who knew Henry Gass, claimed that he did. Whether Darrow paid or not, he is most certainly responsible for arranging young Frank's entrance into this prestigious school and for changing his life.

Meanwhile, in 1898 a sum of $10,000 had been noted in the will of Judge William A. Goodwin of Nashville as a donation for Sewanee. The income from this original money was to be used to educate young men who were too poor to pay for their own tuition.[19]

~

On Tuesday, June 13th, Frank Gum rose early, ready to begin his new life. Mr. Darrow, in a fancy black carriage, with his black coachman, John Murray, at the reigns, rode straight from Oak Manor at the far end of Maney Avenue to the Gum home at the other end of the avenue.

It is interesting to picture the scene that fateful day as Frank prepared to leave for Sewanee. At thirteen, he was still a little fellow, a child really. He was going on a grand adventure, and nothing would ever be quite the same again. Standing on the porch to bid him goodbye were nineteen year-old Mary, sixteen year-old Emmett and little brothers, Willie, ten, and Allie, seven.

Will Gum was there also. One can only imagine how he felt, seeing his middle son riding off in a grand carriage. Frank was being given an opportunity that any young man in Murfreesboro might envy. Perhaps, Will warned him not to waste it, but Will did not need to worry. Frank was eager for his new life to begin, and Will was likely relieved that he would have one less mouth to feed.

With a click of the reins, the horses moved ahead as the Gums waved their dear brother goodbye. Of the five children, Frank was the lucky one. He would not have to live with deprivation or worry anymore, nor would he have deal with his father's anger or alcoholism. But with this gift, came a responsibility to the rest of his family. It was a responsibility that Frank would not forget.

On a paper that all Sewanee Alumni are asked to fill out regarding their Personal History is the question: "Who or what influenced you to choose Sewanee?" Frank's brother, Will, would later fill in the answer: "Godfather, Mr. Geo. M. Darrow." Although church records of his baptism do not exist, it appears that Frank was baptized at St. Paul's before he left Murfreesboro.

On the same paper, Frank's home address is listed as "6 Main Street." Frank was living on Maney, and apparently the numbers on East Main have changed from that time, or Will didn't remember them. Still, we have to wonder, what address was Will referring to—his grandmother's home, the brick cottage or the store? For avocation, Will wrote "singer."[20]

Some have questioned George Darrow's interest in Frank. In studying Darrow's life, it is clear he had a general interest in young people and a desire to help them. He and Tempe never had any children of their own, though they later adopted Tempe's niece.

By the early 1900s, George Darrow would become involved with the local schools. At the end of each year, students were tested and given prizes for merit. For the subject of history, two or three of the students

Courtesy Tempe Thompson

with the highest grades were called to the Darrow home to be closely questioned by Mr. Darrow. His vote was the deciding factor as to who received the prize.

In the early 1920s, Florence Cox McFerrin was one of the students called to Mr. Darrow's home. She later recalled that Mr. Darrow was a man of average height, who was kind, but also very intent on his purpose. She and the other students were extremely nervous because being called to the Darrow home was considered a very important event.

Mr. Darrow befriended many neighborhood children during his years in Murfreesboro, sometimes buying them little gifts, as he did for young Kacky Butler Holden, the granddaughter of Mary Elizabeth Murphey, Maria Baugh's youngest sister.

~

That first trip to Sewanee must have seemed like an amazing dream to young Frank Gum. Frank had ridden the train before, but on those trips he and his brother were working to earn a few extra coins. Now, Frank was a regular passenger, riding with the richest man in Murfreesboro. The journey to Sewanee was sixty-one miles, but on the train the journey would have been swift.

Mr. Darrow was a charming man, who knew how to engage young Frank in conversation as the train rolled along. Then, without warning, they ascended steeply to the top of the mountain, which overlooked a patchwork of farmland in different shades of green. The train screeched as it pulled to a stop in the Sewanee station. They had arrived!

Descending from the train, an old hack with an old horse was waiting for them. They were taken several blocks, along avenues lined with trees, green lawns and lovely homes. In a matter of minutes, they had arrived on the Sewanee campus. The school must have seemed a sort of fairytale land to Frank, with its large stone buildings looking like ancient England. There were also old rustic buildings made of logs, in a kind of mystical forest. Some buildings had steep roofs, while others were built with large verandas. All were surrounded by woods and, in some places, by wildflowers. Frank had never seen anything so beautiful. The University at Sewanee was a town unto itself.

Turning down a lane, the carriage stopped before a large log house. Here, Mr. Darrow and Frank left the carriage. This was the home of Vice Chancellor Wiggins, the man George Darrow had written to about Frank.

Benjamin Wiggins, a graduate of Sewanee, was passionate about his Alma Mater. Although his photos show a rather severe and intense man, with ice blue eyes and a mustache, Mr. Wiggins was friendly to Mr. Darrow and Sewanee's new student. After a short conversation with Frank about his responsibilities, he was shown around the campus. Then, Frank was taken to the building where he would be living for the next few years and introduced to his house mother.

The Sewanee Inn.
(Courtesy University of the South)

Frank Gum and the other fine, young lads entering Sewanee Grammar School were housed at a place known as the "Sewanee Inn." A portion of this building dated back to 1869 when the school first opened after the Civil War.[21] In 1899, the building contained both classrooms and dormitories for the grammar school students.

Each residence on campus had a house mother, who looked after the boys and attended to their needs. Many of these women were widows of Confederate soldiers. Now in their sixties and seventies, these house mothers seemed ancient to the young students. Nevertheless, the women had great love and affection for the boys, and their care helped make Sewanee feel like home.

There were four trains a day to Sewanee, so Mr. Darrow likely returned to Murfreesboro that afternoon. Frank Gum was left to find his way around this strange, new world.

~

The University of the South at Sewanee was founded in 1857. It had been the dream of Episcopalian Bishop Otey that the institution would one day become a great University like Harvard or Yale; a learning center in the South, which would bring forth the finest men. In his speech that June day in 1857, Bishop Otey said,

> "We contemplate no strife save a generous rivalry with our brethren, as to who shall furnish to this great Republic, the truest men, the truest Christians, and the truest patriots."

The University had only begun to be built when the Civil War broke out. In 1861, Bishop Leonitus Polk dedicated the spot and a local farm boy used thirty-eight oxen to pull a six-ton cornerstone up the 2,000-foot mountain on his father's wagon. In the midst of the war, the Yankees blew the cornerstone to bits and set every home on the mountain ablaze. Polk (as told in *Part 1*) joined the Confederate Army, and was shot dead through the breast as he sat overlooking a battle in Atlanta.[22]

At the close of the war, nothing of the original University existed. According to the agreement for the land donated to the university, if a school was not in existence by 1869, the property would be returned to the original owners. As a result of this threat, Bishop Charles Todd Quintard, who was then practicing medicine in Memphis, took it upon himself to try to save the University.

Bishop Quintard asked the Episcopal Churches of the North to help. Then, he traveled to England to plead for assistance from the British church. Quintard let it be known that his goal was to found a school in the style of Oxford University. The Archbishop of Canterbury became interested, and as a result, Bishop Quintard received generous gifts of money and books from many of the English churches.

Over the next years, using the local limestone and sandstone, Sewanee took on the appearance of a grand and ancient English town in the midst of the woods. A library, hospital, classrooms, fraternities, dining halls and inns were among the many buildings raised.

The first structure rebuilt on the campus was that of the little frame chapel named St. Augustine in honor of the first Archbishop of Canterbury. This chapel was the heart of the campus, and the place where Frank Gum would perform his "services," singing twice a day for prayers.

Sewanee's location, on top of the 2,000-foot mountain, had been chosen purposely. The founders desired a place where young men could study;

learn ideas and morals for their future without the distractions of the outside world. Those who chose to settle in the village atop the mountain of Sewanee needed the permission of the Vice-Chancellor. He controlled the area as much as the local police, deciding which tradesman would be allowed to have their shops there, who might lease or even build homes, and who could be buried in the cemetery.[23]

Among the tradesman invited to stay in the town were two French tailors, who had arrived at Sewanee in 1870. For many years, Monsieur Pillet, easily recognized by his "dapper frock coat" and high silk hat, made all the uniforms for the students on campus.[24] Although Monsieur Pillet and his partner, Monsieur Farbre, died a few years prior to Frank Gum's arrival, their tradition was certainly carried on.

On entering Sewanee, two uniforms were made for young Frank. The weekday uniform was a gray suit in military style with a black stripe down the outside of each pant leg, and a gray jacket banded in black around the neck and sleeves. The dress uniform was made of the same gray cloth, but the jacket had a tailcoat and was decorated with fine gold braid and brass buttons across the arms and chest. Dress uniforms were worn on Sundays, and for special occasions.

At Sewanee no boy was considered more or less important than anyone else. They were all Sewanee boys, judged by their behavior and their code of honor toward God, country, school and one another. The uniform and values afforded every boy an equal chance. For Frank, the school at Sewanee meant freedom from the dark shadow under which he had been living for so many years.

At same time Sewanee was an Episcopal school, it would always carry a strong military feel, from the uniforms to the strictly polite manners. There were parades, and marching to church services each Sunday as the band played "Onward Christian Soldiers."[25]

The first members of the faculty had been trained at Heidelberg, Cambridge and the University of Virginia, West Point. The professors all wore black gowns, and there was a certain dignity about them. Rev. William Alexander Guerry was the chaplain in charge of the choir.[26]

To be at Sewanee in summer was a great relief from the humid heat of Murfreesboro. In fact, many people came to Sewanee to escape the summer heat. It was for this reason that the early Trustees decided the

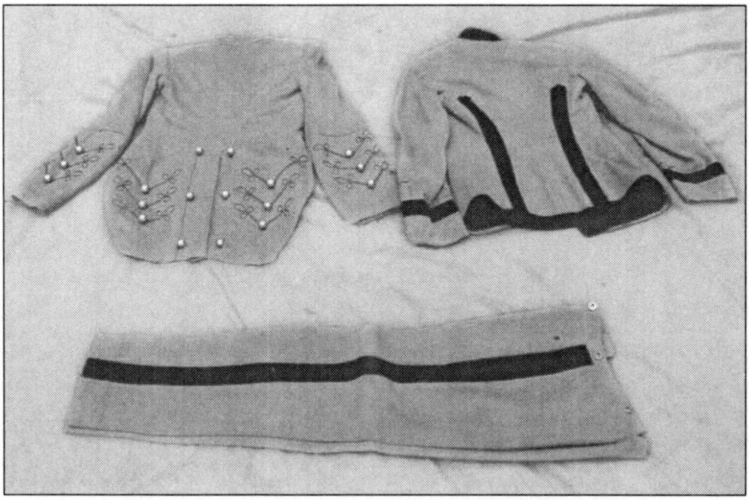

Sewanee Uniforms of Charles Carter Swope, age 8, who entered the Sewanee Grammar School in 1907, two years after Frank Gumm left.
(Courtesy of Carter Swope)

The Choir at Sewanee, Sopranos include John Gass, Henry Gass, Charles Gloyer, Frank Gumm, Carl Judd, Silas McBee, Charles Puckette, Stephen Puckette and Ferdinand Rodgers. Frank Gumm should be one of the boys in the front row, but has yet to be identified. Rev. W.A. Guerry, M.A.B.D. is the Chaplain. Below, St. Augustine's Chapel. Courtesy University of the South

school year should include summer, and the yearly break should be taken in winter.

The Lenten term of 1899 had begun in March. Frank was a late arrival in June, but he caught up quickly. His schedule included early chapel services, followed by the grammar school classes in English, Latin, History, Mathematics and Greek. Classes in Geography, Religion and science were also offered.[27] Although listed as "grammar school" classes at that time, in the present time these classes would be termed "junior high" and "high school."

In 1899, Frank Gum joined approximately 126 young boys in the grammar school department. That term the entire University had about 516 students. Other departments in the school were academic, theological and law. While 102 of Sewanee's students hailed from Tennessee, there were also students from Mississippi, 57, Louisiana, 47, Alabama, 46, Texas, 46, Georgia 49, Florida 39, South Carolina 38, and other southern states, 50. In addition, there were seven students from foreign countries.

If Frank was homesick, he soon learned that there were other young boys at Sewanee like himself; boys with similar poor backgrounds. One student in Frank's class was Henry Gass.

Henry's father, John Gass, had also attended the Sewanee Grammar School. Later he become the rector of St. Luke's Church in Atlanta. Sadly, Mr. Gass died at an early age, leaving behind his wife and three small children: John, Jr., Henry and Ivy. A short time after Mr. Gass's death, Henry's mother married Bishop Bratton and took Henry and his siblings to live in Jackson, Mississippi. When the boys were of age, Mrs. Bratton, determined that her sons receive a Sewanee education like their father, packed her family up and moved them to the Sewanee.[28]

Henry was the smallest boy in class and spoke in a high, nasally voice that made everyone laugh. Henry was also the smartest boy in the grammar school, and like Frank, he and his brother, John, sang in the choir. Henry and Frank soon became the best of friends. Another boy in the choir, Charles Puckette, also became good friends with Frank and Henry. When not busy with their classes, these three boys "ran around together."[29] Eventually Charles McD. Puckette worked for *The Chattanooga Times*, and later become Managing Editor for the *New York Post*.

Frank, Henry and Charles had a busy schedule. They began their day by singing for the morning services at St. Augustine's Chapel. Then, they went to their classes. After their noon meal, the choir sang for another service, which was followed by music practice.

In Murfreesboro, Frank had always been a friendly, outgoing chap, whom everyone liked.[30] The same was now true at Sewanee. It didn't take long before everyone knew who he was. Along with that, his pure soprano voice was unforgettable. He was at home now, a truly happy young man.

During Frank's first two years at school, there were continual improvements to the campus. In 1899, the dormitories received water, pumped inside for the first time. An electric plant soon followed.

The town had learned that in order to protect the springs, which gave them their water supply, the forest growth on the 5,000 acres of University land must also be protected. When the village first was built, all the trees had been cut down and the wells had run dry. Now, it was the custom to plant one tree for every tree cut down. In addition to the wooded land, produce for the students was grown on a portion of the campus, making the school self-supporting.

Shortly before Frank Gum came to Sewanee, it was decided that the grammar school needed a suitable dormitory. George W. Quintard, of New York, the brother of the late bishop, heard about Sewanee's need and offered $50,000 to build the building. In July of 1899, one month after Frank Gum arrived at the school, the cornerstone was laid. It was hoped that the building would be completed by March of 1901, but due to the size of the enormous stone building, the University ran out of funds. Eventually, J.P. Morgan of New York donated the needed amount. The building was not completed until 1907.

The fall of 1899, the University of the South reached a high point in sports when the Sewanee Tigers football team won every game that season. Everyone on campus felt the spirit of school pride. From October to December, the Tigers' scored 12–0, outscoring their opponents 322 to 10. In December, they were awarded the Southern Intercollegiate Athletic Association title.

~

When winter came that first semester break in December 1899, Frank's train fare home was likely paid by Mr. Darrow as Frank had no money of his own, and his family had little to spare. That first visit home may have felt strange. Frank was eager to see his family, but he had changed, and viewed his family's living situation with new eyes. His education, surroundings and friends were giving him a new reference point in the world.

The rest of the year, Frank was just as happy to stay at school. William Alexander Percy, a student at the same time as Frank Gum, would later say that while living at Sewanee, he dreaded those trips away from the beauty and peace of the mountain.

Life at Sewanee was ideal and as the years passed, Frank gained a sense of pride about himself. On his trips home, people would later recall seeing him as he walked along the street, singing or whistling with his coat slung over his shoulder and his hat pushed back on his head. Life had been good to him, and he was an optimist, fully expecting the best. Mr. Darrow would have every reason to be proud of him.[31]

In 1900, the directors opened a medical school, and Dr. J. B. Murfree, the Gum's old neighbor, now an eminent physician and surgeon, was invited to teach. The medical school would be the best attended school at the University. Whether Dr. Murfree knew Frank was there or saw him is unknown.

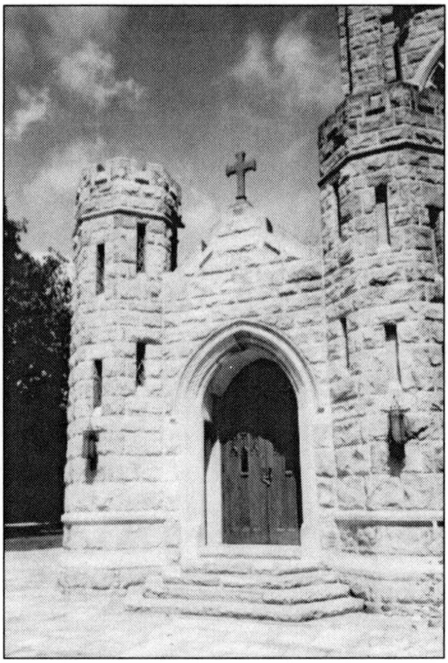

Besides Frank Gum's regular performances with the choir at St. Augustine's Chapel, there were also special seasonal performances. These events were attended not only by those at the University, but by off-campus visitors as well. On these occasions, the school newspaper, the *Sewanee Purple*, would review the performances, as they did for the Easter Service on April 17, 1900:

> "...The music was not easy of execution. It was the best church music that is sung by the best in the land, and our organist and choir have full right to grow extremely conceited about their performance last Sunday. To speak the truth briefly, the music was by odds the best that has ever

> rung through that chapel, so far as we know ... Master Frank Gumm of Murfreesboro sang with accuracy and purity of tone the solo part of Stainer's "They Have Taken Away My Lord."

Although Sewanee was an Episcopalian school with high moral standards, it was anything but stuffy and boring. There were plenty of parties in the houses of the village. William Alexander Percy, who was one grade above Frank, hints in his book, *Lanterns on the Levee*, that on occasion, there were also games of poker and drinks of "mountain dew" brought up from the village below. But most of all, there was passion for the beauty in literature, music and ideas.

The students put on many plays, and because there were no girls in school, in the tradition of old time theatre, the boys usually played the female roles. Sometimes, however, girls from neighboring schools were brought in to play the female roles.

A review in the *Sewanee Purple* of October 9, 1900 describes one play Frank appeared in *The Seven Little Dwarfs*. Frank was given the role of the prince and received an excellent notice:

> "The prince was duly and instantaneously amorous as he should have been in the person of Master Frank Gumm."

Around this time, Frank began to spell his last name "Gumm" with two *m*'s. Whether this was a result of copying the *Sewanee Purple*'s spelling of his name is unknown. In any case, during the next few years, other family members would begin to follow his lead.

~

Living at Sewanee, Frank continued to grow in happiness. He did well in his classes, and his vocal abilities were carefully nurtured as he traveled the road from boyhood to young adult.

Sewanee was beautiful in winter, with dustings of snow on the cedar forests. In spring there were flowers of every color: red, yellow, pink, violet, blue and purple. The students often wandered through the woods, thinking, reading and practicing their songs, instruments and theatrical pieces. William Percy recalls coming upon a young man one day, practicing his declamation piece:

"...One afternoon of thick yellow sunshine, I was audience to another who stood on an abandoned windlass with tulip trees and a blue vista for backdrop reciting pentameters, which though you may never have heard, we thought too rich and cadenced for the race of men to ever forget."[32]

The description, which could have been of Frank Gum, or any young man at Sewanee, opens a window into the life young Frank led. At the age of fifteen, Frank was involved in "declamation," reciting speeches from memory, and on June 21st, 1901, two years after entering the grammar school at Sewanee, he received a medal for Declamation. It was an honor of which he was so proud, he never forgot the date.

Thirty-five years later, Frank wrote his boyhood friend, Henry Gass,

Boy, I will never forget the six years I spent at Sewanee; they were six of the happiest, most beautiful years of my life.[33]

Chapter 20

Legal Matters, 1900–1903

WHILE FRANK GUM WAS AWAY AT SCHOOL, MANY ASPECTS OF THE OLD life in Murfreesboro changed. In the summer of 1900, there was an outbreak of typhoid fever up in the Blackman Community, and on July 30th, Clemmie's brother, Charlie, died of typhoid. Two days later on August 2nd his wife, Lizzie, died. A short time later, their daughter, Mary Ann, also died. Left behind were nine children ranging in ages from twenty-two to six years of age. The children would later divide their inherited land between them. Some of it was good for farming and some not. At least one of Charlie and Lizzie's descendents still lives and farms on this land today.

When Frank Gum came home in December for his 1900–1901 winter break, he noted one surprising change in Murfreesboro. The streets were no longer dark at night, but lit by electric lights. The power came from a new plant on the property of Dr. J.H. Reed.

Another surprise would have been, seeing Mr. George Darrow driving around in his new-fangled, one-seat horseless vehicle which was operated by a lever. Because of the dusty roads, Mr. Darrow was well-covered with a hat and goggles, but able to maneuver around narrow areas quickly. Being the first person to own an automobile in Murfreesboro, Darrow was no doubt the talk of the town.[34]

Meanwhile, though it could not be said the Gums were poverty-stricken, Will seemed unable to rise above his financial state. On December 12th, 1900, he sold his one-eighth interest in his father's property on Maney Avenue to H.B. Williams. The sale garnered him $50. At the same time he conducted this sale, he made sure that he would be able to buy back the share of his father's property during the next months.

By early 1900, Jere Gum had moved to a small place a few blocks from his home on the Shelbyville Highway. To help cover his expenses, he took in a boarder, twenty-one year-old Frank Wastrial. At the same time, seventy-three year-old Jere was working at a bank as a watchman.[35]

Meanwhile, Jere and Martha's children had all moved out on their own. Nannie and Ed Rion were living in a small house on Maney Avenue near Main, and were very involved with Baptist Church. In 1896, E.T. Rion had been named the Sunday School Superintendent.

By 1899, Ed Rion was having a lovely new home built for his wife at 330 Lytle Street. It was a grand red brick home designed in something of a Jeffersonian style. Built entirely on one floor, it included a broad covered porch, large entrance hall and ten rooms, including a spacious front parlor with high ceilings and elegant molding. The home was completed around the time Nannie gave birth to their first child, Edwin Rion, Jr., who arrived on July 28, 1900.

Nannie's sister, Bettie Fox, gave birth to a son in December of that same year. Officially, his name was John H. Fox, but he would always be known to the family as "Jack." Susie Finlayson had announced the birth of her first child, a daughter, Mildred, down in North Carolina in September 1899. With Lucy, Charles and their four sons, Roy, Clair, Charles and Harry, living next door, Suzie wasn't lonely.[36]

Courtesy Claire Rion Weber

Down in Atlanta, John Gum, Jr. and his family were doing quite well. He and Lucy seemed to enjoy living at the Peach Tree Hotel and had no desire to live anywhere else. John, who, in the future, would follow his father, using the name "Jere," had become something of a distinguished business man in Atlanta. As General Sales Agent

Rion Home on Lytle Street.
(Courtesy Nancy Lee Dismukes)

for the Mitchell Wagon Manufacturing Company, John traveled a good deal, managing the southeast portion of the United States from Missouri to Florida. His name appeared fairly often in the Atlanta *Constitution*, and, like his nephew, Frank Gumm, John, Jr. was now spelling his name "Gumm."

On 20th of February 1900, a lengthy letter from John Gumm, Jr., appeared in the editorial section of the *Atlanta Constitution*. In it, Mr. Gumm says that Atlanta should let go of some of her landmarks in favor of putting up new buildings and a new railway depot.

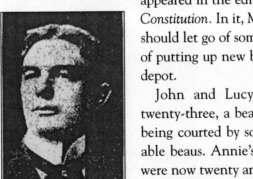

John A. Gumm, Jr.

John and Lucy's daughter, Annie, now twenty-three, a beautiful and popular girl, was being courted by some of Atlanta's most desirable beaus. Annie's brothers, Trigg and James, were now twenty and seventeen.

The Gumm family's youngest sibling, John H. Gum had been discharged from his service in the Spanish–American War the end of October

1899. Johnny, who was mustered into Company H as a private in June of 1898, had been transferred to Company B, and like many men in that war, became ill in the line of duty. After his discharge from the army in San Francisco, California, twenty-five year-old Johnnie Gum decided to join his brother in Atlanta.

1901

In 1901, Jere Gum gave his children permission to sell the Gum family home to a widow, Mrs. Elmyra Thompson. On June 29th, Mrs. Thompson paid the Gumms $600 (=$15,600) in cash, with notes of $200 (= $5,171) each due in 1902 and 1903. The transaction was witnessed by John A. Gum, Sr., his children and in-laws. Will Gum, whose name appears on the sale, apparently had been able to buy back his share of the property.[37]

The buyer, Mrs. Thompson, was a strong woman of devout Methodist faith, who, since her husband's death, had been living in Bell Buckle with her five children. The children, Eva, Allie, William, Joe Miller, and David, ranged in ages between eighteen and four. Once the Thompsons were established in the old Gum home, it did not take long for the Gum children to become acquainted with them. Robert Emmett Gum, in particular, could not help noticing Mrs. Thompson's beautiful, fifteen year-old daughter, Joe Miller.

The Thompson family had a rather illustrious past. Their ancestors had played an important role in the history of Rutherford County. The children's father, David Smith Thompson, was a descendant of the Smith family, who, in 1812, had joined the Jarratts in founding the Salem Methodist Church. He was also a Methodist minister.

Elmyra Thompson, who was related to her husband through the Smith family, came from a family that was possibly even more illustrious than her husband's. Elmyra was the daughter of William "Bill" Granville Crockett and the granddaughter of Overton Washington Crockett, a distant cousin of the famed Davy Crocket.

In 1814, Overton and his brother, Fontaine Posey Crockett, were on their way to serve in the Battle of New Orleans under General Andrew Jackson when General Smith invited them to stay overnight at his mansion, Springfield. It was then that Overton and Evalina Smith, who was

The Salem Methodist Church, established in 1812, was built as a log church was built in 1814, on land deeded by Robert Smith. The present church, built in 1903, replaced the 1834 brick structure, but retains part of an original brick wall in its facade [Taken from the TN Historical Marker 3A-196]

only fourteen at the time, first met. After the war, Overton returned to Springfield and romance blossomed.[38]

Elmyra's father, Bill Crocket, had served as both sheriff and Mayor of Murfreesboro. Elmyra America Crocket, born on February 2nd, 1853 was one of Bill and Elizabeth Jarratt Crockett's six children. She and David Thompson married in 1876, the same year David was licensed to preach. Three years later, Rev. Thompson was serving as a traveling minister, and one year after that, as deacon. On the weekdays, David earned his living by farming. Then, in 1887, the family moved to Beech Grove where Rev. David Thompson became the first minister of the Beech Grove Methodist Church.

Sadly, life took its toll on Rev. Thompson. Along the way, he contracted tuberculosis, a common illness in this damp southern location. He died on January 2, 1896, at the age of forty-six.[39]

Jack and Maria Baugh's family were members of the Salem Methodist church. Maria Baugh passed away in 1898, but the Baughs likely knew the Thompsons. In addition, the Thompsons were also well-acquainted with the Howlands and the Jacobs who lived in the small community of Beech Grove. Elmyra probably learned about the Gum home from one or more of these families.

Emmett Gum, now eighteen, was a good looking, energetic and industrious young man. For a time, he worked in a drug store near the square. Like his brothers and sister, he was also musical and, possibly, earned some money singing. In a 1937 news article, Aunt Nannie Rion recalled,

> "There were four boys and a girl in the family, and each of them was a good singer. They sang quite a lot for the entertainment of their friends, at concerts and local entertainments, but Frank was the only one who ever "did anything" with his talent. Professionally, I mean."[40]

1902

When Frank came home for his 1901–1902 winter break, church records show that January 5th, he was a communicant at St. Paul's, whose congregation now stood at thirty-seven members.

The previous day, Frank's sister, Mary Gum, who was now twenty-one, had gone down to Horace Palmer's office and signed a deed which read in part:

> *For the consideration of the sum of one dollar to me paid, the receipt of which is acknowledged ... Mary B. Gum, has this day bargained and sold and does hereby transfer and convey unto H.E. Palmer all the right, title and interest ... in and to the following described lot lying in the 2nd Ward at the Town of Murfreesboro.*

The lot described was the land on Main and Maney which the children's grandmother had left them. The deed stated that Mary was in debt to "W.T. Gum, Guardian for my brothers in the sum of $160." Although the document was written as if Mary owed her father, this debt was the money Will Gum expended to repair his children's property and had yet to receive from the court. By having Mary sign this "deed," which stated that the money owed was bearing interest, Will was attempting to force the court's hand to repay him.[41]

Mary, now twenty-one, was no longer protected under the children's trust. Though her father had likely pushed her to sign this legal agreement, it seems she had done so willingly. She had been assured that her father would receive his money, and she would not loose her inheritance. Horace Palmer, who was a fair man, had agreed to draw up the legal papers.

On March 28th, 1902, Rutherford County had the worst flood in its history. Although most of Murfreesboro, which is built on a small hill above the rest of the county, was safe, the surrounding area's homes, bridges, fences and cattle were all swept away. Power lines were also downed. It would take months to try to repair the damage and there was a great deal of suffering.[42]

On April 1st, three days after the flood, Will Gum and the children appeared before the Rutherford County Court. The court noted that "Frank A. Gum is residing temporarily at Sewanee, Franklin County, where he is attending school."[43] The following day, J.L. Myer was deputized by the sheriff of Franklin County to deliver a subpoena to Sewanee, summoning fifteen year-old Frank Gum to appear at the courthouse in

Murfreesboro. So, Frank boarded a train and came to town for a day or two.

One matter of business before the court that April concerned the remaining property owned by the children on Main and Maney. Recently, Will Gum had spoken to Mary, Emmett and Frank about the possibility of selling the land. Once again, the store had burnt, and since they could not afford to rebuild it, and the lot was bringing in no income, and it was a drain on them "by way of taxes." A buyer had been found for the lot who was offering a substantial amount of money—$2,000 (= $51,400).

The interested party was not a stranger. He was Charles H. Byrn, the son-in-law of Mrs. Alabama Richardson and the husband of Allie Richardson for whom Allie Gum had been named. Mr. Byrn, who was born near Milton in 1856, was a successful Murfreesboro businessman. He owned a wholesale and retail hardware store in town and was also on the board of directors for the First National Bank of Murfreesboro. He and his wife had three children and were eager to build a beautiful home in the heart of Murfreesboro.

Charles H. Bryn.
(Courtesy James R. Roberts)

Meanwhile, during this same session, the court was considering whether or not Will Gum should receive the $160 he had spent on the children for their "maintenance and support."[44] The court noted that Horace Palmer, who was the trustee for the case, otherwise known as *W.T. Gum et al v. R.E. Gum et al*, had been "subpoenaed to court more than five days before the hearing" but had failed to appear.

On April 14th, Frank Gumm was called to court again. On April 16th, Emmett and Frank, both being over fourteen years of age, were asked to sign a statement for their guardian ad Litem, Andrew Lytle, that they

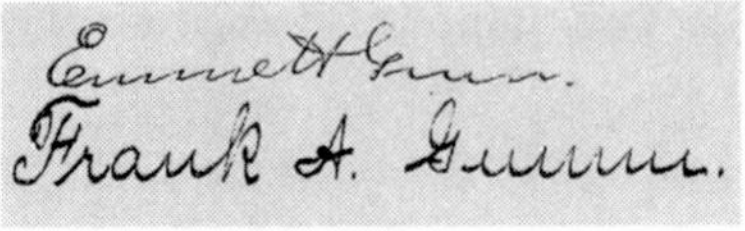

understood the remainder of their inherited property was worth more in cash, and they agreed to sell it. *Notice that Emmett has signed his name with one "m" and Frank has adopted his new signature.**

That April, the Rutherford County Court went over every detail of the Gums' living situation. On April 17th, all records concerning the Gum children were reviewed. The expert opinion of two witnesses regarding the Gum properties was also taken. The court noted that the taxes owed by the Gums to the State, County and municipal government were $208.22. These were taxes that had not been paid for four years. In addition, the estimated repairs needed on the Gum home would cost approximately $250 to $300. It was stated that if the land their grandmother left them was sold, after paying their taxes and repairing their home, the children would have an additional $1,500 to invest for their future. In addition, Mr. C.H. Bryn had agreed to pay any legal costs involved in the sale.

That same day, Will T. Gum was asked to take the stand. Now forty-eight, Will stated his relation to the children, giving his minor children, the boy's ages as 19, 15, 12 and 9. Regarding his children's property ownership and his own financial state, Will said:

A: The said minors have no property except the lot in question, the dwelling and lot mentioned in the bill and $160 which came into my hands as their guardian as process of insurance upon a former building which was a store upon said lot.

I have no property and have no regular or permanent employment. As a matter of fact, I have expended the whole of the $160 and more for the benefit of said minors in furnishing necessary clothing and board. I had no means but said $160 and such means as I could earn and accumulate. (= $4,120)

I have taken a note of my daughter, Mary B. Gum for said $160 security mortgage in her interest in the lot, but I think the court will direct that I be credited with said amount and this cancel said mortgage. I received said $160 in January 1902, and it is 4/5 of the previous insurance received on account of a fire, which destroyed the buildings that formerly stood on the lot.

* Courtesy Rutherford County Archives

> The rent for the cabin in the south of the lot is consumed in paying the wash or laundry bill of the family, so that there has been no revenue or income for the children since said fire occurred last October. Counting from October, this insurance $200 (= $5,140), in all, has paid the board and clothing and other necessary expenses of the family and it has also paid $25 for papering and finish work on the house, about $10 for building a coal house, $4.15 for three years insurance and also $59.45 of a bill of cost in a suit which I bought for the benefit of said children against the men of Murfreesboro.*
>
> Of course, I could have added money which I carried and borrowed in my own name. One of the boys, Robert Emmett was at work till about January 1, 1902, and of course, his earnings helped to support him. Since that time he has had no employment. We have all lived together in the same dwelling. It is thus seen that I have expended for my children in repairing, insuring, taking care of their property and maintaining and supporting them with the $200 of insurance money received … I had insurance on the property burned but it had run out and I had not the means to renew it in time to prevent the loss.[45]

Will further states that his biggest loss was the storeroom, which he had built with the money he borrowed in his own name. He had used the store rent to repay the loan, and because of that, he hadn't had money for insurance on the storeroom. About the land where the store was built, Will said,

> "The lot is low and has been much accustomed to overflow (flood). To be used as a residence the lot will have to be filled up with much earth."

On April 18th, the family was back in court, and once again the property sales idea was reviewed. The first witness was J.G. Mosby, who stated,

> "I know the complainant Mary B. Gum and the defendants, Robert Emmett, Frank A., W.W. and Allie R. Gum. I know the lot in question … and I believe that $2,000 for the lot is a good price."

---

* This suit has not been found, but may have been the same case the children's grandparents filed against the Mayor and Alderman, for cutting through their property to put a street in.

"I must say that the rental value of said lot and cabin would be about $4 or $5 per month. The lot corner really has no rental value except possibly as a garden."

About the house the Gums were living in, Mosby said,

"I have examined the said dwelling and I find that the premises are in need of repair. The dwelling needs to be painted, the fences need to be repaired and in some places replaced. The chimneys need to be repaired and in some parts entirely replaced as they are split apart; there are three rooms and a dining room, which is also used as a kitchen.

I understand that Mr. Gum desires a small kitchen and in my opinion it would not be a waste of means to invest a small amount in building a kitchen. I did not examine the inside to see whether the dwelling needed painting on the inside."[46]

That day, April 18th, the Rutherford County Court agreed to the sale of the children's lot, and a "Decree Confirming Sale of Realty," a seven page document, was written. With their property (which comprised nearly half a city block) sold, it was the end of an era, but for the Gum children it meant the end of debt and worry.

Richardson and Richardson, who were handling the case on Will and Mary Gum's behalf, asked that Will be paid out of the proceeds and that "Mary B. Gum be acquitted and discharged of all liability."[47] Although at one point the court had questioned whether Will Gum should be "paid for the care of his own children," in the final report, the Clerk & Master, Hickum Weakly, recommended that Will Gum, "being a man of no means with no permanent or regular employment & using his own means & earnings in the maintenance and support of his children … be credited…"[48] Mr. Weakly also recommended that the repairs on the family home be done.[49] Once the money from the sale was dispensed, the court noted that $10.00 would go to pay the guardian ad Litem.

In the coming days, the Gum family would see the place they once called home, the place where Pa's store had stood and where Mammy Ran and Jane had lived, cleared. Mr. Bryn hired a man to fill in the corner, which Will Gum had described as "low." The wagoner agreed to load the dirt for five cents a load. It took 500 wagonloads of dirt to make

The Bryn House on East Main.
(Courtesy James R. Roberts)

the ground on the corner level. The wagoner nearly went broke because it cost him more than 5 cents a load to obtain that much dirt, but in the end, Mr. Bryn compensated him. The corner seems to have been a sinkhole, which even today shows some problems. It was a spot which Will T. Gum had been unfortunate to build on.

To make sure his house would not sink, Mr. Bryn had the builders dig ten feet below the basement level and lay a bedrock foundation. A stone basement was placed on top of this. Because of Mr. Bryn's careful planning, his house is one of the few in the area which has not sunk over the years.

While Frank was away at school, he likely received letters from his family telling him of the fascinating new developments with their old property. On his return home, he would find the Gum house on Maney a much nicer place to live and, standing on the old Baugh lot, a veritable mansion.

~

With the court's permission, on August 18th, Will Gum used the money from the sale of the Maney and Main Street property to buy a nice, white house several blocks north, on Bell Street, as an investment property for the children.[50] The property had been owned by Captain James Oslin for about twenty years. It was sold to the Gums by its recent owner S.S. Butler, who was living in Texas.

This house was even nicer than the one the Gums were living in. Testifying in court, a nephew of Captain Oslin's, H.O. Parker, stated that it was "unusually well-built," containing "a large amount of red cedar lumber … It has a bath room and water closet, comfortable sitting and bed rooms, is a two–story frame building, containing six rooms and a kitchen." Because the house needed about $200 in repairs, Will had been able to purchase it for $1100, leaving a surplus of $400 (= $10,300) in emergency funds.[51]

After completing the work on the house, Will had no trouble renting it. The rent, approximately $12 a month (= $309), would bring them some cash to live on.

Once again, Will Gum wanted to get paid for his work, and entreated Mary to sell her share of the property in order to force the court to pay him. On August 23rd, 1902, Mary B. Gum signed a deed similar to the earlier one.

> *For and in consideration of the sum of one Dollar cash to me in hand paid, the receipt of which is hereby acknowledged, and the further consideration hereafter expressed, I, Mary B. Gum, have this day bargained and sold and do hereby transfer and convey to W.T. Gum in trust my undivided interest in the following described real estate: A certain house and lot in the fourth ward of the town of Murfreesboro being the same conveyed to me and my brothers by S.S. Butler … bounded on the north by Burton or Boyle Street, East by Howse, South by Huggins, West by Walnut Street.*[52]

The debt owed to Will Gum was again $160. Will wanted his money by January 4th of 1903. It is interesting to note that on this document, Mary has changed her name to "Gumm."

1903

On his 1902–1903 winter break, Frank Gumm learned that Emmett had asked the beautiful and gentle Joe Miller Thompson to be his bride. Emmett was now 19, and Joe Miller was 16. They had little money, but

Robert Emmett Gum and Joe Miller Thompson about the time they were married. (Courtesy David Richardson)

they were in love. On January 22, 1903, possibly while Frank was home on winter vacation, the couple was married.[53]

Joe's mother, Elmyra, was apparently not that pleased with the marriage, but in the end she accepted Emmett. A short time after their marriage, Emmett and Joe left town. Traveling south, the couple settled in Pensacola, Florida where Emmet got a job as an insurance salesman. Murfreesboro had not been a good place to earn money. In addition, Joe Miller's health was delicate and the couple hoped that the warm Florida sunshine would be the answer to her health problems.

Another Gum wedding took place during this time. Although the Murfreesboro Gums were not invited, they learned that Cousin Annie in Atlanta had married "one of Atlanta's most popular young businessmen," Walter Sylvanous Parker. The *Atlanta Constitution* announced that the couple was married on April 21st, stating that it would be a quiet wedding, "with no attendants or reception."[54] Following the wedding ceremony, the Parkers left on a two week "wedding trip," which culminated in Washington, D.C.

The reason John Gumm, Jr. wanted the wedding kept private was the fact that Lucy Trigg was not well. She had been having mental difficulties for some time. Within the next year or two, Lucy would be confined to the State Sanitarium in Milledgeville, Georgia, where she would remain until her death at the age of seventy-eight in February of 1935.

That October, the Gumms of Atlanta had another embarrassment that was far less private. In fact, it made the local papers. Johnny Gumm, who was still living in Atlanta, owed the local "clothes pressing establishment" on Peachtree and Alexander streets $5.00. When he went to pick up his clothing that Monday morning without the money, the shop owner refused to release his clothing. In response, according to *The Atlanta Constitution*, twenty-six year-old Johnny assaulted the proprietor with a rock, hitting him several times.

The proprietor finally gave in. John H. took his clothes and left. Halfway down the block, he realized that he had left some articles of clothing behind. When he returned for them, the owner "turned the tables" on him by closing the front door and blocking it with the big clothes presser. There was a phone next to the door, and barricading himself between the door and the clothes presser, the owner called the police. When Officer Lindsay arrived, Johnny Gumm was arrested.[55]

No further reports about John H. Gumm have been found. His life appears to have been sad, but brief. Eventually, he returned to Murfreesboro, where he died in 1913 at the age of thirty-six. He is buried next to his parents at Evergreen Cemetery.

In 1903, Will Gum was fortunate enough to obtain a position with the Haynes Brothers Staple and Fancy Groceries in Murfreesboro. He certainly had the experience for this job, and Mr. Haynes had faith in him. In December, Mr. Haynes gave Will the legal right as "Guardian of Haynes Bros." to represent the store in court.

The case was against H.W. Pennell for $33.00. Apparently, Mr. Pennell had not paid his bill of $11 for the months of October thru January.[56] Whatever the reason, the judgment received was in the favor of Haynes Bros. Will Gum, having done his job, was able to collect the amount due. Now, nearly fifty, it seems Will had rectified his ways, and was leading a responsible life.

Chapter 21

Endings & Beginnings

In 1904, the Gum family continued to grow and change. On February 6th, Aunt Bettie Gum Fox gave birth to her fifth child, a little girl whom she named, Martha, for her mother.

A little over a month later, on March 21st, seventy-six year-old John Alexander Gum passed on to the hands of his maker. It was a sad day for his children. He had been a good father, but life had not been easy for him since Martha's death seven years earlier.

That summer, word reached the family that Emmett and Joe Miller were parents. On July 20th, Joe had given birth to their daughter, Mildred Yneistra Gumm, named in honor of a Pensacola family who had befriended them.

Life in this small Florida town seemed idyllic for a time. The winters were mild, the living was easy, and the couple made many friends. Joe and Emmett, who were very much in love, were filled with joy over the birth of their baby girl. But there was one blight to their happiness—Joe Miller was not well.

Perhaps, she had always been somewhat delicate, but now Joe had a cough that was constant, and she was often feverish. The fever passed for a time, but it always returned. Despite the warm climate, it soon became apparent that Joe was not getting better. These days she ate very little. At some point, she was diagnosed with tuberculosis, the disease which had killed her father.

Late in 1904, Robert, Joe and Baby Mildred moved back to Tennessee. Perhaps Joe wished to be closer to home or by now was too ill to take care of Mildred. Emmett and Joe moved to 1513 Church Street in Nashville, where Emmett found a job as an insurance agent.

~

At Sewanee, life was sweet for Frank. In December of 1903, he completed his grammar school education. Returning from winter break in January, he began his college studies, which included English, Latin, German, History & Politics, and Mathematics. Electives were Greek, General Science and Physics.[57] In addition, Mr. Darrow had arranged for him to have private voice lessons. With time and experience, his passion for singing had only grown. Frank Gumm was now a finely trained singer, who easily stood out in a crowd.

Marguerite Rather Gass, who knew Frank as a child in Murfreesboro, and visited Sewanee during these years, said of him, "He had a beautiful baritone voice and led in all of the university dramatic and musical productions. He was very highly thought of ... at Sewanee."[58]

In the spring of 1904, Frank became the "end man" in a Sewanee Minstrel group which traveled around the area. Performing for the public and receiving applause for his work, whetted his desire to be on stage. It was something he had always wanted, and now he felt ready. Yet, as much as he wanted to be a performer, Frank would be forever haunted by the memory of his father's inability to support his children. Whatever his desires, Frank would always put the insurance of a good income first.

That June, Frank took part in the Sewanee Dramatic Club's production of William Shakespeare's *Twelfth Night*. Many other theatrical pieces were put on the boards between 1903 and 1905; however, the records for most of these were not preserved. Because of that, *Twelfth Night* is the only theater record found for Frank Gumm in college.[59]

~

In 1905, Frank had two more years of schooling to complete before graduating. He had completed his sophomore year, which had essentially the same classesas his freshman year, only a level higher in complexity. But after finishing the June to December 1904–1905 semester, Frank left his home of six years, the "happiest years of his life," and returned to Murfreesboro.

There are many possible reasons for Frank Gumm's early departure from Sewanee. In later years, his friend Henry Gass would say he wanted to pursue his career. Still, considering all the factors in his life at this time, it appears that Frank returned to Murfreesboro because his father, Will, was in failing health, and his younger brothers, Will and Allie, needed his help.

Frank had been given a wonderful gift—a great education. He had lived a life stress-free, a life far better than any of his siblings, but he realized it was now time for him to think of the people back home.

Mary had taken it upon herself to help by signing away her inheritance so her father could get his money. Older brother Robert Emmett had a child, and a wife in failing health. Sixteen year-old Will W. had quit school and gone to work, and now little Allie, a strapping boy of thirteen, was also planning to leave school. Though there is no known documentation stating why Frank left school, by the spring of 1905, he had returned to Murfreesboro and found a job.

For a short time, Frank lived in the family home on Maney Avenue, but things were not the same. Frank was now a young gentleman who knew how to dress and act, and who had grown accustomed to living in certain peaceful, pleasant and intellectual surroundings. Will Gum (who still spelled his name with one "m") also may have been supplementing the family income by bringing a boarder into the four-room house. For whatever reason, shortly after Frank's return to Murfreesboro, his Aunt Bettie Gum Fox "took him in."[60] At that time, the Fox family was in a living in a fairly nice house near the corner of College and Maney Avenue with their four children: William, 15, Anna Lee, 11, Jack, 5, and Martha, 1.

In later years, Jack Fox would tell his son, Henry, that Frank Gumm had been his buddy. Since Jack was no more than six or seven then, he must have meant that his cousin, Frank, spent time playing with him.

Jack's son, Henry Lee Fox, when speaking of his grandfather, for whom he was named, described him a "gay old blade." Mr. Fox, of course, was referring to the original connotation of the words, meaning someone of a colorful nature, who liked to go out on the town and have fun.

Jack Fox, six, and Martha Fox, two. (Courtesy Mary Cole)

Bettie Gum Fox was a strong woman, who was also very much a lady. Her granddaughter, Betty Fay recalls that when she slept in her grandmother's bed as a child, it smelt of violets. Bettie Fox had inherited the high energy of the Gums. She was a strong-minded, tough lady, who sat in a rocker and smoked one cigarette after another.

Fox family notes state that during this time, Frank Gumm worked as a clerk in the Rutherford County Courthouse by day and sang at night. Though no public records have been found to confirm Frank's court position, it may have been arranged by the family attorney, Horace Palmer, or even his Uncle Henry Lee Fox, who held this same position after returning from the Spanish–American War.

Returning to Murfreesboro after a life of order and beauty, must have seemed strange. Once again, there was the incessant sound of the train horns calling day and night, and the terrible heat of summer. It would be strange as well, to see the huge house, almost like a castle, and the pristine lawn where Pa's store used to be. He could never walk by the spot on Main Street where the brick office building had once stood without thinking of his mother. And he could not see the Murfree home, where he had been born, without remembering another time.

If Frank had a desire to move on with his life, and sing in vaudeville, he knew this was not the time for it. His father, Will was failing, and he, along with his brothers, Willie and Allie, were still considered minors in regards to their inheritance.

~

In early November of 1905, it became clear that the beautiful Joe Miller was not going to live long. Her round, youthful face and body had become skeletal, her cheeks sunken in and when she coughed there was green sputum and blood. She coughed incessantly, and Emmett was helpless to stop it. It was heartbreaking for twenty-two year-old Emmett to watch his beautiful, eighteen year-old wife fade away. Joe Miller longed to see her little girl, but knew she never would.

Joe Miller was diagnosed with miliary tuberculosis, a disease which, even now, if not treated quickly, is 100% fatal.[61] On November 11th, 1905, Joe Miller Gum passed away. She was nineteen years old, and she left behind a sixteen month-old daughter.

Emmett escorted her body back to Murfreesboro where she was buried at Evergreen Cemetery in a lonely plot not far from his mother, Clemmie. Elmyra Crockett Thompson insisted that she would take care of little Mildred. Sad and restless, Emmett soon gave up the rooms in Nashville and returned to Murfreesboro.

~

One year later, toward the end of November 1906, William Tecumseh Gum died. He was fifty-two years old. There is no record of the cause of his death, but we can imagine that the years of drinking and troubles had worn him down.

Ten years later, in Atlanta, Will's brother, John Alexander Gum, Jr., who was only a year younger than Will, would show himself to be a strong and handsome man. At the time Will died, however, he was likely thin and worn, being almost unrecognizable from handsome young man who had once courted Clemmie Baugh.

Whatever his children felt about their father, he was had been their only parent for the last ten years; the one link to their mother and the big house on East Main. Now, he was gone. Dressed in his dark suit, he would lie still and at peace in a pine box, laid in the front parlor of the little house on Maney Avenue. Will's brothers and sisters would all come to look at him and pay their respects. None of them could truly know what Will's five children had endured over the last decade.

We can imagine Mary, Emmett, Frank, Will W. and Allie standing before the coffin, looking down at their father. What memories, happy or sad, what tears or lack of, what prayers offered up that night before his burial will never be known. Frank, looking at his younger brother Allie, may have felt a sadness for him, and, then, for Will W., too. They could not remember any other life than the one they had with their father.

The three eldest Gums had memories of happiness and security, for they shared a past in the big house when Ma was alive and well, and when Pa was someone they looked up to. Then, Grandmammie was alive; the protective angel watching over them. Mammy Ran was in the kitchen cooking, always there with a chuckle and a sweet and a tender pat on the back. Those hands had seemed safe to come to with the little falls and tears. That was before they knew what trouble was. Will and Allie scarcely had memory of that.

Never again would Will Gum come in the door with alcohol on his breath and a scowl on his face, yelling at them for nothing at all. No more fear. Oh, the feeling of strange sadness and helplessness when those who were most powerful in our lives are suddenly rendered weak, and then, gone; when all our complaints about them mean nothing. Then is the true lesson of life learned. Perhaps the greatest loss is the person you never really got to have. Now that period of their life—with all its resentments and regrets—was over.

With all the troubles of Will's life, there were still tears to be shed, for, perhaps without knowing it, his life had been so much less than it could have been for the once energetic, good-looking, young man who was full of ideas and who had promised himself he would do better.

On the day of the wake, there was music in the little house. Then, Will's brothers and sisters gathered around to remember the days when Will was a young man, his antics and things he did that would help the children to know who their father had been. But bitterness would prevail. Will Gum was not one of the memories they handed down to their children.

The next day was the service at Evergreen Cemetery. Will was laid to rest next to his only wife, Clemmie W. Gum. He had known many people during his life and his funeral may have had a fairly large gathering. That day, Emmett was there with tears in his eyes. A few feet from his father's fresh grave was the grave of the beautiful Joe Miller; two such deep wounds of different kinds.

Following the burial, Emmett headed to Maney Avenue to visit with baby Mildred, now two. Her sweet coos brought sunshine into his life. Before long, Emmett would leave Tennessee, never to return.

Following the funeral, Aunt Nannie's husband, Uncle Edwin Rion, went to court and was appointed "guardian for Frank Avent Gum, Will Wade Gum and Allie Richardson Gum, minor children." His bond was $1,000.[62] From now on, he would also represent them in regards to their estate.

A few months after Will's death, in March of 1907, Frank Avent Gumm turned twenty-one. Several weeks later, in April, he appeared in court and received a final settlement for the money which had been held in an account.[63]

~

After the passing of their father, Mary and Will W. began to attend St. Paul's Church regularly, and decided to become official members. Since Frank first began singing at the Episcopal Church back in 1897, his siblings had often attended St. Paul's rather than the Cumberland Presbyterian Church, but perhaps while their father was alive, they had not felt free to change churches.

On May 10, 1907, Will Wade Gumm was baptized along with several other new members. Mary Gumm and Mrs. Robinson stood as witnesses for him. Mary and Will were not the only members of the Cumberland Presbyterian Church to join the Episcopal Church that day. There were several other Cumberland Presbyterian Church members joining as well.

That same day, Mary and Will Gumm were confirmed by the Bishop of Gailor, along with the other former members of the Presbyterian Church, who were possibly friends of theirs: Miss Rachel Johnson, Miss Rosalina Soffentius, Mr. Eugene Joseph Sebastian and Edwin Mason.[64] John Henry Diley served as Clergyman for this event and Mary and Mrs. Robinson stood up as witnesses for Will W. Gumm. Signing the church register, Will now spelled his name with two *m*'s.

In October, Frank Gumm stood as a witness for the baptism for two year-old Frank Waldron Alexander, the son of Eugene Alexander. He also stood as a witness for a two month-old Howard L. Burgdorf. Frank Gumm was an integral part of the church at this point, and likely a member of the choir as well.

After returning to Murfreesboro, there is no record of any interaction between the Darrows and young Frank, though they likely spoke to one another at church. Perhaps, Mr. Darrow was not pleased that Frank had left Sewanee early. In addition, the Gumm family was considered lower class; not acceptable among the society of the Darrows and their friends. Meanwhile, the Darrows were dealing with a tragedy of their own, one that began only a few months prior to the time Frank was sent to Sewanee.

~

Tempe Darrow's Swope relatives were an odd and intense group of people. Tempe's uncle, William Carter Swope, lived on a large plantation in Courtland, Alabama known as Rocky Castle. Living with him were his wife, Mary Wesley Carter, and their four children: Annie, Clay, Tempe and Carter.

In February of 1899, a huge storm was brewing, but Mary Carter Swope had decided she wanted to buy something in town and, against all protests, would not be deterred. The servants absolutely refused to take the one-seat phaeton and ride to town, so, in a passion Mary jumped into the phaeton and rode off.

With the intense rain coming down, the local creek rose in a flash flood. Mary was swept away and drowned. Left behind were her grief stricken husband, William, three young children and a baby. In later years, there would be stories of the "Blue Lady" down in Courtland, Alabama who haunted Rocky Castle, crying as she looked for the four children she left behind. Eventually, this "castle" was razed.[65]

William Swope moved the children to his parent's plantation in Mississippi. Then, in 1907, William died. By now, two of the children, Annie and Clayton, were adults, but the youngest two, Tempe, who was fifteen, and her little brother, Charles Carter, eight, still needed to be cared for. The Darrows brought Tempe and Carter to Oak Manor, but they quickly decided that raising young Carter would be too much for them.

Although no child below the age of ten was accepted at the Sewanee Grammar School, Mr. Darrow, with his connections to the school, made arrangements for the eight year-old to attend. Carter was delivered to Sewanee, and was soon wearing a tiny version of the military uniform and carrying a little wooden rifle.[66]

From the Soule College Yearbook

Meanwhile, Tempe, now nearly a young woman, was enrolled in Soule College, Murfreesboro's finest school for the education of young women. Her life would be filled with parties and travel. Later, the Darrows adopted her and willed her their entire estate. Carter, however, remained an orphan, receiving nothing other than his fine education.

~

Sometimes on his way to work, Frank stopped in front of the Byrn house, which was surrounded by a beautiful garden. Enjoying the view, he would often see Mr. Bryn's daughter, Annie, playing outside and stop to talk to her. Annie, Mrs. A.R. Richardson's lovely granddaughter, was a beautiful little girl with golden curls. Perhaps Frank told her how he used to live there, and play on the very same grounds when he was a child. It must have seemed so awfully long ago. Like his godfather, Mr. Darrow, Frank may have dreamed that one day he too would own a house like the Bryns' home, and mingle with the best people in town.

Walking two blocks to the Square, Frank passed the statue of the Confederate soldier and, then, turning right, walked half a block north. A few doors off the square, just before reaching College Street, Frank entered the lobby of the Princess Theatre, a two-story building of medium size and elegance. It was not a large theatre for city standards, but quite a nice size for Murfreesboro. Frank played organ for the silent pictures and sometimes entertained the audience with song.

Now that he was back in Murfreesboro, Frank connected with many old friends, and made new ones as well. Persons who remembered him later described him as "always happy" and "laughing." The ladies considered him "handsome and very, very charming ... He had dark hair, dark

Annie Bryn Roberts.
(Courtesy James R. Roberts)

eyes and was of medium height, medium build." Another friend noted that, "he was well-read, a good conversationalist. I couldn't say enough nice things about him."[67]

Frank's wonderful voice got him invited to a lot of parties. As one lady explained, "In those days, young people didn't date the way they do now, but on a Sunday afternoon the whole crowd got together, usually at one of the girl's houses."[68] It was said that the music began when Frank arrived. At some gatherings among family and friends, Frank, Mary, Will and Allie all sang together. [69]

In 1907, the Tennessee Baptist College for Women had just opened. They often had parties and it was not long before Frank was invited to attend one of these events. It was a chance to have fun and meet some of the prettiest girls in town.

At one of the Tennessee Baptist College parties, Frank found himself smitten by a beautiful, southern belle, eighteen year-old Nene White. Nene was an exotic looking girl with beautiful long, dark hair and black eyes. In fact, she was so exotic looking that some suggested she might have Indian blood—a thought she would have scorned.[70]

Nene was majoring in music at the college, and when Frank heard her sing, he knew it was meant to be. Together, they sang amazing duets. For her part, Nene thought Frank had the most beautiful voice she had ever heard.

Nene White in 1915 on her wedding day. (Courtesy Gloria Shacklett Christy)

After they had known one another a short time, Frank asked her to marry him.[71]

Raised by her grandmother, Nene was serious about her Baptist upbringing and beliefs. During this period, much of Murfreesboro was dry, considering alcohol the work of the devil. After the fatal addictions to alcohol that many of Rutherford County's early citizens suffered, including Frank Gumm's own great, great grandfather, Norton Gum, this is not surprising.

Frank, however, was a young man of high spirits, who enjoyed parties and enjoyed taking a drink. Perhaps it was in his blood, alcohol making him feel exceptionally well, but Miss White did not approve. In response to his proposal, she told him, "no." Frank adored her, and begged her over and over to be "his girl," but to no avail. As fond as she was of him, for who could not be fond of Frank, she knew he was not the man for her. And that was that.

Heartbroken at having been turned down by the girl he thought was meant to be his wife; Frank was ready to move on.

Chapter 22

Mr. W.D. Fox & Tullahoma

BETTIE GUM'S FATHER-IN-LAW, WILLIAM FOX, WAS WHAT THEY CALLED "black Irish." He immigrated to the United States from Ireland during the Great Famine (1845–1852), during which over a million Irish citizens died.[72] It is said that William Fox came to Tennessee because of the cattle business "trade in stock" that he had with Nathan Bedford Forest.[73]

In the mid-1800s, William Fox moved to Rutherford County where he met his wife, Tennessee Rowton, who was also of Irish descent. The couple was married August 20th, 1859 and had eight children: William R. born in 1860; Henry Lee, 1863; Maggie, 1865; Walter Dennis, 1870; Kate, 1872; Thomas, 1875, and Joseph, 1878. Another child, John, died when he was a few years old. The eldest son, William R. Fox, made an excellent name for himself beginning in 1884 as the proprietor of a livery, feed and sale stables just off the Murfreesboro square.[74] By 1900, some of the William and Tennie's children had moved away, and some, like their eldest son, William R., had died.

Bettie and her husband, Henry Lee, seemed happy enough. After working in the banking business in Nashville, Henry Lee Fox joined his brother-in-law, Edwin T. Rion, in the insurance business. They opened an office for the Rion & Fox General Insurance Company in a building just off the Murfreesboro Square.

Henry Lee was well-respected in Murfreesboro. To locals, he was known simply as "The Colonel." He and Bettie were active in the First Methodist Church, where Henry Lee served as trustee, steward and, later,

1905 Calendar for the Rion & Fox Insurance Co. Ed Rion, Jr. and Stewart Fox, son of W.D. Fox. (Courtesy Nancy Lee Dismukes)

chairman of the board for the congregation.

"The Colonel" was a high-ranking Mason and a charter member of Al Mynah Shrine Temple. He was made a Master Mason in 1896. In 1897 and 1898, he was worshipful master of Mount Moriah Lodge No. 18 in Murfreesboro. In 1900, he was "exalted" in Pythagoras Chapter No. 150, Royal Arch Masons and in 1904 became a member of Murfreesboro Commander No. 10 Knights Templar. Henry Lee returned to the banking business in Nashville around 1905, and while there, received the Scottish Rite degrees.[75] Throughout his life, he would remain active with the Masons.

Henry Lee Fox in the 1940s.

On Frank Gumm's alumni paper for the University of the South at Sewanee, his brother, Will, noted that Frank was a Mason. Frank probably became a Mason during the time he lived with the Fox family, with Henry Lee as his sponsor.

Although no one in the family knew for sure, it was suspected that Henry Lee Fox was a member of the Klu Klux Klan. It seemed that every time something with the Klan occurred, Henry Lee was not at home.

Bettie Fox stayed at home and took care of the children. She also kept busy with social, church and charitable activities. The Fox family had a cook and a maid to help with the care of the house. No white family in Murfreesboro at this time, even one with a fairly modest income, would

Bettie Gum Fox.
(Courtesy Aaron Todd)

think of doing their own shopping or cooking.

Along with the high energy of the Gums, Bettie Fox had inherited the generous and caring side of this family. She had a great desire to help those in need. In future years, Bettie Fox would be among the first to help organize a chapter of the American Red Cross in Rutherford County.[76] She was also the first woman social worker in Tennessee, traveling into the hills outside Murfreesboro, to places where houses were built with sticks and boards, and had no running water or heat. It was Bettie's job to see that the children in these place had the medical care they needed, food to eat, and were attending school.

One of the stories that Bettie love to tell, and which family members often repeated, involved a visit to the hills outside Murfreesboro where many of the poorer people survived by making moonshine. Bettie was visiting one of these small houses in the hills one day when she noticed that the baby was teething. When she asked the father whether the child was eating, he replied, "It helps if you put a little whiskey on the bisket."[77]

There would also be a time in later years when the Colonel decided to go to California "for his health."* One day he just disappeared, leaving Bettie in charge of the family. He was gone a long time; a year or more. Then one day, he reappeared at dinnertime (lunch), sat down at the table

* Some family members say he may have had tuberculosis.

and said, "Mrs. Fox, will you please pass the butter." Such was life in the Fox household.[78]

With all the adults and children living in the Fox home, there was always something going on. Jack was full of fun, Martha, even at two and three, was a little lady. But it was eleven year-old Anna Lee, who particularly impressed Frank. She was a very lively, funny girl, who said whatever came into her head, and usually it was something very clever. Frank, who had inherited the Gum's humorous streak, must have enjoyed living with this very entertaining family.

Sometime around 1905, Henry Lee Fox went to work for the City Savings Bank of Nashville. In next year or so, Bettie and the children followed him to Nashville, where by 1910, they were living at 106 9th Avenue South.

While living with his Aunt Bettie and Uncle Henry Lee, Frank became acquainted with the Colonel's eclectic brother, Walter Dennis Fox. Walter D. or "Walt," as he was called by his family and friends, was a real estate man who had married into the much respected Ewing family. Walt's mother-in-law, Ada Ewing, owned the Princess Theatre on the Square, and hired Frank as manager of the theatre. Frank must have been quite happy in this job. Folks later recalled seeing him during this time, as he walked through the streets of Murfreesboro, whistling or singing on his way to work.

The former Princess Theatre.

All the members of the Colonel's family were colorful characters, but perhaps none were more colorful than Walter Dennis Fox. Henry Lee was tall and thin; a serious fellow with a dry sense of humor. His younger brother, Walter

Dennis was truly a handsome man with full lips, dark hair, and dark, intense eyes.

Walter D. Fox was educated at the University of Kentucky, after which he attended Jennings Business College in Nashville. Like his older brother, Walt worked in Nashville for a time, in the very responsible position of secretary for the Nashville Railway & Light Company.

While Walter D. Fox was extremely good businessman, his real distinction was his interest in the theater. Walt was a playwright. His most notable play was a tribute to Tennessee's hero, Sam Davis, a play written entirely in Shakespearean verse. His other plays, such as "The Harlequin of Dreams," "Jean Lafitte," and "Passing the Love of Women" were mainly romantic and historical plays. In addition, he had written a few short stores and poems.

Aside from his work as a dramatist, Walter Fox was a whirlwind of energy. In the twenty years since his graduation from school, he had worked as a bookkeeper for the first National Bank, managed the Murfreesboro Waterworks, and was a writer and editor for the *Murfreesboro Free Press*, a newspaper founded in 1878 whose motto was "The Greatest Good to the Greatest Number." Under Walter D. Fox's leadership, the periodical became a respected newspaper.[79]

In 1892, Walter Fox won the hand and heart of Josie Ewing, one of the most sought after "belles" in Murfreesboro. Beautiful Josie, with her blonde hair and blue eyes, is said to have had men coming to court her in "droves."[80]

After the wedding, Walt moved into the Ewing family mansion on High Street. Also living in the home was Josie's beautiful mother, the former Ada Byron Hord and Josie's paternal grandfather, Judge E.H. Ewing. Josie's father had passed away two years before the couple married.

At the time, there was nothing unusual about Walter D.'s moving into his wife's family home. As stated by Mrs. Ridley, one of Judge Ewing's granddaughters, in her book *Falling Stars*, after the "War Between the States," many extended members of a family would live together, and the Ewings, with their large home, were used to this.

In 1894, Josie gave birth to a son, J.E. Fox. A little over a year later, Josie died giving birth to their daughter, Margaret. Three years after Josie's death, little J.E. died of typhoid fever.[81]

Walt and his daughter, Margaret, continued to live with his mother-in-law and Judge Ewing. With the entire family under one roof, and Walt constantly busy with real estate and writing, daughter Margaret was well taken care of and able to receive all the love and attention she needed.

In 1900, the Soule College for Women decided to put on one of Walter D. Fox's plays and invited him to direct it. Sarah Antoinette Bell, a senior student from Augusta, Georgia was cast in one of the roles. Not long after this, Sarah and Walt fell in love. On June 12th, almost immediately after Sarah's graduation, the couple was married. Sarah was eighteen and Walt, thirty-two. As the new Mrs. Fox, Sarah joined Walter D. under the Ewing's roof.

In later years, Sarah would tell her children about living in the Ewing home. Each night at dinner, old Judge Ewing, would quiz her about what she knew.[82] Judge Ewing, whose grandparents were among the first settlers in Nashville, was born in 1809. He became a licensed attorney in 1830 and a partner of James P. Grundy. Now nearly ninety, Judge Ewing often spoke of the history he had lived through and the historic figures who had been his friends, men like Daniel Webster and Francis Fogg.[83] Somehow, Sarah managed not to be too intimated by the old Judge.

In 1902, Sarah Fox gave birth to her first child, a son, Stewart Bell Fox. That same year, on April 24th, old Judge Ewing passed away. These events, along with other factors would lead to further changes for the Fox family.

In 1903, Ada Ewing found that the big, house on High Street, which had been built in 1856, needed far more repairs than she could afford to make. Mrs. Ewing owned two-thirds of the property, which included a four acre estate and Walter D. Fox's daughter, eight year-old Margaret Fox, owned the other third. Ada Ewing wished to sell the estate to W.D. Mooney, former headmaster of the Battleground Academy in Franklin. Mooney was preparing to open a school in Murfreesboro, and he wanted to buy the estate and use the house both as his residence and a school while he built a larger school on East Main Street.[84]

Because Margaret was a minor, it was necessary that she be represented by a guardian ad Litem in the sale. Ada Ewing and W.D. Fox went to court to settle this matter.[85] Once the sale was finalized, Walter D. Fox, his wife, Sarah, and the new baby moved into a small house nearby. Mrs. Ewing and Margaret became boarders in one of the mansions on East Main.

Walter Dennis Fox.
(Courtesy of The Knights of Pythias)

Sometime around 1908, Walter D. Fox ventured out to the countryside and crossed the border down into Coffee County, in the area of Tullahoma. Here, he made a surprising discovery. Traveling down winding roads that once had been Indian trails, crossing over hills and streams, Walt happened upon something unlike anything he had seen in Tennessee. Standing a hillside, he heard the rushing of water. Looking below, he saw a paradise of waterfalls and vivid greenery beyond imagination. Walt decided to call this place, "Ovoca" for the River Ovoca in County Wicklow, Ireland, where his family had originated.[86] As a man of literature, he thought of a poem by Thomas Moore, *The Meeting of the Waters*:

There is not in the wide world a valley so sweet,
As that vale in whose bosom the bright waters meet.

Seeing the beauty and peace in this spot, Walt, in his way, began to think of what good this land could do for others. He had suffered the loss of a spouse, and now he imagined Ovoca as a place of peace and healing for the widows and orphans of the Knights of Pythias, a fraternal organization to which he belonged.

The Fraternal Order of The Knights of Pythias was founded after the Civil War. Its purpose was to reconcile the brothers of the North and South through works of common charity and brotherhood. Some of the principles of the Phythians include making "Benevolence, Kindness, Generosity and Tolerance a reality."

In 1904, Walter D. Fox had been given the position, Keeper of the Records and Seals for the Knights of Pythias in Tennessee.[87] On approaching the members of the organization, they agreed that building a home for the widows and orphans of the Knights would be a project which they would fund, and which he could oversee.

The Knights raised the money to build the homes. By late 1908, plans had moved forward. Walt and Sarah were ready to move to Tullahoma, just a few miles from Ovoca. From here, Walt would supervise the building of the Ovoca village.

~

How Frank Gumm began his association with Walter D. Fox is unknown. Walt's family was under the impression that the two men started a newspaper together. Although there is no evidence of this, Walter D. was the editor of the *Murfreesboro Free Press*, so it seems likely that this was the paper on which they worked together.

Walter D. Fox moved his family, which now included seven year-old Stewart and a new baby, Josephine, to a rented house on Polk Street. His thirty-six year-old unmarried sister, Katherine, joined them. At what point Frank was offered a job as Walt's secretary is not known, but it appears the Gumm family was ready for a change.

Frank Gumm was now twenty-three years old and had been out of school for nearly four years. His father was dead, Emmett was living in Michigan, and Will, now twenty, had moved to Port Beat, Mississippi, where he was working as a Depot Agent for the railroad. Sixteen year-old Allie had left school and was working. Neither Frank nor Mary had found the person they wanted to marry. In fact, Mary, at twenty-nine, was likely considered an old maid and had little hope of marriage.

Murfreesboro was really just a small farm town, which had an opinion of all of the Gums, both because of their father and other things they could scarcely know about. The idea of leaving town with the cultured and well-educated Walter D. Fox may have been just the thing. It would be Frank Gumm's ticket to a new life.

The polite society of Rutherford County has its own customs and formalities, some of which persist today. Persons intending to do business inquire first of the other person's well-being and that of their family. When that conversation has been completed, they begin their talk of business. In 1909, the formalities would have been more marked, and when Frank Gumm was asked if he would be interested in accepting a position as Walter D. Fox's secretary, he would have responded in a manner equally formal.

"Sir, it would be a most favorable position. I would be pleased and honored to accept it."

As an educated Sewanee man, Frank Gumm had to be impressed with Walter D. Fox. For three years in a row, Mr. Fox had been listed in the *Who's Who of America*. Working for him was an honor.

Frank may have moved to Tullahoma earlier than previously thought. As evidence for this, the Rutherford County Tax Record Book shows that for the year 1908, F.A. Gumm of the 6th Ward owed a poll tax of $1 and a school tax of $2. His record is marked "unpaid." The logical reason for this would be the fact that Frank was no longer living in Murfreesboro.

By late 1908, or early 1909, the Gumms had rented their home, packed their belongings and left for Tullahoma.

~

Tullahoma lies approximately 45 miles south of Murfreesboro, 26 miles from Sewanee and 14 miles from Winchester, where Uncle Joe Baugh once lived. Uncle Joe had past away in 1901. Cousins Ashton and Henry Baugh were now living in Birmingham, Alabama. Ida and her husband, John Hannah, had moved to Muskogee, Oklahoma, for Ida's health. Cousin Emma, who was married to Fred Whittlesly, had six children, and was living in Minnesota.

In 1909, Tullahoma was a busy town. It had grown greatly following the Civil War, mainly because of the railroad which transported goods to and from the town. Besides this, Tullahoma was known both for its educational institutions and its spas. Travelers came from all over to treat illnesses and improve health in the hot springs. The Jack Daniels whiskey factory was twelve miles south.[88] There were also many factories springing up in the area. In the future, sporting goods such as baseballs and mitts would be made in Tullahoma.

During the early 1900s, Tullahoma was a happening place. Although the downtown area had been destroyed by fire four times in the 1890s, it was now completely rebuilt. The town, built on flat land, boasted that its Main Street was the widest street in America. The railroad ran down the middle of Main Street. The depot, where trains stopped to pack and unload many times a day, kept the town extremely busy.

Gumm home in Tullahoma. (Courtesy Margaret Collier)

The Gumms rented a house at 207 E. Lincoln Street, a couple of blocks from Main Street and the railroad. Directly across from their new residence was St. Barnabas Episcopal Church, which looked like a miniature copy of the stone buildings at Sewanee. The house itself was a small, white frame cottage with two bedrooms, a parlor, a kitchen and front porch. The Gumms were located conveniently to the Walter D. Fox, being just around the corner, from their residence on Polk Street.*

Allie Gumm was able to procure a job as "express rider," spending half his the time in Tullahoma and the other half as a boarder in their old home in Murfreesboro. The job seems to have entailed delivered things between the two towns. When the census taker came to Murfreesboro in 1910, he caught Allie at home on Maney Ave. Then, when the census taker in Tullahoma arrived at the Lincoln Street home, Allie was there.

Mary set about making the little cottage a home, cleaning, hanging curtains and putting up a few pictures. She kept house for Frank and Allie. Perhaps in her spare time, she joined the ladies church organization of the St. Barnabas.

Frank Gumm joined the St. Barnabas Church Choir and by the time he left Tullahoma, he was choir director. Although a later article claimed he was the choir director for the First Christian Church, that church has no record of Frank Gumm and was across town, a good distance on foot from where the Gumms lived.

During this time, St. Barnabas choir had a quartet, of which Frank Gumm was a member. The quartet was quite popular, and in addition to singing for church services, the group was also hired to sing at parties.

Ever social and full of energy, Frank wasted no time getting around, meeting people and seeing the lay of the land. Singing was something he could not do

* Due to the fact that the street numbers had been changed and no one knew the formula, the author was unable to find and photograph the Fox residence.

without; it was a passion. Once word got out about Frank's beautiful voice, which had developed into a rich high baritone, he was in demand. Along with the quartet's activities, he was found jobs as a soloist at the local movie theatres. Comments about Frank in Tullahoma concur with those in Murfreesboro, "his voice, once heard, was not something easily forgotten."

The first time the Gumms saw Ovoca, they must have been amazed. From Lincoln Street, they traveled two miles in a horse-drawn carriage. Traveling along a winding trail, a sudden veer in the road took them down a country path that rolled with deep dips and rises. It was beautiful country. The burble of springs mingled with the sound of songbirds, and the air was sweet with fragrant leaves and wild vegetation.

After a mile or so, the path along the edge of a hill opened into a wider area of rolling hills. Adjacent to the road, a bubbling stream flowed beneath ancient trees. Here, the carriage stopped, the occupants got out and walked up the hill.

With Walt as their guide, the Gumms followed until they heard the sound of rushing water. There below, Walt pointed out a tropical paradise

undreamed of, with waterfalls amidst rocks, ponds and brilliant, green vegetation. Ovoca was truly an amazing place.

Rising above the waterfall, were rolling hills. Walt showed them where the homes, hospital and school were going to be built. A group of men were now in the process of clearing the land and leveling off the portions where the buildings would be constructed. Altogether, Ovoca comprised 400 acres of land. In addition to the waterfall and stream, there was also a large lake with several ponds. It was pristine land, practically untouched since the Indians had hunted and camped there.[89]

Plans for Ovoca included a number of homes for widows, a home for orphans and a central hall. In addition, there were to be summer cottages which could be rented by the Knights of Pythias for their families. Walt was having a home built on the site for his family. He had decided this was the place he wanted to raise his children. In addition, the workmen were building fences and a grand stone entrance.

During the day, Frank Gumm took care of the duties for the Knights of Pythias, traveling between town and Ovoca fairly often. Since Walter D. was still editor of the *Murfreesboro Free Press*, Frank also had a hand in that. This may have been his first effort and education in writing for a newspaper—something he would do fairly consistently over the next twenty years. Being around Walter D. Fox was an education. It was one Frank wanted to take full advantage of. He had certainly met his match in education, energy and creativity.[90]

Ed Rion was a member of the Knights of Pythias and in the summer of 1909 or 1910, Nannie Rion, her children, Ed, 9, and new baby, Virginia, along with some other family members came to Ovoca on vacation. It was nice for Frank, Mary and Allie to have this relaxed time to visit. It was a custom the Rion and Fox families would continue long after the Gumms were gone.

Living in Tullahoma, Frank was much closer to Sewanee than he had been in Murfreesboro. His thoughts may often have turned to the happy days at his Alma Mater. He may even have gone to visit, but at this point his old friend, Henry Gass, was studying at the University of Oxford in England, on a Rhodes scholarship, the first student from Sewanee to receive such an honor. If Frank regretted leaving school

The Rions on vacation in Ovoca about 1913, Nannie (center), Virgina to her right, and Ed, Jr. far right. Other two ladies may be Gums or Wades. (Courtesy of Nancy Lee Dismukes)

before graduation, he was not one to linger or mourn over what might have been. With the energy inherited from his Gum and Baugh lines, he was looking for new opportunities.

Starting life afresh in another town was fun for Frank. After a local talent agent heard him sing, he received numerous jobs, both private parties and theatre performances. Young, handsome, and full of energy, it seemed the sky was the limit.

Frank would always have a flare for the theatrical and ambitions for the stage. Though he never seemed to feel free enough to throw caution to the wind and risk all for a career on the stage, Frank was continually drawn in that direction. Every person who heard him sing thought he was one of the most exciting performers they had ever seen. "There he goes, singing down the street," folks in Tullahoma would remark.[91]

Meanwhile, in the spring of 1910, the Gumm siblings decided to sell the house at Walnut and Burton their father, Will, had bought as an investment property. On March 25th, they sold it to R.A. Rushing and wife for $2,000.[92] (= $46,205) This meant that each member of the family would receive a nice amount of money.

Nannie Gum Rion with daughter, Virginia, and son, Edwin Rion, Jr. circa 1913.
(Courtesy of Nancy Lee Dismukes)

~

Much has been made of Frank Gumm's departure from Tullahoma and the south. It has been suggested that he got into some kind of trouble or was asked to leave. While these rumors may be true, no information concerning their truth has been found, and the events, as they occurred, were not as previously described.

Frank Gumm had come to town to work with his Uncle's brother, a job which may have been temporary. By 1911, Walter Fox had completed his home at Ovoca and moved his family from Polk Street in Tullahoma to the new house in the country. At this point, it is possible that Walter D. Fox no longer needed Frank's services. Frank certainly did not want to live in the country. Likely, he was ready to move on, expand his boundaries and fulfill his dreams.

~

Following Joe Miller's death, Robert Emmett Gumm had gone through a very difficult time. Joe Miller's mother, Elmyra, or "Mur" as she was called, had taken over the care of Mildred. Without the responsibility of his child, at a certain point, Emmett fled his painful memories.

Sometime between 1905 and 1909, Emmett traveled north in search of work and a new life. According to family stories, he found some work in vaudeville. Eventually, he ended up in Chicago, where he took a job as a soda jerk. It was here that he met a young woman who caught his attention.[93] She certainly was not beautiful in the way Joe Miller had been. She was strong and angular, and—perhaps, what attracted him most of all—she was funny.

Emma Belle Smith was born in Montana in the late 1880s. She didn't like to say her age, and when she pronounced her maiden name she said, "Smythe" because, as she put it, "Smith" was "too common."[94] Belle was about twenty-one when she met Robert Emmett Gumm.[95] He felt secure with Belle and asked her to marry him. They were married sometime around 1910.

As a Southerner moving North, Emmett was ready to change his life. For one thing, he no longer used the name "Emmett." Perhaps Belle disliked the name, but for whatever reason, from here on he would be known as Robert E. Gumm or "Bob."

Robert found a job selling soap for the N.K. Fairbanks Company.[96] The brand he sold was called "Sunday, Monday," probably because in those days most people took their baths only on the weekends. As a traveling soap salesman, Bob's job took him to Ironwood, a busy mining town. By 1910, Bob and Belle were happily settled in this prosperous area.[97]

Frank and Robert Emmett had always been close. Of all the Gumm siblings, they were closest in age and interests. After Robert left Tennessee, the two brothers kept in touch, despite the distance between them. Even so, they missed the camaraderie of the old days. Now, while Frank was trying to decide what his next step would be, Robert suggested that the family come up to Ironwood for a visit, and to meet Belle.

That January, Robert Gumm had purchased the Eagle Restaurant and renamed it "The Eagle Café." The cafe was situated on the main street of town, Aurora Street, and Bob had great hopes for it. The local paper reported that this was not his first experience in the restaurant business. Bob told Frank there were a lot of opportunities up in Ironwood. The town even had four theatres with live entertainment.

So, early in March of 1911, Frank, Allie and Mary boarded a train and headed north. Along the way, they may have stopped in Vincennes, Indiana to visit their Uncle Jack Baugh who had recently relocated there.

Since the 1890s, one by one, the members of Jack Baugh's family had left Murfreesboro. The south, particularly Rutherford County, was still in a state of depression from the Civil War. Uncle Jack had remained behind until 1907, when the family farm was sold. Then, Murphy George brought his father, who was now old and penniless, to live with him. In September of 1911, Murphey would marry Katherine Cunningham.

Traveling north must have been a great adventure for the Gumms. Once again, with the exception of their brother Will, the entire family would be together.

Life in Ironwood was certainly different from life down south. In March, it was already warm down in Tullahoma, but when Frank, Allie and Mary arrived in Ironwood, it was still winter. The family enjoyed seeing "Emmett," meeting Belle, and experiencing life up north. Frank and Mary were favorably impressed—enough to consider moving to Ironwood. Allie, however, decided that he would rather stay in the south.

Nearly nineteen, Allie was ready to set off on his own, but he would not be alone. Brother Will had recently moved just south of the Tennessee border to Huntsville, Alabama. He wrote Allie that the town, which originally had been a prosperous cotton town, was quite busy and had many job opportunities, so Allie made a decision to join Will, the brother he was closest to.

Returning to Tullahoma, the Gumms packed up their belongings. Then, Frank and Mary traveled north, and Allie, south. Before Frank left Tullahoma, he made sure to leave his new address with the school at Sewanee—Ironwood, Michigan.

~

After Frank left, Walter D. Fox continued with his plans, completing much of his dream village for widows and orphans. In the spring of 1912, less than a year after the Gumms departed, Walt caught influenza. He was laid up for a week. Then, for three agonizing days, his family watched as he sank into a final sleep. He was forty-two years old. He left behind a young wife, and three children. The youngest child, Walter Dennis, (who would later change his name to William), was eleven months old.

It was a terrible, sad shock for Frank, when he learned of Walt's death. Walter D. Fox was still a young man, a vital man with much to give. The tragedy of his early passing affected everyone who knew him.[98]

Mr. Fox's dream would be completed. The orphanage opened in 1918, and the property was used for the Knights of Pythias Widows and Orphans until 1976.

The year 1912 was one of great loss to the Murfreesboro Community. On April 24, 1912, Murfreesboro lost her most beloved citizen with the passing of seventy-six year-old Dr. J.B. Murfree. Dr. Murfree, probably the most beloved citizen in the town's history, had touched so many lives with his kindness and fine medical care. It is said that his funeral was the largest event ever seen in the town.

Two months later, on June 11th, Horace Palmer, who was now a Judge, passed away at the age of fifty-seven. Considered one of the most influential people in Murfreesboro, his early death was deeply mourned.

Dr. Murfree and Horace Palmer had been important in the lives of the Gumm children, but now, led by fate, they had all left Murfreesboro.

Chapter 23

Journey Away from Home

IRONWOOD WAS A SMALL, BUSTLING TOWN 18 MILES SOUTH OF LAKE Superior. The town bordered on Hanover, Wisconsin, separated from it only by the slender Montreal River. Ironwood owed its existence to the discovery of vast amounts of iron ore deposits in the hills. The railroad, which came to town in the 1880s, had been the town's lifeline to prosperity.

Frank and Mary settled at 125 E. Aurora Street, not far from Robert Emmett's Eagle Café at 109 Aurora. Eager for success, Frank was soon working as an office clerk for the Oliver Iron Mining Company.[99] As unlikely as the job seemed for someone with his vocal talents, Frank was intent on rising above his impoverished childhood and making money. In this prosperous town, where people looked for entertainment in their free time, it would not take him long to find a singing job as well.

Mary Gumm's life had also taken a new turn. Mary was engaged to be married. Her suitor was a man six years older than her, a letter carrier from Murfreesboro named Oscar McPeak. Perhaps the two had met when he delivered mail to the Gumm home. It seems that their attachment had been formed prior to the Tullahoma move. Although Mary had not lived in Murfreesboro for at least two years, somehow their courtship continued.

Oscar McPeak came from a poor family. He was the son of Reverend Gervis McPeak, a farmer and Methodist minister. Gervis, who was born in Crittenden, Arkansas in 1837, came to Tennessee with his first

Rev. Gervis McPeak

wife, Elizabeth Powell, in the 1850s. Shortly giving birth to their son, Flavious, in 1858, Elizabeth died. When the Civil War began, Gervis returned to Arkansas and joined the Confederate Army.

After the war, in 1867, Gervis McPeak settled in Lebanon, Wilson County, Tennessee, where he married twenty-one year-old Lucy Ann Lannon. Gervis and Lucy had four children: Laura, born in 1869, Oscar, in 1874, Mabel, in 1878, and May, who was born in Mississippi, in 1890.[100]

Rev. McPeak was licensed to "preach the Word" in 1871. He would continue in his calling for the next forty years.[101] Meanwhile, the illnesses Rev. McPeak contracted during the Civil War (likely intestinal bugs among other aliments) continued to plague him. As time went by, his condition became so debilitating that, though he continued to preach, it was impossible for him to work. As a result, the McPeak children did not have an easy childhood. Rev. McPeak liked to say that they grew up "poorly, but honorably."[102] Late in life, he reported that on average he made no more than $150 a year. (= $3,878*)

Oscar's older, half-brother, Flavious, had been quite successful working for the Bank of Commerce in Nashville, where he handled stocks and bonds. In 1894, Flavious moved to Texas, where he continued to work with stocks and bonds. He also founded the Mount Olivet Cemetery in an area outside Fort Worth known as Arlington Heights.[103] Possibly, during these years Flavious helped his father financially from time to time.

During Oscar's childhood, the McPeaks lived in Mississippi, and then in Memphis where Rev. McPeak set out to preach the Gospel and save souls. By the late 1890s, the McPeaks had returned to middle Tennessee and settled in Carthage, where the local newspaper, *The Liberty Herald*, often reported on not only Rev. McPeak's preaching, but on the comings and goings of his son, Oscar.

---

* 2010 calculations come from http://www.westegg.com/inflation/

In 1897, *The Liberty Herald* reported a rather mysterious case involving Oscar McPeak. That September 2nd, the Lafayette Bank in Carthage was robbed. Missing was $12,000. Also missing were the casher, identified as William Beckwith, son of the late Judge, and the clerk, Oscar McPeak.[104] No further information has been found on this case, but shortly after this event, Oscar's sister, Laura, married William Beckwith. The marriage did not last long. It appears they divorced, and from that time on Laura used her maiden name.

The McPeak family eventually settled in Murfreesboro, and by 1910, were living on East Bell, several blocks north of East Main, and just around the corner from the Murfree sisters.

If Oscar had wanted to marry Mary Gumm prior to 1910, the financial situation of Rev. McPeak's home may have stood in the way. Oscar's earnings were probably something of a necessity for the family. By 1911, however, Oscar's oldest sister, Laura, was working in a dry goods store and his middle sister, Mabel, was married. Perhaps, at last, Oscar felt free to leave home. When Mary Gumm moved to Michigan, thirty-six year-old Oscar McPeak knew he would have to marry her, or, perhaps, never see her again.

There was one other reason Oscar may have finally agreed to wed Mary. If calculations are correct, by June of 1911, Mary Gumm was nearly three months pregnant. According to U.S. Postal records, one month before the marriage, on May 16th, 1911, Oscar resigned his position as a Murfreesboro letter carrier.

Oscar and Mary in 1918. (Courtesy of Bill Gibb)

The *Ironwood Times* reported, that on June 17th, "Mr. Oscar

McPeak of Murfreesboro and Miss Mary Gumm of this city were united in marriage at the home of the bride, 125 E. Aurora Street." Presiding over the ceremony was Rev. William B. Goombe, pastor of the First Methodist Church. Mary had agreed to marry in her husband's faith, rather than her own.

Mary, at thirty-one, had probably despaired of ever being married. Now, at last, her dream had come true. After the wedding, the happy couple left on a short honeymoon trip. When they returned, Oscar and his new brother-in-law, Robert E. Gumm, became partners in the Eagle Café.[105]

~

As mentioned previously, Frank spent his days working for the Oliver Iron Mining Company. Before long, he was spending his nights singing. The first time the citizens of Ironwood heard Frank Gumm sing, they took him to their hearts.

There were approximately five theaters in Ironwood, as well as an opera house. W.F. Kelly, who managed the Temple Theater, was always looking for the best talent. After hearing Frank Gumm sing, and seeing the audience's response, Kelly hired him. Frank lucked out with this job because Kelly managed not one theatre but five—two in Michigan, two in Wisconsin and one in Minnesota. The Temple Theatre in Ironwood was at 125 Aurora Street (not to be confused with 125 E. Aurora where Frank, Mary and Oscar lived).

Frank's nightly schedule was a tight one. He began the evening in Ironwood, singing "a couple of popular songs" before the start of the first picture show. Then, he would hurry out and hop a streetcar for the seven minute ride to the Temple Theatre in Hurley, Wisconsin, less than a mile away. After repeating his performance before another eager audience waiting for their picture show, Frank hopped back on the streetcar and returned to Ironwood, where he performed for a new audience, waiting for the second picture show. When the weather and business were good, Frank was asked to ride the streetcar out to a third theatre in Bessemer—a trip of seven miles.

W.F. Kelly's Temple Theatres were much larger and fancier than those Frank had performed in previously down south. Kelly's theatres, especially the one in Ironwood, were full-fledged theatres with an orchestra.

The May 9, 1945 Ironwood Times *claims that all the "big shots" were in this photo: A.L. Picker, Theodore Steinmetz, Fritz Steinmetz, W.F. Kelly, Walter Miles and Louis Guyer (the only one identified as 3rd from the left). Frank Gumm is fifth from the right with a light cap on his head (or 7th from the left). A poster in this photo is said to state that Frank Gumm is being featured in a song titled,* Then You'll Remember Me. *Unfortunately, an original of this photo has yet to be found.*

The Ironwood Temple Theatre orchestra was conducted by a fine musician, A.L. Picker.

Sometimes, Frank and another singer, Walter Miles, joined forces. Walter, who was described as a "wonderfully clever bass singer," like Frank, had a trained voice. Although he lived in Auburn, New York, with his wife and little girl, he made his living touring. According to the memory of a mutual friend of theirs, when Frank Gumm and Walter Miles sang together, they "brought down the house" with a "technique that made women and children cry." The friend also stated that "Men in the house were jealous of the 'Gumm–Miles' technique with women in singing sentimental songs."[106]

People who knew Frank during his time in Ironwood described him as a handsome man about 5′8″ and 140 pounds. His hair was dark and his eyes "brown, flecked with green."[107] He dressed simply in black, but wore a white collar and a light cap, which set him apart.

Bob, Frank and Mary, all happily ensconced in Ironwood, were pleased to learn that that down in Huntsville, Allie and Will were also doing well.

The brothers had joined forces and were rooming together just off the town square. For a time, both worked as clerks in the town square. Eventually, Will W. found a job with Mitchell Shoe Company, and Allie became a traveling salesman.[108] The brothers were happy sharing this new life together.

~

As auspicious as the beginnings in Ironwood seemed, they did not last long. By late summer, what had seemed a neat family arrangement was quickly unraveling. By now, Frank was managing Mr. Kelly's Temple Theatre in Ironwood. Mr. Kelly also had a theater in Duluth, Minnesota called "The Happy Hour Theatre." In early July, Frank traveled to Duluth, possibly on business for Mr. Kelly. In any case, now twenty-six and having saved some money, Frank decided that he wanted to have his own theatre.

Twenty-one miles west of Duluth, in the somewhat prosperous town of Cloquet, Frank found what he felt was a great investment. In July of 1911, Cloquet's newspaper, *The Pine Knot*, announced that F.A. Gumm was taking over the management of not one, but two theatres: the Bijou and the Diamond. Frank seemed to be intent on following in Mr. Kelly's footsteps. But Frank was not doing this just for himself. He had another idea; he planned to go into business with his brother, Robert.

Cloquet, which was incorporated as a village in 1884, had just become a city in 1905.[109] In 1910, with a population of 7,031, the city formed a consumer cooperative that would become one of the strongest in the nation. This may have been what drew Frank to the area.

Cloquet was also a divided city. The area built around the railroad and sawmills was rough. For the single male workers there were seventeen bars and a red light district.[110] The main part of the city centered around the church and family life. The 20th century was still young and a good percentage of people were suspicious of vaudeville and moving picture shows, considering them the same as burlesque, immoral forms of entertainment. Theatre owners often had to do a great deal of work to convince local citizens that their theater was entertainment for the family, and in no way immoral.[111]

On August 30th, the local paper announced that R.E. Gumm, who had been in the "theatrical business in Chicago," and was "connected with United Theatres Co." would arrive from that city on Monday. The new firm owned by F.A. & R.E. Gumm would be known as "Gumm Bros." Although Robert had worked for a theater company when he lived in Chicago, it seems this news story was one that Frank delivered to the paper in order to enhance their images for the citizens of Cloquet.

That same day, the local paper carried a long article about the plans for the Parlor and the Diamond theaters under their new ownership. The article was clearly written by Frank Gumm, who was in a hurry to get the word out and get business going. Frank mistakenly began the article with the impersonal "they" and concluded it personally with "we."

The Bijou was to be used as a "Photo playhouse" only. At this theater a new film would be shown every night. The Diamond Theatre was to be a moving picture and vaudeville house. There would be three reels of "good film subjects" and an illustrated or spotlight song every night. Admission would be 5 and 10 cents. Frank may have planned to do some of the performing himself.

In addition, the article announced that Mrs. Cora Metcalf, a well-known music teacher and pianist would play piano in the Bijou. Frank made it known that Mrs. Metcalf was the widow of a Mason with three small children to support. Being a Mason himself, he no doubt felt an added responsibility to help her. The article stated that Mrs. Metcalf would teach music to anyone who wished to learn. Besides piano, she offered lessons in violin, guitar, mandolin, banjo, trap drums and voice! The Metcalf family was living in the Wright Hotel.

Frank made it clear that the theatre intended to cater to the "younger set." There would be a children's matinee every Saturday afternoon, and a prize of $1.50 to the person arriving with the largest potato. (= $34.65) "The potatoes will be given to the poor," Frank writes.

To gain attendance, Frank concludes his article with many interesting offers including the fact that any lady accompanied by a person with a ticket on October 2nd would be given free admission. The news article took up an entire newspaper column and concluded with announcements for "amateur night" on Fridays and a "Dance" every Wednesday. As a final enticement, Frank writes, "A *new stunt will be pulled off—watch for it.*"

On September 9th, the *Ironwood News Record* announced that orchestra leader, A.L. Picker, who had been working at Mr. Kelly's Happy Hour Theater in Duluth, and would be "succeeding Frank Gumm" as manager of the Temple Theatre.

That September in Cloquet, Frank Gumm made a formal announcement on the front page of *The Pine Knot* informing the public of the Bijou's new management. Although the article states that Frank and Robert had purchased the theatres, in truth, they were only leasing them. Signing his announcement "Frank A. Gumm," he writes,

> "Nothing will be said or shown in this house that can possibly offend the most refined taste. We shall do everything in our power to please the people of Cloquet and beg of you a trial."[112]

Perhaps someone had warned Frank about the likes and dislikes of Cloquet's citizens. It seems clear that Frank was trying, in every way he could, to please the local citizens and gain their patronage. It would not take long for him to learn, however, that the average citizen in Cloquet was not easily convinced. Family men and local churches called for strict moral codes. Perhaps the large number of single men and the existence of the red light district mad them even more were suspicious of outsiders. Frank, with his southern accent and outgoing manner, did not fit in. Nevertheless, he kept trying.

The same day Frank Gumm's front page announcement appeared, there was an advertisement announcing the Bijou's upcoming acts. That week the Oberman Trio with monologue and singing was performing. The following week a vaudeville act known as "the Scotch Lassie and Her Lad," a singing, talking and dancing act by McDonald & Genereaux was set to perform. An article showing some sympathy for Frank Gumm also appeared. The author wrote,

> "Mr. Gumm impresses one as a very capable young man in his line of endeavor and most desirous of pleasing the theatre-going public of Cloquet."

Obviously, the citizens of Cloquet were quite particular, and Frank and his brother, Bob, were not having an easy time.

The October 7th paper announced that Mrs. R.E. Gum would be arriving in Cloquet the following Wednesday. Robert and Belle were boarding with Mrs. T.H. Bertram on Avenue D.[113]

"Have you noticed the class of pictures exhibited in the Diamond lately?" asked *The Pine Knot* of October 14th. Under the listings for the

Bijou Frank noted, "We show three new pictures every night with new music and singing. The prices are always 5 & 10 cents." Frank also advertises a popularity contest for Sunday evening, and adds that they will "have no public dances in the future." Apparently, there had been complaints.

Meanwhile, Robert had not fully settled his business in Ironwood. On October 28th, the *Ironwood Times* announced that Robert E. Gumm and Oscar McPeak had sold their interest in the Eagle Café to John Parent, who planned to have the Café open day and night.

The Gumms seem to have been thought of fondly in Ironwood. When Robert made a return visit, the paper announced that he was "traveling between Cloquet and Ironwood, trying to arrange things at both ends." It was not until early November that Robert and Belle finally settled over the East End bakery on Cloquet Avenue.[114]

Robert Gumm had seemed happy in Ironwood prior to the time his siblings arrived. How well he got along with Oscar McPeak is a matter for question. Robert sold the Eagle Café only months after Oscar became a partner. While Frank Gumm remained friendly with Oscar, so far as we know, once Robert and Oscar parted ways, there was never any interaction between them again.

On January 3, 1912, Mary's baby was born. The baby was a boy and his parents rejoiced. The baby's official name is not known. Mary simply referred to him as "Totsy."

Five months after leaving Ironwood, in March of 1912, Oscar was reinstated in his old job as letter carrier in Murfreesboro. Where he and Mary lived, or what Oscar did for employment between October and March is not known.

~

Frank Gumm, like his father, Will, so many years earlier, had big dreams. However, Frank was not a patient man and within months he found that the Cloquet venture was not going nearly as well as he had hoped. While Frank and Bob continued to book talent and advertise the shows, financially, the venture was a huge disappointment. As reported by *The Pine Knot*, on November 25th, to supplement his income, Frank had "taken a job as a stenographer in J.E. Dieson's law offices."[115]

There have been suggestions as to why Frank Gumm moved from place to place in his early adulthood. The fact is that during this time, much of America was on the move. With railway transportation at its height, new cities were springing up and there were plenty of jobs. All these things afforded the young, energetic and the adventurous new opportunities.

Although there may have been trouble for Frank in Cloquet, it also seems fairly clear that he found life in this small, restrictive town, not to his liking, and, financially, not viable. Finding a singing job in a larger city would be much more to his liking, and that is exactly what he did.

On December 16th, *The Pine Knot* announced that F.A. Gumm had given up his interest in the Cloquet Theatres. R.A. Fleischbein (who actually owned the theatres) and R.E. Gumm were forming a new company called, the Cloquet Amusement Company. The article noted that Frank Gumm made "a host of friends and won the hearts of theatre-goers with his excellent singing at the theatres." In conclusion, it was revealed that Frank was going to visit friends in Ironwood before he moved to Chattanooga, Tennessee, where he would "remain."

This article may have been a way of closing Frank Gumm's chapter in Cloquet and letting the citizens know that he was moving far away. Frank did visit his friends in Ironwood, a place where he would always be welcome, but he never went to Chattanooga.

Chapter 24

East or West

WHETHER FRANK EVER INTENDED TO GO TO CHATTANOOGA IS NOT known. He traveled east, over 160 miles, to visit friends in Ironwood. Then, retracing his tracks, he traveled west to Superior, Wisconsin, only 21 miles east of Cloquet. On the 16th of December, the Cloquet *Pine Knot* reported that Frank Gumm was "singing in a theater in Superior."

Built on the banks of Lake Superior, the city of Superior sat on the northwest tip of Wisconsin, just across the lake from Duluth, Minnesota. Traders had been traveling through the area since the early 1600s, but it was not until 1852 that the town was platted and the first log cabin built. The 1880s brought the discovery of iron ore in the nearby regions. Twenty years later, Superior was a bustling transportation hub, accessible by boat and train. Besides iron ore, the city had the means to transport high quantities of grain and timber.

Superior was certainly one of the busiest cities that far north. In 1910, the population had reached 37,643. With a good sized, working population and winters tempered by the lake affect, local citizens were always looking for entertainment. As a result, there were quite a few theatres where jobs could be had.

When Frank arrived in town, it was December, and, as fate would have it, he found that theatre owner, Ray Hadfield, needed a singer for his December shows. Six years earlier, Hadfield, who would later be referred to as "father of the movies" in Superior, had opened his first moving picture theatre in Duluth.[116] "Doc" and R.H. Hadfield, brothers, also owned several theatres in Superior, including the Orpheum on Tower Street. If things went well with Hadfield, Frank would be able to work his theater circuit and earn a living singing. But for now, Mr. Hadfield had a particular job in mind; he wanted Frank to pair with his newly hired, classically trained soprano, Maude Ayres.

In 1911, Maude Ayres was a lovely young woman of twenty. Born in Orange, New Jersey, her family moved to Superior when she was five years old. Maude had been singing publicly since her childhood. After graduating from high school, she traveled to New York where she studied music at Julliard. She and Frank hit it off right away and soon were singing a program of solos and duets for the Orpheum's Christmas season.

On December 20th, the *Superior Telegram* reported:

> Manager Hadfield's picture palace is now giving the best show that has ever been given in Superior. High class photoplays, two illustrated song singers, an orchestra, a pipe organ and a modern theatre....
>
> Miss Maude Ayres and Frank A. Gumm ... are doing much to add to the popularity of the new picture palace as both are artists of far more ability than is generally found in this line of work.

One week later, on December 28th, the *Superior Telegram* announced a program with several new films at the Orpheum. "The Logging Industry in the Northwest" [is] a picture that has special interest for all people in this section," the paper said. The other pictures playing that week were: "Cow-girl Pranks," a western, "The Stranger," and "The Girl and the Half-back." The latter was a football picture. The article noted that "an added feature to this picture is the duet sung by Miss Ayres and Frank Gumm ... it brings out the proper spirit for the game." Concluding, the writer noted,

> "The illustrated songs by Miss Ayres and the Orpheum orchestra and pipe organ add to the merit of the production. These features place the Orpheum theatre in a class by itself..."

As the news article stated, Frank and Maude were working ma
song illustrators. This job required a singer to stand before a movie
where pretty, colored picture slides illustrating the song and the song lyrics were shown. It was song illustrator's job to lead the audience in song as they pointed out the lyrics with a long wooden pointer. In the old days, people loved this kind of participation. They also liked it if a beautiful lady or a handsome young man with a beautiful voice were leading them. Frank, being a very social person with a lot of energy, likely enjoyed the opportunity to interact with the audience in this way.

Besides his busy theater schedule, Frank Gumm appears to have been very active on the social scene. Soon after he arrived in Superior, he met seventeen year-old Katherine Francis McGraw. Katherine was the sixth child of Irish-American parents, Frank and Mary McGraw. Mr. McGraw, a real estate agent, had moved his family to Superior several years earlier.

How Frank and Katherine met is not known, but in a whirlwind courtship, Frank asked her to marry him. Katherine, a Catholic, was willing to marry Frank, but it seems he was always putting the date off. Finally, she gave up.[117]

Four years later, while in New York, Katherine McGraw met vaudevillian, Joe E. Brown. They were married on December 24th, 1915. It was a marriage that lasted for sixty-seven years, until the comedian's death in 1973.

~

Early in 1912, something else happened to Frank Gumm. Ray Hadfield, with his many theatres, kept Frank and Maude busy traveling from one place to another. One day, while Frank was singing onstage, he looked down into the orchestra pit and found himself fascinated by a pretty, young girl playing the piano. She was so small, she almost looked like a child, but as she played, her little hands flew over the keys like a virtuoso. Then, she looked up at him with her "flashing black eyes" and he was smitten.[118]

After the show, Frank asked the theatre manager to introduce them. Her name was Ethel Milne and she was eighteen years old. Though she was not beautiful, Ethel had a beauty about her. Her flawless alabaster skin was accentuated by her dark eyes, long lashes and the black curls, which framed her face. She also had a lovely smile.

Like the moving picture stars of the day—Mary Miles Minter, Mary Pickford and Lillian Gish, Ethel was tiny, 4 foot 11, but like the film heroines, she was also strong and every bit a spitfire. Frank could not help admiring her. Unlike the girls he had known at home, Ethel was all business. He soon found that she had energy and wit to match his and, perhaps, what he lacked—a drive to succeed.

Frank, Maude and Ethel became good friends. They spent a lot of time going around town together. Mr. Hatfield sent them to perform in many different locations. The more time Frank spent with Ethel, the more entranced he became by this young, dark-eyed girl. He wanted to know her better. Ethel, for her part, was equally attracted to the tall, dark, handsome gentleman with the beautiful voice that had a slight hint of the south in the way he spoke. It wasn't long before she invited him to meet her family, which was a revelation in itself.

~

The object of Frank's fascination was not a Superior girl. Until she was about fifteen, Ethel's family had lived in eastern Michigan, in the county of Marquette. She was born Ethel Marion Milne on November 17, 1893 in the town of Marquette, a major port on Lake Superior. The main source of income for the town was the shipping of iron ore. Marquette is also the fifth snowiest city in the United States, receiving on average, 141 inches of snow every year.

Ethel's father, John Milne, worked as an engineer for the railroad. At the age of nineteen, he joined the Grand Trunk Railroad. Two years later, he was working as a fireman, shoveling coal on the Duluth South Shore and Atlantic railroad. Eventually, John was promoted to engineer, "driving the train from the right-hand seat, where most of the train's signals are."[119]

John Milne met his future wife around 1890, likely in Marquette. She was Evelyn Fitzpatrick. Born in New York State on June 4th, 1868, she was the fifth child of Hugh and Mary Fitzpatrick's brood of ten. John and Eva were married on February 4, 1891.

FRANK AVENT GUMM.

Shortly after their marriage, the Milnes moved into the house at 509 West Washington Street in Marquette. Here, their three eldest children were born. Their first child, Dorothy, arrived in 1892, followed by Ethel in 1893 and John in 1895. Dorothy died when Ethel was about three or four. Experiencing the loss of her closest sibling at such an early age no doubt left its mark.

The Milnes moved several times during Ethel's childhood. For a while, they lived in Ishpeming, and, then, in Republic. Finally, they settled in Michigamme, where they rented a home on Railroad Street. The Milne family lived here the longest of all their homes, staying eight years until they moved to Superior.

During Ethel's childhood, brothers and sisters arrived with regularity every one to two years. Twin boys, John and Charles were born April 1st, 1895, however, Charles died in October at the age of six months. Mary Civila was born September 11th, 1896, Robert, September 21st, 1897, Franklin, February 13th, 1899 and Fred, October 21st, 1900.

The U.S. Census record for 1900 shows a house full of small children with Ethel, 7, John, 5, Mary, 3, Robert, 2, Franklin, 1, and, of course, a baby on the way. Ethel and her siblings were very close and would remain so throughout their lives. Being the oldest, Ethel took on some of the responsibility in caring for the little ones. Eva certainly had her hands full. In 1900, John Milne's twenty-one year-old brother, George, also was living with the family, and working as a Bell Boy. The last Milne baby, Norma Elizabeth, would be born six years later on September 24th, 1906, when Ethel was twelve.

The town of Michigamme, laid out and built by the Michigamme Mining Company, was nestled among the rolling hills, along the inlet shores of Lake Michigamme. At the time the Milnes lived there, the population consisted of a little over 1,000 people, most of whom worked in the mines and for the lumber mills. Although the town was situated on the edge of the northern wilderness, during the eight years the Milne family lived there, it was a very active place. There were two hotels, four general stores, a sawmill, broom factory and pool hall, all built from the tall timber woods outside the town.

The area surrounding Michigamme is truly beautiful. Amidst the rolling hills, and sometimes rocky landscape, tall evergreen trees, and other hardwood forests thrive. Although the winters are brutal, in springtime, quantities of wildflowers bloom everywhere. In summer, the late night skies reveal the amazing northern lights. Wildlife, including a good-sized moose population, wolves and, of course, fish from the vast Lake Michigamme, abound.

Working for the railroad, John Milne earned a fairly good income and provided well for his family. But John had other interests. Both he and Eva were very talented musicians. Each carried on the respective traditions of their musical heritage; the music of Scotland and Ireland.

John played the violin, and Eva, the piano. During the early years of their marriage, the Milnes sometimes toured the local area with "an old fashioned medicine show."[120] As the Milne children arrived, John and Eva passed their musical knowledge on to them. Each child was taught to sing and to play at least one instrument. The children also learned to dance the Highland fling, and Irish step-dance. Music was an intrinsic part of their lives, and every place the family lived, they provided musical entertainment for the local residents.

When it came time to make their performances known to the public, Mr. and Mrs. Milne believed they would get more attention through "trouble" than good behavior. John and Eva often put on a show for the town by having knock-down drag-out fights which concluded with John chasing Eva down the street, brandishing a cane. Sometimes, Eva would turn the tables on her husband, and hit him on the head with "a tin pitcher." The family knew they had achieved their goal when town folks came to hear them sing. And the town folks did come, wondering if, possibly, they might see another row between this firey couple.[121] In private, the Milnes laughed about these events, paying little attention to what people said about them.

By 1911, Ethel and her seven brothers and sisters were living at 1626 Oakes Avenue in Superior, having moved from 1914 N. 19th the previous year. For a decade or more, the Superior City Directory shows that the Milne family moved nearly every year. In the 1911–1912 volume, Ethel Milne was listed as a pianist for the Bijou Theatre.

~

When Frank Gumm finally met Ethel's fascinating family, he was as delighted with them as they were with him. Frank felt very much at home with this friendly, music-loving and somewhat comedic family. The Milnes, who were very impressed with Frank's beautiful singing voice and good manners, welcomed him into their midst.

By now, Frank had asked Ethel to marry him and she had accepted. Both had ambitions for the stage. Their partnership would be more than just a marriage. Testing their musical abilities together, they were sure they could create a successful act.

In later years, Maude Ayres would give several versions of the events that followed. In all of her accounts, she was surprised to learn that Frank and Ethel planned to be married. "I didn't even know anything was going on between them," she later said.[122]

Maude, a treasured friend to the couple, was invited to their engagement dinner one evening in March of 1912. The dinner took place at the back of the Orpheum stage, between shows. Ethel, who knew how to make something out of little, had prepared a feast. Seated at a card table with a white table cloth, the three performers enjoyed a meal that included champagne, "fried chicken, salad, rolls" and, even, "a wedding cake."[123]

It was a lovely evening, but meanwhile, Maude couldn't help wondering about the rumors she had just heard regarding Frank. "Everybody in Superior was talking about it...," she later said."[124] The rumors entailed the fact that Frank was interested in other than just female companionship and that something inappropriate had occurred between him and another man, possibly back in Cloquet. Maude wondered if Ethel knew about it. It seemed difficult to believe that she had not heard the rumors as well.

On March 30th, *The Pine Knot* announced that Frank Gumm "left this week to locate in Portland, Oregon after spending the winter at Superior. He visited old friends in Cloquet a few days prior to his departure for the west."

Frank had only been in Superior a little over three months, he was engaged to be married and all had seemed well, but apparently things were not going as planned. According to Maude Ayres, Frank had to get out of town and "get out fast" because he had been accused of being a "pervert."[125] His visit to Cloquet had been to bid his brother, Bob, and sister-in-law, Belle, goodbye. One cannot help wondering if they too had heard the rumors, and if Frank was being threatened, why he felt safe enough to visit Cloquet.

Five months after Frank Gumm left on his journey west, Robert E. Gumm sold out his interest in the Diamond and Bijou theatres of Cloquet and moved fifteen miles away to Duluth. Apparently, Cloquet was not to his liking, or the pressure of Frank's reputation had been too much to handle.

Bob found an opportunity, managing the Majestic Theater at 24 East Superior Street in Duluth. On August 9th, 1912, *The Pine Knot* stated that Mrs. Gumm had gone on ahead of Mr. Gumm to the "Zenith City" and that any Cloquet resident who wished to visit the new theatre would be "extended a most cordial welcome."

~

In March of 1912, Frank Gumm was traveling far from the girl he had hoped to marry, and the town in which he had found full-time work as a singer. Some accounts state that he joined a vaudeville troupe when he left town and, on this tour, stopped in many states along the way. If this is true, the tour may have included Ironwood. An Ironwood resident later recalled that Frank was in town around this time, arriving as part of a vaudeville troupe. From there, it seems that he traveled south; one of those southern stops being Atlanta, Georgia.

While in Atlanta, Frank visited his Uncle Jere Gumm and Jere's new wife, Katherine. Cousin Annie, who was happily married to Walter Parker, had given birth to a son, Jere Alexander Parker in 1908, following by twin boys in 1910. Sadly, the twins both died one year after their birth. Then, in March of 1912, Annie had one more son, David Gumm Parker. Since David's birth, Annie had not been well. Previously, she had led a very active social life and her name had appeared fairly often in the local newspaper's society column. Now, she spent most of her time in bed at the family's elegant home on Ponce de Leon.

In June, Annie Gumm Parker passed away at the age of thirty-four. In the obituary notice, placed in the *Atlanta Constitution*, among those invited to the funeral services were John H. Gumm and Frank A. Gumm. From this notice, it appears that Frank had been in town to visit the family shortly before Annie's death, but now they had no idea how to reach him.

Frank's tour took him through many other states and concluded in the most exciting American city at the time, Portland, Oregon.

~

In 1912, Portland, Oregon was a Mecca, one of the most happening places for opportunity in the entire United States. Frank Gumm was a go-getter. If there was something happening or an opportunity out there, he was going to find it, so it is interesting that he ended up in Portland.

In 1905, the Lewis and Clark Exposition Fair was held outside Portland, and in 1907 the Oaks Amusement Park opened with over 350,000 visitors, an unheard of number at that time. By 1909, the Portland to Seattle Railway was completed and a bond was posted for the building of a bridge, which opened in 1910.

Portland was like early San Francisco in the Gold Rush. It was a major port and people from all over were coming there. Buildings were going up and there was entertainment galore. On entering the city and walking around, Frank must have been amazed by the size of the place. There was activity every where he looked.

Frank went to work for the People's Amusement Company, a corporation intent on opening a chain of quality silent picture theaters throughout the northwest. Frank was given the job of managing the Crystal Theatre at 125 North Killingsworth and Albin. The theatre, which no longer stands, was opened in 1911 under proprietorship of twenty-four year-old Harry Fleishman. A few blocks away, at 1196 Kirby Street, Frank rented a room in a large home which recently had been turned into a boarding house. Once again, he was thrown into a situation with people he did not know, but this time, most of them were performers.

The Portland of 1912–1913 was completely different from any place Frank had previously lived. The city was by far bigger than any place he had visited. It was one huge amusement park. There were fairgrounds and Ferris wheels, beaches and brothels and workers of every nationality. The ebb and flow of people did not stop; Portland was a boom town.

This was the kind of excitement young Frank had been craving. He made friends with a couple of fellows, likely young men in similar professions to his own, and the three of them went around the town together. Frank kept a couple of pictures of himself and his friends fooling around in Portland in his personal scrapbook. These small souvenirs are the only indication of Frank's life in 1913.

In the future, this period in Portland would stand Frank in good stead. A friend in Lancaster, California was later surprised by Frank's theater connections. Every time a theatrical troop came to town, Frank always seemed to know at least one person in the group.[126] It was astounding how many performers he knew.

Yet, despite all the excitement and fun in Portland, Frank could not forget the girl he left behind, Ethel Milne. Her dark hair, dark eyes and lively personality stayed with him. During this time, the pair kept in touch by letter.[127] If others had turned him down or given up on him, Ethel had not. She was still waiting.

While Frank was gone, the Milne family moved again; this time to 1809 Hughitt Avenue. Meanwhile, Ethel was listed in the Superior City Directory as "musician Orpheum Theatre." Possibly, she was playing more than one instrument. The following year, John Milne, who was listed as Engineer for the DSS&A Railyard, moved the family once again to 912 North 18th Street.

Finally, nearly a year and a half after he left Superior, Frank Gumm made the decision to return. He said he was "miserable" without Ethel.[128] Whatever had been in his mind about life and the future before this, Ethel had changed all that. Frank found that he wanted to be around her all the time and despite being a couple thousand miles away, he could not get her out of his mind.

~

On his return, Frank apparently lodged with the Milne family. They all adored him and were thrilled that he was going to be a member of the family.

Happily, Mr. Hadfield agreed to rehire Frank and soon he and Maude Ayres were singing together once again. Besides playing the Orpheum, they toured other local theatrical houses, as well as the small lumberjack and mining towns of Minnesota and Wisconsin.

Looking toward their future, Frank and Ethel started working on their own vaudeville act, for which Ethel created the arrangements. Frank felt they would be a winning combination. The couple had big dreams. They would tour the areas outside of Superior and, when they were ready, they would travel east to Chicago. Frank already had their marriage license in his pocket; it was just a matter of finding time for the wedding.[129] Meanwhile, Hadfield was keeping them very busy.

~

When the local paper announced the wedding of Frank A. Gumm and Ethel Marion Milne, it stated that on his return to Superior, he had taken a job at the Parlor Theatre, and Miss Milne, who had also been out of town, had, by chance, been hired at the rival Lyric Theater across the street, thus fate had caused their paths to cross.

Between family tales, old news stories and memories, the truth may be difficult to discern. What seems certain is that Frank Gumm returned to Superior because of Ethel. Were it not for her, he might have continued his travels or simply stayed in the booming city of Portland. The couple was in love, and with absolute faith in their love for one another and their ability to meld their talents, the future looked very bright.

Approximately one month after his return to Superior, on a bitterly cold day, the 22nd of January 1914, to be exact, Frank Avent Gumm and Ethel Marion Milne were married. The entire Milne family attended the ceremony, which was conducted by newly ordained Episcopal minister, J.J. Crawford. The couple's friend, Alfred Street, stood as best man. It is uncertain as to where the marriage took place. Speaking about the wedding in a 1937 interview, Ethel does not mention a church.

Fred Milne would later recall how beautiful his sister looked that day and how happy Frank was. The entire Milne family rejoiced that two people, so well suited, had found one another and were very much in love. After the wedding that morning, the couple went back to work.

Just before the show that night, Frank told Maude that he and Ethel had been married that morning. Maude was very surprised; nevertheless, she was happy to join her friends after the show to celebrate their wedding.

In a little over a month, the three friends would part. Frank and Ethel would move on to follow their dreams. Maude would remain in Superior and continue to perform, finding work in light opera. The following year, Maude would marry her former high school classmate, Victor Holman.

A few weeks after the wedding, the *Ironwood Times* reported on the Gumm marriage. Frank was still dear to the hearts of Ironwood's citizens.

Chapter 25

Happy Beginnings

FRANK GUMM'S CONTRACT WITH RAY HADLEY ENDED IN LATE FEBRUARY. Meanwhile, he learned about a job from a couple on vacation in Superior. Mr. and Mrs. C.E. Aikens, a middle-aged couple from Grand Rapids, Minnesota, who had thoroughly enjoyed Frank's performance that day, and later told him and Ethel about a new theatre that had just opened in their delightful little town. The proprietors, Barlow and Bentz, were looking for someone to manage it and provide good entertainment. The Aikens thought it might be an excellent opportunity for the young couple.[130]

Frank followed up on the information, and on March 5th, the *Itasca County Independent* announced that "the services of Frank A. Gumm had been procured as "singer and manager." In addition, the article stated that Mrs. Gumm "will take charge of the music at the Grand."[131]

The Aikens offered the Gumms a room in their home, rent free. They were pleased to help bring such fine musical talent to their town.[132] They also knew that rooms for rent were difficult to find. With a job and a place to live, the future looked bright.

Meanwhile, the Gumm siblings had all agreed to sell the family home in Murfreesboro. None of them planned to live in Murfreesboro, and there was no sense in keeping it.

The home was sold to C.R. Cawthorn for $1,750 (=$38,500). Mr. Cawthorn made a payment of $580 in cash. There would be two promissory notes of $583 (= $12,800) each at six percent interest due in the next two and a half years.[133] In order to sign the papers, each member of the family appeared before a notary public in the state where they were living.

Robert Emmett and wife, Belle, appeared on March 2nd, 1914 in Louisville, Jefferson County, Kentucky. Mary and husband, Oscar McPeak, appeared on March 9th in Birmingham, Jefferson County, Alabama. Will and Allie Gumm, both still living in Huntsville, Madison County, Alabama, appeared before a notary there on March 12th. Just prior to moving to Grand Rapids, on February 14th, Frank and Ethel Gumm appeared before a notary in Superior, Douglas County, Wisconsin.

In July of that year, Frank learned that his youngest brother, Allie, had married Miss Minnie Overton, a twenty year-old young lady from Huntsville.[134] Minnie, the eldest daughter of a policeman, was a Baptist and would remain so. Allie, likewise, retained his membership in the Episcopalian Church.

Less than one year later, on March 3rd, 1915, William Wade Gumm married a schoolmate of Minnie's, Miss Frances Stamert. Now, all of Will and Clemmie Gum's children were married.[135]

~

Back in Grand Rapids, Frank and Ethel were doing quite well. They lived in a beautiful little town, and the kindness of the Aiken family had helped to make the early months of their marriage much easier. The Grand Rapid's town folks, in general, were very friendly and thoroughly enjoyed the programs created by the Gumms. In fact, they were so successful at the New Grand, that the town's older and smaller theater, The Gem, soon went out of business.

The Gumms were not running the New Grand by themselves. The theater's co-owners, Mr. and Mrs. Bentz worked with them. Mrs. Bentz took the tickets and Mr. Bentz ran the films, leaving the Gumms to the more creative part of the venture; Frank, to promotion and Ethel, to playing background music for the silent pictures. On weekends, when the theatre was often filled to capacity, the couple performed between pictures, just as they had in Superior.

By summer, the Gumms were making enough money to rent a house in town. Yet, as winter approached, they had other thoughts. Possibly, Frank was dreading the long winter. In addition, the warm applause of

Grand Rapids' citizen had boosted their confidence. The couple had not yet given up their dreams of vaudeville, and now, they decided to pursue those dreams.

Frank and Ethel made up a story, telling Messrs. Barlow and Bentz that they wanted to spend the winter with Frank's parents down in Florida. In their place, they offered the services of Ethel's brother, Jack, as manager, and Mary, who was now working in a theatre in Superior, as pianist. Barlow and Bentz agreed to their leave.

With the security of knowing they had a job to fall back on, the Gumms made some connections and set up a short vaudeville tour on the Michigan/Wisconsin Gus Sun circuit. From there, they would go to Chicago and see what fate had in store.

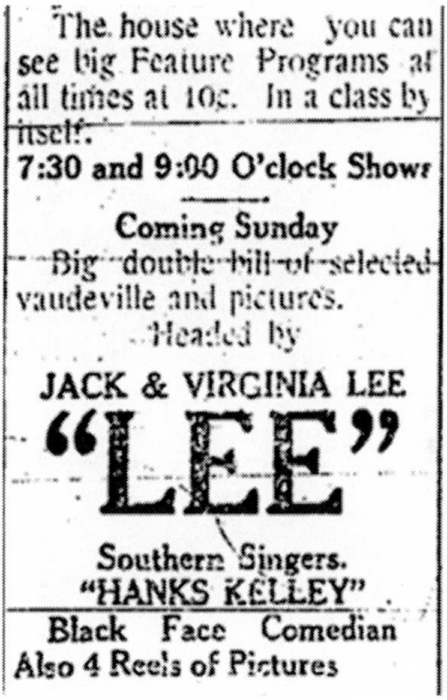

The house where you can see big Feature Programs at all times at 10c. In a class by itself.

7:30 and 9:00 O'clock Shows

Coming Sunday

Big double bill of selected vaudeville and pictures.

Headed by

JACK & VIRGINIA LEE

"LEE"

Southern Singers.

"HANKS KELLEY"

Black Face Comedian

Also 4 Reels of Pictures

Billing themselves as *Jack and Virginia Lee, Sweet Southern Singers*, the Gumms sent off on a new adventure. Each night, dressed in old-fashioned costumes, they went on stage, and sang the popular songs of the day. Still very much in love, it was an exciting time for the young couple.

The most popular songs that year were love songs like, *Let Me Call You Sweetheart*, *Dream Girl*, and the recent hit by Al Jolsen, *You Made Me Love You.* It has been said that Ethel Gumm was a professional dancer. Frank was a good dancer as well. Since most theaters at this time had, at the very least, a small band consisting of four pieces, it was not necessary for Ethel to stay behind the piano for every number. It is possible, as later photos reveal, that the couple also added a bit of movement to their act.

For almost three months, Frank and Ethel traveled, visiting small towns throughout Michigan and Wisconsin. In most of these theatres, the act was performed between pictures. Author Gerold Frank was able to preserve some memories of the Jack and Virginia act in his book, *Judy*.

Photo from 1925 reveals something of the charming and chivalrous style of their early Jack and Virginia Lee, Sweet Southern Singers act.
(Courtesy Itasca County Museum)

The Jack and Virginia Lee act began with the curtain rising to reveal Ethel seated at the piano. Frank would then introduce himself:

> "Good evening ladies and gentleman. My name is *Jack Lee, and this is Virginia Lee, my wife.* (Virginia bows and smiles.) *Virginia will now open our program by playing "Alexander's Ragtime Band." I would like you all, please, to observe how small her hands are.*"[136]

At this point, Ethel would turn to the audience with a sweet smile, and raising her palms toward the audience, turn them to the right and left so everyone could seen her tiny, dimpled hands. Then, she would turn back to the piano and begin to play the ragtime melody, her fingers flying over the keys, playing the syncopated melody with amazing speed and precision. Naturally, the audience broke out in big applause.

The Jack and Virginia Lee act contained both duets and solos. While most of the songs were the new hits of the day, Frank also enjoyed singing songs about the old South like *Sewanee River*, and religious songs such as *The Old Rugged Cross*.

During the early years of their marriage, the Gumms sang two songs that would later be forgotten with time: the somewhat patriotic and jaunty song with the long title, *There's a Maid in America, Made in America, a Maid for Every Boy* and a song that seemed just made for them, *Mary, You're a Little Bit Old Fashioned*. The latter song was about a slightly older, more experienced man courting a young and innocent girl. In the second verse, the couple is married and "Mary," having had "lots of fun" is a bit less innocent.[137]

Met by enthusiastic applause everywhere they went, in late January the couple decided they were ready to take the next step and head to Chicago. They had pinned their hopes on this. From there, possibly, they might reach New York.

But, no sooner had the couple arrived in Chicago, than Ethel fell seriously ill with influenza. It was clear they could not continue. Frank managed to get Ethel on the train and back to the Milne house in Superior, where she was so weak she could barely rise from her bed for three weeks. It was said she had "near-pneumonia." During this time, a visit from a doctor revealed another fact; Ethel was not only sick, she was expecting.[138]

A couple of weeks after Ethel's recovery, the Gumms returned to Grand Rapids and received a warm welcome. From now on, Grand Rapids would truly be home.

Chapter 26

Grand Rapids

Grand Rapids was incorporated as a town in 1891, twenty-three years prior to the Gumm's arrival, but for hundreds of years before that, this land of lakes and forests had been the home of the Ojibwa (Chippewa) Indians. After the territory was ceded to the United States in 1855, homesteaders began to settle the area.

Early visitors to the territory had noted the vast forests of tall timber. In a short time, loggers and hunters began to populate the land now known as Itasca County. The real advantage of this northern Minnesota location was the Mississippi River. Grand Rapids was founded on the northernmost navigatable point of the river; the Mississippi made this a potentially a profitable spot. From here, loggers could float the tall timber downstream, and, then, ship it to places far south. The same was true for the fishermen, who shipped quantities of lake fish to inland areas via the Mississippi.

When the Gumms settled in Grand Rapids, it was not much more than a charming village surrounded by pristine forests and lakes. In some ways, Itasca County could be compared to Rutherford County at its beginnings, and while Grand Rapids could certainly be compared to Murfreesboro, but instead of a courthouse as the focal point, in 1895, this northern town had built a grand, Richardson Romanesque three-story Central School in its town center.

From the Gumm's point of view, Grand Rapids was comfortably small, with enough activities and social life to keep them busy. Full of energy and enthusiasm, the couple threw themselves into every possible activity.

Being involved in the community was also good publicity for their theatre and shows. At the Episcopal Church, Frank became choir director, while Ethel played the organ. Frank joined the fire brigade, and Ethel held bridge parties. It is easy to see how Mr. and Mrs. Gumm were soon one of the most popular couples in town.

Although Grand Rapids was lovely in late spring and summer, winter in northern Minnesota lasts from October to May, with snow arriving sometimes as early as September. The days are short and often bitterly cold. Temperatures may go to thirty below zero, snowfall sometimes more than sixty inches in a season.

Ethel was used to cold weather, but, for Frank, it was adjustment. Nearly every year, he arranged a southern vacation for the months of January or February. But winter in Grand Rapids, with little else to do, was also a busy time for the theater.

Part of the Gumm's satisfaction with the town was the knowledge that Grand Rapids was a beautiful place to raise children. Despite its small size, the town had everything they could want. It was laid out in such a way that residents were able to walk to the stores, schools and churches.

The Milnes were a close-knit family and so, for Ethel, one of the most important features in town was the railway station, with a direct line Superior. During the time the Gumms lived in Grand Rapids, family members took hundreds of trips back and forth to Superior and, later, Duluth where some of Ethel's siblings settled. Sometimes, Ethel, who had always been very independent, picked up and went to visit her parents by herself. In turn, Ethel's parents, brothers and sisters were all visitors in the Gumm home. Eva Milne and Norma were probably the most frequent guests, often coming to help Ethel with the house and the children.

Of course, the central feature of the Gumm's life in Grand Rapids was the theatre. Under Frank Gumm's management, the New Grand was often filled to capacity with a captive and eager audience.[139] As advertised, the theater had two shows daily; one at 7:30 and one at 9:00. This kept Frank and Ethel quite busy, though, of course, they worked with Mr. and Mrs. Bentz. Sometimes Frank hired an outside piano player to fill in, especially after Ethel had children to care for.

Early in his management of the New Grand, Frank had the idea of holding amateur shows on Fridays. This attracted not only those who wanted to perform, but also the friends and family members who wanted to see them.

One of the first nights Frank instituted the amateur show, he invited Robert and Wayne Gilbert, to sing. These two young men were brothers that Frank had been told sang in the Methodist church choir. That night, Frank joined the brothers on stage, strumming his ukulele. Dressed in white flannels with red vests and straw hats, the three men sang, *By the Light of Silvery Moon*. They were a hit, and Frank continued to have amateur nights every Friday.

~

In the spring of 1915, Frank learned that his youngest brother, Allie, and wife, Minnie, had welcomed their first child. Allie Richardson Gumm, Jr. was born April 23rd. The following year, in August, the couple would have their second child, another boy, James Wade Gumm.

Meanwhile, there was excitement at home in Grand Rapids as Ethel prepared to give birth to their first child. On September 24th, the baby, a girl, was born in the modern way, at the Itasca Hospital, a few blocks from the couple's new home. They named her Mary Jane. In 1902, the popular comic strip character, Buster Brown, had a sister named Mary Jane. Later the Buster Brown Shoe Company gave the name, "Mary Jane," to a style of little girl's shoes with straps.[140] Possibly, the name was just one Frank and Ethel thought was cute.

After Mary Jane's birth, Frank took over some of the piano playing for the pictures while Ethel recovered. The Milnes all came to visit, anxious to see the new little girl. A month or so later, Ethel bundled up the new baby and boarded the train to Superior for a visit with her family.

On her return performance at the New Grand, she and Frank sang *The Old Gray Mare*, a new 1915 hit, and a song with much pathos, about the pitfalls of theatrical success, *There's a Broken Heart for Each Light on Broadway*. Strangely, the song foreshadowed Ethel's own sorrows. In 1915, it's the melancholy air may have touched audiences as they thought of the 1,198 innocent men, women and children who had been killed that May when a German submarine torpedoed the U.S. passenger ship, the *Luisitania*.

The war in Europe had begun with the assassination of the Austrian Arch-Duke by a Serbian national in 1914, approximately six months after

Ladies and babies of Grand Rapids, the winter of 1915. Ethel Gumm and baby, Mary Jane, are second from the right. Ethel is the shortest mother. (Courtesy Itasca County Museum)

Frank and Ethel were married. From there, the conflict spread throughout Europe as the allies took sides. Americans, with ties to so many of these nations, did not want to be involved in the war, but it was looming nearer and nearer. The sinking of the Luisitania and the loss of 128 innocent Americans, had served to stoke the fires.

~

By 1917, life seemed quite good for Frank and Ethel Gumm. In fact, the New Grand was doing so well that, according to the local newspaper, Frank and Fred Bentz had the original New Grand had torn down, and were building a 450 seat theater in its place.

The new theatre was designed and built specifically for use as a theatre. It was constructed of brick and concrete, with a real stage measuring 18′x23′ for live performances. The local paper stated that the new theater was going to be fitted with "opera chairs," "steam heat," and a "special "11′x14′ foot gold fiber screen, providing a soft, restful light."[141] Grand Rapids was about to have a new state of the art theater, and the Gumms were thrilled.

While they waited for the theater to be completed, Frank was busy planning an exciting program for the grand opening, which was scheduled for April 12th. Meanwhile, the shows and films continued in another location.

On March 20th, the night of Frank's thirty-first birthday, Ethel arranged a surprise party. That night, Frank came home from "the show" to find sixteen male friends and a house full of delicious food, music and birthday cards.[142] To all eyes, the Gumms were a wonderful, happy couple who worked very hard and were bound to succeed at anything they tried.

Plans and hard work do not guarantee the future. As sure as the Gumms were, life had its own surprises in store. On April 6th, only six days before the opening of the New Grand, Congress voted to declare war against Germany and her allies. A good many Americans had protested against becoming involved in a war, but the sinking of seven U.S. merchant ships by German submarines, as well as the German Foreign Minister's attempt to have Mexico become their ally against the U.S., were the final straws. President Wilson called for war, and the vote by the United States Congress made it a reality.[143] At the same time they voted for the war, Congress also passed the Selective Service Act. Over the next two years, 2.8 million men would be drafted, with an average of 10,000 soldiers being sent to France per day. Now, things began to change swiftly.

On April 16th, hundreds of people assembled in Grand Rapids to watch Navy recruits depart by train. Frank had a good friend who joined the service, and the two kept in touch, writing from time to time about what was going on in the barracks and what was going on in town. Frank liked to keep in touch with his friends, writing newsy and somewhat humorous letters. One letter, now held by the Judy Garland Birthplace, contains inside tales about persons from Grand Rapids, one of whom who got "the clap."

When the first draft notice appeared in Itasca County on June 5th, men between the ages of twenty-one and thirty were registered for the draft. Since Frank was now thirty-one, he was not called. Meanwhile, 2,266 men registered in Itasca County that June. By September, the draft board changed the age classification and called for men between the ages of eighteen and forty-five.[144] However, no draft card for Frank Gumm has been found.

Down in Huntsville, Alabama, on the 5th of June, Frank's two youngest brothers Will and Allie Gumm were called before the draft board. Allie stated on his draft card that he was working as a garage manger for C.M. Skinner. He was described as being of medium height with black hair and brown eyes. Will, a salesman for Myerson Shoe Company, had gray eyes and brown hair. At the time Will applied for the draft, he was sick. Neither of the brothers was drafted into the war.

On July 4th, Ethel gave birth to the Gumm's second child, another girl. Dr. Hursh, who was delivering the baby, was supposed to be giving an Independence Day speech at a celebration downtown. When he arrived late, he told the crowd that Mr. Gumm would "have to explain" the reason for his tardiness.[145]

The Gumms named their new daughter, Dorothy Virginia; her first name was in memory of Ethel's sister. No one ever called the little girl Dorothy. Perhaps that was due to superstition. Instead, she would always be known as Virginia or "Jimmy."

A short time after Virginia were born, Frank Gumm gave the diamond ring he wore on the fourth finger of his right hand as a down payment for

Allie Gum and wife Minnie with children, Baby Elizabeth, James (center) and Allie R., Jr. around 1918.
(Courtesy Bill Gibb)

shared ownership of the New Grand with Frank Bentz. Apparently, Barlow wanted out. Frank had put all of his savings into the ring. He enjoyed the way it sparkled in the stage lights as he strummed his ukulele.[146] But investing in the theatre was another step in solidifying his family's future.

That September, close to Mary Jane's second birthday, Grand Rapids saw another one hundred and sixty men leave town for France.

By 1918, in the midst of worry about war, a deadly influenza epidemic had taken hold and was quickly spreading across the United States. It was thought that the war conditions—many men living in close quarters—may have hastened the spread of the virus. The virus, which became known as "The Spanish Flu," was most deadly to young, healthy adults.[147]

On September 25th, 1918, the first influenza cases were reported in Minnesota. Within less than a week, there were 1,000 cases.

Meanwhile, fires were raging in the northeast corner of Minnesota. Cloquet was burnt to the ground. Hundreds were killed in Cloquet, and in the small villages outside the city. Thousands of homes were destroyed. It had been a very dry year and as the fire spread, there were "massive evacuations." This led to further worry that more people would be exposed to the now rampant "Spanish Flu." The National Guard was called in to hand out clothing and, to dig massive graves for the dead.[148] Frank Gumm must have wondered if anyone he knew in Cloquet had been killed.

By November, Minnesota was in a state of extreme emergency. Hoping to slow the flu epidemic, officials declared that places where people gathered were to be shut down until further notice. This included schools, churches and theaters. That very day, 400 new cases of the flu had been reported in Minnesota. The day the ban was announced, many ran out for one last hour of entertainment. The following day, Frank closed the theater. Now, all they could do was wait.

In a close community like Grand Rapids, the Gumm family made do as best they could. Everyone was suffering, but worry about the virus was greater. The closure of public places lasted for six weeks. Within that time, the spread of the virus slowed and the ban was lifted. World-wide, the epidemic killed more than 20 million people.[149]

~

Robert Gumm did not receive his draft notice until 1918. He and Belle had left Duluth shortly before Frank's marriage in 1914. For a short time, they lived in Kentucky. Then, realizing there were greater opportunities in the north, they settled in Indianapolis, Indiana, where Bob found a job working as manager for an exhibitor film company.

On September 12th, of 1918, Robert Gumm appeared before the draft board. His record states that he had blue eyes and was balding with light brown hair. The burn on his right hand was noted as a distinguishing mark, being described as a "deformed at the little finger from burn."[150] Robert Gumm was not drafted.

Elmyra Crocket Thompson

The Thompson children, Allie, Birkle, Billie and Howard. Mildren Gumm, 2nd from the left.

By now, Robert's daughter, Mildred, was living with her grandmother, "Mur," in Hereford, Texas. Mur's youngest son, David, had moved there with his family, and Mur followed. The Thompson family's weakness for tuberculosis was better fought in a hot, dry climate. Joe Miller and her father were not the only victims of this disease. In 1924, Joe's sister, Allie, also would die from the disease.

Robert missed his daughter, but growing up next to her cousins, with the continued love of "Mur" seemed to be the best thing for her. Although rather shy, Mildred was a happy little girl. In Hereford, she and her Thompson cousins were like one big family. Robert wanted her to have a secure, happy childhood, not one full of worry as his had been.

Mur, though rather a rough woman, was also very kind-hearted.[151] She wrote Bob and Belle frequently about the little girl.

Dear Children, I will send you some of Mildred's little pictures to let you have an idea how she looks. I have neglected having any made. This is a groop (sp) Mildred, Allie Murfree & Allie's two little boys... Excuse their appearance. They were in the yard at play. The place is 330 Allen Ave. ... Mildred is a mighty sweet child. Wish you could *see her. Love to both of you from "Mur"*

As Mildred reached her teen year, she came north to stay with Bob and Belle for extended periods.

L. to r. Mildred, Bob and Belle. (Photos courtesy David Richardson)

Chapter 27
Mary

THE U.S. POSTAL RECORDS TELL A DISTINCT TALE OF OSCAR AND MARY McPeak's travels. After leaving Ironwood, they were not happy in Murfreesboro and, soon, decided to move south, near Mary's brothers, Will and Allie. Oscar's youngest sister, May McPeak, had married J.F. McWilliams in 1910, and was also living in Huntsville. Oscar's transfer was approved, and on July 1st, 1912, he began work as a letter carrier in Huntsville.

Mary must have been happy to be close to her younger brothers once again, but for some reason the McPeaks didn't stay in Huntsville. A little over five months after moving to that city, Oscar transferred again, this time further south to Birmingham where he started work on December 16th, 1912.

Birmingham was a much larger city than any the couple had lived in prior to this time. It was also the city where Oscar's sister, Mabel, had been living with her husband, Eugene Newsom for the past ten years.

Eugene H. Newsom, who was also from Tennessee, had found success working for a shoe manufacturer in Birmingham. The Newsoms had two little girls: Sara, born in 1904, and Marie, born in 1906.

Though it is uncertain whether Mary knew, her cousin, Ashton Baugh, the son of Joseph Baugh, was also living in Birmingham. Ashton was married to Marie Alice Walmsley. The couple had had four lovely children: Clara, Ashton, Henry and Anna. Ashton's eldest child was the same age as Frank Gumm and his youngest, a year younger than Allie. Ashton's brilliant brother, Henry Baugh, had suffered a mental breakdown and was institutionalized in Tuscaloosa, Alabama where he remained until his death in 1930.

The first year in Birmingham seems to have been full of joy and contentment for the McPeaks. In 1913, Mary gave birth to a second child whom she affectionately called, "Babe."

What joy and happiness there was in the McPeak house with these two small children, Totsy and Babe. Mary kept in touch with family in Murfreesboro, and with her brothers, telling them of the babies' progress. In particular, she often wrote to sweet, compassionate Aunt Nannie Rion, who was the nearest thing to a mother Mary had.

During their years in Birmingham, the McPeaks moved several times. Usually, they lived in rooming houses, or small, furnished apartments. With the money Oscar was earning, they were able to buy a few nice pieces of furniture and make their rented rooms feel like home. Oscar loved Mary and wanted to provide well for her and the children. Having had a difficult childhood, Mary was patient and grateful for the things Oscar gave her.

In July of 1913, Oscar McPeak's status with the Post Office had changed from "temporary-additional" to "Regular carrier" giving him an increase of salary totaling $1,000 per year. (= $21,777) Having a bit more money may have afforded the family a trip north to visit Oscar's mother and Mary's relatives in Murfreesboro. Still, it appears that the family had little money to spare.

December of 1913 arrived, and Christmas was just around the corner. At work, it was Oscar's job to deliver the mail to the residents of north Birmingham. Although mailboxes had become mandatory in 1912, many persons still did not have a mail box. As a result, letter carriers often waited at a resident's home for as long as an hour in order to personally hand a piece of mail to the addressee.[152]

On December 20th, Oscar set out to deliver a Special Delivery letter addressed to Mrs. E. S. Rhine in north Birmingham. Arriving at the Rhine home around 11 o'clock in the morning, he found that Mrs. Rhine was not at home. He waited a short time, and when she did not return, he carried the letter back to his post office, Boyle Station.

Just before he arrived at the station, Oscar took the envelope out of his pocket and noticed that the seal on the envelope had opened. Looking inside, he saw four single "silver certificate" dollars. (= $87.00) It was then that temptation struck. He removed the money and put it in his pocket. Then, he took the letter into the post office, and dropped it off with the clerk, Mr. Pierce.

As soon as Mr. Pierce picked up the envelope, he noticed that the back flap was no longer sealed. Checking the enclosed letter, and realizing that the money that should have been there was gone, Mr. Pierce ran out of the station after Oscar, and brought him back to explain what had happened. Once inside, Oscar was sent to his supervisor, Mr. Russ, who convinced him to return the money.

Oscar told Mr. Russ that the envelope was already open when he took the money. Nevertheless, once he handed the four silver certificate dollars over, he was arrested. He had broken the law, noted as Section 195 of the Penal Code—it was the same as robbery.

Mary was devastated when the news reached her. Oscar was not held in jail, but two of Oscar's friends, Mr. Tribble and Mr. Williams, agreed to pay the three hundred dollar fine should he not appear at his trial, set for the spring of 1914. Meanwhile, Oscar was without a job.

In the midst of all this, another tragedy was in the offing. Birmingham was a big city and had afforded the McPeaks many pleasures including museums, concerts and beautiful parks to walk in. But along with these advantages, there were dangers, which might occur anywhere, but seemed more prevalent in the big city. Disease spread quickly, and in the days before antibiotics, an illness could be easily fatal to a small child.

So it was that without warning, two year-old Totsy became ill. Babe soon followed. The children must have been quite ill because even without much money, Mary took them to the infirmary where the doctors advised her that Babe was not in danger, but Totsy must stay.

On January 3, 1914, Mary wrote to her Aunt Nannie in Murfreesboro:

Dear Aunt Nannie:

Rec'd your letter and remembrance and I was so glad to hear from you. Totsy is much better and Dr. thought he could leave infirmary today and it is his birthday. Look for him as soon as can stand the trip. Babe coming with him.

Love, Mary[153]

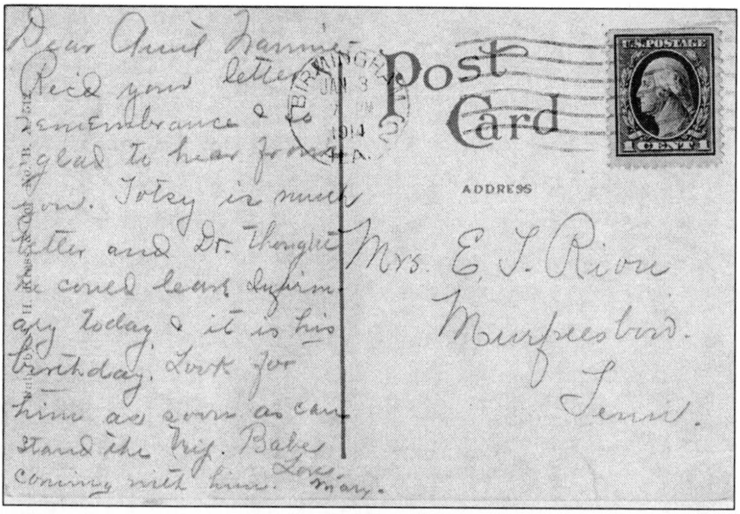

Mary Gumm McPeak's postcard to Aunt Nannie Rion, Jan 3, 1914. (Courtesy Joy Rion Nelson)

Mary had survived many difficulties in her life, and somehow kept remained strong. But now, when at last she was truly happy; the unthinkable happened.

Historically, no records of these children exist. There is the postcard from Mary. That is all. We can only guess that the children died. Except for two unmarked graves at Evergreen Cemetery in Murfreesboro—which may be theirs—no record or grave has been found. The children simply disappeared. The devastation that Mary and Oscar suffered during this time is difficult to imagine.

During this same periord, the McPeaks learned that Frank had married Ethel Milne. In February, the sale of the Gumm house in Murfreesboro would certainly have done something to alleviate their financial distress. Likely, a good portion of that money went to pay for Oscar's attorney.

Oscar McPeak's trial was set for March 2nd. The case was tried before the U.S. District Court for the Northern District of Alabama. It was a trial by jury. There were two counts against Mr. McPeak. The first count stated that he had broken the trust placed in his hands as a U.S. Mail Carrier. The second count stated that he had embezzled $4 from the contents of a letter entrusted to him.

Oscar McPeak had given a written confession and was convicted. His sentence was thirteen months in prison. On October 3rd, 1914, he turned himself in and was held in the Birmingham jail, awaiting transport to the prison. The prison he was being sent to was in Atlanta, Georgia—the State Penitentiary. His arrival must have been a daunting event.

The Georgia State Penitentiary was built in 1902. It is a huge fortress that covers 300 acres, the size of a football field. Accommodating 1,200 prisoners, the prison has housed many famous persons including, Al Capone, Eugene V. Debs, Carlo Ponzi and Bernard Madoff.

On entering the massive building, Oscar McPeak had to fill out a large amount of paperwork, which included information on whether his parents were living and his religion. Thankfully, Oscar's father, Rev. Gervis McPeak had passed away the previous year. His son's shame would likely have been more than he could bear. Oscar's mother, who still lived in Murfreesboro, may never have been told of her son's crime for her name does not appear on the list of correspondents during his stay in prison.

Oscar must have felt great shame. He had grown up the son of an honorable father and mother. Did he need money to pay for his children's doctor bills? Or had he simply wanted to buy Mary and the children some presents for Christmas? His reasons for stealing remain a mystery, but by his foolish action, he brought more pain and hardship to the wife he loved than he could ever have imagined. On the prison's record

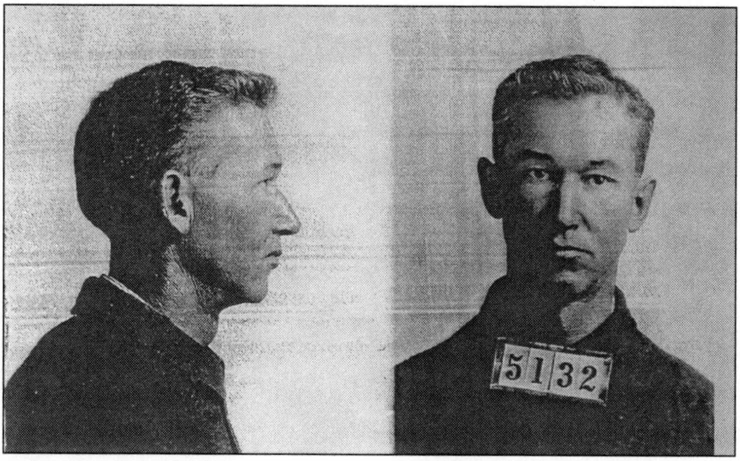

Oscar McPeak's mug shots, Inmate #5132, Atlanta Federal Penitentiary. (Courtesy National Archives and Records, Southeast Region, Morrow, Georgia)

regarding his wife, Oscar wrote that Mrs. Oscar McPeak was living at 2305 11th Avenue, N. Birmingham, Alabama.

Following the paperwork, Oscar was fingerprinted and photographed. His height was listed as 5'7", his weight 117 pounds and his eyes, chestnut, and his hair, gray with some chestnut. He was then stripped of his clothes and belongings and dressed in striped prison garb. Oscar was 39 years old and his world had come crashing down, all through his own hands.

Now completely alone, Mary found refuge in Pensacola, Florida. For the next six months, she would reside in a house at 316 Guillmarde Street. Although it is unknown whether this situation was arranged by family, possibly her brother, Bob Gumm, who had once lived in Pensacola, or her landlady, Mrs. Judy, who came down to visit while Mary was there. In 1911, this home was owned by R.G. Green. In 1916, the residence was owned by a Mrs. Holbrook. It seems most likely that Mrs. Holbrook was the person Mary stayed with.

The Penitentiary kept a list of the correspondence prisoners received during their incarceration. Included in the notations were the names, their relation to the inmate and their whereabouts. Mary was the first person to write Oscar. During the first month, she sent a letter every five days. By the end of the 1914, she had written her husband eighteen letters. Unfortunately, none of these letters seem to have survived.

Others who wrote Oscar during this time include his attorneys, Bondurant & Smith, a friend who was trying to get him a job, his sisters, Mabel Newsom, and May McWilliams, and brother-in-law, Frank Gumm, who wrote him from Grand Rapids in November, shortly after Mary Jane was born.

Oscar found the prison hellish. No sooner had he been incarcerated than he began an intense lobby to be released on parole. Early in November, only a month after arriving, Oscar found himself in trouble with prison authorities. It began when the cigarette papers he ordered were not delivered as requested. In those days, most people rolled their own cigarettes. Oscar wanted white papers and had been given brown because, they said, he did not have enough money for white papers. In addition, he had only received one packet of papers, and claimed he had paid for two. When Oscar became upset, prison authorities confined him to his cell.

Oscar McPeak was not a hardened criminal. Many people in Birmingham liked him and thought he had seen the error of his ways. Oscar applied for parole almost immediately, and by the 6th of November letters were being written to the Circulation Manager of the *Birmingham News*, attempting to get a job. A copy of an unsigned letter in Oscar's file states that in order for a prisoner to be released on parole, they must have "employment with a definite wage until the end of the parole," so as "not to be forced to return to crime for a livelihood." Oscar wrote Judge Grubb that prison, "…has been a lesson I shall never forget and I assure you I shall never appear before you in your official capacity again…"[154]

Early in 1915, Oscar McPeak received many letters of encouragement. Mary was now writing him every two to three days. By the end of spring, she had written him thirty-one letters, beginning January 1st of 1915. Frank Gumm wrote Oscar that January, mailing the letter from Minneapolis. Other letters Oscar received were from businessmen, friends and co-workers.

On February 24th, 1915, Oscar McPeak wrote to his landlord, "Friend Judy," about the rooms the McPeaks were renting in his home. In his letter, Oscar says that their bank account has been closed and he is uncertain when he will be released. Having no money to pay rent, "unless I am working," he tells Mr. Judy to continue to rent their rooms for another month. "Mary will notify you in time as to when we can take them." Oscar adds that he hopes "the people are taking good care of their furniture."

In March, Oscar, who had been recommended for parole because of good conduct, had apparently fallen ill. The prison's doctor ordered that he be given another blanket to keep warm.

May 4th, 1914, Oscar McPeak's parole approval was received. Two days later, Oscar McPeak was released from prison. Taking the train to Birmingham, his first line of business was to report to W.S. Dunston at the *Birmingham News* regarding his new job, working on the circulation desk of the newspaper. Oscar's salary would be approximately $36 a week, nearly double what he had made working for the U.S. Post Office. (= $774.00)

Oscar McPeak was soon named Circulation Manager of the *Birmingham News*. It was a job that seemed to suit him, and he declared himself on the straight and narrow. He and Mary were going to start life over. In one of his letters, Oscar wrote that he intended to follow every step in order to be released from parole. On August 16th, he achieved that end.

Mary and Oscar remained in Birmingham for several years. Then, in 1918, they moved up the mountain from Birmingham, to the peaceful town of Anniston, where Oscar McPeak became to circulation manager of the *Anniston Star*.

The couple settled down in a small house (which no longer exists) at 128 East Ninth Street.[155] A few blocks away was the beautiful Grace Episcopal Church, and a few blocks further, on West Eleventh Street, were the offices of the Anniston Star newspaper. Anniston offered a much easier and more pleasant lifestyle for the couple, who were now 44 and 38.

Grace Episcopal Church

~

The young men of Anniston were volunteering for the war right and left. It seemed as if nearly every young man was leaving town for Europe. Fort McClennan, just outside the town, was gearing up to become a big army base. On September 2nd of 1918, Oscar McPeak was called to report to the draft board. Mary must have been very nervous that day about the outcome of his interview. On his draft paper, Oscar listed Mary as his closest relative, stating that he had no children. Oscar was not drafted.

During this time, Mary continued to mourn her children. At the same time, she kept busy visiting her brothers and in-laws. In March of 1918, Mary took the train, which was a quick ride from Anniston, to visit her sister-in-law, Mabel and her friends down in Birmingham. Following that, she rode up to Huntsville where she visited Will and Frances, and Allie and Minnie. Minnie had just given birth to a little girl whom the couple named Elizabeth Baugh Gumm.[156] Mary was happy to help her with the children while Minnie was recovering. According to the *Anniston Star*, this visit was quite lengthy; Mary did not return home until May 10th.[157]

In July, Mary and Oscar traveled to Huntsville together. Allie and his wife, Minnie, were having a family reunion of sorts. Minnie's parents were there as well as some of the Baugh relatives from Tennessee. Everyone was anxious to see Allie and Minnie's new baby girl who was now about four months old.

Allie had just bought his first camera and was eager to capture the family on film. During the party that day, he kept busy making family members pose in various groups. He loved his new camera.

As joyous as the occasion was, it was obvious that Mary had changed. Somehow, she didn't seem her old lively self. And as much as she loved seeing Allie's three children, Allie, Jr., now 3, James Wade, 2, and baby Elizabeth, her heart ached for her own lost children. Allie had Minnie and Mary for a photo together, conjuring up happier times.

During the months that followed, the *Anniston Star* kept track of the McPeak's comings and goings, and their frequent visitors. In July, Will and Frances Gumm came up to Anniston and spent some time with the McPeaks. Oscar's sister, May, her husband, Joe McWilliams and their little boy, three year-old, Joe, also came to stay for a while.

July 1914, l. to r. Minnie, Baby Elizabeth, Allie, Allie, Jr., Minnie's mother, Nannie Overton, James, (in front) Oscar, Mary, Minnie's father, Jim Overton. (Courtesy Bill Gibb)

The McPeaks seem to have been a very lively, social couple who enjoyed being in the midst of activity. Since travel by train at this time was affordable and easy, it appears that many people took advantage of this transportation, in order to stay close to their family and friends. Mary and Oscar also made new friends in the town of Anniston. Everyone who met them seemed to like them and treasure their friendship.

In the fall, Mary found not feeling well. It is not known if she went to the doctor, but perhaps she shared some of her feelings with her brother, Frank, because around this time, he decided that he should bring the family for a visit.

Mary and Frank had not seen one another in quite a while, possibly since they parted ways in Ironwood. Frank told Mary and his brothers that he would be bringing Ethel and the girls for a long visit. They would board a train just as soon as they wrapped up the Christmas shows at the New Grand. Once again, the idea of escaping at least a portion of the Minnesota winter was very attractive, but most of all, he wanted to see Mary and have her meet Ethel and the girls.

A few days after New Years, Frank and Ethel with three year-old Mary Jane and nineteen month old Virginia arrived in Anniston. The family stayed with the McPeaks for nearly a month, enjoying the mild

Allie's photos. Above left, Oscar McPeak, Will Gumm, Allie Gumm, Right, Minnie & Mary Gumm. Below, Allie (left) with some of his Baugh relatives in Huntsville, AL family reunion. Uncertain as to who they are.
(Courtesy Bill Gibb)

weather and their time together. Then, on January 26th, the *Anniston Star* announced that the Gumms and Mrs. McPeak would be traveling together to Huntsville.

Time has not recorded the events of these days. We can only imagine that Frank, Allie, Will and Mary shared memories and enjoyed one another's company while the northern and southern cousins played together. Of course, as southern wives, Minnie and Frances looked Ethel over. Her manners were quite different than theirs. She was far more direct, less soft and less subservient to her husband than a Southern wife would be. In later years, Minnie Gumm said, "I always liked his little wife—but, you know, she was a northern girl."[158]

By February 28th, Mary, having bid Frank and his family goodbye, was back on the train to Anniston where she would welcome her sister-in-law, Laura McPeak, for a visit.[159] The McPeaks returned with Laura to Birmingham on March 3rd, spending the weekend with family and friends before returning home.

In April, Mary, who was feeling terribly ill, finally went to the doctor. His findings were not good. He suspected a tumor and told her she must have surgery.

Oscar and Mary's families were both informed and Mrs. Gervis McPeak, Oscar's mother, made plans to come down from Murfreesboro to help with the house and Mary's care. Will and Frances Gumm also came to stay, being terribly worried about the state of Mary's health. Without children, they were much freer to travel at a moment's notice.

The surgery was performed at Sellers Hospital in Anniston. As it turned out, the operation was long and difficult. The tumor was much larger than they had previously thought and from all that can be gathered, Mary's prognosis was not too good. Nevertheless, they removed what they could.

On May 5, 1919, the *Anniston News* reported that Mrs. McPeak was recovering well from the surgery.[160] Mary had to stay at Sellers Hospital for at least several weeks. On her return home, both she and Oscar held on to the hope that this operation had cured her.

Now, a multitude of good wishes were sent her way and many visitors came to call. On June 23rd, Oscar's niece, Miss Sara Newsome, who was now fourteen, came to stay for a while. The newspapers reported that Mary McPeak was recovering her strength.

While Mary had been so desperately ill in the hospital, Oscar had traveled south to New Orleans on business for the paper. It appears he was trying to work on a deal. However, perhaps learning from the doctor about the seriousness of Mary's conditions, things changed.

Mary and Oscar did not stay in Anniston very long after her surgery. Oscar made the decision to move them just the other side of the mountains to Rome, Georgia.

~

Rome was a small, but lovely city, built—like Rome, Italy for which it was named—on seven hills. Nestled between two rivers, the Etowah and Oostanaula, the city contains a series waterways and bridges which add to its charm. The Etowah cuts through town on one side, merging with the winding, non-navigatable Ostanaula at the far end of town where these two rivers form a third river, the Coosca. The confluence of these three rivers sometimes causes the waters in Rome to flood.

During the Civil War, Rome became a center for medical treatment. Following the Battle of Atlanta, 1100 wounded solders were sent to Rome. The citizens turned the city into one great hospital, even using churches and other buildings for the wounded. At the close of the war, William Tecumseh Sherman burned every building in Rome, with the exception of those being used as hospitals. In 1908, Rome's Harbin Hospital was ranked among the best in the South and by 1919, when the McPeaks arrived, there were seven hospitals in the city.

Besides its hospitals, Rome was busy cotton town and cultural center. The streets were carefully designed and lined with fine buildings. The town had its own opera house where local citizens congregated to enjoy concerts, and traveling companies performing Europe's great operas.

The McPeaks settled in a small house on the 2nd Avenue, only a block from the Etowah River, in the center of town. Early each morning, Oscar would set off on foot, walking three blocks to the offices of the *Rome News* where he had taken over the job of Circulation Manager, the same job he held in Birmingham and Anniston.

On their arrival, Oscar, who was now making a fairly good living, hired a maid to take care of the house. Mary was not well enough to take care of the house. Meanwhile, Oscar's mother had joined them, helping where she could, but at seventy, Oscar did not want her to keep house.

The people of Rome were down-to-earth and friendly and shortly after their arrival, the McPeaks were invited to many social events. Oscar's job at the *Rome News* enabled him to become acquainted with many of city's citizens. Mary also received many invitations from the local ladies. Life in Rome could have been the best Mary had known, but it was not to be.

After moving to Georgia, Mary's health quickly began to decline. Oscar took her to see some of the best doctors in town, but nothing they did seemed to help. Although Mary's medical records have been lost to time, everything about her case seems to point to cancer. Her pain was growing worse, and her weakness increasing.

Each day after work, Mr. McPeak came home, hat in hand, and climbed the stairs to the bedroom where she lay. Sometimes, he would find her sitting in a chair, looking out the window at the river and the cemetery hill beyond.

"How are you, dear Mrs. McPeak?" he would ask anxiously.

It grieved Mary to see him so. Once she was stylish and laughing, brushing his coat, straightening his tie, and helping in so many ways. Now, there was nothing she could do. She did not want to trouble him. He had suffered enough. Each night, Oscar and his mother prayed for Mary's recovery, and Mary put on her bright smile for them. But each day, she felt less hopeful.

In September, Mary could already feel winter in her bones. She had thought and thought about what to do. Now, she even tried to end her life, not once, but several times. Each time, she failed. Her body was wracked with pain and trying to hide it was becoming more and more difficult. Oscar called the doctor in, but there was nothing he could do.

It was dark on the morning of September 23rd when Mary finally found the strength to get out of bed. She had spent part of the early morning hours writing a note. In fact, Oscar had risen at 4 AM to check on her and had seen her light on. Now, she laid the envelope with his name on the window sill where the maid would be sure to see it when she came in her room.

Poor Oscar, she knew it would grieve him, but she could not stand the pain any longer. Soon, she would be too weak to walk or help herself, and, soon, she imagined, she would only be able to lie there screaming in agony until she passed out of this life. There was nothing good left for her, nothing more she could offer. She must go for the good of everyone.

Down the stairs she crept slowly, so that no one would hear. Each step wrenched her insides so that she thought her legs would fold beneath her, but she held on. Only a little further and it would be over.

There was barely a light in the sky when she went out the door, closing it softly behind her. The maid would arrive at 5 AM and there was not a moment to waste. Mary was wearing her dark gown, a sign of morning for the babies she had lost four years earlier.

Then, as she walked down the street, she saw it. There. There was the bridge; the slight curving bridge. "Oh God, please help me!" she cried, as she pulled herself step by step up the curve of the bridge.

Down below the river swirled and pushed against the shore. It had rained recently and the river waters were high and rough. How far was it down? She could not think. There was only the thought that once over the edge, her troubles would be gone. Her pain would be gone. Oh, Totsy! Oh, Babe! Dear mother . . . they would all be waiting for her.

~

The maid came quietly through the door at 606 2nd Avenue, just as she did almost every morning, except Sunday. Mr. McPeak would be rising soon and she must have the hot coffee and breakfast ready for him. There was old Mrs. McPeak, his mother, who would rise a bit later, and then there was poor, dear Mrs. McPeak upstairs in bed. What a dear and lovely soul she was. Lila knew how she suffered and how she tried to hide it from her husband; such a sad, sad tale.

The house seemed extra quiet this morning for some reason. Lila built a fire in the wood-burning stove. Then, she built fires in the dining room and sitting room so that they would be comfortably warm for Mr. McPeak and his mother. She would just go up now and check on Mrs. McPeak. She knew she did not sleep well and, perhaps, she would like a bit of warm coffee.

On entering the room, Lila stared in disbelief at the bed. Mrs. McPeak was not there. Had she gone to the hospital or suddenly gotten well and gone into another room? Perhaps she was with Mr. McPeak? No, no. There was something white sitting on the window sill. It was addressed to Mr. McPeak. What was it? She took the envelope and anxiously knocked on Mr. McPeak's door . . .

They had looked now for many hours. A whole group of men had gone up and down the river, looking for a body and they had found nothing. Mary McPeak, the charming lady with the dark hair, cheery brown eyes, lilting voice and smile; she had touched all who met her with her kindness. She had been so weak. Perhaps she had found a place to sit in solitude. But where? Everyone kept hoping that she had not gotten far; not jumped in the river as her note said she would. But a little after 2 o'clock, the word came. She was found. Tom Byrd and Frank Brookshire found her body lying at on the edge of the river. She was dead; drowned in the Etowah River.

Etowah River Bridges

They carried her to the Daniel Furniture Company, which was only a block away. The store carried rugs, stoves, furniture, but also coffins. An inquest was called for three o'clock that afternoon. They concluded that because of "bad health" and "mental disturbance," Mrs. McPeak had ended her life by "stepping" from the Second Avenue Bridge. In the back of the building, the furniture company provided embalming. Mary was readied for burial and her brothers were sent telegrams. It would be a terrible shock for all of them.

Poor Oscar, such a good man, everyone said. The McPeaks had come to Rome so recently, hoping to start a new life. The paper commented on what a fine couple they were and what a sad tragedy this even had been. A terrible tragedy.

Oscar bought a plot for two of them, high on the hill of the Myrtle Hill Cemetery. Their plot would overlook the town of Rome, including the river where Mary died. It was across from Mrs. Woodrow Wilson, who had only been buried there in 1914.

The *Rome News* announced that the funeral would take place on Thursday; the time was "pending the arrival of Mrs. McPeak's brothers."[161]

Mary Gum McPeak's Funeral, written on back, "Sister Mary's Grave, Rome, GA, Mytle Hill, Sept 26, 1919.
(Courtesy Joy Rion Nelson)

Frank had received the news and boarded the train the next morning. There, on the side of the hill in Rome, the four brothers watched the burial of their sister, who had been too young to die. Mary's husband, Oscar, was a broken man.

This terrible event must have sent Frank into a deep, dark depression. It was a shock for all of Mary's brothers and the family at large. As children, Mary had always been there to take care of her brothers, but none of them had been able to help her in her darkest hour.

~

Shortly after the funeral, Oscar moved from the house on 2nd Avenue to a residence on 8th Street where he would not have to cross the 2nd Avenue bridge to go to work. He could not bear the thought of Mary's painful last days in that house, nor bear to pass the spot where she had thrown herself into the swirling waters of the Etowah River.

After Mary's death, Oscar's unmarried sister, Laura McPeak, came to help keep house and care for their aged mother. Oscar continued with his job at *The Rome News*, but as kind as all the citizens of Rome were, life was not the same without Mary.

Oscar did not recover from the tragic death of his children, nor the loss of his wife. In 1920, he was still living in Rome at 606 East 6th Street with his seventy-three year-old mother, Lucy, and his fifty year-old sister, Laura. Then, in 1924, while visiting Lexington, Kentucky on business, Oscar McPeak took a 38 caliber revolver and shot himself in the left temple. His body was found in a room at the Tyler Hotel. On the dresser was an envelope addressed to his sister, Laura in Murfreesboro. It read in part:

> *Have gone the limit. Health and money gone. Only a short time till the end anyway and do not want to drag on and be a burden to you and mother when you have so much on your shoulders. You and I both will be better off. Insurance receipts enclosed.*[162]

Oscar McPeak was buried along side Mary at Myrtle Hill Cemetery. After his death, his co-workers at the Rome News commented on him with fond memories. Following her mother's death in 1929, Laura McPeak lived over the Women's Club in Murfreesboro, where she sometimes worked. She passed away in 1963.

Endnotes
Book 2—Young Frank Gumm

1. Interview with Carter Swope/Swope & Family Papers

2. $10,000 in 1890 would equal $.... in 2003.

3. So named because the bishop at that time was very tall and this was the only comfortable bed for him when he came to town. Interview with Thelma Woods, Nov 30 1983 for paper by Louise Ledwith, p. 6

4. http://www.oaklandsmuseum.org/history.html

5. Hearthstones, Caneta Skelley Hankins, Oaklands Assn., 1993, p. 44 (Rachel Maney 1826–1911)

6. U.S. Census, 1870, St. Anne's Parish, County of Allenrole, VA, P.O. Charlottesville, p. 96

7. Falling Leaves by Elizabeth Howse, p. 71

8. Swope/Darrow Family Archives

9. *Falling Stars*, Elizabeth Howse Ridley Ibid, p. 71

10. Ibid, p. 72

11. A History of Saint Paul's Episcopal Church: One Hundred Years, Murfreesboro, TN, compiled by Carole M. Carroll, 1992

12. History of St. Pauls Episcopal Church, by Carole M. Caroll, 1992

13. Early East Main, Louise Ledwith, History 490 paper, 1983, p. 2

14. TN paper (not marked) 1937, Clipping in Sewanee file, *Judy Garland Breaks Into Film*, Ed Cherry

15. *Judy* by Gerald Frank, Harper & Row, 1975, p. 6

16. Judy

17. As reported by Jimmy Gumm in Gerald Clarke's book, Judy, Frank Gumm later told his daughters that he ran away.

18. The Nashville Tennessean Magazine, March 27, 1955, p. 8

19. *The History of the University of the South*, Sewanee, TN, 1900, p. 354

20. Frank Gumm File, Archives, University of the South, Sewanee, TN

21. LINEBAUGH book on The University of the South

22. The Nashville Tennessean Magazine, June 9, 1957, *To Furnish the Truest Men* by Louise Davis, p. 12

23. Ibid, p. 18

24. Ibid, p. 18

25. Ibid, p. 18

26. Chattanooga News-Free Press, Sunday, Sept 6, 1992, *Father of Judy Garland Went to Sewanee* by John Shearer, p. E-2

27. Letter from Edward J. Tribble, University of the South Archivist to David Dahl & Barry Kehoe, 1972

28. *A Tale of Two Families*, lecture paper by John Gass Branton, p. 1, Archives, University of the South, Sewanee, TN

29. Note from the Sewanee Files, Charles McD. Puckette, The Chattanooga Times

30. The Chattanooga Times, June 26, 1969, Mrs. Henry Gass

31. *Young Judy*, David Dahl and Barry Kehoe, Mason Charter, NY 1975

32. Lanterns on the Levee, William Alexander Percy, Louisiana State University Press, Baton Rouge, 1941, 1968, 1973, p. 98

33. Letter by Frank A. Gum to Professor Henry M. Gaas, March 1934, Courtesy of University at Sewanee

34. Rutherford County, Mabel Pittard, Memphis State University Press, 1984, p. 98—Exact date of car is unknown. 1900–1903

35. U.S. Census for 1900, Rutherford County, TN, District 254, Enu. 114, Sheet 8

36. U.S. Census, 1900

37. Rutherford County Property Records, Book 42, Page 195

38. Hearthstones, Mary B. Hughes, Mid-South Publishing, 1942, p. 43

39. http://www.familyorigins.com/users/h/a/r/Cynthia-Ann-Harp-NC/FAM01-0001/index.html

40. Tennessean, 1937. Unmarked clipping from Sewanee Files

41. Rutherford County Records Book42, p. 597–598

42. Rutherford County, Mabel Pittard, Memphis State University Press, 1984, p. 99

43. W.T. Gum vs. Mary B. Gum? April 2, 1902
44. Rutherford County Records Book42, p. 597–598
45. W.T. Gum W. T. Gum et al vs. R.E. Gum et al, April 18, 1902, p. 3–4
46. J.G.Mosby, appeared in court April 18, 1902
47. Sales Decree W.T. Gum et Al. vs. R.E. Gum et. Al, April 18, 1902
48. Report of Clerk & Master, Hickum Weakly, April 17, 1902, Ent. Bk X, p. 438
49. Book X, p. 438, April 17, 1902
50. Rutherford County Property Record Book 42, p. 597–598
51. Deed of sale from S.S. Butler to Gum Children on August 18, 1902
52. Rutherford County Property Record Book II, p. 472
53. Rutherford County Marriage Records Book, p. 445, #1613
54. The Atlanta Constitution, Atlanta, GA, April 12, 1903, p.
55. Ibid, Tuesday, October 20, 1903, p.3 "Took His Clothes By Force"
56. RU Cty Court Case Haynes vs. H.W. Pennell, Dec 10, 1903
57. Letter to David Dahl & Barry Kehoe from Edward J. Tribble, University Archivist, University of the South, Sewanee, TN Sept 12, 1972
58. University of the South press release, June 24, 1969
59. Ibid, p. 2
60. Stated by Bettie Gum Fox's grandson, Henry Lee Fox, 2005
61. http:www.ehow.com/list_6109916_signs-symptoms-miliary-tuberculosis.html
62. Rutherford County Court Records Book SS, p. 516, December 1906
63. Ibid, Book SS, p. 577
64. Taken from St. Paul's Church Register 1898–1908.
65. Carter Swope, NYC interview, 2004
66. Carter Swope, NYC interview regarding his father
67. The Nashville Tennessean Magazine, March 27, 1955, p. 8
68. Ibid
69. Young Judy, David Dahl & Barry Kehoe, Mason Charter, 1975, p.
70. Bill & Minerva Shacklett, Gloria Shacklett
71. Sara Shacklett Tinsley
72. http://en.wikipedia.org/wiki/Great_Famine_(Ireland)
73. Henry Lee Fox, interview notes 2003–2005
74. Goodspeeds History of Tennessee 1888
75. The Nashville Tennessean, February 1952, obit
76. Daily News Journal, May 21, 1944, Front Page Obit
77. Story as told by Henry Lee Fox, Aaron Todd, and Jack Todd

78. Story told by Henry Lee Fox

79. Notes from Margaret Fox Hester, taken from TN State Archives, Family File, Obituaries, *A History of Rutherford County*, C. Sims, P. 113, *Who's Who in America*, Vols. 1902–1912

80. Falling Stars by Elizabeth Howse, ie Mrs. G.S. Ridley, p. 13. Mrs. Ridley's mother was a cousin to Josie Ewing.

81. Letter from Margaret Fox Hester, 2006, & gravestones at Evergreen Cemetery, Murfreesboro, TN

82. Stories from the grandchildren of Walter D. Fox and Sarah Bell

83. Biographical Appendix, p. 1031, *Falling Stars*, Elizabeth O. Howse, p. 4

84. Those East Main Street People and Their Houses, C.B. Arnette, 2006, p. 216–217

85. W.D. Fox and others vs. Margaret Fox, RU Cty Court, 1903–1917

86. Tullahoma Time-Table, The Official Publication of the Historic Preservation Society of Tullahoma, Inc. VII, No. 1, April 1986, p. 25

87. Who's Who in Tennessee, 1910?, p. 65

88. http://en.wikipedia.org/wiki/Tullahoma,_Tennessee#History

89. Ovoca pamphlet from the early 1900s. Coffee County Historical Society and periodicals

90. Walter D. Fox's descendants believed that Walter D. and Frank Gumm started a newspaper together. No evidence of this has been found, but the fact that W.D. Fox was editor of a paper explains this idea.

91. Coffee County Historical Society, May 1974, p. 15—other reference misplaced

92. RU County Property Record Book, #51, p. 447

93. Information from Geri and Richard Gumm, daughter-in-law and grandson or Robert Emmett Gumm

94. Information from the Robert Gumm family which includes: the fact that at a certain point Belle's father was the oldest living Mason and received a letter from President Franklin D. Roosevelt. Have been unable to find her family in the census.

95. Interview with Geri Gumm, Robert E. Gumm's daughter-in-law, 2005.

96. The Ironwood News Record, January 21, 1911, p. 13

97. Michigan, U.S. Federal Census 1910,

98. NEWs Obituary 1912

99. Ironwood Daily Globe, Ironwood, Michigan, November 3, 1939, p. 6

100. Records contained in the family book, Mount Olivet Cemetery & A Collection of Information About the Flavious G. and Johnnie Clara McPeak

Family 1894–1936, by Howard H. McPeak, 1987. Thanks to Harold McPeak for kindly sharing this "private publication" with me.

101. This comment based on the copy of a note from Rev. McPeak.

102. Taken from Flavious McPeak's family history

103. Mount Olivet Cemetery & A Collection of Information About the Flavious G. and Johnnie Clara McPeak Family 1894–1936, by Howard H. McPeak, 1987

104. The Liberty Herald, Smith County, The Times, September 2nd, 1896 http://www.tngenweb.org/dekalb/Liberty_Herald/herald110.htm

105. Ironwood Times, June 1911, p.

106. Ibid, p. 6

107. This latter description came from Judy Garland herself.

108. City Directories of 1914–1916

109. http://en.wikipedia.org/wiki/Cloquet,_Minnesota Get Happy by Gerald Clarke, p. 12

110. *Crossroads in Time: A History of Carlton County, Minnesota*, Francis M. Carroll, Carlton County Historical Society, 1987, Chapter 9

111. Interview with Carlton County Historical Society, 2010

112. Pine Knot, Sept 16, 1911

113. Pine Knot, October 7, 1911

114. Pine Knot, November 18, 1911

115. Cloquet Paper November 25, 1911

116. Young Judy, p. 18

117. Judy Garland, The Secret Life of an American Legend, David Shipman, Hyperior, 1992, p. 5; Additional research from U.S. 1913 census, and Joe. E Brown internet sites

118. Judy by Gerald Frank, p. 7

119. Stars Fell on Michigamme,(Back Then column) by Larry Chabot, Marquette Monthly, Sept. 2003; www.mmnow.com/ Monthly, Sept. 2003; www.mmnow.com/ m_archive_folder/03/0309/back.then.html

120. Ibid

121. Judy Garland, The Golden Years, Rita Piro, Great FEATS Press, p. 3–4

122. *Blaine Grads Treasure 75th Reunion*, Debs Kreig, The Evening Telegram, Superior, WI, 7-18-1985, p. 17

123. Get Happy, Gerald Clarke, p. 13

124. Get Happy, Gerald Clarke, p. 14

125. Ibid, p. 14

126. Interview with Glen Settle, Lancaster, CA 2003

127. Judy Garland The Golden Years by Rita E. Piro, Great FEATS Press, NY, p. 4

128. Judy Garland The Golden Years by Rita E. Piro, Great FEATS Press, NY, p. 4

129. Superior ....

130. Judy Garland, The Secret Life of an American Legend, David Shipman, p

131. *Itasca County Independent*, March 5, 1914, Front Page, See *Rainbow*, p. 21

132. Rainbow, Christopher Finch, p. 21

133. Rutherford County Record Book No 58, p.184–185

134. Marriage Certificate from the State of Alabama, Madison County, July 2, 1914, p. 551

135. Marriage Certificate from the State of Alabama, Madison, March 3rd, 1915, p. 285

136. Judy by Gerald Frank, p. 7

137. These songs with detail notes may be found on the recording, *Made In America, Vaudeville Songs—A Tribute to the Gumm Family*. © 2005

138. Get Happy by Gerald Clarke, p. 15

139. Judy Garland, David Shipman, p. 7

140. http://en.wikipedia.org/wiki/Mary_Jane_(shoe)

141. Grand Rapids Companion, 1991 GR Centennial Committee, p. 169–170

142. Itasca County Independent, March 24, 1917, Judy Garland, D. Shipman, p. 8

143. http://en.wikipedia.org/wiki/World_War_I#Entry_of_the_United_States

144. Grand Rapids Companion, p. 235

145. Young Judy, Dahl & Kehoe, p. 29

146. Judy by Gerald Clarke, p. 8

147. http://en.wikipedia.org/wiki/1918_flu_pandemic

148. http://blogs2.startribune.com/blogs/oldnews/archives/45

149. http://blogs2.startribune.com/blogs/oldnews/archives/43

150. WWI, U.S. Draft Card Registrar's Report, Card # 1343, 13-3-15-C

151. Memories by Elmyra Thompson's granddaughter as told to the author.

152. Online history of the U.S. Postal Service

153. Postcard of Nannie Rion,, courtesy of Joy Rion Nelson

154. #3935, United States versus Oscar McPeak, December 1913, National Archives Records, Southeast Region, Morrow, Georgia,

155. This house no longer exists. Address taken from Oscar McPeak's draft record.

156. The Anniston Star, March 27, 1918

157. Ibid, May 9th and 10th, 1918

158. Judy, Gerold Frank, p. 7

159. Grand Rapids paper of January 4th stated that the family would be gone six weeks.

160. The Anniston Star, May 5, 1919

161. Ibid

162. Lexington Leader, Lexington, KY October 28, 1924, p. 12, col. 7

Those Gumm Girls

The Judy Garland Birthplace, Grand Rapids, Minnesota.

Chapter 28

1920

It was March, and the snow was coming down. Ethel had told him to stay home, but Frank was determined to bring the new pianist at the Lyceum Theatre in Deer River her first pay check, so he hopped in his new Ford Model-T and headed down the winding two-lane road through the woods. That winter season had been one of the snowiest in Grand Rapids history, already topping 50 inches, and winter wasn't over yet. As Frank reached the half-way point between Grand Rapids and Deer River, the flurry turned into a blizzard. Well, there was no turning back now. To keep from sliding off the road, he slowed the engine and hung on. He would make it, but what an adventure!

Frank was proud of his new automobile. He had bought the shiny, black Model-T with the oval window in the back a few months earlier. Business at the New Grand was good, so they could afford it, and since automobile prices had come down, a lot more Americans were buying them. Frank loved the freedom this "horseless carriage" afforded him; having an automobile made him feel rich.

After buying his Model-T, Frank Gumm and Fred Bentz had expanded the business, adding two more theatres, the Lyceum fourteen miles northwest of Grand Rapids, and the Eclipse, just six miles east in Coleraine.

When Frank finally arrived at theater that evening, Ruth, the new pianist was busy playing the Lyceum's "battered, old piano." Seated in the house, a crowd of about thirty people were intently watching the flickering action on a movie screen that looked like "an old bed sheet."

Frank Gumm and his car around 1917.
(Courtesy Judy Garland Museum)

The audience probably would have been larger if it wasn't for the storm raging outside.

When the film concluded, Frank handed Ruth her first paycheck, a grand sum of $7.00 (= $74.90). Then, the projectionist showed slides of the Gibson Girls, while Frank entertained the audience with a performance of "Let Me Call You Sweetheart." Outside, the wind was howling and, inside, Frank "rocked the building, singing." In later years, Ruth Gunderson would say, "I considered . . . Frank Gumm a living doll."[1]

That year, 1920, Frank was busier than ever. Traveling between three theaters kept him on his toes, but it also meant a fairly good income for the family. In June of the previous year, Frank and Ethel had purchase the house they were living in from Daniel and Annie Gunn for "$1 and other valuable considerations."[2]

Besides the needed income, Frank, with his gregarious personality and high energy, liked to be on the move. Recently, he had taken a job, writing a column for the local newspaper, *The Independent*. Since part of his job entailed gathering news around town, most mornings he stopped at the town's confectionary shop for a dish of ice cream. Mabel MacAdam later recalled that while he was there, he usually sang a few songs at the piano.[3]

At least once a month, if not more, Frank and Ethel still performed at the New Grand. In the summer, when the weather allowed, they traveled to some of the neighboring towns, where they performed their *Jack and Virginia Lee—Sweet Southern Singers* act.

Although Ethel was an exacting housekeeper and an excellent cook, she had so many responsibilities these days that Frank agreed she should hire a housekeeper. For a time, Inga Mooren, a Swedish girl who lived some twenty miles away, came to live with them. When Ethel played background music for the 7:30 picture show, and Frank, for the second show at 10:30, Ina, who slept in the summer kitchen, was there to watch the girls.[4] With two shows a night, seven nights a week, the Gumms were continuously busy.

Ethel seems to have managed the household in a manner similar to the way her mother, Eva, had managed hers, and like her mother, she taught her daughters to sing and dance. By the time Mary Jane and Virginia were five and three, they had learned to sing together in two-part harmony.

That year, the girls made their stage debut, appearing in one of the New Grand's Friday night amateur shows. Naturally, the girls charmed everyone with their performance, and they soon became regulars on the New Grand stage. In addition to coaching the girls, Ethel also made their costumes.

Along with all the other activities in Grand Rapids, twice a year, the community put on a theatrical production. Ethel usually helped produce the show, and with her expertise, chose the music for these events. She and Frank kept abreast of the latest Broadway hits and popular songs. One year, when she was unable to obtain the sheet music for a particular Broadway song called "Money, Money, Money," she wrote a new set of lyrics.* Of course, Mr. and Mrs. Gumm both appeared in these theatrical productions, and, like everything else they did, were a big hit.

Before radio or television, the general population actively sought ways to entertain themselves at home. Many homes had a piano or musical instrument of some kind, and families would gather together to sing. People also invited their friends over for parties, so they could have some fun. Mr. and Mrs. Gumm were exceedingly active in this way; they were known to have some of the best parties in town.

In the early years, an upright piano stood in the front parlor with Frank's ukulele on top, ready to be taken down at a moment's notice for a quick musical number. Ethel played at least three instruments besides piano, including the accordion. Mr. and Mrs. Gumm seemed to be born entertainers with the ability transition seamlessly from socializing to performing. Although Ethel was sometimes looked upon as a little overbearing, without a doubt, she and Frank were loads of fun to be around.

Bridge parties were also very popular during this period, and Ethel enjoyed having them at her home. In fact, one week she hosted four parties. At every bridge party, she provided what the local newspaper report called, "dainty" snacks. With all their activities and talent, it is not surprising that Mr. and Mrs. Gumm were soon socializing with the "best people" in town.

---

* "Money, Money, Money" from Mary, a 1923 Broadway production by Louis A. Hirsch and Otto Hardback.

~

Local memories of the Gumms in Grand Rapids recall a happy, carefree couple, but one young man who met them around this period saw another side. Marcus Rabwin, the son of Russian immigrants, had grown up working in his father's movie theatre in a small, northern Minnesota town, Eveleth. The summer of 1920, Marcus had taken a job as a film salesman, trying to persuade theatre owners to rent Hodkinson pictures, instead of the big name studio pictures.

One day, while traveling on the train through northern Minnesota, Rabwin was advised by some older film salesman to avoid Grand Rapids and the man who ran the only theatre in town, Frank Gumm. One salesman described Mr. Gumm as "nervous," with a "hair-trigger temper." It would be a waste of time, he was told, to try to sell Mr. Gumm anything because "he hated salesmen."[5] Despite the salesmen's comment's, Marc liked the idea of a challenge, so when the train stopped in Grand Rapids, he got off.

In later years, it seems Marc Rabwin dramatized his first visit to the New Grand, describing it as a "one-story, clapboard building with a painted sign." The truth is that in 1920, the New Grand was a new brick building with a "seating capacity of 450."[6]

Marc found Frank Gumm in the lobby, making popcorn, while he took tickets from the people coming in to see the show. Most surprising to Marc was the fact that Frank Gumm had a southern accent. He did seem edgy, advising Marc to "stay out of his way until he had time to talk to him.

Later, they went into the theater's tiny office, where Frank paced, fidgeted and, in a flash, got so angry, his face turned purple. Marc, soon to be a medical student at the University of Minnesota, suspected that Frank was hyper-thyroid, something he would talk to him about later. Meanwhile, the two men hit it off.

Besides his high energy, nervous personality, Marc Rabwin found that Frank Gumm was also warm and charming, with quick humor and a ready laugh. That night, Frank Gumm invited him to have dinner at the family home and stay over-night because, he said, there were no decent hotels in town. Marc Rabwin was all of nineteen when he met the Gumms. It was a friendship that would last throughout Mr. and Mrs. Gumm's lives, and the life of the baby that was yet to be born.[7]

~

One of the songs Frank and Ethel Gumm enjoyed singing during this time was a Walter Donaldson–William Jerome hit, *Back Home in Tennessee.** The song spoke of the happiness felt in returning home to Tennessee where there are "roses 'round the door," and family and friends waiting to greet them. In 1920, as the winter season approached, Frank and Ethel made plans to travel south, this time with the children.

The end of November, with a foot of snow already on the ground, Ethel left Mary Jane and Virginia at home with Frank while she traveled to Superior to visit her parents. On the 4th of December, Frank boarded the train with his daughters. The family was reunited in Superior, and from there traveled south to Tennessee. Despite the fact that Murfreesboro can be fairly cold in December, nevertheless, the weather was mild compared to Minnesota. When Frank bundled the girls onto the train, temperatures were already averaging 16 degrees; going south was a nice break for everyone.

For a week or two before Christmas, the Gumms stayed with Uncle Ed and Aunt Nannie Rion. The Rion's son, Ed, Jr., now a handsome young man of twenty, was living at home with his new bride, Aileen Jaccard. As a wedding present, Mr. and Mrs. Rion had given the couple a small store on East Main Street, just across from Middle Tennessee University. The Rion's daughter, Virginia, now eleven, was a pretty girl with long curls. Likely, she enjoyed playing with Mary Jane and Virginia.

During their visit, the Gumm sisters performed some of their songs and dances in the Rion's front parlor. All the relatives were there, including Aunt Bettie, Uncle Henry and their youngest daughter, Martha, who was now a young lady of fifteen. Everyone was delighted with Frank's darling little girls.

Anna Lee Fox, whose presence Frank enjoyed so much when living in the Fox family home, was not there. Recently, she had married Mr. Paul

---

* *Back Home In Tennessee*, words by Wm. Jerome, Music Walter Donaldson, 1915, Waterson, Berlin & Snyder Co.

The Rion Family, Ed, Jr., Ed, Sr., Aileen, Nannie and Virginia. (Courtesy Claire Rion Weber)

Mertz, who was an insurance salesman from Pennsylvania, where the couple now lived.

Jack Fox, twenty-one, was a WWI veteran. Recently, he had married Mary Bodie, a Mississippi belle, whom he met on his way home from the war. Jack and Mary were living with the Fox family in their new home on South Tennessee Boulevard. Mary had just given birth to their first child, Van, that August. Also living with Henry Lee and Bettie was Henry Lee's mother, Tennie Fox.

Coming back to Murfreesboro with his wife and children, brought Frank memories of his own youth. He took the girls to see the big house on East Main where he was born, the corner where his father's store once stood, and the little house on Maney Avenue from which he had embarked on a new life at Sewanee. The spot where the brick tenement once stood was now owned by one of the Ransom brothers, and an elegant home had been built there.

The Fox Home

Another surprise was the fact that the Darrows no longer lived at Oak Manor. Instead, they were living in the grand mansion they had built on the corner of East Main and High Street, now called Highland. Meanwhile, the grand Oak Manor had gone into decline.*

Following their visit with the Rion and Fox families, the Gumms boarded the train and traveled to Huntsville. It had been Frank's wish to spend Christmas with his brothers this year. Since Mary's death, remaining close to Will and Allie seemed even more important. Aunt Nannie would later write to her daughter-in-law, Aileen, that Frank remained close to his brothers his entire life.[8]

~

The following January in 1921, Frank Gumm went south by himself. Leaving the average 12 degree temperatures of Grand Rapids on the 22nd, he stopped first in Indianapolis where he visited with Bob and Belle. From there, he traveled to Murfreesboro, and finally to Huntsville. He was gone several weeks, and returned home the second week of February.

Although Frank may have wanted to escape the freezing temperatures up north for part of the winter—a condition which may have irritated his troublesome ear—it is clear that his relationship with his siblings was also one of the most important elements of his life.

The balance of 1921 seems to have passed much like the years before it. In September, Frank and Ethel traveled to Minneapolis where they gave their yearly performance at the County Fair. Janey and Jimmy were probably left with Ethel's parents, which not only made things easier for them, but gave the couple a little vacation.

Then, sometime between October and November, Ethel Gumm discovered that she was pregnant. Almost immediately, she decided that she did not want the baby. During the early weeks of November, she tried every home remedy she knew to terminate the pregnancy. Nothing worked. Finally, she and Frank drove to Minneapolis to seek out the help of their young friend, Marcus Rabwin at the University of Minnesota.[9]

Late one night, Marc heard a knock at his door. Opening it, he was surprised to find Mr. and Mrs. Gumm, who had traveled nearly 200 miles to ask for his help. Although they didn't use the word, it was clear they

* Oaklands was restored in the 1950s and is preserved as a museum.

were asking for an abortion. They made the pregnancy sound like an accident, and insisted they only wanted two children.

Rabwin refused to help. Not only was abortion illegal, he told them, it was terribly dangerous. He thought Ethel should go ahead and have the baby. "After the baby's born," he said, "you wouldn't take a million dollars for it."[10]

In later years, Judy Garland would tell a similar story, stating that her mother had tried to end the pregnancy on her own, but she had been born anyway. Why a mother would tell her child that she had tried to abort her is another matter, but it does seem that this baby was meant to be. It would be a much sadder world had Ethel Gumm succeeded.

Although, according to Marcus Rabwin, Frank stressed that their problems were financial, this was hardly true. The Gumms had enough money and were living quite comfortably. It has been suggested that something deeply unsettling occurred between September and November; something that made Ethel not want this baby. Until now, the family had seemed quite happy.

After their visit with Marcus Rabwin, Ethel accepted the fact that the child was coming. Frank was her first love, and she wanted the marriage to work. For his part, Frank loved his family, and was committed to making Ethel happy. The couple now hoped that the baby would be a boy. They decided to call him, Frank Gumm, Jr.

On June 9th, Ethel went into labor. Frank helped her into the Model-T, and raced through town, across the railroad tracks and the bridge over the Mississippi River. To the left, sitting on a slight hill is the red brick Itasca Hospital. It was here, on June 10th, 1922 at 5:30 AM, in a small room on the second floor, that Ethel Marion Gumm gave birth to her third child.

Chapter 29

A New Baby

ALONG WITH THE VOICES IN THE ROOM, THE FIRST SOUND THAT MET the newborn baby's ears was the sound of the Mississippi rapids. Before the rapids were tamed, the rushing waters could be heard quite clearly through the hospital walls.

The fact that the baby was a girl may have been a disappointment to her parents, but it was a disappointment that did not last long. She was a beautiful baby, and they loved her. In keeping with the original plans for their child's name, her parents decided to call her Frances Ethel Gumm.

Mary Jane, six, and Virginia, four, were thrilled with their new little sister. In the tradition of the Gumm family, they called her "Baby" or "Babe." From the very beginning, Frances Ethel Gumm charmed everyone she met.

When Grandma Eva came to visit and help Ethel, she took to calling the baby, "Fanny." Many of the family, including Frank and Ethel followed suit during the first two years of the little girl's life. Her two year-old portrait and Frank's alumni card at Sewanee both attest to this fact.

Ethel, who was never one to lounge about or rest, was soon back to work, playing piano for the silent pictures at the New Grand. While she played out front, the new baby slept peacefully in a box back stage. This was how little Fanny Gumm spent the first year or more of her life, surrounded by love and music.

Frank was not around a lot. Managing three theaters and writing a news column kept him fairly busy, but he usually came home before the girls went to sleep, to kiss them goodnight and sing *Danny Boy*, or another of his favorite songs to them.

Meanwhile, Ethel kept to her schedule. When she wasn't at the theatre, she coached Janey and Jimmy, worked for the community theatre and wrote songs. A visitor to the Gumm household around this time remarked that it seemed Ethel was always writing songs.[11]

Even if she was not much of a housewife, every one who knew Ethel Gumm at this time admired her. The local opinion was that she was a very nice woman, who was willing to help anyone she could. Now that the Gumms were so much busier, some of the time, Frank hired other performers and pianists to work at the New Grand in their place.

~

In 1922, Frank Gumm took out a loan with the bank to improve the family home. One large improvement was to remove the wall between the enclosed front porch and the parlor, making it one large room. At the same time, he had the workmen put in windows across the front and side corner of the parlor. This renovation brightened house. In summer, much like the South, a shower of pink clematis blossoms, growing on a trellis at the front corner of the house, could be seen through the windows. The new windows also made it easier for Ethel to watch the children while they played outside. With the parlor enlarged, the Gumms replaced the upright piano with a baby grand.

As little Fanny grew older and began to walk, Ethel was often too busy, or perhaps too distracted, to mind Baby all the time. Sometimes, she asked their next door neighbor, Mrs. Morris, who had just moved to town in 1923 or one of the other ladies to watch Fanny. Sometimes, the neighborhood children played with Fanny, carting her around in a baby carriage.[12]

In those days, town of Grand Rapids was a safe place for children. There were few automobiles and those who owned them did not drive faster than 5–10 miles an hour. The Gumms lived in an area of family homes, bordered by farmland, woods, ponds and lakes. The one exception to this was Mr. Gunner Smith, a blacksmith, who had his shop across the street. The mustachioed Mr. Smith had a wooden leg, which was fascinating to the local children. They loved to peek in and watch him

Baby Frances Gumm, 1923.
(Courtesy Dahl/Kehoe Archives)

as he chewed tobacco and hammered the hot iron until "a shower of white-hot sparks" flew over him.[13]

The Gumms' street was full of children, and the parents thought nothing of letting their offspring run wild. In any case, there was always at least one mother, if not more, keeping an eye out for everyone else's children, as well as her own. Because of this, Ethel apparently felt free to let Baby Frances run around when she was a little over a year.

During this time, one neighbor found Baby was running around, badly in need of changing. Unsure of where Ethel was, the neighbor took Baby inside, and finding that she had no diapers handy, replaced her diaper with a kitchen towel.* This incident, which seems to have occurred more than once, may be responsible in part for the lyric in Roger Edens' *Born in a Trunk,*

And they used a make-up towel for my didee ...†

~

* It seems Judy must have known about this situation, for in the song, Roger Edens seems to have based some of the lyrics on Judy's own life. Otherwise, it is wild coincidence!

† *Born In A Trunk,* Roger Edens © 1954

While Ethel's relatives were constant visitors to the little white house in Grand Rapids, it seems Frank's family, who lived quite a distance and had little money, did not visit. His brother, Bob in Indianapolis, was the closest, but in 1922, Bob and Belle had a reason of their own not to make the journey. On March 5th, 1922, after twelve years of marriage, Belle had given birth to a son, Richard Earl Gumm.

Richard was not the only cousin to the Gumms born in 1922. Ethel's brother and sister-in-law, Jack and Margaret Milne, who had been married in 1919, had a son, Robert, on the 23rd of March. Their first child, John, Jr., was born the previous year.

Jack, Jr. had recently moved to Duluth, where he had a job as a clerk, working for the Duluth Mesabe & Iron Range Railroad. Jack Milne was also a very talented singer with a beautiful Irish tenor voice. In addition to his job, he moonlighted at the Golden Gate Nightclub, and sang for weddings, funerals and Sunday church services. He also sang for synagogue services. While visiting the Gumms in 1923, he performed on the New Grand stage and received an excellent review. Like his sisters, Jack was a wonderful pianist, but according to his son, never took lessons. He was simply able to play by ear.[14]

Franklin and Fred Milne at the train station in Superior.
(Courtesy Dee Milne)

Ethel's sister, Mary Civila married Jack Glyer in 1919. Jack was a talented singer and the couple, who had no children yet, sometimes worked in vaudeville. Like Ethel, Mary played the piano and sang.

Grandma Eva loved her grandchildren and came to visit often, sometimes bringing Ethel's youngest sister, Norma, with her. Norma, who was now sixteen, had inherited the family tendency toward weightiness. Eva's rich cooking likely contributed. By her mid-teens, Norma was well over 200 pounds. Nevertheless, she had a nice singing voice and, like other members of the family, was pursuing a career in vaudeville. When Ethel's family was in town, they helped with the house and the children, as well as performing in the theater.

Grandma Eva. (Courtesy Dee Milne)

Although Ethel was usually too busy to do a lot of housework, like her mother, she was an excellent cook. Along with her wonderful sweets and jams, Ethel's tasty dishes included heavy gravies, and things that would stick to the ribs through the cold Minnesota winters. When Grandma Eva came to stay, she spent hours making "pasties"—a stew of meat and potatoes cooked in a crust.

For a time, Ethel Gumm hired an older woman named Bella Nelson as a housekeeper. Bella lived in an old house behind the Gumm property, but according to town legend, there was something about Bella that scared all the local children. Nevertheless, the Gumms seemed to like her.

As Baby grew a bit older, Ethel sometimes put Janey and Jimmy in charge of looking after their little sister. On one of these occasions, the older sisters had plans to raid a local farmer's orchard. Undeterred by being saddled with their baby sister, Mary Jane and Virginia decided to take her along. Their objects of their desire were some luscious, red, ripe cherries. Perhaps they were hoping their mother would make them a nice cherry pie.

So, the girls set off on a journey of two blocks, with the wagon and Baby Fanny in tow. As the story goes, Janey and Jimmy had almost filled the wagon with cherries when the irate farmer showed up. Scared, Janey grabbed Baby and threw her into the wagon on top of the cherries. Then, the two girls ran for their lives. By the time they got home, as grown-up "Frances" later described it, she was so covered with the sweet, red juice of ripe cherries; she "looked like a cherry tart."[15]

Although little Frances Gumm made her official debut at the age of two and a half, it is apparent that she had been singing much earlier. Some records state that she was singing "Jingle Bells" the Christmas of 1923 at the age of a year and a half. Growing up in a home where life centered around music and performing, she was exposed to music and responded to it in the same way most children learn to speak or take their first steps.

One day, Frank was playing piano in the front parlor, while Baby Fanny and her little friend were playing nearby. Perhaps Baby was trying to sing along. For whatever reason, Frank called the two little girls over to him and attempted to teach them, *My Country 'Tis of Thee*. The other little girl could only absorb a small portion of the tune, but Baby was able to learn the entire song. Frank was so excited by how quickly she picked up the tune and lyrics that he called Ethel and the girls to come in and listen. This was her first song, and, to Baby's pride, everyone in the family exclaimed, "Baby Gumm is good!"[16]

Chapter 30

Back Home in Tennessee

In September of 1923, Frank received the shocking news that his youngest brother, thirty year-old Allie Gumm, was dead. Allie had contracted strep throat, which led quickly to pneumonia. He was only ill a few days before he was gone. Minnie was left with three children, Allie, Jr., 8, James, 6, and Elizabeth, 5. Once again, a Gumm parent had died tragically young.

On the 22nd of September, Frank left Grand Rapids to attend Allie's funeral.[17] He remained in Huntsville for two weeks, trying to absorb what had occurred and help Minnie in her terrible time of grief.

To support her children, Minnie got a job with Montgomery Ward. Later, she would go to work at Dunnavant's Department Store, a large, high-end clothing store where she worked altering clothing until 1965. The inherited love of music would continue with Allie's children. Elizabeth's son, Bill Gibb, would later recall that his mother loved to walk around the house singing.

How deep Frank's grief was over the loss of his sister and youngest brother, can only be imagined, but while he and Ethel lived in Grand Rapids, Frank would continue to make every effort to visit his siblings and their children each year.

~

The winter Baby Fanny was two she became ill with a terrible ear infection. Ethel rushed her to the hospital, and held the screaming child down, while the doctor lanced her ears.

(above) Alle with Minnie and the children. (Below), Minnie and the children around the time of Alle's passing. (Courtesy Bill Gibb)

Due to his poverty stricken childhood, Frank's early ear problems had never been completely been cured. Baby's parents would make every effort to see that hers were. When she came home from the hospital, Baby was given the "home remedy" for earaches. For most of the winter that year, she sat in the front parlor on the sofa with a pair of socks hanging over her ears. The socks were filled with hot salt and tied together so that the heavy end of each sock hung over her ears. Judy Garland later described herself as looking "like a cocker spaniel."[18]

A musician acquaintance once noted that Baby Frances' ear condition may also have been instrumental in the placement of her voice. "Because her ear condition affected her hearing," he said, "she placed her voice where she could hear it."[19] Since persons hearing Baby Gumm sing when she was as young as two noted her unusual ability to project, this analysis may be, at least in part, correct.

One neighbor, Mrs. Minor, who often babysat little Frances, later recalled that Ethel often sat in the front parlor holding the singing two year-old on her lap. Even though Frances was inside, Mrs. Minor could hear her singing clear across the street.

By now, Frances loved to sing and whenever Janie and Jimmy put on one of their backyard shows, they would put her to work. In a short time, the two year-old's song repertoire expanded. That spring, Baby Frances made first formal singing debut at the Itasca Dry Goods store annual "Style Show." What she sang has not been recorded for posterity.

During this time, Ethel Gumm, who had recently lost a lot of weight, suddenly fell ill. The cause was found to be a large goiter. On Marcus Rabwin's advice, she was sent to Rochester, Minnesota for surgery.

While Ethel was away, Frank took the girls to the theatre with him. One night, he had booked a child trio called *The Blues Sisters*. The group consisted of three little girls, very much like the Gumm sisters, between the ages of five and nine. Baby watched the show sitting on her father's lap, and when the youngest girl came forward and sang a solo, Jimmy said she could see the wheels turning in her little sister's head. "Daddy," said Baby, whispering to Frank, "Can I do that?" And Frank had said "yes."

~

That summer, the Gumm family made an unscheduled trip south. This time, it seems they hopped into Frank's Model-T Ford and drove.

Betty Baugh.
(Courtesy Curry Wolfe)

Although the Grand Rapids papers make no mention of this summer trip, there were several people down south who recalled seeing the family the summer Baby turned two.

Stopping first in Indianapolis, the family visited Bob, Belle and little Richard. Then, they traveled to Vincennes, Illinois where they met Frank's Baugh cousins. Uncle Jack Baugh had passed away in 1913 at the age of seventy-eight. After a bad fall down the stairs of his son, Murphey's home, Uncle Jack had been confined to bed for several weeks, where he contracted pneumonia and died.[20] At his request, he was buried at Evergreen Cemetery in Murfreesboro next to his wife, Maria, and his parents.

Murphey George was happy to reminisce with Frank about family and the old days in Murfreesboro. Nine years older than Frank, he recalled many things about their grandmother, Mary Ann Baugh, and Frank's mother, his Aunt Clemmie, in a way that Frank could not. Murphey George also had a very strong Tennessee accent which may have been difficult for Ethel to understand. Murphey's accent was so strong that when the children in his daughter Betty's class were asked if any of their parents came from a foreign country, Betty raised her hand.

While the adults reminisced, the Gumm girls, eight, seven and two, visited with Betty Baugh, ten. Recalling the visit later, Betty said she thought her cousins a bit stand-offish.

The Gumms' visit in Indiana was brief. They had a long trip ahead of them. Arriving in Murfreesboro, Edwin and Nannie Rion were apparently out of town, because in later interviews, Aunt Nannie said that Frances had never been to Murfreesboro. The Fox family, however, was home, and Anna Lee, who was there at the time, later recalled that little Frances, who was barely two, was already singing. If the Gumms visited Jefferson Springs, where the Fox family had a summer cottage, they may also have stopped in Jefferson to visit some of their Wade cousins. There were so many relatives and old friends to see on this trip, and everyone remarked on what a lovely family Frank had.

On this trip, rather than imposing on the Fox family with their full house, and perhaps on the advise of his cousin, Murphey, Frank took the family down Manchester Pike near Old Millersburg, where Aunt Eliza Pruett's, son, Ashton, and his wife, Lizzie Alice, had a farm on Hoover Road. Ashton, who was two years older than Frank, may have been a cousin he played with as a child. In any case, the Pruett's took the Gumm family in.

The Gumms were accustomed to visiting the south in winter, but by now the weather was quite warm. Staying in the country, where people still lived in old log homes without the advantage of electricity, running water or ventilation systems, was quite different from life in the grand Rion home. The Pruetts also did not have the luxury of servants as town folks did, and likely, Ethel was feeling the effects of the heat and humidity. This may explain why Alice Pruett later complained that during the Gumm's visit, she had to do all the cooking and washing for this family of five people.

On the hot summer afternoons, while the family picnicked in the shade of some old trees, Baby Gumm climbed up on a nearby log and sang as if she were on the stage. As Alice Pruitt later put it, "Judy Garland could stand on a tree trunk and sing like a birdie, when she was only two years old."[21]

Rumors abound that the Gumms also visited the Gum Community, staying with Frank's distant cousin, John Gum and his family in their Sears and Roebuck house. Although this is possible, it seems hardly likely. Frank was barely acquainted with his country cousins, if that, and apparently, these country cousins did not think much of him.

Traveling south, Frank took the family to Sewanee in hopes of visiting with his old school pal, Henry Gass and his family. Henry was now married to Marguerite Rather, one of Frank's former Murfreesboro schoolmates. After attending New College at Oxford, Henry had returned to Sewanee in 1912, where he became a professor at the Sewanee Grammar School. In 1922, he took a position at the college as a professor of classical languages.

Frank and Ethel Gumm swimming with their daughters Mary Jane and Virginia. Date and location unknown, but was probably taken by Alle Gumm. (Courtesy Bill Gibb)

Unfortunately, Frank had not written Henry to let him know they were coming, or if he had, Henry had not received the letter. Mr. and Mrs. Gass were taking their usual summer vacation in Wisconsin, and had rented their home. Frank left a note for them, and showed his family around the Sewanee mountain campus, where the temperatures were much cooler then below. "We always hated that we missed them," said Mrs. Gass said many years later.

From Sewanee, the Gumms traveled to Huntsville, where Allie's widow, Minnie Gumm, was still residing with her three children. By now, Allie, Jr. was nine, James, eight and Elizabeth, six. Frank was happy to see his children playing with their Gumm cousins. Will and Frances lived only a few doors down on Green Street.[22] The Gumms had a nice reunion. The bond Ethel formed with Will, Frances, Minnie and Minnie's children during these early visits was one that would not be broken.

Refreshed and, no doubt, tired by their long trip, the Gumm family returned to Grand Rapids and resumed their usual schedule.

Chapter 31

Baby Takes a Bow

By the time Baby Frances was two, Mary Jane and Virginia were seasoned performers, appearing regularly on the stage of their father's theater. In addition, the three little girls often came to the theater to watch the picture shows, and the performers Frank hired. Life for the Gumm family centered around the theater, and without a permanent babysitter, it was often necessary to bring the children to work.

The first two years of Baby Fanny's life, her presence in the theater was not been a problem. But once she turned two, Frank found that trying to control her at the same time he ran the business was impossible. Fanny wanted to run where she wanted and the place she wanted to be most often was on the stage. Since he and Ethel were too busy to watch her, Frank sometimes gave their neighbor's son, Bernie Morris, who already had several little jobs around the theatre, a quarter to hold Baby on his lap. The most important part of this job was not to let Baby get on stage while her sisters were up there.

The Morris family and the Gumm family, as neighbors, were well acquainted with one another. Mrs. Morris often babysat Frances, and Bernie and Mary Jane were in the same class at school. When Bernie was cast in the school play as Prince Sunshine opposite Mary Jane's Cinderella, Mrs. Gumm told him to come over to the house for a dancing lesson. Bernie would later refer to Ethel Gumm as "a professional dancer." She taught the two children, who were about eight or nine at the time, an appropriate dance for the play, possibly, a minuet or a waltz. Mary Jane and Bernie were rehearsing the dance while Mrs. Gumm demonstrating the finer points when Bernie heard a small but determined voice pip out, "I want to do that TOO!" It was two year-old Frances. Eighty years later, Bernie was still able to imitate her distinctive way of talking.[23]

Now that Baby could sing, Mary Jane and Virginia often included her in their little backyard shows. She also sang at family events. Although she had not appeared on stage yet, the two year-old was already honing her skills.

When Grandma Eva came to visit that fall, she was delighted to see how well little Fanny was already singing. What particularly impressed her was how intently her granddaughter listened to a song and was able to replicate it after hearing it only one or two times.

Whether in Duluth or Grand Rapids, every afternoon Grandma Eva sat down at the piano and sang her favorite songs for her grandchildren. Two of the songs her grandson, Bob Milne, later recalled hearing were *Ramona* and *Who Killed Cock Robin?* And whenever Grandma Eva sang, Bob, his brothers, sisters and cousins, all sang along.[24]

On Thanksgiving of 1924, Grandma Eva was in the audience of the New Grand with Fanny sitting on her lap. Sisters Janey and Jimmy were up onstage singing one of their numbers and Eva could feel little Fannie squirming. Enchanted with her granddaughter, Eva put Fanny down so that she could join her sisters onstage, as she so obviously wanted to do. But Baby knew what was what in the family and immediately walked over to Ethel, who was seated at the piano just below the stage.

"Mama," said Baby, "I wanna sing too!"

"Not now, Baby," said Ethel. "You can sing another day."

Baby knew not to cross Ethel and did not go on stage that night.

After Thanksgiving, Ethel began rehearsing the girls for the New Grand Christmas celebration. She thought of a unique way for Baby to make her stage debut, and had the girls practice until it was perfect.

Then, to Baby's delight, Ethel sat down at her sewing machine and began to work on a little, white dress for the show. Copying the fashion magazines with pictures of Broadway stars she had seen in magazines, Ethel created a soft cotton top and added to it a very stiff short skirt with layers and layers of net; the kind found in ballet dresses. She covered the layers of net with a simple piece of cotton fabric. To finish the dress

Frances Ethel Gumm, age 2.
(Courtesy Itasca County Historical Society)

off, she added a huge tulle bow to the back. The bow was so big that when tied, it almost appeared to be angel wings.

Baby was thrilled and would forever remember the love with which her mother made this dress. Now, at last, she was going to be just like the rest of the family; she was going to sing with her sisters in Daddy's theatre!

The day finally arrived. Janie and Jimmy were wearing rather plain dresses with long coats and Baby was there in her white net dress. Ethel fixed her hair in Mary Pickford curls and added to her outfit long white socks and black patent leather shoes for dancing.

It was December 24th and the theater was full that night. Everyone in town was there, all in the Christmas spirit, ready to celebrate and enjoy the special evening that the Gumm family had prepared.

As the lights came up on the stage, Ethel played a lively opening. The song was a new hit by Gene Austin, Jimmy McHugh and Irving Mills, called *When My Sugar Walks Down the Street, the Little Birdies Go Tweet, Tweet, Tweet.** Not in their usual fashion, Janie and Jimmy were standing tightly plastered together as they began to sing:

I know a thing or two,
And I'm telling you,
I've got a wonderful girl.

Since the girls were usually dancing up a storm, the audience likely wondered what was happening. Yet, Janey and Jimmy Gumm were obviously bubbling over with excitement about the surprise that was going to take place on stage. Then, the girls came to the phrase,

When she is by my side,
I'm so filled with pride,
I want the whole world to know—

At that moment, the older Gumm sisters parted and revealed their tiny baby sister with her little white dress and dark curls. A sound of surprise and delight ran through the audience as Baby Gumm began to dance in step with her sisters, her little voice blaring out, and every bit as loud as theirs, if not louder. Now, for the first time, the three little Gumm sisters moved together, singing,

When my sugar walks down the street,
All the little birdies go Tweet, Tweet, and tweet!

One thing that surprised people most about Baby's performance that night was her complete lack up fear—her confidence. And, in addition to that, this tiny girl could be heard! The song finished to uproarious applause.

---

* *When My Sugar Walks Down the Street, The Little Birdies Go Tweet, Tweet, Tweet,* ©1924 Ireneadele Music

It is said that Janey and Jimmy performed two more numbers that night, but no one remembers what they were. What is remembered is that Baby Gumm had a solo singing "Jingle Bells."

Baby came out and began to sing her solo with her mother at the piano. Ethel had given her the little bell she sometimes used to announce dinner, and every time she sang the words "Jingle Bells," she rang the little bell. The applause Fannie received as she finished, pleased her greatly. There were all these people staring at her with big smiles on their faces, applauding!

When the song was over, Fannie decided she was not ready to get off the stage. She was having fun. She wanted to try it again and see if she could get the same response. She began to sing the song a second time. Applause again! It worked! So, she started to sing again.

Mama was playing the piano, but as they neared the end of the song she told Baby, "Get off!" Baby looked toward the wings and there was Daddy waiting. "I wanna sing some more," she told her mother. She was having too much fun. Now, she launched into her fourth chorus.

By now, the audience was laughing, and Baby finished to BIG applause. It was bigger than before; Baby Gumm decided that she was just going to keep singing! She really liked this now. Daddy was standing in the wings and telling her to get off, and Mama was telling her to get off as well, but she was laughing. Baby had an audience full of people who loved what she was doing and she loved it. Standing center stage, fearless, with the blood of her pioneer ancestors running through her veins, Baby Gumm launched into a sixth chorus of "Jingle Bells"!

At this point, Frank Gumm was laughing so hard, he had tears streaming down his face. But after a nudge from his brother-in-law, Fred Milne, he decided it was time to take matters into his own hands. Out he strode across the stage and threw little Fanny Gumm over his shoulder. The audience let out a burst of laughter, but nothing was going to stop Baby. She belted out those last few notes, ringing her bell, "Jingle all the way!" over his shoulder, making a grand exit to huge applause and laughter.

That evening at the New Grand became a legend in the family, the town of Grand Rapids and finally, throughout the world. At the age of two and a half, Frances Gumm had found her calling.

During the spring of 1925, the little Gumm girls, now a trio sang at a number of birthday parties and small events around town. In July, the *Deer River News* noted that Mr. and Mrs. Gumm as well as their "three delightful daughters" performed at the Lyceum Theater. The paper referred to them as "the Gumm girls" and the "Gumm sisters." In each report, it was stated that the sisters were "clever" and had pleased a large audience.[25]

~

Hindsight is 20/20, as they say. While Christmas Eve of 1924 was later looked on as predicting the future greatness of Frances Ethel Gumm, to the other kids in the neighborhood, Baby Gumm was cute, but just another kid running around with a dirty face.

Frances seemed to be a healthy baby, but in 1925 she suddenly became seriously ill. With a high fever and the inability to keep any food or liquid down, the little girl soon faded almost to nothing. As her sister, Jimmy, later recalled, her arms and legs were little more than sticks.[26]

Late one Tuesday night, Frank and Ethel realized that they were about to loose the precious little girl, who was, by now, the light of their lives. The couple bundled her in blankets, jumped into the Ford, and headed to Duluth in the middle of a snow storm. (Someone must have been home to look after Janey and Jimmy.) Undeterred by the weather, the Gumms drove 80 miles in the dark through a blinding snowstorm. Arriving at the St. Mary's hospital, even the specialists did not think the little girl would survive, but miraculously, she did. Her parents must have prayed that night.

One week later, Mr. and Mrs. Gumm returned home with their daughter. Realizing how easily they might have lost her, they treated her with great care. Baby Fanny was coddled and given everything she wanted.

That year, Frank Gumm also became quite ill. It was found that he, had an "ingrowing goiter;" possibly worse than the one Ethel had had. Marcus Rabwin arranged for Frank to be admitted to the hospital in Rochester, where they removed the goiter. Ethel stayed with him, while her mother and Norma took care of the children. After a week, Ethel returned home, but Frank was forced to remain in Rochester another two weeks in order to have the wound in his throat properly dressed.[27] When he returned, he seemed much calmer, but during the next months, he began to gain weight.

Despite the fact that both Frank and Ethel had surgery, they remained people of high energy. Eleanor Downing, a child who came to the Gumm home to play with Jimmy, recalled that Ethel was always running; she never just walked. Even in the high heels she wore to make herself taller, Ethel was ran up and down the stairs of the Gumm home.

That spring, Janey and Jimmy had a backyard circus show where Frances performed the new hit, *Tie Me to Your Apron Strings Again.**

Although the Gumm girls played with the other children and were fit in well with their peers, in other ways Mary Jane and Virginia were looked on as quite remarkable. When asked about her friends later in life, Jimmy's friend and classmate, Eleanor Downing said, "They were the stars of the town."

~

In early 1925, while attending to business at the Lyceum Theater in Deer River, Frank happened to visit the local photographer, Mr. Enstrom, at his studio on the main road through town. Whether Frank had seen some of Mr. Enstrom's work, or just wanted photos is not known, however, he made an appointment with him to have the entire family photographed.

Elstom's Studio in Deer River, MN

On a sunny day, sometime between late spring and early autumn of 1925, the family packed up their show costumes and piled into the car for a ride down to Deer River. That day, Mr. Emstrom took a total of 16 photographs. Mr. and

* *Tie Me To Your Apron Strings Again*, w. Joe Goodwin, m. Larry Shay ©1925

Mary Jane (left) and Virginia Gumm (right), 1925 Elstrom Studios. (Courtesy Itasca County Historical Society)

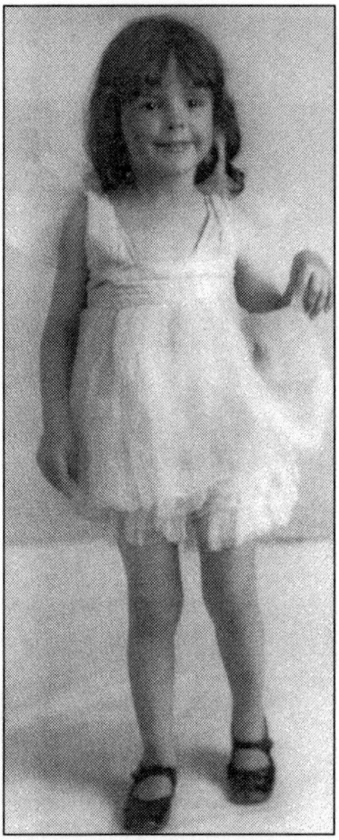

Mrs. Gumm were photographed as a modern couple, and in their antebellum show garb. At thirty-two, Ethel still had a youthful appearance, though she had gained some weight, changed her hair style and seemed more serious than her previous photos. It was Frank, however, whose appearance had changed the most. At thirty-nine, he had become somewhat portly, and balding, his appearance closer to a man of fifty.

Mary Jane and Virginia wore two sets of costumes for their photos. The girls posed first with their baby sister in the outfits they had worn for the Christmas show. Later, Janey wore her flapper costume and Jimmy, her newsboy costume.

For all of her photographs, Baby Frances wore the little dress she had worn for her debut. This time she had apparently forgotten or refused to wear her socks. Her photographs reveal a coy and charming tot, who looks directly into the camera with a maturity and seriousness far beyond her years. These photos are the truest record we have of the Gumms of Grand Rapids.

In later years, photographer Enstrom would gain some degree of fame when a photograph he took of a journeying laborer praying over his meager meal was widely distributed.

~

In 1997, this author and house historian, Jim Sazevich, entered the Grand Rapids bus station to see a tall, elderly man behind the counter. On the wall behind him was a unique poster of a tall, skinny man running with a Greyhound bus.

"Say, is that you, sir?" asked Mr. Sazevich.

"Yes, it is."

Are you from here?"

"No, I moved here in 1922."

"Do you recall a family that used to have a theatre down here by the name of Gumm?"

"Oh, yes," said the man. "I visited that theatre many times. Boy, those girls could sure dance."

It is interesting that our elderly friend recalled the Gumm girl's dancing more than their singing, but his comment does open a window to the past.

Chapter 32

Living with the Gumms

Ethel Gumm had long needed some help with the house, but most of the help she found was short-term. Then, when Baby was three, Ethel learned of a new program sponsored by the state of Minnesota that seemed just right for the Gumm family.

Living in northern Minnesota, there were many families in isolated areas. Usually, these areas had a one-room schoolhouse for grades 1 through 8, but that was all. Few of these children ever went to high school. To remedy this problem, the state of Minnesota instituted a program to bring these young people from the north woods into the towns where they could further their education. The state requested that the town families to take the students under their roofs. In exchange for their room and board, the students would be asked to do housework, care for younger children, or any other chores that might be needed.

Ethel applied for the program and was sent a young girl of seventeen, Wilma Hendricks. Wilma came from a large and loving family of nine children. She had never been away from home, and even though she was able to return home for a weekend every two weeks or so, being away from her family was quite difficult for her.

In later years, Wilma could not quite remember which room in the Gumm home she slept. Going up the stairs from the front parlor, there was a hall, a bathroom, a small room where Janey and Jimmy slept, and the large front bedroom where Frank and Ethel slept with Baby Frances. Ethel had a desk was set up for Wilma in the upstairs hallway, a quiet,

out of the way place for her to study, and which would not interfere with the very active Gumm household. Wilma may have been given a cot to sleep on in the girls' room.

Wilma thought all three Gumm girls were quite sweet and adorable, especially Baby. She had never seen such a darling little child. Baby was chubby with big brown eyes that were almost black, rosy cheeks, a rose bud mouth and, when her mother curled her very fine hair, beautiful dark curls. Baby just had a way about her.

It was fall when Wilma arrived, and soon the weather was quite cold. Wilma's day began early. First, she had to get herself ready for school. Then, she laid Janey and Jimmy's long underwear out on a dining room chair just outside the kitchen where it would be warm. Standing outside the kitchen, near the heat from the stove, Wilma helped the two oldest girls dress for school. After that, they ate breakfast and were off. The schools were only about two or three blocks away.

At noon, Wilma returned to the Gumm house with Janey and Jimmy where they all ate lunch. One day, Wilma was sitting in the dining room where Ethel often sewed clothing and costumes for the girls. It was just a moment to be quiet, think about her school work, and her family at home. But Ethel was all business.

"Now you see, Wilma," said Ethel, "if you weren't sitting there mooning over your soup, you could have had the dishes done by now."[28]

Wilma got up, went into the kitchen and threw her soup down the drain. Then, she washed the dishes and went back to school. She was not used to being spoken to like that and it hurt. She was already lonely enough as it was.

At night, when Mr. and Mrs. Gumm were at the theatre, Wilma was in charge of getting the girls to bed. Janey and Jimmy were pretty well-behaved, but Baby was a problem. She did not want to go to bed, especially when she knew she could charm someone like Wilma!

First, she was hungry, so Wilma fixed her a cup of her favorite Thompson's hot chocolate malted milk and a piece of bread with Ethel's famous peach and pecan preserves. Ethel did know how to cook! While Baby was eating, she would climb up on the counter (just to show off) and walk along the edge, putting her sticky fingers all over the cabinets above the counter. The counter was double her height and made her almost as tall as Wilma. Before Baby went to bed, Wilma had to make sure and wash her sticky finger prints of the cabinets.

"Now Baby, you have to go to bed."

"No!"

"Baby, your Mama will be very angry at me if I don't put you to bed."

"No! I'm not going to bed," Baby told her.[29]

Wilma carried Baby upstairs, got her dressed in her white nightie and put her on her potty chair to make sure there were no accidents in the night. One night when Baby was especially insistent that she was not going to bed, she told Wilma,

"Wilma! I could just slap you!"

Wilma was very surprised at the feistiness of the little girl. "Where did she learn to talk like that?" she wondered.

Like most children, Baby was up and down, giggling and playing until she fell asleep. Then, Wilma would have time for her studies.

There was one thing Ethel Gumm made completely clear—Wilma was not to come downstairs at night after she and Mr. Gumm came home from the theatre. That was their private time to be together. And in the morning, she was to be quiet.

On Saturdays, if Wilma stayed in town, she would ride in the car with Mrs. Gumm over to the theatre and watch the girls perform onstage. That was a great treat, but still, she found she needed time out of the house, and she was always glad when her father came to take her home.

One day, when Mr. Hendricks arrived to get Wilma, he was standing in the front parlor, waiting for Wilma to get her things, when Mrs. Gumm came into the room and asked,

"Would you like to hear Baby sing?"

Mr. Hendricks looked down at the tiny girl, and thanked Mrs. Gumm, but felt compelled to tell her,

"I would love to hear her, but I'm hard of hearing, you know. I really don't think I'd be able to hear her."

Wilma would never forget the sight of those three as she came down the stairs with her bag. Her father was sitting on the edge of the bench closest to the stairs, Mrs. Gumm was playing piano, perched on the other end, and sitting in the middle was Baby, with her dark hair and dark eyes, and from those cupid lips that big voice singing, "Five Foot Two, Eyes of Blue."* That day, Mr. Hendricks heard every word Baby sang, and for years afterward would tell the story of how he sat next to the three year-old future Judy Garland and, despite his deafness, was able to hear her sing.

Five Foot Two, Eyes of Blue was one of the top hits of 1925, and a favorite song of Baby Frances. In later years, one of the neighbors recalled that she would often go to the house of a lady who made especially good cookies and say, "I can sing *Five Foot Two* for a cookie!" Even at the age of three, Frances was learning that her singing had value. Wilma later said that Gumm family's favorite song was *Carolina in the Morning*. It was the song which they all sang.

Christmas time came soon enough, the schools closed, and Wilma happily left Grand Rapids for the north woods. She rejoiced in the fact that she would have a wonderful two-week vacation with her family, during which she would celebrate her eighteenth birthday. Once she was home, she began to realize just how much she had missed the love and support they gave her. The Gumms were a very nice family, but Wilma was a sensitive girl, and working for Mrs. Gumm was not easy. Ethel Gumm was extremely nice to those people who were her peers, but she didn't seem to have much patience for others, like a young, homesick student who was helping to take care of her house and children. She was busy with things far more important.

But Mrs. Gumm had been thoughtful. Before Wilma left, she gave her a Christmas present. When Wilma got home, and unwrapped her present, she found a pair of warm slippers. The only problem was the slippers were far too big for her feet, so she couldn't wear them.

After the winter break, Wilma returned to the Gumm house feeling refreshed by the love and companionship of her family. She was determined to make a new start. The little Gumm girls were very sweet, and she loved them. It was also loads of fun to see them perform in the theater.

---

* *Five Foot Two, Eyes of Blue*, lyrics. Sam M. Lewis & Joe Young, music, Ray Henderson, ©1925 by Leo Feist, Inc.

Most of all, she couldn't help loving Baby. She loved her as if she was her own little sister.

Not long after Wilma returned, Ethel turned to her one day and said, "Wilma, where are the slippers I gave you for Christmas?"

Wilma had to admit to her that the slippers were just too big for her feet, to which Mrs. Gumm replied,

"Well, I don't care. I want you to wear them when you are in the house. We can't have you clumping around down here in the mornings when Mr. Gumm and I are trying to sleep."

For Wilma, that was the final straw. Mr. Gumm had always seemed nice and supportive, but he wasn't around much. Whether she meant it or not, the comments Mrs. Gumm made hurt and insulted her. No one in Wilma's family spoke to her like that, and she didn't want to let anyone else speak to her in that way either.

When the chance presented itself, Wilma approached the coordinator for the state program. Informing her that she was not happy in the Gumm home, she asked if they had another situation for her. As it happened, they did. There was a nice family with one child who had offered to take in a student. The representative suggested that this might be a better situation for her. Living with the Gumms, Wilma never seemed to have enough time for her studies. This position would probably give her the time she needed. If she wanted the new situation, the coordinator told her, she could leave the Gumm home right away. Wilma said she wanted it, and was ready to leave.

When Wilma returned to the house and informed Mrs. Gumm that she was leaving, Ethel was not happy. Obviously, by now she had come to depend on Wilma's help, and Wilma was giving her very little notice. Ethel let her know that she was going to tell the people in charge of placement certain things about her and give her a bad reference.[30] Wilma said she didn't care. She left the house for her new situation and never saw the Gumm family again.

Years later, Wilma Hendricks married Bob Casper, and in 1940, they had a little girl of their own. Sadly, at the age of three their daughter died. As the years passed and Wilma watched the girl she had once taken care of become known to the world as Judy Garland, she couldn't help feeling proud. This little girl had grown up to do beautiful things.

Seventy years after leaving the Gumm home, Wilma returned to Grand Rapids for the opening of the Judy Garland Birthplace. While there, she shared her memories of the past and, along with others, helped to make Judy Garland's first home authentic for the public.

~

Apparently, Ethel found someone to help with the housekeeping, and everyone continued with their normal routines. That winter, as Judy later recalled, she made snow angels with her sisters. Falling back in the snow, waving their arms and legs back and forth to make the shape—Janey, Jimmy and Baby would run upstairs and look out the window to see the angel forms in the snow. Each night, she continued to have her Thompson's Hot Chocolate, which she adored, and Ethel's sweet peach and pecan preserves.

Besides preventing Baby Gumm from going onstage, the Gumm's neighbor, Bernie Morris, would have another claim to fame with regards to Judy Garland. One winter day, all the kids in the neighborhood were out having a huge snowball fight. They had taken sides, and it was war. Bernie thought he would do one better than the other kids, and wipe out the opposite side. He put a rock in a snowball and threw it with all his might. The rock hit little Frances in the head, near her eye. Down she went, crying. When Janey and Jimmy saw that Frances had been hit by a rock, they hugged and kissed her, and took snow and put it on her head. Then, they ran after Bernie and beat him up. That day, he learned that he better not mess with their little sister.

Although Frank's business often kept him away from home, whenever he was there, he loved to spend time having fun with his girls. When Marc Rabwin came to the house, he observed Frank playing jacks on the floor with Janey and Jimmy. Frank also had his bedtime ritual with the girls. All three girls remembered their father singing "Danny Boy" to them at bedtime.[31] To young Frances, however, this memory became a bond representing something special between her and her Daddy.

Once she was dressed in her "little white nightie," Frances would climb up onto her Daddy's lap, and he would sing "Danny Boy," to her and another song which seemed to mean a great deal to him, *Nobody Knows the Trouble I've Seen*. The song, an old Negro spiritual, had first been

From the "Garlandia" Collection of Wayne Martin

written down as a choral arrangement around 1913.[32] Frank may have known a variation of it much earlier. Some of the lyrics are: [33]

Nobody knows the trouble
I've seen
Nobody knows but Jesus
. . . .
Sometimes I'm up, some-
times I'm down
Oh yes, Lord.
Sometimes I'm almost to
the ground,
Oh Yes, Lord.

To many, this might seem like a nice, old hymn, yet knowing Frank's life, how deeply the lyrics of this song rang true for him. Who can know what thoughts he had as he sang this old, spiritual to his daughter, who came to him with unconditional love.

~

Mary Jane and Virginia loved their baby sister, but there were times when they had their fill of her and didn't want to be bothered. One of these times occurred when Aunt Norma was babysitting. Janey and Jimmy had gotten some special candy at school that day, and when they walked through the door eating it, Baby began to cry that she wanted some. The girls ignored her and continued to eat the candy while Baby wailed.

When Aunt Norma came in and witnessed the Jimmy and Janey's behavior, she called them "selfish" and told them, "Give your baby sister some of that candy!" In a huff, rather than share it, Janie and Jimmy both threw their candy on the floor and marched upstairs with Aunt Norma behind them, intent on locking them in their room as a punishment.

Coming downstairs, Norma found that Frances had stuffed the remainder of both candy bars in her mouth. She didn't care that it had been on the floor.[34]

~

Mary Jane and Virginia had a couple of friends who were sisters, just like them. June and her sister were about their same age, and the four girls liked to play together. They also sat together at the theatre.

One day, the girls attended the latest community theater production in which both Frank and Ethel Gumm had leading roles. The five girls, including Frances, were sitting in the front row. June wasn't sure if Frances, who was about three or four at the time, knew the people on stage were her parents because they were all made up and in costume.

Then, all of a sudden, in the middle of the play, Mrs. Gumm came onstage, pulled out a gun and shot Mr. Gumm. He fell to the floor, rolled over and played dead.

At that moment, Baby, stood up and said in a loud voice that could be heard by everyone in the theater,

"YOU CAN'T DO THAT TO MY DADDY!"

With that, Mr. Gumm rolled over as if he was not quite dead yet, winked at Baby and made a little motion for her to be quiet. Then, he died again.

The older girls were mortified. Thinking that everyone in the theater must be looking at them because of Baby's outburst, they slid down in their seats. June said she was never sure if Baby knew the shooter was her mother. As funny as the event was, Baby Gumm's response shows her deep connection to her father, and her desire to protect him, probably in the same way he protected her.

During the summer, Frank took the girls down to Lake Pokegama to go swimming. Pokegama is the largest lake in the area; the place where most families go for a picnics and swimming. Baby was three now, and Frank asked Bernie if he was a good swimmer. When he answered in the affirmative, Frank paid him half a dollar to teach Baby to swim.[35] The local paper notes that on August 21st of this year, the Gumm Sisters performed at a picnic on Lake Pokegama.

When the weather was finally warm, the Gumm girls had lots of fun playing with the neighborhood kids, and when Ethel called them to come inside to rehearse, they didn't want to go. Since nearly everyone in town attended their performances, it was important that the girls had new songs and dances to present. Janey and Jimmy had a lot of work to do.

Finally, Ethel found a solution to the problem. She baked cookies, made lemonade and invited all Janey and Jimmy's friends to come inside for a treat while they watched the girls rehearse. With all their friends inside eating cookies and waiting for them, Mary Jane and Virginia had little choice but to rehearse. They used the small landing of the stairs as their stage, while the children in the neighborhood sat on the floor below.

During this time, Mr. Gumm continued successfully with the Friday night amateur shows. The New Grand saw a great variety of talent. One year, Eleanor Downing's older sister sang a classical piece with Mr. Gumm.

If there were any problems during this time with Frank and Ethel's marriage, their children were oblivious to the fact. To the girls, these years in Grand Rapids would always be remembered as idyllic. It seemed as if the happy days in the little white house would go on forever, but by 1926, the Gumms' days in Grand Rapids were numbered.

Chapter 33
The Move to California

DURING THE EARLY MONTHS OF 1926, THE THREE LITTLE GIRLS WERE kept busy performing at least twice a month at the New Grand. They also performed for special events, such as Washington's Birthday Dance for the Masonic Order in Coleraine. That April, the Gumm family traveled to Virginia, Minnesota where they performed as an entire family under the name *Jack and Virginia Lee and Kiddies*. A month later, the local paper noted that *Jack and Virginia Lee and Kiddies* would be appearing at the Grand Theatre in Bemidji on May 28th and 29th. Ten days later, on June 8th, Mr. and Mrs. Gumm and the three little girls boarded the train and headed out west for a vacation in sunny California.[36]

Two days after beginning their journey, the Gumms arrived in Devil's Lake, North Dakota where Frances celebrated her 4th birthday. That night, as the orchestra began to play the dance hit that was sweeping America, the *Charleston*, Frances jumped up from the dinner table and began to dance. The patrons, wowed by this tiny girl and her ability to execute the Charleston's intricate steps, showered her with pennies.[37]

Originally, Frank and Ethel had planned to take the trip by themselves, but the thought of going without the children made them so "blue," they decided to take the girls along.[38] At the same time, they decided to make the first part of their trip a working vacation. Traveling west, the family performed ten dates in eight theaters between North Dakota and Los Angeles.[39] For the girls, it was a great adventure.

Frances, 4, with her sister, Virginia, 6 at Lake McDonald in Glacier National Park, Summer 1926. Taken by the Gumms' friend, Victor Gray, who the Gumms got off the train to visit.
(Courtesy Judy Garland Museum)

Frank wrote a detailed description of their trip for *The Itasca County Independent*. In his column, he states that from Devil's Lake they traveled to Harve, Shelby, Whitefish and Kalispel in Montana. Then, they worked two days in Cashmere, Washington and one day in Leavenworth, "at the foot of the Cascades." For all their work, the Gumms earned $300, which gave them some extra spending money.

Jimmy Gumm, in describing their trip, later said that on arriving in a town, "Daddy would go to ... a theater and offer to play a show that night. That's how it was done then."[40]

Billed as *Jack Lee and Virginia Lee and the Three Little Lees*, the act began with Frank and Ethel's performance, during which the girls sat out front and applauded. Then, the girls performed their act, while Ethel played from the pit, and Frank applauded from the house. Of course, there were some exceptions to this.

One of the numbers the girls sang was called, *In a Little Spanish Town.** For this song, Mary Jane and Virginia wore Spanish hats with little balls

---

* *In A Little Spanish Town ('Twas On A Night Like This)* w. by Sam.M. Lewis & Joe Young, M. Mabel Wayne, ©1926 Leo Feist, Inc.

hanging around the brim. They would sing the song, and then Frances, wearing harem pants with the same little balls, came out and did a belly dance. Because Ethel was in the pit playing for the girls, Frank had the responsibility of making Baby's costume change in the dark wings. One night, rushing to change Baby's clothes, he got the pants with all the little balls so tangled, Baby never made it onstage.[41]

Frank and Ethel tried to make this vacation fun for the girls, but as happy as it was, there was a dark side that little Frances seemed to sense. Her parents knew that life was going to change, but had yet to tell the girls. For her solo in the show, Ethel had chosen a song recently recorded by Marion Harris, one of the most popular female recording artists of her day. The song was titled, *I've Been Saving for a Rainy Day, and began:**

You never knew when skies are bright
How soon the storm will rise,
And just when everything's alright,
You get a big surprise.

The first lines of the chorus were:

I've been saving for a rainy day,
All the sunshine that you gave me …

The middle of the song had a very sad recitative where the singer speaks to the man who has left her. She has just received his letter, telling her that he still loves her and wants to return. The final lines of the chorus conclude that even if he leaves:

* *I've Been Saving For A Rainy Day*, w. Arthur Swanstrom, ©1921, M. Dorothy Clark, Fred Fisher, Inc.

*"I am glad I've got that golden sunshine,
I've been saving for a rainy day."*

Judy Garland later said that her mother performed the song so convincingly that it broke her heart, and she would sit out in the audience, crying uncontrollably. Frances was a sensitive child, and perhaps without knowing it, she sensed that her secure and happy life in Grand Rapids was about to end.

Interestingly, on this trip the family was traveling a similar route to the one Frank had taken back 1912 when he left Ethel in Superior to work for the People's Amusement Company. The family stopped in Seattle, Washington to vacation, and from there traveled to Portland Oregon where Frank looked up some of his old friends.[42] During these months, Frank seems to have been retracing the steps of his life.

From Portland, the Gumm family went to San Francisco and then down the coast to Los Angeles. The beautiful sites along the West Coast—the Pacific Ocean, the bright sunshine and adobe cottages were all quite new to the Gumms.

Arriving in Southern California toward the end of June, the Gumms met up with Marcus Rabwin and his parents, Frank and Rose, who had recently joined their son in California. Also living in there home were

Courtesy Gordon Stevens

Marcus Rabwin's two sisters and a brother. Although some biographies have stated that the Gumm's stayed with Dr. Rabwin's father, this seems to be untrue.

During the last two weeks of vacation, Mr. and Mrs. Gumm and the girls enjoyed picnics by the ocean in the wonderful California sunshine, and attended a concert at the Hollywood Bowl. They also did the sort of things that other tourists do, such as visiting Hollywood and taking a tour of movie star homes.[43]

In those days, California was still a pristine dream-like place to be. Earlier, most films had been made in New York, but by the mid to late 1920s, Hollywood and Los Angeles with its beautiful climate and unlimited land had become the home base for movie companies and a Mecca for those with dreams of stardom. In 1926, there were at least four major studios in southern California and a host of other creative ventures.

One of the things Frank Gumm did while they were in Hollywood was to try to find the girls' favorite movie star, Fred Thompson. Frank, Ethel and the three little girls went from studio to studio trying to figure out where he worked. Eventually, they found him at MGM, then a small studio with a few sound stages. The Gumms were standing outside the studio gates when Fred Thompson himself drove up. Frank, whose outgoing personality never failed to charm strangers, hailed the star saying, "My kids of have been dying to meet you!" Frank charmed the star, and the entire family soon found themselves inside the MGM studio gates. They were given a tour, met stars and even witnessed some films being made.[44]

While they were in town, Ethel also managed to get the girls into a show at the Earlander's Mason Theater. The event was a Special Saturday Afternoon Kiddie Matinee, starring the Duncan Sisters. Vivian and Rosetta Duncan were vaudeville performers who had appeared on Broadway and the London stage. They were best known for the musical act they created based on the characters of Little Eva and Topsy from *Uncle Tom's Cabin*. Some of the performances Janey and Jimmy had given in Grand Rapids were based on the Duncan Sisters. Likely, they had the Duncans' sheet music and records at home.

After the show, the three girls met the Duncan Sisters, who had encouraging words for them. They were especially impressed with little

Frances, and took down Mr. and Mrs. Gumm's name and address, asking that the family to keep in touch with them.

Finally, on July 17th, the Gumm family returned home with enthusiastic plans to move west. Frank and Ethel had not been happy when they left on vacation, but now they had great hopes for the future. Moving to California would truly be the beginning of a new life.

~

That July, shortly after the family returned from their trip, Frank Gumm's family came to Grand Rapids for a month long visit. Bob, Belle and their three year-old son, Richard, arrived from Indianapolis. At the same time, Will and Frances traveled up from Huntsville. Somehow, Frank and Ethel were able to make room and accommodate everyone. Likely, the summer kitchen was fitted for one family, while, possibly, Frank and Ethel gave up their room for the others. Since it appears this was the first time anyone in Frank's family had visited, it was an important event.

One evening, after the children had been put to bed, Frank, Bob and Will began to talk about the past. Seven year-old Jimmy, who couldn't sleep, crept out into the hall, and listened. Uncle Bob was talking about Murfreesboro and Aunt Mary, who everyone spoke of in hushed tones. Jimmy probably didn't remember meeting her when she was two. There was much Jimmy didn't understand in this adult conversation, but she was fascinated by what she heard, and never forgot some of the details. Later, she repeated them to her little sister, Frances, and, long after that, to author, Gerold Frank.

Uncle Will said that Aunt Mary died by throwing herself in the river. Daddy was upset because she killed herself. It was a sin, and maybe it meant she wouldn't go to heaven. Jimmy thought her father said Aunt Mary had been courted by a rich suitor, the same man who had paid for her father's education, but this man could never bring himself to ask for her hand in marriage. There was also something about wasting away in a wheel chair.

Of course, Jimmy was only seven, and not quite sure what she had heard. The girls saw Mama's relatives all the time, but Daddy's relatives were from the South; they seemed strange and mysterious to the girls. Janey, Jimmy and Frances wondered about their Daddy's past. Sometimes, they would spend long periods of time pouring over his old scrapbooks, trying to imagine the life he had lived long before he married Mama. It was all very romantic. Their daddy, with his soft accent and Southern charm, was different from anyone they knew.

~

In later years, Ethel would say that the family moved west to get away from the high heating bills. The cold did seem to affect little Frances far more than sisters and, in truth; the years between 1917 and 1920 were some of the coldest in Grand Rapids' history. Yet in later years, another story would be revealed about why the family left their home and moved to California. Without wishing to cause a fuss or hurt anyone in the family, according to some, the Gumms had been asked to leave because of Frank's behavior toward a certain young man in town. Once again, the contradictions of Frank Gumm's life appear. He was someone that people adored and remembered fondly. But supposedly, at the same time his news stories on the family adventures out west appeared in the local paper, he was being asked to leave town.

Leaving Grand Rapids would not be an easy task. Frank had to make arrangements for all three of the theatres he managed. The return of his investment in the New Grand, the Lyceum and the Eclipse would be necessary for the family to survive the first months in a new location. When Frank finally found an investor, Fred Bentz gave up his share at the same time.[45]

Frank and Ethel decided not to sell their home. People were always looking for homes to rent in Grand Rapids. It was a sound investment, and maybe they would come back one day. Meanwhile, it would be necessary to sell or give away most of their furniture and the belongings they didn't need. Perhaps, some items could be put into storage until later. The Gumms looked on the positive side. There were so many opportunities out in California; they couldn't wait to start their new life.

Summer passed quickly and as autumn arrived, the Gumms were rushing to finalize their move. They wanted to leave before the first snow fell. On October 8th, 9th and 10th the family gave their last performances at the New Grand, which were billed as *Gala Farewell Shows*. Then, during the last seventeen days, a series of going away parties were held for the family. At most of these, the Gumm sisters performed for their hosts. The final

Nannie Rion and granddaughter, Claire, 1925. (Courtesy Claire Rion Weber)

party, given by the Powers family, was held on the October 24th. Three days later, Frank, Ethel and the three girls left Grand Rapids. Although from time to time, various members of the family would return to visit, but they would never again come back as a family unit.

Riding in Frank's car, the Gumms headed to Duluth where they stopped at Jack's house. Ethel's father, mother and sister, Norma, had moved back to Marquette—probably because of Mr. Milne's job with the railroad.

Leaving the girls with their cousins, Frank and Ethel boarded the train to Tennessee. He wanted to see his family one last time. Once they moved to California, they would likely not be returning. This trip would also give them some time to come to terms with the large changes ahead.

On this trip, the couple visited the Rion and the Fox families. Then, they traveled south to visit Minnie Gumm and her children. Will and Frances, who had moved to Birmingham, came up to see them. Will was working as a shoe salesman at Odems, a job he would hold for the next twenty years.

Returning to Duluth, Frank and Ethel were greeted with one last going away party. From all accounts, it seems that the goodbyes were very difficult, especially for Ethel's family. All these years, the family had been little more than a couple of hours away from one another. Now, they were uncertain as to when they would all be together again. The Gumms and the Milnes were saying goodbye to a way of life.

From Duluth, Frank drove the family all the way to Kansas City, Missouri where some of Ethel's family was living. It was agreed that Frank would leave Ethel and the girls there, while he went ahead to California. Once he had a place for them to stay, he would send for them.

Within a week or so, Frank sent word for Ethel and the girls, and they boarded the train. He was probably lonely because it seems when they arrived, the family had to stay in a downtown hotel for a couple of weeks. By mid-November, the Gumm family had moved to a charming Spanish bungalow at 3254 Glen Manor in the Atwater district of Los Angeles.

Jimmy, Frances and Janey on the steps of their first California home, on Glen Manor Street, 1926. (Courtesy Dahl/Kehoe Archives)

Photos taken at this time show everyone, with the exception of Frank, dressed to the hilt. Mary Jane and Virginia have grown much taller, and both have flapper hairstyles, cloche hats and dresses that were likely the height of fashion. Baby Frances has also grown, and her Mary Pickford curls have been shorn in favor of a 1920s style. She appears a tiny bundle in a white fur coat. In one photo, Ethel wears a huge hat, like the movie stars of the time. In another, despite her fashionable clothes, she is shockingly thin. Frank, in his white shirt, seems to be the most relaxed and happy.

Despite whatever illness or stress Ethel experienced during this time, she had lost none of her zest for living. Like a kid in a candy store, she was now surrounded with seemingly limitless theatrical possibilities for the success of her girls. Almost immediately, she set off to get them some gigs. For the next five months, the Gumm sisters joined Ethel Meglin's Dance Studio and Booking Agency.

That Christmas, the girls appeared in the *100 Clever Children in the Twinkle Toe Kiddie Review* at the huge Loews State Theatre in downtown Los Angeles. The excitement over this event, and the new found talent connections, may have made up for some of the loneliness the Gumms felt that Christmas. For the first time, they would miss the lively goings on with Milne family.

When Frank Gumm first arrived in California, he had the idea of starting a newspaper, but it was soon evident that he would not be able to earn a living with this idea. At the same time, he was scouting the area surrounding Los Angeles for a theatre. Unlike the places he had lived before, Los Angeles is a widespread area encompassing Hollywood, beach towns, desert towns and the foothills. In the towns closest to Los Angeles, the homes were too expensive, and so were the theaters. The move to California and the delay in finding a theater had eaten up a good deal of the family's savings. After several months, Frank began to get nervous about how little money they had left.

That spring, Dr. Rabwin told Frank about a town he had recently visited, and persuaded him to take visit it. The town was about an hour or two from Los Angeles.[46] It seemed to be a nice place, and it had a theater right in the heart of town. Unable to find anything else, Frank decided to give it a try. Although the town was out in the desert, about eighty miles from Los Angeles, at least it would not be isolated in drifts of snow during the winter. Frank found what he was looking for in the town of Lancaster.

Chapter 34
Lancaster

LANCASTER WAS A SMALL TOWN; AN OASIS ON THE EDGE OF THE CALIFORNIA desert. Although the desert area of Lancaster was the exact opposite of Grand Rapids, it had a beauty of its own. Settling there, the Gumms felt like pioneers. No more the long, white winters. In spring after the winter rains, the landscape was covered with miles of golden poppies and other desert flowers. However, the summer, with temperatures as high as 120 degrees, was an adjustment for the Gumms. Except for the Joshua trees and nearby farms, summer's landscape was barren.

Founded in the 1870s when the railroad made the town one of its stops, Lancaster was basically a farming town. The artisan wells, allowed the desert to become green. Outside town, there were about forty farms,

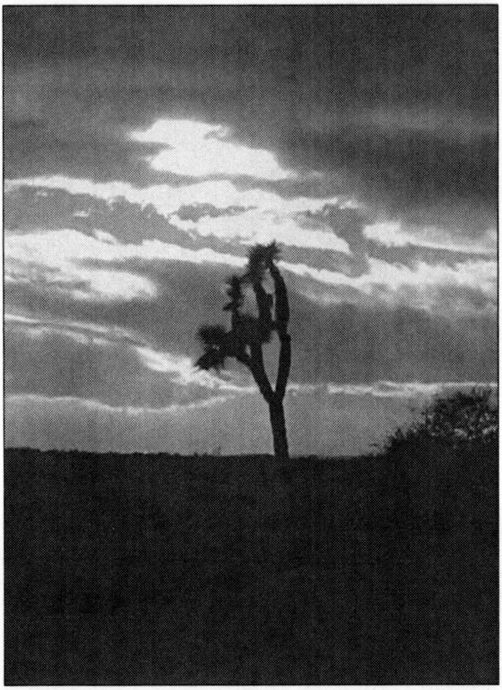

each containing approximately one hundred acres. Farmers here grew alfalfa, corn, almonds, peaches, clover and grains. Some of the farmers also raised chickens and turkeys.

The town of Lancaster encompassed one square mile. Most of the businesses were on Lancaster Boulevard, the main street in town. There was a theatre, garage, candy store, barber shop, produce store and clothing store. The farmers and their families came to town on Saturday, during which most of the town's business occurred. On that day, the farmers sold their goods and bought the supplies they needed, whether machinery, clothing or food. After conducting their business, these folks stayed in town to seek out some entertainment at the local theatre. Lancaster was similar to Murfreesboro in this way. These were people Frank Gumm could understand.

On Frank's first visit to Lancaster, he had been pleased to find that the town had a good sized theatre was for rent. Once he inspected it, however, he was shocked by the theatre's condition. It was terribly run down and dirty. Even more shocking was the sight of the present renter, an old vaudevillian, standing out front, holding his hat for patrons to throw money in as they entered.

As Frank mulled the situation over, he realized that the town and the theater had real possibilities. In this small town outside Los Angeles, he would be able to rent the theater for an affordable price, and with 500 seats and a ready audience, the family should be able to make a good living. In addition, the theatre contained a nice-sized stage, which meant the Gumms would be able to do shows, just as they had in Grand Rapids.

The owner of the Antelope Valley Theatre, was Mr. Witford B. Carter, one of the town's leading citizens.[47] Mr. Carter, a twenty-four year-old farmer with a chicken ranch, had built the theatre several years earlier. The two men met and settled on an agreement. Frank was happy now that he would once again have his own theatre. Being this close to Hollywood might also mean he could get first run or previews of new films.

~

On May 11th, the Gumm sisters performed at the Wilshire Masonic Hall in Los Angeles. The event was a benefit for Mississippi flood victims. Following the show, Ethel and the girls packed up and moved to Lancaster where Frank had rented a house on West Lancaster Boulevard, the far side of town. It was a simple home, smaller than what they were used to, but it would do for now.

Eleven days later, on May 22nd and 23rd, the Gumm family gave their first performances at the Antelope Valley Theatre. By then, Frank had the place looking like new. In addition, he made sure the big event was well-advertised, with a story about the family, which appeared on the front page of *The Antelope Valley Ledger-Gazette*. The citizens of Lancaster were similar in attitude to the citizens of Cloquet; they were suspicious of theater folks. Realizing this, Frank stressed that his theater was family-oriented. In his advertisement, he announced that he was using the first show as a means of "introducing the family to the good people of Lancaster and Antelope Valley."

Jimmy Gumm would later say that in the beginning, the parents in town didn't want their children playing with the Gumm "show kids." However, once they saw that Mr. and Mrs. Gumm were nice, normal people, that attitude changed.

The week after their first performance, the Gumms received a positive review in the *Ledger-Gazette*. Mr. and Mrs. Gumm were paid a compliment on their "musicianship," but it was "the little daughters" who "completely won the hearts of the audience with their songs and dances."[48] The Gumms were in business.

With money coming in, by summer Frank was able to modernize the theatre with new seats and an Artic Nu-Air cooling system. He also built a box office and hired a local woman to sell tickets. The Valley Theatre—Frank's new name for it—was now like new, and a far more attractive place for local residents to bring families.[49]

With the exception of the *Better Baby Contest* that October, for the next sixteen months, the Gumm sisters performed almost exclusively in Lancaster and neighboring towns. Since Frank had to make most of his income on the weekend, Fridays and Saturdays were working days, not only for Frank and Ethel, but for the girl as well.

Janey, Jimmy and Frances were used to living in an area with lots of other children to play with, but after leaving Grand Rapids, their only contact with children their age had been while performing. Once they were settled and started school, Janey, now 12, and Jimmy, 10, made friends with a couple of boys, Marcus and Frank, who were either invited or showed up at the house one day while Ethel was out shopping.

Shortly after they arrived, Ethel returned in the family car. Hearing her pull into the drive, there was no time to waste and no escape for the boys, so the girls hid the boys in the front closet. Mama would not like it, if she knew anyone had come into the house without her permission.

As usual, when Ethel came in, she was in a hurry. Then, at some point, Baby, who had been quietly watching the whole series of events, piped up, "Mama, why are Marcus and Frank in the closet?" Janey and Jimmy got in a lot of trouble after that. It would not be the only time Baby got them into trouble.

Now, just as they had in Grand Rapids, the Gumms became an integral part of the town's activities. They attended St. Paul's Episcopal Church regularly, and before long, Frank was playing the organ and leading the church choir. A resident later noted Ethel didn't seem to care much about church, but in the early days, she and the children were regular attendants.[50] Other members in the choir included William and Laura Gilmore, and the Storey family. The minister, Reverend Boyd Parker, originated from Canada, and his wife, Eliza, from England. The couple had a boy and a girl who were around the same age as Frances.

That June, Frances turned five, and a month later, Virginia had her tenth birthday. For their performance at the theatre July 4th (Virginia's birthday), the entire Gumm family sang a new song written by Ethel, called "Rocky Mountain Moonlight."[51]

Their first summer in Lancaster, Janey, Jimmy and Frances spent a lot of time in the cool air of the theatre. While their mother played piano up front and their father took care of business, the girls watched the latest films of the silver screen. That year, among the films released was *Annie Laurie* starring Lillian Gish, a picture the girls had seen being filmed on their first trip to Hollywood. Other films were *My Best Girl* starring Mary Pickford and Buddy Rogers, and *Kid Brother* starring Harold Lloyd. Among the most popular films were those starring a dog that had been rescued in France during WWI, Rin Tin Tin. The girls also may have enjoyed *Mickey's Circus*, the first of a new Mickey McGuire series adapted from the *Toonerville Trolley* comic strip.[52] The film was a debut for a little boy who would soon be known as Mickey Rooney.

Some of the pictures shown on the "silver screen" during these years can only be described as art masterpieces. Their images shown in darkened theaters around the world awakened emotions of courage, fear, joy, love, lust, and patriotism, backed only by the sound of piano music. The Gumm sisters spent more than the usual amount of time taking in these images of romance and heroism.

In between the films, the girls sang and danced. These summer performances were a special attraction for the local kids and their parents. The Gumm girl's performances almost guaranteed an audience. By now, performing was a way of life for the girls. Mary Jane and Virginia enjoyed their performances, but for young Frances, they were serious business.

In December of 1927, the children put on a Minstrel Show. Mary Jane and Virginia performed their version of the Duncan Sisters, singing *Rememb'ring*. Bringing up the rear, five year-old Frances, in tribute to Al Jolsen, sang his greatest hit, *My Mammy*, on one knee. The tiny girl gave it her all and the audience responded with cheers. People were couldn't help noticing her unusual fervor for one so small.

In 1928, Frances suddenly fell ill with the same illness which nearly took her life years earlier. This time, the illness progressed much more quickly. In desperation, Frank and Ethel called their friend, Dr. Marc Rabwin. Now the resident surgeon at Los Angeles County General Hospital, Dr. Rabwin pulled strings and arranged for Frances to be admitted to the pediatrics ward. Ordinarily, she would have had to be poor to be admitted to this hospital, but Dr. Rabwin knew this might be it the only chance to save her life.

An ambulance was dispatched immediately to Lancaster. Frank and Ethel rode in the ambulance with Frances. She would remain in the hospital for nearly a month, even after the infection was stopped, because she had been so weakened by her illness. Frances was so emaciated after she left the hospital, that Peg DeVine, who had befriended the Gumms when they first moved to California, cried the first time she saw her.[53]

~

One year after the Gumm family moved to Lancaster, with the theatre operating successfully, Frank began to look around for a nicer house. Frances would begin school in the fall, and he wanted to find something that was closer to the school, and more convenient to the theater.

The streets in the old part of town were named alphabetically for trees. After Antelope, there was Beech, Cedar, Date, Elm, Fern and Fig. On this particular day, as Frank turned at the corner at Cedar and Newgrove (now 2nd), just opposite the Lancaster Grammar School, he couldn't help noticing the large, two-story house with a well-manicured lawn. At the front corner of the house stood a trellis, six feet high with shower of pink roses. Sitting on the front porch in a swing seat was a pretty teenage girl with blonde hair. Frank headed up the walk.

"Good afternoon, Miss," he said tipping his hat.

"Good afternoon, sir."

"My name is Frank Gumm. And I was wondering if you might know of any houses in this area that are for rent."

"Oh no, Mr. Gumm, there are not many houses for rent around here."

"Well, if you hear of one, would you let me know? I am the manager of The Valley Theatre, and I would very much like my three little girls to live closer to the school. Here is my card. Please, give me a call, if you hear of any homes for rent."[54]

"Yes, Mr. Gumm, I will."

"I appreciate that so much. Thank you!"

Then, with a tip of his hat and a kind of shuffling step, Mr. Gumm walked back to the street and around the corner.

The Walsh Home on Cedar Ave in Lancaster about 1926.
(Courtesy JoDee Hunt)

"A very nice and dapper man," fifteen year-old Dorothy Walsh thought to herself.

There had not been any houses for rent in the area for quite some time, but as fate would have it, within the next few weeks, the family who lived two doors from the Walsh family moved out. The Walshes notified Mr. Gumm of the vacancy, and before long, the Gumms and the Walshes were neighbors.

The house the Gumms rented was a one-story, three-bedroom home, slightly larger and nicer than the earlier house. The best part about it, of course, was the fact that it was near the school, the theatre and in a real neighborhood with lots of children.

Although Dorothy Walsh had just turned fifteen, and was three years older than Mary Jane, and five years older than Virginia, the three girls hit it off right away, and were soon fast friends. Dorothy was happy to have such an interesting family move into the area. She had lived in Lancaster all her life. Her father, Frank Walsh, worked in real estate. Her mother, Kathryn, stayed at home and took care of her and her brother, Bob, who was one year younger than her. Although the Walsh family

Dorothy Walsh.
(Courtesy Dorothy Walsh Morrison)

had no theatrical aspirations, Dorothy loved to play the ukulele, and both she and Bob were good singers, having appeared in the light opera productions at school.

Shortly after the Gumms moved, in thanks for finding their new home, Mrs. Gumm invited the Walsh family over for dinner. "Mrs. Gumm was "mean cook," Dorothy later said. The meal was delicious, and the conversation over the dinner table was "delightful." Ethel was so friendly and full of fun, that Dorothy felt lucky to have such interesting neighbors. In addition, she couldn't help noticing the littlest sister, who was a tiny five year-old and had big dark eyes. The little girl made her presence felt with a charm all her own. After finishing off her meal, the little girl, whose name was Frances, asked her mother,

"Is there a broom in the closet?"

Dorothy wondered what in the world little Frances was talking about. Was she going to sweep up after dinner?

"Yes, there is, Frances," replied Mrs. Gumm.

Then, she left the room and returned with exquisite slices of peach pie. Cooked in with the peaches were pecans. The whole combination was absolutely wonderful.

Dorothy realized that little Frances' question had been a way of asking if there was any dessert. The question so charmed her, that she later used this expression when she had a family of her own.

When Dorothy and the Gumm girls became better acquainted, she often came over in the evenings to stay with Mary Jane, Virginia and Frances while their parents were at the theater. During these evenings, Dorothy, Janey and Jimmy talked and played games. Little Frances, however, remained quiet for the most part, just watching and listening to them.

Dorothy and her brother, Bob on their front lawn about 1926–29. Note the vacant land across the street; the area was still very countrified.
(Courtesy Dorothy Walsh Morrison)

Dorothy playing with Frances and Mary Jane Gumm.
(Courtesy Laureli Lunn)

Now that the Gumms were settled in a close-knit neighborhood, Frances, who would soon turn six, adjusted quickly. Before long, she was running around with all the other children. In the year and a half since the family left Grand Rapids, she had changed. She was no longer a chubby baby; she had grown taller, and had long, skinny legs.

Dorothy and the girls had fun during these days in Lancaster. The Walshes' front yard had a big umbrella tree for shade, and in the summer they would often sit under it and eat pieces of watermelon on toothpicks. At night, they lay outside on the grass and looked up at the stars while Mr. Walsh spoke to them of constellations.

As Dorothy put it, he believed in God, but he had a scientific mind, "He didn't believe in all the trimmings. He asked how man knew what's in the Bible."

The first time Dorothy attended the theater and watched the family perform on stage, she was delighted. "Frank was a sweetheart," she said. "He sang Minstrel songs, up-tempo songs and hymns." Dorothy thought Frank was a tenor, though in actuality, he was a high baritone with a wide range.

Dorothy was amazed by Ethel. "She knew her stuff and was constantly busy—really overly busy." While Ethel was playing piano for the silent pictures, to Dorothy's amusement, she'd also have a book propped up on the music stand and be reading at the same time. Every now and then she'd glance at the movie screen to make sure she was keeping up with what was going on.

During the next few months, the Walsh and Gumm families became very close. When Thanksgiving and Christmas came around, they spent them together. "We were family," Dorothy said simply.

Lancaster's winter occurs during January and February. Since the town is in the high desert, they usually get snow one day a year. But most of the time, winter means rain. Winter is also the time when the winds come blowing down from the mountains and across the desert surrounding the town. Storms blow dust, sand and tumbleweeds into town, and at night, the wind howls.

Dorothy, who had lived in Lancaster her entire life, was used to the winter weather, but for five year-old Frances, the sound of the wind was new. She cried and screamed in terror. "Make it stop!" she said. Dorothy tried to comfort her, but to little avail. "She's such a sensitive child," she told Mary Jane.

Glen Settle was a classmate of Dorothy Walsh, and one of her best friends. The pair had sung together in school operettas. Dorothy liked Glen so much she would have liked to date him, but her father didn't want her to.

Glen lived about six blocks from the Walsh home. His father worked for the railroad, and the Settle home was built right along the railroad tracks. The Settles had ten children, seven boys and three girls which meant they didn't have that much money. Dorothy's father told her that if she went out with Glen, she'd end up living on the railroad tracks too. So the two, remained close friends, "like brother and sister," as Dorothy put it. Nevertheless, Glen often stopped by to visit Dorothy, so it wasn't long after Gumms moved in that he met Mary Jane and Virginia.

Glen thought the two older Gumm sisters were lots of fun. As he put it, "they had lots of personality." Glen's future wife, Sue Miller, was in the same class as Mary Jane, and the two girls became very good friends.

Glen Settle, 1929.

The first time Glen attended The Valley Theatre under Frank Gumm's management, he was able to see the entire family perform. In later years he would compare Frank's singing style to a cross between Perry Como or Bing Crosby and Nelson Eddy. Frank sang like a crooner with classical training. The songs he sang most often were Minstrel songs. Glen also compared the passion and intensity with which Frank sometimes sang to the great Paul Robeson. "He was a very expressive singer," he said.

Ethel Gumm had a "low voice," and when she and Frank sang together they had great harmony. Glen supposed that was because they had worked together for so many years. "They sounded wonderful together," he said. During Mr. and Mrs. Gumm's set, Ethel remained seated at the piano. If Frank had a solo, he would stand at the front of the stage, but when the couple sang together, "he came around and stood next to her."[55]

As much as Glen admired Mr. and Mrs. Gumm as performers, nothing could compare to their youngest daughter, Frances. According to Glen and several other people in town, "she was louder than everyone else in the family put together!"

Carl Bergman, who Frank hired to do the lighting for The Valley Theater's shows, ran the spotlight on Frances and her sisters while they sang. Later, Carl kept those lights. Some of the lights and other things from The Valley Theater are now said to be at the Oceanside Museum in California.

For most of 1928, the Gumm sisters and their parents performed locally. By now, the family was truly a part of Lancaster, and looked on as one of its assets. Frank, Ethel, and the girls were often asked to perform for local clubs like the Kiwanis and the Masons, as well as at private parties. The girls even rode on a float in the Alfalfa Festival Parade.

The Gumms were also quite social during this time, and hosted a cast party for the local production of *The First Year*. The Gumm sisters performed at that event, as well as in March at Frank's forty-second birthday for which Ethel had a big party.[56]

Birthday parties were a large part of Lancaster's social life, particularly for the children. Now that Mary Jane, Virginia and Frances had many friends, in addition to being invited to others' parties, they had big birthday parties of their own. Some people, like Barbara Webb Ralphs, kept the little presents Ethel selected for the guests at her daughters' parties.

As she had in Grand Rapids, Ethel continued to arrange dinner and bridge parties. One of the couples with whom Frank and Ethel played bridge was William and Laura Gilmore. Laura was about the same age as Ethel, and had been born in Minnesota. When she was a girl, her father moved the family to North Dakota where, for a while, she taught school under her maiden name, Laura Keenan. Prior to the California move, one of Ethel's friends in Grand Rapids had asked her to look up her cousin in California. Later, Ethel realized that her cousin was Laura Gilmore.[57]

Born in Nebraska City, Nebraska in 1888, Bill Gilmore came from a large, Irish Catholic family. Bill had a degree in electrical engineering. After his marriage to Laura, the couple moved to West Virginia, where he worked for a coal company. The Gilmores moved to Lancaster around the same time the Gumms arrived. Bill had a job as an electrical water pump salesman, an item much in demand in the area. Like the Gumms, the Gilmores had three children: Bill, Jr., who was born in 1919, Ruth, born in 1921, and John, or "Jackie," as he was known, born in 1924.

~

In 1927, a huge change occurred in motion pictures. For years, the industry had been working on bringing sound to the pictures, but that year, with the release of *The Jazz Singer*, everything changed. Although most of the film was silent, in the middle, Al Jolsen spoke his signature line, "You ain't heard nothing yet," and then broke out into song. For the first time, the sound was coordinated with the picture and was recognizable, and of decent quality. With a star like Jolson leading the way, and breaking box office records, nay-sayers stopped laughing. Soon, everyone in the industry was scrambling to follow suit. It was clear that it would only be a matter of time before pictures in general had sound.

While Ethel concentrated her energies on Lancaster during 1927 and most of 1928, she was growing tired of the dusty, little town. Once the Valley Theatre was earning them a viable income, Ethel was ready to take the girls, who by now had become polished performers, down to Los Angeles.

In August of 1928, in order to escape the oppressive summer heat and relax, Ethel took the girls down to Santa Monica for a couple of weeks' vacation. While they were there, she heard about an audition for a local radio show, "The Kiddies Hour." Dressing the girls to the hilt, she drove them over to the local department store where auditions were being held.

The Gumm Sisters were just the sort of act the radio station was looking for, and they got the job. From August through October of that year, each week the girls sang on the Los Angeles Radio Station, KFI, performing such hits as *Avalon Town* and *You're the Cream in my Coffee*.[58] They received a great response. In September, legendary cowboy film star, William S. Hart, made a request for the Gumm sisters to sing *There's a Long, Long Trail A-Winding*, to which they complied. Later, on her weekly television show, remembering that time, Judy Garland would sing this song again.[59]

Although Ethel may have been more at peace with her marriage now than she had been previously, she had no intention of staying in Lancaster. Seeing her girl's success on the radio, she began to dream of bigger things. During this time, she reconnected with Ethel Meglin, who by now had created "The Meglin Kiddies," a group of 300 talented kids. On September 18th, the girls were performing as part of Mrs. Meglin's "Kiddies" at the Ladies Aid Charity Fete which took place at Pickfair—the home of the Hollywood's most famous film star couple, Mary Pickford and Douglas Fairbanks.

Ethel Meglin, like Ethel Gumm, was a woman of boundless energy who knew how to push. Once the Gumm Sisters signed up with Mrs. Meglin, they were kept busy, performing at community centers, the Los Angeles

Children's Hospital Ward, and, finally, at the Shrine Auditorium for *The Los Angeles Examiner's All Star Christmas Benefit.* Backstage, Mary Jane, Virginia and Frances rubbed shoulders with famous stars like Joan Crawford, Myrna Loy and Tom Mix. One hundred of Mrs. Meglin's 300 Meglin Kiddies performed that night. The full capacity of the Shrine is 6,500 people. This was likely the largest audience Frances, now billed "Baby Gumm," had ever performed for.[60]

The next week, the girls appeared with the Meglin Kiddies again, this time at Loews's State Theatre in Los Angeles for the Christmas Show. Dressed as Cupid in a long ruffled gown with pantaloons, Frances sang *I Can't Give You Anything But Love, Baby*, and received her first review. The reviewer for the *Los Angeles Record* wrote: "One small miss shook these well-known rafters with her songs à la Sophie Tucker."

Bishop Theatre
Tuesday and Wednesday
JULY 16-17
EXTRA ADDED ATTRACTION
The Three Gumm Sisters
(IN PERSON)
now with the famous Meglin Kiddies of Los Angeles, and avail
able only during vacation times, will appear in HARMONY SONGS
TAP AND ACROBATIC DANCNG.

The Gumm Sisters in 1929. (Courtesy Dahl/Kehoe Archives)

On New Years weekend, the Gumm girls were back in Lancaster, recreating their performance on the stage of their father's theater. Although Frank had not wanted Frances to perform in the Los Angeles shows, as always, he supported his daughters by attending their performances.

The year 1928 concluded with everyone feeling quite happy and looking forward to the wonderful unknown things which might be in store for them. Meanwhile, Ethel Gumm, like most stage mothers, had been bitten by the bug. Once applause is heard, the hunger for it grows even greater.

Chapter 35

Transitions and Friends

IN JANUARY OF 1929, THE GUMM SISTERS CONTINUED TO PERFORM WITH the "Meglin Kiddies." By now, Mary Jane, at thirteen had reached the awkward age, and Virginia, at eleven was on the edge of it. Still, it had taken years for the girls to become the trio they were, and Ethel realized there was no time to waste.

That February, despite any protests Frank may have had, Ethel had made up her mind what she was going to do. On March 1st, *The Ledger Gazette* announced that Mrs. Gumm and her daughters were "leaving" town to live "indefinitely" in Los Angeles, where "the girls may pursue special studies." The article also noted that they would be spending their weekends in Lancaster so that she could "furnish music" for the theater.

Ethel and the girls moved into an upstairs apartment at 1814½ Orchard Street, near Washington and Vermont.[61] Although Mary Jane and Virginia missed their friends during the time they were gone, they missed their father most of all. Nevertheless, they followed their mother's plans without complaint.

Over the next few months, along with their theatrical studies, the girls performed with the Meglins at such venues as the Shrine Auditorium, Graumans Egyptian Theater and the Figueroa Playhouse. Mrs. Gumm paid for her daughter's theatrical lessons by playing piano for Mrs. Meglin's classes.

Meanwhile, at least one weekend a month, the Gumm Sisters performed on their father's Valley Theater stage. On May 16th and 17th, the whole family performed in what was billed as *The Second Annual Minstrel*

John Milne, Jr. later in life. (Courtesy Robert Milne)

Show. This time, Uncle Jack Milne, using his railroad pass for a free trip out west, was visiting from Duluth, and joined in on the fun.

By now, Jack and his wife, Margaret, had seven children at home (eventually they would have fourteen). In addition to his railroad job, and freelance gigs, Jack would soon have a radio contract with the Goodrich Tire Company of Duluth, appearing on WEBC Radio as a featured soloist. During his years on the radio, Jack Milne became known as the "Goodrich Silvertone Tenor."[62]

The Minstrel Show of 1929 opened with the entire cast singing *When We Turn Out the Hometown Band.* The Gumm Sisters' big number was *Old Man River*, which all three girls performed in blackface.

Around this time, Ethel moved back to Lancaster with the girls. Although they were in constant demand down in Los Angeles, the "big break" Ethel had hoped for was not occurring and likely the stay in L.A. was more than the family could afford. Meanwhile, their sojourn "down below" had earned them one big break—their first film.

In June, the day after Frances Gumm's seventh birthday, The Gumm Sisters made their film debut singing, *In the Good Old Sunny South*, a number which appeared in *The Big Revue*, a Mayfair Pictures, Inc. production, the company owned by Mary Pickford and Douglas Fairbanks.

That summer, the girls worked every few days, both by themselves, and as part of *The Meglin Kiddies*. Most of their appearances, including one at The Bishop Theater in Bishop, were not too far from home. Of course, once *The Big Revue* came out, their billing went up a notch.

When the girls weren't performing, Ethel drove them the 70 to 80 miles down to Los Angeles for dance lessons. After seeing the other acts downtown, she had become aware that the girls needed more professional dance training if they were going to compete or get any work in Los Angeles. Sometimes she invited Dorothy Walsh to come along. Ethel seemed to like having Dorothy with them. She and the girls got on well, and because she was a bit older, she could help keep the girls in line while Ethel concentrated on the business side of things. Dorothy felt like one of the sisters. The only difference between them was the fact that the Gumm girls were dark haired with dark eyes, and "Dottie" was blonde-haired with blue-eyes.

During her time with the Gumm family, Dorothy observed that Frank and Ethel Gumm were different in every way. Although Frank was certainly a hard worker, he was relaxed and easy going, while Ethel was impatient. Her temper could flip in a second and you did not want to be at the end of that temper. Sometimes Frank seemed to walk with a little shuffle, almost as if he was tired. Both Frank and Ethel were a little overweight; Dorothy thought that was probably a result of Ethel's good cooking.

~

The main street in town, Lancaster Boulevard, was only a few blocks from the Gumm home on Cedar Avenue. Down Lancaster Boulevard was the Valley Theatre, Harris' Clothing store on corner, and a small restaurant with seating for 20–30 people. There was also a pool hall two doors down from the theatre, and on the other side of the theater, a barbershop and a garage with an auto parts store. A dozen or so stores lined the opposite side of the street as well.

Glen Settle's brother, Bill, had a produce store on Tenth Street West and Sierra, which he owned with Whitford Carter, the owner of The Valley Theater. The store, known as the Antelope Valley Produce Store, was right near the theater. While Glen was in high school, he worked there on the weekends. After he graduated in 1929, he worked there almost every day from 8 AM to 9 PM. On Saturdays, the store closed at 6 PM.

Mrs. Gumm was a frequent customer at the produce store, and whenever she came in, she was in a hurry, as if she could not wait to get out of there. Glen thought, "She always seemed to be on her way somewhere." If Mrs. Gumm asked for the groceries to be delivered, Glen was the one who delivered them, and he soon learned that he had better be careful with what was put in the Gumms' box. Mrs. Gumm was very particular. One day Glen gave her a bad tomato, and she let him know about it. Nevertheless, Glen enjoyed visiting the Gumm home. Whenever he went inside, it seemed there was something interesting going on—it was a lively place.

One thing that struck him was Frances. She had such a big voice on stage, but she was very quiet whenever he saw her at home. She seemed to be just observing what was going on, but never in the midst or part of it.

In a small town like Lancaster, everyone knew everyone and Glen saw Mr. Gumm fairly often. In the summertime, traveling acting companies came to town. These touring companies would put up a tent in the downtown area and perform, alternating two or three shows for a period of two or three weeks. Then, they would pack up and move on. The summer touring companies were really competition for The Valley Theatre, so Frank must have had mixed emotions about them.[63]

One day, Glen was talking to Frank when the Galvin Players arrived. Right away, Frank went down to see them, with Glen following along. To his surprise, it seemed Frank knew every actor in the group. Frank Gumm knew so many people; Glen thought he was rather amazing.

~

In the fall of 1929, the stock market crashed. In a short time, a good portion of the country was sent into a deep depression, with thousands out of work. For a time, Lancaster—as a farming community-remained seemingly unaffected. In addition, the film business seemed to thrive. If someone had a nickel or a dime, they were happy to go to their movies just to escape their worries. Meanwhile, most of America was suffering.

In November 1929, *The Ledger Gazette* noted that "Frank Gumm had signed a contract with RCA Photophone," a company which would install "talkie equipment" at the Valley Theatre. Soon, Frank would not need a pianist to play background music for films.

Despite was a short period of rest and family togetherness, from this point on, Ethel Gumm was a woman on a mission. She wanted to get her girls out of Lancaster. While the Depression, a truly frightening situation, should be taken into consideration, it is also true that Ethel, a creative and talented woman of thirty-six, was dissatisfied with her life. The life in Lancaster was not what she had signed on for when she married Frank, nor when they moved to California. She wanted something better for her family and for herself. And only eighty miles away in Los Angeles, there was a completely different world, a world of possibilities, an emerald oz where dreams came true.

Dorothy Walsh would later feel that Ethel had been misunderstood. She described her as a woman full of energy and ideas; a woman who was "always doing something creative. She had big plans for the girls because she wanted to take care of them," Dorothy explained. "Judy wanted to perform," she added in regards Judy's later complaints that her mother pushed her on stage. "Ethel was only doing what Judy wanted."[64]

After Ethel saw the girls achieve success on the radio, and in the Meglin Kiddie film, she was certain that even greater success could be achieved; her girls would be able to live lives of fulfillment and financial security. From here on, she began taking the girls down to Los Angeles—several weekends a month. Sometimes, she took Frances by herself.

By late 1929, the Gumm girls were receiving bookings throughout the Lancaster area, and as far as Long Beach and Covina. If Ethel was unhappy with her life at this time, it only showed itself with her determination to see her girls succeed.

Between November and December, the girls filmed three movie shorts with *The Vitaphone Kiddies*. The company was a subsidiary of Warner Brothers, and the girls went to the Burbank studio to work on the pictures. Frances was given two solos, *Blue Butterfly* and *Hang onto the Rainbow*, a remarkable feat considering the fact that she was chosen from so many children.

During the time they were filming, the girls had no less than thirteen appearances throughout Los Angeles and in Lancaster. Meanwhile, the girls were older now, and Mrs. Gumm severed their relationship with the Meglin Kiddies. Instead, she signed them up with an organization known as *Hollywood Starlets*. The Gumm Sisters were billed as *The Hollywood Starlets Trio*.[65]

For their first gig, they performed downtown Los Angeles at the opening of a new toy department in the Walker's Department Store. While they were performing, Frank went down to Union Station to pick up Grandma Eva, who had taken the train in from Minneapolis for Christmas.[66] The girls gave their final performance of the year for the annual Christmas Dinner-Dance at The Los Angeles Country Club in Beverly Hills.

While life was exceedingly busy and exciting for Ethel, it had slowed down for Frank. With Ethel and the girls gone much of the time, he was lonely. Outwardly, the Gumm marriage seemed as strong as it had been, but the break was deeper than most people realized.

~

In February of 1929, while appearing in the play *Cinderella*, which starred her sisters, Virginia and Mary Jane as Cinderella and the Prince, Frances became acquainted with a girl three years older than herself, Ina Mary Ming. Ina Mary lived several blocks away from the Gumms. Her mother, Clara, worked as a bookkeeper for the telephone company, and her father, Sam Ming (a Scotch name), worked as a foreman for the Edison Company. Also living in the Ming home were Clara's two children from a previous marriage, Lorene Lundy, who was four years older than Ina, and Will Lundy, who was two years older.

Everyone in the family called Ina, "Muggsie," possibly because she was such a tomboy. Muggsie called Frances, "Babe." Although the girls were two grades apart in school, it didn't seem to matter. They enjoyed doing the same things. Neither of them liked to play with dolls. Instead, they climbed trees, played games, and rode their bicycles around town. Nearly every day after school, and every bit of free time they could find, they were out playing together. Of course, Frances had to go home every afternoon to practice her singing. Besides singing, Ethel was also teaching her to play the piano. Sometimes, Ethel took Muggsie along on their trips to Los Angeles, so Frances wouldn't be so lonely.

One day, when Muggsie and Babe were out together, they came upon some cement that had just been laid and was still soft. The girls took their shoes off and ran through it, leaving behind a trail of footprints. Neither girl ever told their parents for fear of punishment. This cement is now preserved at the Western Hotel in Lancaster.

Another time, the girls were playing in Ming's yard, which right next to the Gilmores. The Mings had a big, old tree in the back yard and Frances was climbing up in it. Muggsie's brother, Will, was there, and all of a sudden he saw Ethel Gumm running down the street, begging Frances to get out of the tree. She was so afraid she'd fall and get hurt.

During her early years in Lancaster, Frances had fallen out of a swing, and injured her neck so badly, it was reported in the local paper. Although most people, like Will Lundy, thought Mrs. Gumm was over protective of Frances, her worry is understandable. Frances was small for her age (the smallest in her class), and considering how many times she had come close to death, Ethel worried about her well-being.

Will Lundy was a friend of the Rev. Parker's son, Boyd. Sometimes, he went to church with Boyd. Eventually, Boyd talked him into joining St. Paul's Episcopal choir. Every Sunday, Frank Gumm played the organ at St. Paul's and led them in song. When Will finally became a member of the church, Frank Gumm stood up as his godfather.

Although Frances loved to sing, like any child, there were times when she didn't want to perform. One day, a talent scout came to Lancaster and picked her out for a screen test. Ethel was so excited and prodded her, but she didn't want to go down to Hollywood. She was so tired of traveling; she just wanted to stay home and play with Muggsie. To Frances, Muggsie was her only real friend. Muggs seemed to understand how she felt about things, and was always there for her. At this point, Frances felt at home in Lancaster.

Both Dorothy Walsh and Muggsie Ming were aware of the intense fights between Mr. and Mrs. Gumm. When Dorothy lived in Lancaster, she could hear the Gumms fighting two houses away. Later, when Mr. and Mrs. Gumm were fighting, Muggsie would stand outside with her best friend, "Babe," sometimes crying along with her. They waited for Mr. Gumm to play the piano and sing a love song. That was a sign the fight was over, but to Muggsie, the songs always sounded sad.[67] Sometimes, Frances was allowed to stay over at Muggsie's house, where she was able to relax and get away from the tensions at home.

Of course, life in Lancaster was not all bad. The renovated Jazz Café was just down the street from the Valley Theater, and almost every day, "Daddy" would take Frances there for a treat. Everyone who saw Frank and his youngest daughter together recognized something special between them. Mary Jane was her mother's girl. Virginia seemed to be a cross between parents, but Baby was definitely Daddy's girl. Some would say that they were most alike—their liveliness, sense of humor and sensitivity to others. Frank was a hard worker, but he also believed in enjoying life.

At Christmastime, Charlie Wakefield, who ran the soda fountain and candy store, made candy canes. Then, he and Frank joined together to give the children in town free candy canes and a free showing of Rin-Tin-Tin movies. The Kiwanis, a business club, also put on events at Christmas, for which the Gumm Sisters sometimes preformed.

In summer, all the kids went down to swim in the Olympic-sized pool, which cost 25 cents admission. A local teacher recalled seeing little

Frances with her long skinny legs walking down the middle of the street on her way to and from the pool. Babe and Muggsie used to run barefoot in the shadow the telephone poles, so their feet wouldn't burn in the 100-plus degree heat. Sometimes, Frank came down to see the girls at the pool, and would throw a handful of pennies in the water, which sent everyone scrambling to capture them. These were the fun and happy days that Frances did not want to leave for the auditions in Los Angeles.

~

1930

When Dorothy Walsh graduated from high school in 1929, her father decided to move the family to Pasadena so that she and her brother, Bob, would be able to attend Pasadena City College.

Dorothy Walsh, 1929.
(Courtesy Glen Settle)

The Gumms, who were doing quite well, decided they would like to rent the Walsh home. The house was a California artisan home, built by the president of a bank. It was a sturdy home with beautifully crafted rooms of fine wood. Designed to keep the heat out; the windows had copper weather-stripping, and the roof was metal. The house also contained seven large bedrooms, which meant there would be plenty of room for Ethel's family to visit. Already, Grandma Eva was spending a good portion of the year with them. Now, she and Norma, or anyone else who visited, would be able to have their own room. The house also had a music room, which was certainly something unique for the Gumms.

Almost a year after Dorothy's family moved to Pasadena, Kathryn Walsh complained about a very bad head and neck ache. The doctor told her it was nerves. It wasn't. Mrs. Walsh had polio.

Dorothy and Bob were sent to live in a mountain cabin for two weeks in order to protect them from the possibility of catching the polio germ, which was believed to be extremely contagious. Mr. Walsh stayed behind, daily visiting his wife who was confined in an iron lung. A short time later, Mrs. Walsh passed away.

The Walsh family was devastated, particularly Dorothy, who had lost her mother without ever being able to say goodbye. In a short time, she had left her childhood home and friends, and lost her mother. During this time, Glen Settle took the streetcar down to Pasadena to visit her.

In the months that followed, Dorothy kept in touch with the Gumms. Along with her father and brother, they had become her family, and she was a part of theirs.

~

In February 1930, Frank Gumm's sound equipment for the new talkie films finally arrived and was installed. *The Ledger-Gazette* congratulated Frank for this new advance in technology and for "having faith" in the Lancaster community. The advertisement by local townsmen reveals that in 1930, Frank Gumm was looked on with great respect by the local citizens and town leaders.[68] Now that the Valley Theater would be showing "talkies," except for the girls' weekend performances, Ethel would be free to use her time in other ways.

When the Gumms first moved into the Walsh home, Ethel seemed more content with her life in Lancaster, which made Frank quite happy. She opened a dance and music studio in town, and rented a large, rounded metal building that looked very much like a Quonset hut. The building was located out on Lancaster Highway, just on the edge of the desert. In a short time, Ethel had about twenty pupils, including

The Lancaster building where Ethel Gumm taught dancing.

Muggsie Ming and Ruth Gilmore. Mrs. Gumm also tried to get Will Lundy to join. He later said, "She tried to get me into the class, but that was not my strong suit."[69]

Mary Jane and Virginia assisted their mother with the classes at the studio, but since they were busy a good deal of the time, Frances was frequently called upon to demonstrate dance steps for the students.

Following in Ethel Meglin's footsteps, and using some of her best students, Ethel Gumm formed a dance troupe called *Rainbow Girls*. On weekends, the *Rainbow Girls* performed on the stage of the Valley Theater. Dorothy Walsh later said that they rehearsed so hard for the new "chorus line" that everyone was hurting, and Mary Jane sprained her ankle.[70] It seems the dance troupe didn't go much further than that. Families in Lancaster were not that interested in seeking stardom (or even show business) for their children. It was just fun for the young people involved. During this time, Muggsie and her friend, Ruth Gilmore, also appeared at the Valley Theater in a kind of acrobatic act.

Sue Miller, a classmate of Mary Jane's, was one of Ethel's students. Sue was a very pretty girl with dark hair, and during this time, she and Mary Jane became very good friends. Meanwhile, Sue and Glen Settle were dating.

Around this same time, Glen, who was a big strong fellow, a star of both the high school football team and the basketball team, met a movie star who asked him if he would like to go out with her. Because he was dating Sue, Glen told her "no." When Frank Gumm heard about the incident, he thought it was terribly funny, and was forever kidding Glen about the fact that he had turned down a date with a movie star.[71]

Sue Miller.
(Courtesy Glen Settle)

Glen thought Mary Jane was the least attractive of the three Gumm sisters. Virginia was definitely the most attractive, and the most popular with the boys. "She also had the most personality," he said, "and because of that, all the boys were going after her." For a while, Glen's younger brother, Irving, dated Virginia.

One time, Glen and Sue went down to Los Angeles to see the Gumm girls at the Paramount

Theatre. When Mary Jane and Virginia spotted the couple sitting in the audience, they got the giggles. Glen guessed they hadn't expected to see their Lancaster friends in L.A.

A few years later when Mary Jane changed her named to Susie, Glen figured that maybe it was because of her friendship with Sue Miller. Eventually, Glen and Sue were married.

Since Glen was 4 years older than Mary Jane, six years older than Virginia, and eleven years older than Frances, in later years his memories of what occurred in Lancaster during these years was clearer and had more perspective than many of Frances' school chums.

Now that the Gumms had a bigger house to live in, Grandma Eva came to live with them. She and Ethel's father, John Milne, were divorced. For a time, John Milne, Sr. lived in a rooming house in Duluth. Then, Jack Milne built a place on the back of his house for him to stay.

During the early 1930s, Eva and Norma ran a bakery back in Superior. The two women baked bread and rolls which they delivered to homes around the city. Eva liked to cook, and everyone who knew the Gumms in Lancaster, always remembered the delicious donuts she made to sell to the neighbors. Bob Herbert, one of Frances's classmates, would bring her a magazine and she would pay him with half a dozen donuts. Visitors to the Gumm home said that when you walked through the door, the house smelt delicious.

~

1931

Beginning in 1931, whether at the Valley Theatre or "down below" in Hollywood, the Gumm Sisters were busy nearly every weekend. They appeared frequently in Beverly Hills, and sometimes traveled as far as San Diego. When they could get away with it, Mary Jane and Virginia (who Lancaster residents seemed to refer to by their full names) stayed in town. Mary Jane, who was now fifteen, and Virginia, who was thirteen, wanted to socialize and go on dates. Virginia would later say she and Mary Jane didn't need much rehearsal anyway. They learned their steps and "just did it."

Frances was quickly becoming the star of the trio, and Ethel took her down to Los Angeles almost every weekend. Her performances as a cute kid with a big voice were evolving to something much more. She was beginning to reveal a talent far beyond her years, and an ability to move audiences to tears and ovations.

~

In the first grade, Frances had a young teacher, Marta Wilson Peterson. The next year's teacher, Mrs. Thacker, was older. During her first years at school, Frances appeared in many of the school operettas. Glen Settle's nephew, Dick White, appeared in two of these operettas with Frances. In one, she played Betsy Ross, the young woman who made the first American flag; Dick played one of the Indians. For many of the school performances, Ethel played the piano. Barbara Webb's mother also played for many of the productions.

While publicly there has been much focus on how Frank and Ethel doted over their youngest daughter, it is clear that they were equally proud and supportive of their older girls. When Virginia graduated from eighth grade, Ethel was there to accompany her as she sang *Gypsy Love Song* and *Brahm's Lullaby*. Frank also took part in events involving his daughters, and made sure to attend any of their performances he could.[72] In the summer, when Ethel took the girls out of town, he often drove down during the week, when the theater wasn't too busy, to spend a few days with them.

Frances had done well in school the first two years, but in third grade, the constant running to Hollywood—almost every weekend—began to take its toll. In fact, a lot of the kids felt sorry for her.

"Her mother took her to Hollywood on the weekends which made her different from the other kids in class," said Bob Herbert, her classmate. "The other kids were interested in the ball games and happenings around Lancaster. When Frances came back to school on Monday and talked about the movie stars she'd met, some people thought she was showing off. That was her world, but the kids in school would have been more excited if she told them she met Rin Tin Tin. They just couldn't relate."

Dorothy Mumaw Darling, who was also in Frances' class, noticed how she fell asleep at her desk after her long weekends in Hollywood. Dorothy and some of the other kids felt Ethel Gumm pushed Frances too hard. "Mrs. Gumm wasn't like any of the mothers in Lancaster," said

The Lancaster Grammar School's 3rd Grade Class in 1930: Back row, far left, Ralph Dubois, fifth from left, Ed White, Second row from top, far right, Dorothy Mumaw Darling. Third row from top, third from right, Frances Gumm, Front Row, third from right, Bob Herbert. far right, the only Japanese American student in their class, died fighting in WWII.
(Courtesy Dahl/Kehoe Archives)

Barbara Webb Ralphs, whose mother, like Ethel, taught piano. "The other mothers in town seemed more motherly."

While Frances Gumm's schoolmates may have been repeating the things they heard their parents say, it seems a lot of parents in town thought Ethel Gumm was bossy. In later years, some people blamed her for Frank's condemnation, saying she should have been home rather than running down to Los Angeles all the time.

When "Babe's" classmates went to the theatre to hear her sing, they couldn't help being impressed. Dorothy Mumaw thought she could belt out a song better than anyone Lancaster. It was clear, perhaps in hindsight, that it was only her way of life that had pushed her away from them.

Although Frances clearly enjoyed singing, there was a growing division in her world. The things which her mother thought made her important were not the same things her school friends valued. She wanted to be a normal kid and fit in with her peers, yet at home, Ethel had schooled her in the values of show business and stardom, and there was little rest from that. In her heart, Ethel truly believed she was doing the best thing for her daughter, but she failed to realize that neither fame nor money could equal happiness.

As time passed, this division between show business and a normal childhood became a point of great contention between Frank and Ethel Gumm. Muggsie, who came over to play after school, sometimes heard the Gumms arguing over this very subject.

Clearly, Frances was an exceptional child, but Frank had never wanted her to be pushed as a "child star." It was one thing for her to perform in his theatre with her sisters, and quite another for her to be spending her days and nights away from home, singing on a big stage and mingling with show people. He did not approve of that, and he let Ethel know. There would be plenty of time for her to do those things once she was older.

Sometimes, "Babe" told Muggsie about the things that went on when they went down to Los Angeles. Perhaps she had shared her feelings with her father as well. One of her complaints was the fact that her mother was constantly taking her to sing for men who sat there stone-faced while she sang her heart out. She absolutely hated that.

Meanwhile, Ethel felt the time for Frances was now. There were loads of adults with talent, but a little girl who sang as she did was one in a million. If she was going to succeed, they had to do it now, while the momentum was going. Perhaps the one thing Ethel could not face was the fact that promoting her daughter's career was something that gave her a reason for living. She was not happy with her life, but finally, after one argument with Frank, she agreed to keep the girls home during the school year.

In January, however, Ethel happened upon an advertisement placed by dance instructor, Maurice Kussel, who was seeking young performers for his *Stars of Tomorrow* revue. Ethel went to see him and was hired to conduct the orchestra for the new revue. In time, she also gave him a copy of her song, *Deep, Deep in My Heart*, which he helped her get published. It was a lovely song, although it did not go far, possibly because Ethel was too busy with her daughters to promote it.

The girls would remain under the tutelage of Maurice Kussel during the next two years. He was an extremely well-schooled dancer who had appeared both in vaudeville and on Broadway. Kussel was amazed by Frances, and at Ethel's request, agreed to choreograph the Gumm Sisters new act. In exchange this great service which would make the Gumm girls' act shine, Ethel worked for a lower salary.

~

Through the years, socially, the Gumms had continued on with their lives, just as they had in the past. Frank and Ethel still played bridge with the Gilmores, but Jimmy, now a teenager, couldn't help noticing that Bill Gilmore was always looking at her mother.

At some point, Bill Gilmore and Ethel began an affair. When it began, and how long it lasted, is not clear. Muggsie later recalled a day when she and "Babe" were playing hide and seek with the Gilmores, and ran into an old, abandoned building on their property. Babe ran ahead to a room on the second floor she thought was empty. By the time Muggsie caught up with her, an angry Bill Gilmore "pushed them out." Babe had witnessed something disturbing between her mother and Gilmore, but she never would say what she had seen.[73]

The full story of the Gumm and Gilmore relationship seems far too complex and messy to untangle. The friendship between the two families, involved not only the parents, but the children. While Bill and Ethel sustained a secret relationship, outwardly the two families continued on as friends.

To Muggsie and Frances, Mr. Gilmore was a harsh, frightening, and even cruel man. Dorothy Walsh found him "bombastic and dictatorial." "The truth," his granddaughter said, "is that he was a brash Irishman, who wouldn't put up with nonsense." Frances had grown up in a household that was somewhat lenient, and, when Frank wasn't around, Bill Gilmore sometimes took the opportunity to correct her. Her mother didn't interfere, and this became another cause for hurt and resentment in Frances.[74]

Then, sometime between 1931 and 1933, Laura Gilmore had a stroke. Although she survived, she was confined to a wheelchair, and her condition, complicated by bouts of high blood pressure, was serious. Laura was a sweet lady, and those in the know about Bill Gilmore and Ethel felt extra sorry for her. Yet, to the Gilmore family, Bill was a loving husband, who adored his wife, and would do anything for her.

After Laura's stroke, the Gilmores moved about 84 miles away, to the town of Santa Paula. Situated in Ventura County near the California coast, Santa Paula is known as "the citrus capital of the world." Likely Bill found a better situation there, though he may have wished to escape Lancaster as well. Meanwhile, the town was only sixty miles from Los Angeles. The Gumms and the Gilmores continued to keep in touch. Whatever the relationship between Gilmore and Ethel, it did not replace the relationships with their spouses.

Frank Gumm was determined to be a loving provider for his wife and children, no matter what problems he had. He had lived part of his childhood with a father who could not provide for his children, and who was emotionally unavailable. For this reason, if for no other, Frank hung on to his life with Ethel and the girls. He would not be like his father.

People in Lancaster could not help noticing that there was something special between Frank and his youngest daughter. The two of them had a connection, and a mutual understanding. But, no matter how much Frank loved Frances, he could not protect her from the pain caused by the division between her parents; she felt torn between the mother and father who could not get along.

~

Shortly after Mrs. Walsh died, Frank Walsh and his children left Pasadena and moved to Los Angeles. In the midst of the depression, times were hard, and there were few jobs. Mr. Walsh, who was a real estate man, had a good friend who was known as the "mortgage king." This man bought the homes people lost in the Depression. He hired Mr. Walsh to fix them up, during which time the family would live the house. Once the home was sold, the Walshes moved to the next house. Over the next few years, Dorothy and her father moved quite often.

Meanwhile, for two years Dorothy attended Los Angeles City College. Around 1933, the Walshes moved into a big beautiful home on St. Cloud Road in Bel Aire, just a few doors down from Ronald Reagan. Dorothy loved this house, but after a short time, her father's friend said he had sold it to a rich Texan, so the Walshes had to move. A few months later, the Texan lost the house and Walshes moved back in. Of course, they were thrilled to return to this gorgeous home.

Around the same time, Ethel Gumm rented a house in Beverly Hills. The Gumm girls were working a lot, and appearing at some big theatres. Ethel rolled up the carpets in the living room so that the girls could practice their tap dancing, but they made such a racket that the neighbors complained. Pretty soon, the landlord told Ethel that he couldn't have them living there with all the dancing going on, so they had to move. According to Dorothy, "Ethel was always moving."

Whenever the girls were in Los Angeles, Dorothy spent as much time as possible with them. She attended their shows. She also went backstage to help them with their hair and costumes. According to Dorothy, the girls loved to perform and there was lots of excitement backstage. Dorothy was also very lively, and together, she, Janey, Jimmy and Frances had loads of laughs. With her high energy and great sense of humor, Dorothy fit right in.

Although Ethel still made some of the girl's costumes, now that they were in Hollywood, frequently, she bought or rented costumes from the costume companies near the movie studios. These costume rental places had beautiful outfits of all types. By renting, the girls could change their appearance with every performance if they wished, and make their shows even more exciting.

Chapter 36

Goodbye to Lancaster

GLEN SETTLE HAD ALREADY GRADUATED FROM HIGH SCHOOL WHEN HE started playing golf with Frank Gumm. That was around 1930. The fair weather and warm climate made golf a big sport in California. Sometimes, Don Hatfield, Glen's future brother-in-law, joined them. One day, Don brought his camera and took some photos.

Frank had a set of wooden clubs. He also wore the fashionable golfing costume of the day, trousers that fastened at the knee, long plaid socks and a cap. Frank had a great sense of humor, and playing golf with him was always an enjoyable outing. You just never knew what Frank, with his charming Southern drawl, was going to say next.

One day, Glen and Frank drove down to the Griffith Park Golf Course. The course, which lies on hill near the famous observatory, overlooks Hollywood, and is considered one of the finest courses in the area. The date was May 24th, 1930. On their way home, Frank was driving down Hollywood Boulevard when they noticed something going on at Graumans' Chinese Theatre.

"Come on," said Frank, "Let's go down there."

He parked the car and the pair walked down to the theatre.* They soon discovered it was a premiere for Howard Hughes' new film, *Hell's Angels*, starring blonde bombshell, Jean Harlow. A big crowd of people

---

* Although other authors have included Don Hatfield on this trip, the author is basing this on what she was told by Glen Settle.

Glen Settle and Frank Gumm playing golf.
(Courtesy Glen Settle)

was being held back by the police. Klieg lights stretched their bright beams across the sky and a line of movie stars in fancy cars were waiting to walk the red carpet.

Arriving that evening were Buster Keaton, Delores Del Rio, Norma Talmadge, Mary Pickford and Douglas Fairbanks, and Charlie Chaplin. When Frank and Glen got to the theater, the crowd was anxiously awaiting the arrival of Jean Harlow.

Glen noticed that Frank could be very bold and forceful when he wanted to be. After sizing things up, he was amazed so see Frank push his way through the crowd, right up to the front rope. When he got to the rope, Frank didn't stop, he went under it. He wanted to meet Jean Harlow!

"Who are you?" "What are you doing?" "What's your name?" people were saying.

"I'm Rin-Tin-Tin's cousin," said Frank, quick as a whip.

Glen thought Frank was awfully funny. He was always coming up with crazy things like that, which made him extra fun to be with.

~

Antelope Valley High School was the only high school within a hundred miles. There were many farms outside Lancaster, as well as gold and silver mines way out in the desert. It wasn't possible for the young people whose families worked in these areas to travel to school every day, so the Lancaster school had a dormitory where about fifty to sixty students lived during the week. There was one dormitory for the girls and another for the boys.

A few years earlier, the math teacher for the high school was also one of the teachers who oversaw the boys' dormitory. There were rumors that something had occurred with him and some of the boys. There had been complaint, and he was dismissed. After he left, the teacher moved down to a town near San Diego, where another complaint of the same type was brought against him. This time he was taken to court and convicted of child molestation, a crime for which he was sent him to San Quentin for twenty years. That was about 1932. After he was convicted, word eventually came back to Lancaster.

The math teacher's replacement was Jack Workman, who came to Lancaster from Cal Tech where he had been completing a degree. That second semester in high school everything went smoothly.

It was said that one of the complaints came from Lyle Hatley, a boarding school student who attended high school about the same time as Glen Settle. Lyle came from a mining family. His father was a mining engineer, and worked in the silver mines outside town. Lyle had always been a good kid, but according to Glen, after his father was killed in a mining accident, he became a troublemaker. It seemed as if he was always in trouble. The authorities sent him away for a while.

In high school, Lyle started hanging out with Steve Castle, the son of a railroad man from Tennessee. Together, these two were in constant trouble. The police stopped one of them for speeding with a bunch of kids in the car. Later, one of them confessed to holding up a store with a gun. They also robbed a gas station.

The Valley Theater had two kinds of seating. The logue seats, which had a cushion and were more expensive, and the cheaper plain, wooden seats. After school a lot of the high school boys liked to hang out around the block, and then go into the theater. Whenever they went to the theater, some of Lyle's basketball team members couldn't help noticing that Lyle, and sometimes Steve, just walked in and never paid. To some, Lyle seemed to be a "cocky," kid with a chip on his shoulder, who would get away with whatever he could. The boys wondered what was up with him.

~

By the end of 1932, Ethel was finished with Lancaster. On December 21st, *The Ledger-Gazette* noted that after the beginning of the year, "Mrs. Frank Gumm plans to spend the greater part of her time in Los Angeles."

Some thought that part of Ethel's reason for moving the girls out of Lancaster, besides the fact that she hated it there, was because Frances suffered greatly from the pollen and desert dusts. Many nights when she was younger, Ethel had wrapped her youngest child in a blanket as she wheezed and gasped for breath, and driven her for miles. This solution to the problem really did help. Once they had driven far enough away, Frances' breathing would improve.

Another situation affecting most of America at this time was the depression. By 1933, the full effects were being felt everywhere. Frank had even been forced to lower ticket prices in order to keep familes attending the shows. He was hurting for money. In fact, he had fallen behind on his rent.

Meanwhile, rumors about Frank Gumm had begun to surface, and to be passed around among the young men in town. These rumors involved his interest in young men and boys. The girls knew nothing about it, but the teenage boys spread the rumors among themselves for laughs.

Ed White, who was in Frances Gumm's class, heard his dad and his uncles talking one day. One of his uncles said, "Don't let Ed around Frank, he's queer." That was the only inkling he had that anything was wrong. He liked Frances, but she seemed to have no interest in him. She just wanted to play with Muggsie.

Glen Settle's other nephew, Dick White, was also in Frances' class, and used to play piano for her when she wanted to practice her tap dancing.

The song she liked to dance to was *Alexander's Ragtime Band.* Dick did not go to Frances' house much, though when he did, Mrs. Gumm always welcomed him.

The rumors about Frank did not affect Glen Settle much. He had never had a problem with Frank, and considering the troubled backgrounds of the boys believed to be spreading the rumors, he took it all with a grain of salt. Homosexuality was a subject that was new to most kids in Lancaster; they had never heard of anything like that. Glen couldn't help wondering if these boys just liked to make things up. He was also aware that there were a small group of people in Lancaster who didn't like Frank.

In later years, Glen joked with a writer who was researching Frank Gumm, saying "I guess I wasn't his type." The writer, however, took Glen's playful statement seriously. He later called Glen to tell him he had set up a rendezvous for him with another man. When Glen passed the information on to his wife, she had a long laugh. This shows how easily information can be misconstrued.

~

Ethel Gumm centered her life around her girls. She and Frank could no longer seem to agree on anything. They fought so much; it was painful for them to be together.

Will Gilmore helped Ethel feel good about herself. It was good to know that a man could still find her attractive. Perhaps in some ways, he reminded her of her father. She wasn't as young anymore, or slender. Her body had taken on the stocky form of her mother, most notably, the thick calves and ankles. Often she went on oranges juice fasts—nothing to eat for a few days—just drinking orange juice. That kept her going; she could loose that extra ten pounds and look nice in the A-line dresses that were in style.

Ethel could still look pretty when she smiled, but too often she knew she was frowning at life. This was not at all what she had planned. She had planned on a marriage to the man she loved, with a happy family, years of music together. Frank had never failed her as a provider, but her real joy now was seeing her girls up onstage. Frances was not an ordinary child; she had the ability to move an audience. Even at ten, she could move audiences in ways that seasoned performers could not. And Ethel was not going to let her fool around and end up as she had with an unhappy marriage. She, Ethel, would see that Judy became a star and moved with the best people.

Meanwhile, Ethel was determined that while she stayed in her marriage, she would have her own life. She had warned Frank about his behavior. He grew incensed—the idea that he would ever do anything to harm his daughters' reputations.

Working in show business fulfilled Ethel's needs, and made her happy. It made her forget what it was she wanted to forget—that she was growing old and was not happy in her marriage. Not happy might be a mild statement. At every turn she was reminded of how far they had gone from the original dream.

~

As time passed, the rumors about Frank began to spread outside the circle of high school boys, who by now had graduated. One author mentions that a child had even teased Frances about her father. In any case, if Ethel heard anything about that, she would have been even more anxious to leave town. She did not have that freedom in Grand Rapids, but by 1932, Ethel had her own car, a job, and a means of further employment. In addition, she knew that her girls had the ability to earn money with their performances.

The spring of 1933, Ethel moved Virginia and Frances moved to a small house down in Los Angeles. Mary Jane, now in her final year at Antelope Valley High, stayed behind to graduate with her class. Grandma Eva, who loved Frank, was happy to stay at the house with Ethel's sister, Norma. During the next few months, the two women kept house for Frank and Janey.[75]

In April, Frances made an appearance by herself at the Coconut Grove, where she was introduced to the audience by Eddie Cantor. The author's grandparents were present at that engagement, and would later say they had never seen anything like this child's performance. The audience went wild.

Frances, who would turn eleven that year, was proving that her unique qualities were not simply those of a cute baby. Although she was entering what is commonly known as "the awkward stage," was a bit "gangly," and no raving beauty, she had reached new heights as a vocalist. She could sing for a thousand people and touch them with her voice. And she loved it. Ethel had thought once that Mary Jane and Virginia had the talent to make it in the business. Now, all the attention was going to their little sister.

That June, after Mary Jane graduated, she and Grandma Eva joined Ethel and the girls in Los Angeles. Norma was busy with her own career.

The following month, Frank came down to visit the family and was apparently not satisfied with the house Ethel had chosen for them. Instead, he rented a large house at 2605 Ivanhoe in the Silverlake district of Los Angeles. Virginia later described the house as "wild." Sitting on the side of a hill, it was built like a castle, with a terrace all the way around, and a bridge leading up to the front door. Each room was on a different floor. The first floor was the living room, the kitchen, dining room and two bedrooms were above that. The top floors contained more bedrooms. A sauna and gymnasium were on the very top floor.

In August, the Gumm family went to San Francisco, where they performed as a family for the last time. During the San Francisco performances at the Golden Gate Theater, Frances made friends with another young performer, who a secret crush on her—Donald O'Connor. Donald was three years younger than Frances, and, like Frances, part of a family vaudeville act which included his mother and several brothers.

Following this performing vacation, Frank Gumm returned to Lancaster by himself. Although officially, the Antelope Valley paper announced that the Gumm family was residing in Los Angeles, with Mr. Gumm traveling to town several days a week, for all intensive purposes the Gumm parents were living apart. Meanwhile, Ethel was so busy working for Maurice Kussel, she had to ask her sister, Norma, to take Frances to one of her gigs.

Frances was enrolled in Mrs. Lawlor's School for Professional Children in Hollywood. On her first day, she met Mickey Rooney, while helping him to pull a comb out of his tangled hair.[76] They hit it off right away, and Frances was overjoyed that at last she had schoolmates with whom she could relate. Also attending "Ma Lawlor's" was her new vaudeville pal, Donald O'Connor.

Chapter 37

The Chicago World's Fair

THE SPRING OF 1934, AN OPPORTUNITY CAME TO ETHEL'S ATTENTION. Chicago was hosting *The Centennial of Progress Exposition*, otherwise known as The Chicago World's Fair, which opened in 1933. That summer would be the final season for the fair, and there was an opportunity for the girls to perform. The biggest problem would be the long drive and the cost of getting there.

Frank told Ethel he didn't want her driving that far with the girls, but she would not be moved. They were already booked. She and the girls would perform in Colorado, and then drive to Chicago. On their way home, Ethel planned to visit her family in Duluth, and then travel to Grand Rapids, where they would check on their home and visit some friends. (Another factor may have been Ethel's father, John Milne, who was living in the Rail Road Retirement home, just outside of Chicago. Although there are no records of this, Ethel may have wanted to visit him.) Unable to convince her otherwise, Frank gave his wife some money for the trip. Though he could not afford to leave the theater and travel with them, he could do that. In addition, he arranged for Ethel and the girls to stay part of the time with his cousin, Anna Lee Mertz.

Anna Lee and her husband, Paul Mertz, had recently moved from Westfield, New Jersey to River Forest, Illinois. Paul was employed by the Sears & Roebuck Company in Chicago, where he had an executive position.

Three years earlier, Paul and Anna Lee their oldest son, fourteen year-old Allen, to pneumonia. Their middle son, Billy, who was now fourteen, had Down's syndrome. Barbara Ann, who was their youngest child, was just six months younger than Frances. Anna Lee, who her nephew, Henry Lee Fox, later described as "a Mother Hen," wrote to say they would be happy to have Frank's family stay with them.

Ethel hired a woman named Marviola to make four beautiful dresses for her and the girls in their act. The dresses were white, with rows and rows of tiny ruffles, covered with sequins. These dresses required very little ironing, though Jimmy later called them "awful."[77] In addition, the girls had fashionable new hairstyles. Frances wore her hair in curls, and Ethel, perhaps feeling a bit more matronly at forty-one (though recently she had taken three years off her age) had her hair cut short.

The older girls were nearly grown now. Mary Jane would turn nineteen in September, Virginia, seventeen while they were on the road. A few days before they left, Frances turned twelve. Though tiny for her age, her voice was mature. In her recent reviews, she had been referred to as "a small woman," much to her amusement. At twelve, Frances was a seasoned performer, who was able to hold an audience of a thousand or more spellbound. Everywhere she went, she received amazing reviews. As Ethel saw it, she just had not gotten that break yet.

The new act had some great numbers. As a trio, the girls followed their idols, the Boswell Sisters, in their styling and some of the numbers they chose. After working together for so long, the Gumm girls had great harmony. Ethel worked to see that every number was absolutely perfect. Still, she knew Frances was the real draw, the one who set the act apart.

So, a few days after Frances had her birthday, Ethel and the girls set off across the Rocky Mountains on a wild ride to Denver, Colorado where they had a week-long gig at the Tabor Grand Theater. For this show, the Gumm sisters performed with a ten-piece orchestra, opening their act with *Avalon Town*.

The events on this trip, crazy as they were, tickled the Gumms' funny bones. At this first gig, their spotlight cam up on the wrong side of the stage, and they spent the entire number either chasing it, or being chased by it, as they tried to get out of the dark.

Mrs. Gumm and the girls arrived at the next gig in Littleton, to discover that the Blakeland Inn had been raided and shut down by the police the night before. The owner, however, agreed to have the family perform for him and his friends. Everyone was all so impressed by the Gumm Sisters' performance that he not only paid them, he got them another gig in Colorado Springs.

From Colorado, the Gumms drove directly to the Mertz home, where they were relieved to have no more worries for a week. The Mertzes welcomed them warmly. They were amazed by how talented the girls were, but especially amazed by Frances. Mr. Mertz even got Frances a print job advertising Sears and Roebuck's newest stove.

Anna Lee (seated) with Allen and baby, Billy. The woman behind her may be her mother, Bettie Gum Fox.
(Courtesy Claire Rion Weber)

Anna Lee's daughter, Barbara Ann, was a beautiful girl with dark hair and dark eyes, and together, she and Frances had lots of fun. In the future, Barbara Mertz Goenne would say, "Judy was a happy girl with a fine sense of humor."[78] Frances especially loved Anna Lee with her southern accent, and wild sayings. Anna Lee, in turn, reported to her mother, Bettie Fox, and her Aunt Nannie how sweet and unaffected Frances was by all the attention she received. The Mertz and Gumm families had lots of laughs together, but despite the enjoyable time, their performance at the World's Fair was looming. It would be the biggest event they had ever attended—with visitors from all over the world.

Many years later, while speaking to Dorothy Walsh Morrison about the fact that this author had spoken to the Fox/Mertz family, she said, "Ask them if Ethel ever found her music." It seems Ethel was always loosing things and on this particular trip, before they even got to their engagement in Chicago, somehow she had misplaced the folder with all of the girl's music. She was frantic. Where could she have left it? Mary Jane and Virginia must have rolled their eyes because this was not the first time their mother had lost their music. Still, it was a serious matter.

They had come all this way and, now, no music? Mary Jane had, no doubt, written Dorothy about the event, but Dorothy didn't remember how it was resolved.

With thousands of people converging on Chicago, including some of the greatest entertainers of the day, it proved to be an exciting time for the girls. Meanwhile, traveling south to Chicago after their visit with the Mertzes, Ethel and the girls received a bad surprise. The Old Mexico Café where they were to perform was on the outskirts of the fair. Short on money, Ethel asked for an advance of $35. That was the only money she would ever get from the café owner. At the end of the second week, the owner put her off. In the middle of the third week, Ethel and the girls arrived to find the Old Mexico Café boarded up.

When Ethel found the manager, she was told that if she knew what was good for her, she'd forget about the money. Otherwise, she was bound to find herself at the bottom of Lake Michigan. This was Chicago, and there were plenty of tough business owners and underworld people operating there. Justifiably frightened, Ethel decided to move on. Frank had been right to be worried.

Ethel and the girls were staying in a cheap hotel where there were many other performers who had come to Chicago to work the fair. A dance team known as Jack, Mack and Al suggested they go to the Friday night tryouts at the Belmont Theater. There was always someone in the audience from the William Morris Office, they added. That Friday, the girls' performance stopped the show, but by some quirk of fate, no one from the agency had attended that night.

The next day, Ethel was washing the girls' dresses in the bathtub when Janey asked her what they were going to have for breakfast. Their accommodations had a kitchen, and all they found there was one egg and half a loaf of moldy bread. They had hit bottom. Their one resource were the American Express checks which Frank had given them, and which Ethel had sworn she wouldn't use.

The following day, August 19th, Jack Cathcart, a young trumpet player who had befriended Janey when they worked at the Old Mexico together called Ethel to tell her to get the girls over to the Oriental Theater right away. He was working there as a pit musician, and the management had fired one of their acts. They needed another. As soon as he contacted them, Ethel and the girls rushed right out to the theatre.[79]

Apparently, the management didn't have time to audition them. Trusting Jack Cathcart's recommendation, the girls were told to be ready to go on for the second show.

Georgie Jessel was the big name in this show. Jessel, a thirty-six year-old vaudevillian, had been in the business since childhood, and worked with many show business greats. In 1925, he played the starring role in the Broadway musical, *The Jazz Singer*, but lost out to Al Jolsen when it came time to make the film. Billed as a singer, actor, comedian and "Toastmaster General of the U.S.," Jessel's career would ultimately span more than seventy years.

When Jessel announced the girls for their first performance at the Oriental Theatre, he "punched" the name "Gumm," and the audience laughed, expecting a comedy team. The girls weren't funny, but their performance was great and, according to Jimmy, they stopped the show.

When they came off, Jessel told them they had to change their name, but not to worry, he'd come up with a solution. He did. According to the story, between shows Jessel got a call from art critic, Robert Garland. When it came time for the next show, Georgie Jessel knew what to do. He went on stage and told the audience that the next act had three girls "as pretty as a garland of roses." Then, he introduced them as the "Garland Sisters." No one laughed, and the girls decided to keep the name.

For Frances Gumm, this gig was the turning event. Her solo, *My Bill*, a number made famous by the great singer Helen Morgan in *Show Boat* a few years earlier, was the highlight of the act. Seated on the piano, wrapped in a dark shawl from head to toe, only her face was lit by the spot while she sang. When the song was over, Frances removed the shawl during the applause, revealing the fact that she was only a child. Audiences were amazed. As Jessel later said, "She sang like a woman, and a woman that had been hurt." Her performances stopped the show.

To commemorate these exceptional performances, and have better advertising materials, the Gumm sisters had a series of photos taken by one of the leading theatrical and vaudevillian photographers, Bloom. The photos taken of all four women and of Frances alone are classics. Looking at the photos now, the girls were beautifully dressed, and obviously groomed for success.

Meanwhile, the newly named *Garland Sisters* were signed up with the William Morris Agency. Now, at the same time they played the Oriental

Theater, the sisters also performed two shows a day at a Chicago nightclub. There was not much time for fun offstage that summer, but Ethel must have been tremendously proud of the success her girls were having. At the same time, the girls had feelings about something none of them dared say to their mother—they missed their father, and couldn't help wishing he was there to share their success with them.

Back in Lancaster, Frank was not having a happy time of it. With the downturn in the business, and the cost of the house in Los Angeles, he had been forced to give up the family's beautiful home on Cedar Avenue. Instead, he was living in a small apartment on the edge of town which he called a "shack." Hot in summer and freezing cold in winter, Frank was miserable, and alone. Meanwhile, he continued to run *The Valley Theater*, the one sure source of income for the family. Likely depressed much of the time, and possibly drinking to alleviate his sadness, Frank tried to be happy over the girl's success in Chicago. The loss of his family and the state of his finances must have weighed heavily on him.

In Chicago, Frances met up with her schoolmate and pal, Donald O'Connor at the State Theater not far from the Oriental. It seems at one time or another, they had both worked with a Turkish vaudevillian known as Haji Ali. The famed vaudevillian was a regurgitator, who swallowed seventeen nuts and a walnut, and then proceeded to throw up one by one. He also swallowed costume jewelry and, on occasion, goldfish.

The grand finale of his act involved building a fire onstage, and then drinking, first a gallon of water, followed by a pint of kerosene. Alternately, Haji Ali then threw up the kerosene, making the fire enormous, and the water, putting it out.

Donald O'Connor later said that he and Frances believed there must be a trick to this act, and spent some of their free time that summer, looking around backstage, trying to figure out how Haji Ali did his trick. They looked all over for tubes or whatever he might be using, but never found a thing. Their memories of this vaudevillian became a great joke and point of connection for them. Years later, whenever they met they'd greet one another with the question, "Have you heard from Haji Ali?"

After working hard all summer, Ethel and the girls were looking forward to a vacation with family and old friends back in Minnesota. But now that they were signed up with the William Morris Agency, their original plans began to go awry. At the end of August, billed as the Glum Sisters, the girls played the Marbro Theater. From there, they traveled to Detroit for a week's engagement at the Michigan Theater. Getting closer to Duluth, they were booked at the Riverside Theatre in Milwaukee, but from there, they were sent for a one week engagement in Kansas City, Missouri, followed by two days in Jefferson City, Missouri. By now it was almost mid-October. With an engagement less than two weeks away at the Beverly Wilshire, Ethel and the girls resigned themselves to the fact that they had to head home. They had been on the road now for

The Gumm Sisters around 1933 or 1934. Frank sent this photo to the relatives in Murfreesboro.
(Courtesy Claire Rion Weber)

over four months. What Frances did about schooling during this time is unknown.

After all their performances, Ethel and the girls were on a high, but as they approached the Silverlake home that night in October of 1934, nothing meant more to young Frances than seeing her daddy again. As Ethel pulled the old Buick into the drive about three in morning, Frank was standing outside waiting for them. Frances would never forget running to him that night, and the warmth of his embrace. Their togetherness did not last long. Frank was still living in Lancaster, and from here on, the girls would be continuously busy with engagements.

On October 24th, backed by Vincent Lopez and his Orchestra, the newly named *Garland Sisters* played the Florentine Room at the Beverly Wilshire Hotel. This was certainly a swanky gig where any number of stars, agents and other influential people may have seen them.

Their next big gig was a personal appearance at Grauman's Chinese Theatre, where the girls sang prior to the film, *The Count of Monte Cristo*. For this appearance, Frances received a long review in *Variety*, an important benchmark for any performer. Her sisters were only mentioned as a backdrop; nevertheless, Ethel must have been truly excited.

On December 7th, the *Gumm Sisters* performed at their father's Valley Theatre for the last time. It was Christmas and their appearance was expected, but they were finished with Lancaster.

That same month, billed as the *Garland Trio*, the Gumm girls performed their act at the Wilshire-Ebell Theater. The reviews were stupendous. In the *Los Angeles Evening Express*, the headline read, "12 Year Old Girl Is Sensation at Frolics." Ethel could have no doubt now that, whatever the cost, she had taken the right road.[80]

Chapter 38

Frank Gumm—1935

By fall of 1934, the rumors about Frank Gumm had reached Doc Savage. It was a joke in Lancaster that the town had a doctor named Savage and a dentist named Gaskill.* Doc Savage was a good doctor but he was tough. When Glen Settle broke his leg playing football, he about fainted as Doc pulled the bone into place.

Doc, the father of five children, was a strict, religious man, who believed in following the Bible word for word. He was also an influential leader; a leader of morality in the town. One year, he even led a fight against Barnum & Bailey Circus.

Every year, the children of Lancaster looked forward to the arrival of the circus, which stopped in town on a Sunday, between stops in larger towns. That particular year, Doc Savage declared that Sunday should be for God and church alone. People should not be doing anything that day as frivolous as going to the circus, he declared. Naturally, this didn't sit well with the children.

When Doc Savage got wind of the rumors about Frank Gumm and the young boys at the theatre, he went to work. Lancaster was a small town of approximately 1,500 people and, as one her citizens said, once a rumor got started in the town, whether it was true or not, it would be very difficult to turn the tide. The doctor and a few other leading citizens let Frank know that his time in Lancaster was over. If he knew

---

* At the time, dental patients were given gas to kill the pain.

what was good for him, he would pack up and leave; his presence was not welcome.

Mr. Carter, the owner of the Valley Theatre, followed Doc Savage's lead. Although Frank Gumm's lease for the theater was not up, he was told to leave. When Mr. Carter's son was asked about the situation for purposes of this book, he said he didn't want to talk about it. Two things he admitted to were: the fact that once a rumor, true or not, was circulated through the small town of Lancaster, it would be difficult to take back, and that Frank Gumm's lease was not up when he left. According to Scott Schector's book, *Judy Garland: The Day by Day Chronicle of a Legend*, Frank lost his lease because he owed Mr. Carter, $2,000. However, it appears that no amount of money would have convinced Mr. Carter to let Frank stay.

Frank vowed to fight the allegations. He even took an ad out in *The Antelope Valley Newspaper*, but business fell sharply. What mother or father would let their child go to a theatre, or even go themselves, where a purported child molester was the manager? Frank was alone in his fight. No one in town was going to stand up against Doc Savage, and Ethel and the girls were gone. That spoke volumes in itself.

Frank Gumm in front of the Lakeview Terrace home, Silverlake District of Los Angeles, 1934.
(Courtesy Dahl/Kehoe Archives)

Finally, Frank gave in. In a sense, he had no choice. The theater was doing almost no business, and he couldn't afford his rent. On April 7th, Ethel came to town and helped him pack up what was left. A few days later, he was gone.

Before he left Lancaster, Frank went over and gave Glen Settle his golf clubs. Maybe he knew his days of having carefree fun were over, or maybe he just wanted to give Glen a present. Eventually, Glen donated these clubs to the *Judy Garland Museum* in Grand Rapids, Minnesota.

There were a few Lancaster residents who kept in touch with Frank, but life in Lancaster, which had started happily, now had a dark shadow over it. Ethel had gotten her girls out from under as quickly as she could. She had been determined that nothing should mar them or their future.

Don, who photographed Glen and Frank, later married Glen's sister. He died tragically some years later, while he was out hunting. His dog fell on his rifle, hitting the trigger and shooting him straight through the heart. Steve Castle drove into a tree and died in the 1930s. Lyle Hatley served his country valiantly during WWII, and was seriously wounded. He married a Lancaster divorcee with two little girls, and lived in Los Angeles until his death in 1974.

~

Leaving Lancaster in April of 1935 had its bright spot. Frank could now live comfortably under the same room with his girls. A few days after arriving in L.A., he contacted the Rabwin brothers, and all three men went out together, driving around the outskirts of Los Angeles until they found a theater in Lomita, approximately twenty miles from where the Gumms were living. Frank renamed the theater *Garland's Lomita Theater*. By now, he and Ethel were both using the Garland name, a move which could have protected the family, if there were any allegations against "Frank Gumm."

During this time, the family moved a couple more times, first to another home in Silverlake, and then to Mariposa Avenue in Hollywood. If Frank and Ethel argued about their marriage during this time, neither made a move toward divorce. Perhaps, that was for the sake of their youngest daughter. The other two girls were nearly grown, but Frances needed both of her parents. In addition, appearances were important these days;

it would look better to everyone if young Frances did not come from a broken home.

~

In March of 1935, Frank Gumm turned 49. After the trials of the past year, and standing on the edge of fifty, he seemed reflective about his live. One year earlier, he had written a letter to his old friend, Henry Gass at Sewanee, saying,

> Tomorrow is my birthday. I will be 48, and I can think of no better way of celebrating it than by sending you my check in order that I may become, in my humble way, a "paying" member of Sewanee's great alumni.

Around this same time, Frank wrote to his brother Robert about moving south. After taking over the management of the Lomita Theatre, he could see that even without the family performing there, the theatre was going to bring in good money. Frank encouraged Bob to think about moving the family down to Los Angeles.

Bob and Belle were quite happy in Seattle. In fact, Bob had just talked his daughter Mildred and her family into moving to Seattle, so they could all be closer together. Mildred and her husband, Alton Durham, had plans to move with their two little girls in October of that year. All things considered, Bob had no desire to leave Washington.

The Gumm family's life was a whirlwind of activity. Mary Jane and Virginia were both "boy crazy" and dating, as Frank noted in a letter, and "Baby is beginning to give the boys the once over." At the same time, Ethel had the girls constantly running to singing gigs and auditions.

Meanwhile, Marcus Rabwin had married Marcella Bannett, who worked at RKO as David O. Selznick's executive secretary. Selznick, who was married to the head of MGM, Louis B. Mayer's daughter, Irene, soon went to went to work at MGM, taking Marcella with him.

Before Dr. Rabwin married Marcella, he jokingly insisted he needed the Gumms' approval first. At a dinner arranged for that purpose, Marcella met the Gumm girls and heard them sing for the first time. It was her opinion that the older girls had lovely voices, but it was Frances who was incredible. She was definitely star material.

After the Rabwins married, Marcella tried to think of way they could help Frances' career. There was one person they wanted to hear her sing—MGM screenwriter and director, Joseph L. Mankiewicz. He missed the party they gave with the girls, but later attended one of their performances at the Wilshire Ebel Theatre. Watching twelve year-old Frances sing, Joe Mankiewicz felt the same excitement he had felt seeing the great Al Jolsen on Broadway. Mankiewicz now approached Ida Koverman, Louis B. Mayer's assistant. Mrs. Koverman wrote down Frances Garland's name down, but it seems nothing else happened.[81]

That June, Ethel and the girls headed to the Cal-Neva Lodge in Lake Tahoe for an engagement. For a while, Frances, who hated her name, had been playing around with different names. She had tried Alice and Gracie, among others, but while in Tahoe, she hit on a name that was the title of Hoagy Carmichael's new hit, *Judy*. The new "Judy" now declared that she was through with her old name, and didn't want to be called "Baby" ever again. A few days later, Janey announced that she was changing her name to *Susannah*. Ethel didn't approve, but both girls were adamant, perhaps, Frances most of all. She absolutely refused to answer to anything but *Judy*.[82]

Meanwhile, the newly named Suzie had fallen in love with a young trombone player named Lee Cahn. There was a fight with Ethel over the subject, but Suzie was not deterred. Her mother was doing what she wanted on the side with Bill Gilmore, and she would do what she wanted. She was an adult. Ethel just hated musicians.

When their gig was over, Ethel already out in the car with the motor running, when the girls came out and piled in. They were already on the road when Suzie, with her mind on other things, suddenly realized she had forgotten their hats in the room. Under the hats, was their music, so they had to go back. When they arrived, Ethel sent Judy in to get the hats and music. As she walked through the lodge on her way to their rooms, she was stopped by the manager-bouncer, Bones Remer, who said he had some people at the bar who wanted to hear her sing. Although she protested, Bones assured her that he'd talk to her mother. "Just hurry back," he told her.

When Ethel came into the bar, she found that the men who wanted to hear her daughter sing were Harry Cohn of Columbia Pictures, Lew

Brown, songwriter and executive of Columbia, Harry Akst, another songwriter, and Al Rosen, an agent. Ethel sat down at the piano, and when Judy returned she sang *Zing! Went the Strings of My Heart*, one of her best songs, along with several others. Finally, she sang, *Dinah.* As it turned out, Harry Akst had written the song, and asked to accompany her.

When Frances finished, Harry Cohn asked why she wasn't in pictures, to which Ethel responded, "I think it's because she's not pretty enough," a comment which no doubt stung Judy. Before they left, Al Rosen gave Ethel his business card, but once they were in the car, Ethel said, "We'll never see any of them again." They had been to so many auditions and been given so many promises, she no longer believed what people said.

Two weeks later, Al Rosen called Ethel with an audition at MGM for Judy.

~

Dorothy Walsh didn't know about the auditions at MGM that people wrote about in regards to Judy. There had been many auditions for the Gumm Sisters, with many important people. Dorothy only knew about one MGM audition, and that was the one she attended.

The call came one afternoon while she was visiting with the girls. Someone at MGM said they would like them to come down right away for an audition.

Frank was at home, sick in bed with the flu that day. Of late, he had seemed increasingly tired and looked much older. He even seemed to walk with more of a shuffle than he had previously.

Ethel was home, so Suzie, Jimmy and Judy, who were dressed casually but nicely, jumped in the car and headed down to MGM. Dorothy went along for moral support, just as she had for many of their performances and auditions in the past.

When they got to the studio, they were escorted into a small room with a grand piano. The men said they wanted Roger Edens to play, but he wasn't available. There were three men present, probably directors. One of them had a foreign accent. Then, there was Ethel, Suzie, Jimmy, Judy and Dorothy.

With Ethel on the piano, the three girls sang a couple of numbers to start. Then, one of the men, who Dorothy later told her granddaughter was Joe Mankiewicz, said, "Let's have the little girl sing a song by herself."[83] Judy got up and sang, *Zing Went the Strings of My Heart*. She gave it her all, and her voice echoed against the walls of the tiny room. With her final note, the place erupted as the three directors jumped out of their seats, cheering and applauding.

Suzie and Jimmy had come to MGM in high spirits. They were hoping that they too might be signed with a studio contract, but after Judy sang, they knew it was over for them. Once their sister had sung, no one even glanced at them.

A short while later, as they were leaving, one of the directors, the one with the foreign accent, came up to Dorothy, and slipping his arm around her back and under her arm, placed his hand over her breast.

"And what do you do, my dear?" he asked.

Dorothy could not get away quick enough.

"Those dirty men," she thought. She had heard plenty about the movie studios. "Judy is so young. Maybe she'll be safe for a few years," she hoped.

~

On August 12th, the girls filmed *La Cucaracha* for *La Fiesta de Santa Barbara*. Following this, Ethel and Judy went down to San Diego where Frances was billed as "Judy Garland" for the first time.

Meanwhile, Louis B. Mayer's secretary, Ida Koverman, had taken a liking to Judy, and as a result, on September 13th a call was put in for her to come down and sing at MGM for another audition. That day, Ethel was out, playing at the Pasadena Civic Auditorium. Frank took the call. He called Judy, who had been playing in the back yard with her little terrier, Waffles, and without wasting time, they got in the car and drove out to Culver City.

For her first song, Frank, who Judy could not help noticing was nervous, played for her. His piano playing was not up to par, and this time someone called for MGM's musical director, Roger Edens.

Like Frank, Edens had been born in the south and spoke with a deep and gentle Southern accent. Roger Edens was well-experienced with singers. He had come to MGM from New York City where he worked with Ethel Merman. He was not only a pianist; he wrote musical arrangements and songs, and had a keen sense of how to make a singer sound good.

When Edens sat down, Judy asked him, "Can you change keys?" to which he replied, "Can you?"

After Judy sang, this time including the song Maurice Kussel had taught her, "Eli, Eli," Mayer got up and walked out of the room without saying a word.

Judy was used it. It was just one more instance of a Hollywood executive behavior, but Frank was annoyed. "My child is tired," he said. Then, they said their goodbyes and left.

When Ethel got home, Judy off-handedly mentioned the audition. Ethel was horrified to learn that Frank had taken her to MGM just as she was. Nevertheless, a call came in shortly after that; MGM wanted to put her under contract.

On September 24th, Susie's 20th birthday, she announced that she was marrying Lee Cahn. That day, against Ethel's will, she flew to Lake Tahoe. Lee, who, in addition to the trombone, also played the violin and clarinet, was unable to take any time off to get married. The couple was married in Reno. After Lee finished his Tahoe gig, they settled in San Francisco where Lee had a job working with Horace Heidt's Californians.[84]

Ethel did not like musicians and was deeply unhappy over her eldest daughter's choice. The only thing was, by putting her daughters in show business, these were the men they most frequently met and were attracted to. There was nothing Ethel could do about it now, except bemoan the fact and protest.

In the midst of this, on September 27th, Judy's MGM contract arrived. The family gathered around the kitchen table to read it—Frank, Ethel, Grandma Eva and the two girls, Jimmy and Judy. After all the years of working and dreaming, life was changing quickly. Judy would start at $100 a week (= $1,560), a salary that was double the average workman's salary. On her twentieth birthday, she would receive $1,000 a week (= $15,600)—an unbelievable amount of money. In addition, she would receive the finest training and grooming. At last, all Ethel's work had paid off.

Now they were on the road to achieving the dream Ethel had long held for her daughter. Both she and Frank knew that Frances was more than talented. She was a remarkable child, and they had, each in their own way, done what they could to see that Frances received the opportunity she deserved. The dream was coming true. They would not have to struggle anymore. In a time when ordinary people would never think of picking up a phone to make a long distance call, both parents sat down and wrote family members back home excited letters about their "baby's" success.

Three days after signing the contract, Judy Garland spent her first day at MGM. A good part of her early days at the study would include musical coaching with Roger Edens. The rest of her time was spent in the schoolhouse. One happy thing for Judy was finding out that her old school chum from Ma Lawlor's, Mickey Rooney, was now at MGM. Donald O'Connor was also under contract there as well.

Shortly after starting at MGM, the publicity team asked Judy to write her official biography for their files. After they read what she wrote, the publicity department asked her to change it. Dorothy was visiting the day Judy came home with the news.

"They didn't like that I was born in Grand Rapids. They said it sounded boring. Imagine that! They asked me to give them another place."

As a result, Judy rewrote her biography, stating that she had been born in Murfreesboro, Tennessee, a name that sounded better to the MGM executives.[85] Apparently, Judy thought that was quite funny.

In October, MGM sent Judy to a USC football game where she was to sing *Fight on for Good Old USC*. In the middle of her song, the home team ran out on the field and the applause from the stands drowned her out. Later, as she was walking up one of the aisles, she saw Bob White from Lancaster, and said, "Hi ya, Bob!" He was surprised because it was a few years since he had seen her, and to those in Lancaster; the new *Judy Garland* was now a star.

On October 26th, Judy appeared on The Shell Chateau Hour, with Wallace Beery, on the NBC radio station. Beery, a film star, interviewed Judy. Then, she sang. It was a huge event as the station played nationwide. Introduced as "only twelve years old" her singing was tremendous, revealing artistry as both a ballad and jazz singer. Although, she already had everything she needed to be a singer when she signed with MGM, it is clear that Roger Edens coaching brought her performance to a deeper level. He slowed her down and took away the "stik" that Ethel had given her as a cute vaudeville performer. Edens was turning Judy into a serious artist. She was a talent to be reckoned with, no matter the age.

Frank and Ethel were both "over the moon" with happiness about their daughter's success, and to a large degree, it seems that family life now revolved around Judy. Her life was changing at a rate faster than anyone could absorb.

~

On Thursday, November 14th, Dorothy Walsh came over to visit the family. Frank seemed fine, and after dinner, he drove Dorothy home. Frank stopped the car, got out and opened the door for Dorothy. Then, he kissed her goodnight on the lips—as was the family custom.

"We'll see you soon," he said.

"Thank you, Mr. Gumm! See you soon."

Friday, Frank went to work at Garland's Lomita Theatre, but complained of pain in his ears, and left a short while later to go home.

Friday had been a fairly quiet day for Judy, who apparently wasn't expected on the MGM lot. In the afternoon, she went over to visit a friend, but returned for dinner. Jimmy had a date with actor, Frankie Darro, and after kissing her father, who was sitting the sofa reading a paper, she and Frankie went out the door. Judy went up to bed about 9:30.

Frank, who still was not feeling at all well, had rested his head against a pillow on the sofa. His one ear was draining, something it had apparently done in the past, and some of the fluid came out onto the sofa pillow.

A short time after Judy went up to bed, Frank and Ethel followed. Within the next hour, it was apparent that Frank's condition was seriously deteriorating. Whether he collapsed or seemed disoriented is unknown, but Ethel got on the phone immediately and called Dr. Marc Rabwin.

As soon as Dr. Rabwin arrived, he called for an ambulance. By now, Grandma Eva had risen as well and all the lights in the house were on.*

At this point, Jimmy and her date returned. It was just before midnight—the standard curfew for dates in the Gumm family. Jimmy was shocked to see all the lights on. Hurrying upstairs, she found her mother in the process of getting dressed to follow her husband to the hospital.

---

* It should be noted that the Lomita Progress later noted that Frank was admitted to the hospital at 1 PM on Saturday. At this point, it is likely impossibly to verify many of these facts. Jimmy's memories have proved not to be 100% reliable.

Jimmy went into the bedroom, and found Judy fast asleep. She decided not to wake her up. There was nothing they could do, and Judy had a live radio performance the next day.

The next morning, the girls came downstairs to find Ethel, who had just returned from the hospital. In answer to the girl's questions about their how their father was doing, Ethel said, "Not so good." Frank was in a coma, but she didn't want to upset them.

Apparently, it was decided that the girls should not go to the hospital. Whether spinal meningitis had been diagnosed at this point is unknown. This was in a time before antibiotics, and there was little they could do. Meanwhile, apparently only Ethel knew that Frank had slipped into a coma. In those days, children were not allowed in hospitals, and Ethel likely wanted to protect her daughters from seeing their father in this condition. No one could do anything to make him better; they had to go one with their lives.

Frank only had a few hours to live. For Judy, the fact that her father died at such a key point in her life, and that she never had the chance to say "goodbye," would scar her for the rest of her life.

Judy's radio appearance on The Shell Chateau Hour with Wallace Beery would be her second. This appearance would be particularly important because Beery was going to announce her contract with MGM. Ethel left the hospital to get Judy ready. Judy's first appearance only a week earlier had been met with great excitement, and everyone was looking forward to this evening.

Shortly before Judy and Ethel left the house, the phone rang. It was Dr. Rabwin. "Judy," he told her, "I want to let you know that I'm putting a radio by your father's bed so he can hear you sing tonight. Now you go ahead and do the show.... That's the best thing you can do for your daddy. He'll be listening, so 'sing sweetly.'" Dr. Rabwin could tell Judy had been crying, but trooper that she was, he knew she would go on.

That evening, Judy sang *Zing! Went the Strings of My Heart!* with everything she had in her. The audience responded with a huge ovation. Judy, a true pro, was able to pull off the performance with never a hint of the drama behind that moment. After this performance, she was required to travel to Santa Monica and sing at "The MGM Club Dance." How Ethel kept her composure knowing all the while that her husband was dying is unknown.

Mother and daughter returned home late. Since accounts of the days surrounding Frank Gumm's final illness vary, it is uncertain as to whether Ethel returned to the hospital that night. She was likely exhausted after being up for most of the previous 48 hours.

On Sunday, Jimmy and Judy got up mid-morning. When they came down for breakfast, Grandma Eva was in the kitchen. By now, Ethel was already back at the hospital. Cedars and Lebanon Hospital was about 1.12 miles away. In the early afternoon, the phone rang, apparently to tell the family that Frank was sinking quickly, and they should hurry if they wanted to see him. Grandma Eva called a cab.

When Jimmy, Judy and Grandma Eva arrived, Dr. Rabwin met them and explained that Frank was dead. According to the death certificate, he passed away that Sunday afternoon at 3 PM. The family was obviously in shock. As sick as he was, they had not expected him to die.

Recently, a doctor, describing the effects of continual ear infections, was able to explain what most likely occurred to Frank Gumm. Years of ear and sinus infections can erode and penetrate the mastoid bone. Eventually, the bone is eaten away until one day, when an infection strikes; it goes to the lining of the brain. There is little warning of this condition, and when it occurs, even today, little can be done. The patient dies within two days. This was likely the form of meningitis that killed Frank Gumm.

After Dr. Rabwin spoke to them, Grandma Eva took them home, while Ethel remained behind. When she finally came home, she was crying. This was the first time the girls had ever seen their mother cry, and now they all cried together.

~

Frank was gone. Ethel could scarcely believe it. With all her anger and frustration, he had been her first love, and the father of her girls. Now he lay pale and still; so still for a man who was constantly moving, singing, laughing and making others laugh. Part of Ethel must have felt glad that she was free; free of all the worry. But then, there was the terrible grief. They had been married for over 21 years. Now, it was over.

While Ethel lay crying on the sofa with the girls and Grandma Eva around her, the door bell rang. Judy went to answer it, and standing at the door were some of their friends from Lancaster, with presents and big smiles of their faces saying, "Surprise!"

Frank, ever the loving one, had made a surprise birthday party for Ethel, just as she had often done for him. He had told her he was hoping to make up for the past and start anew now that Judy had her MGM contract. Again and again, the doorbell ran, with the heart-broken girls having to announce the terrible news, until finally, a friend kindly offered to stay outside and warn the partygoers. Frank had also invited some of their old friends from Grand Rapids, people Ethel had wanted to see on their way back from Chicago. Now, instead of the birthday party he planned, this evening was his wake. Suzie and Lee arrived from San Francisco. Dorothy Walsh and her father, Frank, were there. Mr. Walsh attempted to comfort Ethel that night; she was inconsolable.

Judy felt sick to her stomach. Still small and young, on the edge of maturity, her life had been so happy. She was going to MGM and singing all the time. At last, she could stay in one place and live with her daddy; have a home like other girls. She and Daddy had been close, and he had been so proud of her. She had known that he would always be there to take care of her and to understand. Now he was gone! Daddy cared about *her.* He was the person she loved most in the world. How could he be gone? It was too much for her to absorb. Judy went into the protected state of shock.

~

Two days later they had the funeral at the Little Church of the Flowers in Forest Lawn. Grandma Eva, who had bought two plots there for she and her husband, insisted that Frank be buried in her plot.

Dorothy Walsh was there in the pew with Suzie, Virginia and Judy. They had always been like sisters, and it seemed right. Dorothy had never been able to see her mother again after she become ill. She could understand the girls' deep pain. Besides that, she had loved Frank as well. Still, learning that he had died of meningitis, she kept wondering. "Frank kissed me on the lips that night," she thought, afraid that she too might get ill, but, of course, she didn't.

Ethel asked Dorothy to watch Judy that day. Poor Judy's face was one of devastation. She stared straight ahead, and then with those tremulous eyes looked toward the coffin.

There was Daddy all laid out in his best dark suit and tie. Oh, Daddy. If only he could rise up out of the coffin and tell her everything was okay, the way he always had. She wanted to touch him, but she was afraid; afraid because the man lying there was almost her Daddy, but not quite.

The people from MGM were coming down the aisle in their fine clothes. They stopped in front of the casket, as if to study Frank. At the sight of them standing there, Judy begun to tremble. They didn't know her daddy. They didn't know what a wonderful man he was. They were only staring at him with an expression she didn't understand, now that he was helpless. Judy threw herself down into Dorothy's lap sobbing. "Poor thing it is too much for her," thought Dorothy. But then she heard what Judy was saying, "Don't let them do that," she cried. "Don't let stare at my Daddy like that." She cried it over and over like one afraid, wishing to protect someone they love.

"Hush, Baby, hush," Dorothy said, leaning over Judy and stoking her hair. "Don't say anything."

"No, I don't want them looking at my Daddy," said Judy looking up at her momentarily with flashing black eyes. It was the most intense Dorothy had ever seen her.

Later, the MGM officials and L. B. Mayor's daughter would tell another story. They said she never cried for her father, as if she hadn't cared so much. Judy, herself, would repeat this story, saying it took her 14 days to cry. But the cries that came out of that little girl in the funeral parlor that day would haunt Dorothy for the rest of her life.

Not too many people in Lancaster were still friendly with the Gumms, but Glen Settle's father and Harry Webb, a businessman across the street from the Valley Theatre, came to the funeral. St. Paul's pastor, Rev. Parker conducted the funeral services in the chapel. *The Lomita Progress* reported that, "The Masonic Order had charge of the services at the grave..."[86]

Courtesy Tom Early

That night, Ethel asked Dorothy and Frankie Darro to stay with the girls. She wanted to go out. They all knew where she was going. She would seek comfort with the man she had been having an affair with, Bill Gilmore. The girls were not pleased. When asked about it, Dorothy Walsh said, "She was sad, but not too sad. She was otherwise occupied."

In later years, Dorothy Walsh Morrison refused to believe the rumors about Frank Gumm. After reading what was written in some of Judy Garland's biographies, she said, "People said things about him because they were jealous and wanted to destroy him. There were rumors that he molested a boy. They would have put him in jail if he had done that! He was so nice. He was the loveliest man. He never would have done anything like that."

~

Frank had been asking his brother, Bob, to move down to Southern California for a while. Now, with Frank's passing, when Ethel asked for his help with the theatre, Bob and Belle agreed to come down immediately and take over its management.

Meanwhile, Mildred and her family had just moved to Seattle to be with Bob. Mildred's daughter, Betty Jane Durham would remember how they drove all night, arriving on Halloween. Now, only a few weeks later, Bob, Belle and Richard packed up and left. It was a great disappointment to Mildred, but it seems Bob felt the greatest responsibility toward Frank and his family.

To help with their transition, Ethel invited Bob, Belle and Richard to live with them for a while. They had enough room. Having "Uncle Bobby" in the house was for Judy like having a little bit of her daddy, and seems to have been the best medicine she could have at the time. Bob had a bit of the southern accent, and Frank's sense of humor. Aunt Belle was hoot, too. And she and Cousin Richard had a great time playing around. They both had the Gumm sense of humor, and loved to roar would laugher. Having the Gumms there turned the house back into a home.

In later years, Judy would think back on the last year of her father's life. She had spent so many months away; those were months she and her father could have shared. That time was lost forever. "I wasn't close to my father," she later said, "But I wanted to be." Eventually, the blame for that would fall on Ethel.

Chapter 39

Tennessee Tragedies

THE NEWS OF FRANK GUMM'S UNTIMELY DEATH SHOCKED AND SADdened his family in Tennessee and Alabama. He had seemed healthy; a man full of energy with much to look forward to. Certainly, no one had expected his passing at the age of forty-nine. To those who knew him, it seemed Frank had it all. He was much loved, talented, charming and caring. Each year at Christmas, he sent the family photos of his girls, and letters telling of their achievements. He was especially proud of Frances. Now the she was reaching the heights of success, she would be without her father.

While the relatives in Murfreesboro grieved over Frank's loss, they would soon have grief of their own. Nannie Gum's husband, Edwin T. Rion had been a loving spouse for over thirty years, but in 1936, Mr. Rion, died suddenly.

Nannie shared the house on Lytle Street with her children, Edwin, Jr. and Virginia. Virginia, who had attended Tennessee College for Women and was a talented pianist, was married to Leumuel Cox. The couple had two children, a little girl, Nancy Lee, and a son, Lee.

Nannie's son, Edwin, Jr., was divorced from his first wife, Aileen, who had taken their daughter, Claire, to live in Missouri near her parents. Aileen brought Claire to visit as often as she could. She also kept in touch with Nannie by letter.

Florence Cox's great aunt, Mrs. Reed, was a good friend of the Rions. She lived across the street, and often took Florence to visit Mrs. Rion, a woman Florence later described as a "rather tall, heavy-set, woman with a big hairdo," but who was also "rather nice looking." Florence added that Mrs. Rion was a very kind woman, and "a good neighbor."

One year after loosing her husband, Nannie Rion's daughter, Virginia, died tragically. The following year, 1938, her son-in-law, Lee, who was deeply grieving his wife, was gone as well. The sorrow and tragedy was almost too much for anyone to bear. Writing to her daughter-in-law about the events, Nannie stated that it was only her faith in God and her desire to raise Virginia's children, Nancy Lee, 5, and Lee, 3, in the way her daughter wanted that kept her going.

Two years later, tragedy would come to the Gum family again, this time to Bettie Gum Fox. That 4th of July, the Fox family had gone up to Jefferson Springs where they had a summer home. Bettie's son, Jack was going through a divorce. His wife, Mary, had taken their daughter, Betty, with her. The two boys, Van and Henry were still living with their father. Jack had a problem with alcohol and had been very depressed, but recently, he had started a new job, was trying to pull himself together.

On the 5th of July, the Fox family returned to Murfreesboro. On the way home, Jack kept saying how depressed he was; he couldn't seem to get over it. When they arrived in Murfreesboro, he went up to his room. Then, just as his fifteen year-old son, Henry, walked through the door, he shot himself in the head.

As can be imagined, the entire Gumm family in Murfreesboro was devastated by this series of events. Tragedy had become so much a part of the family's lives that shortly after Judy Garland died in 1969, a new resident in town, attending at a party, was surprised to hear someone say about Judy, "What can you expect? She's a Gumm."

Chapter 40

MGM 1936–1938

Life after Frank's passing was full, but in the photos taken of thirteen year-old Judy only a week or so after her father's death, one can see the deep sorrow in this little girl's eyes. She was still a little girl when Frank died, but working at MGM, she would not remain one for long.

Eight days after the funeral, Judy sang for a dinner at the Biltmore Hotel. The family felt it was good she had MGM to keep her busy. It was a new life for her, and a distraction from her grief. Nevertheless, fourteen days after their father died, while she and Jimmy were in their shared bedroom, Judy broke down. She cried for two hours straight. Jimmy later said that their father's death had begun to sink; she realized their daddy was truly gone.[87]

In a letter to the Sewanee Alumni Association, Jimmy later revealed that during this time there was a fire in the house. As a result, many of Frank's personal records were destroyed.

Early in 1936, Ethel moved Judy, Jimmy and Grandma Eva to a house in the heart of Hollywood, at 180 South McCadden Place. The move took them away from the sad memories of Frank's last hours; it also led them to a world of more elegant living. The home on McCadden Place was a two-story house, one more befitting an MGM starlet. It also had a swimming pool, which was a first for the Gumms.

Spending her days at Metro-Goldwyn-Mayer was exciting for young Judy. There were so many big stars to see, and so many movie productions, costumes and sets, but she wanted to be a part of them. Since she was two years old, she had always been on stage, performing for an audience and receiving applause. Now, as the months passed with few performances and no film work, her life at MGM became almost unbearable.

In a 1940s interview, Ethel Gumm stated that Judy was so unhappy at MGM during this time, that she had spoken to someone about having her released from her contract—at least until she was older. The person she spoke to told her to give it a little more time. That "little time" made all the difference.

Judy was not happy attending the little schoolroom at MGM either, and told her mother she wanted to go a regular school. Ethel approached the studio executives and was given permission to send Judy to a school of the log as long as she wasn't making a film.

That year Judy attended Bancroft Junior High. Along with the regular courses, she also took sewing and cooking. According to Ethel, "[She] had the best time she's ever had."[88] In 1937, she proudly graduated with about 400 students, wearing the "standard red sweater and blue skirt." People who met Judy during this time, including Caren Marsh Doll, a dancer at MGM who later become one of her stand-ins, all remarked that the thing Judy seemed to want most was a normal family life.

"Of all the people at MGM, Roger Edens was the only one who really cared about Judy as a person," said Dorothy Walsh. Edens who was born in Hillsboro, Texas in 1905, and raised in Virginia, had worked in New York prior to his move to L.A. He was a pit musician for the Broadway show, *Girl Crazy*, starring Ethel Merman. Later, Merman hired him as her arranger, and in 1933 brought him out to Hollywood. Early in 1935, Arthur Freed hired him to work at MGM. Roger Edens was a brilliant musician, who knew talent and knew music. Over the years, he wrote many wonderful songs, as well as many great arrangements.

When Roger Edens first heard Judy Garland sing at her audition for Louis B. Mayer, he knew he had heard greatness. Now that she had lost her father, Edens tried to become a positive force in the life of this young and talented girl.

Although Edens believed that Judy certainly deserved praise, he also found that he had to be critical of her because like most teenagers, she wanted to dress and act like an adult before her time. She also wanted to sing songs that were far too sophisticated. At this point, Edens knew that the unique thing about her was the fact that she was a little girl with a mature voice and delivery. They would use that to her advantage. She had plenty of time to grow up and sing the other songs, but right now, he told her they looked ridiculous on her.

In a sense, Roger now became a surrogate father for Judy Garland, at least musically. Under his tutelage, Judy would be transformed from an amazingly gifted singer, to a world class singer. Ethel taught her daughter well, making sure she hit the mark on every note and stylized her singing. Recently discovered recordings reveal a twelve year-old child with unbelievable ability, but much of her singing also reveals little, showy tricks. Under Edens, Garland became an artist. Her notes are sustained, and her voice reveals heart. It is a voice that is rarer than once in a lifetime.

Judy spent a good deal of time learning new songs with Edens, and it wasn't long before he was taking on more than just her singing. According to one movie magazine article of the time, he also gave her advice about her appearance and dress. Before long, Judy would only take advice from him, and though Ethel might have resented that, behind the scenes, they worked together.

In the spring of 1936, the studio teamed Judy with another young MGM contract player, Deanna Durbin. The pair was called on to make a one-reel test. At the time Judy signed her MGM contact, news articles remarked on the fact that amazingly Judy Garland had received an MGM contract without ever being required to make a screen test. Now, the studio wanted to see how she looked on film.

In the meantime, several film properties were considered, but nothing came through. Finally in June, the studio sent Judy to New York City for a personal appearance. While she was there, two days after her fourteenth birthday, she made two recordings for Decca records with Bob Crosby and his Orchestra: *Stompin' at the Savoy* and *Swing, Mr. Charlie*.

After two weeks in New York, the studio called Judy back to Los Angeles. Having seen her test, they wanted her to make a musical short called *Everybody Sings* with Deanna Durbin.

Two months later, MGM loaned Judy Garland to 20th Century for the film *Pigskin Parade* starring Patsy Kelly, Jack Haley and young Betty Grable. Although Judy was horrified when she first saw herself on the screen, the film proved that she had charisma. Her great musical talent was just as thrilling on film as it was in-person. By the end of September, one year after signing her MGM contract, the studio picked up her option. They were ready to put her to work.

During this time, Judy became acquainted with a young actor named Jackie Cooper. A former child star, Jackie was now a teenager, and like Judy attending school at MGM. Judy invited him to a party at her home, and a short time later, Jackie and Judy became friends.

In the 1970s, Dorothy Walsh Morrison's granddaughter, Laureli Lunn, was given a school assignment to interview a member of her family. Laureli interviewed her grandmother, who told her about her friendship with the Gumms. Ms. Lunn has graciously allowed a portion of her school assignment to be included here. It reveals a little personal inside view of life in the Gumm home.

> *One Saturday afternoon, Jackie Cooper called and wanted to know if Judy would like to go out the next afternoon for a drive and possibly get something to eat. She thought that would be sort of exciting because he was starting to work in pictures himself. So, Sunday morning (Labor Day), Mrs. Gumm was busy with the vacuum cleaner in the living room and Judy was saying:*
>
> *"Hurry! Hurry! Get that vacuum out of here! Jackie will be here any minute and we don't want it to look like a mess!'"*
>
> *All of a sudden, the doorbell rang and Judy shrieked,*
>
> *"He's here, and look at this room!'"*
>
> *Jackie came in and climbed over the vacuum cleaner in the middle of the floor—just like a real person! He was all dressed up in a white suit and looked so snazzy. Judy then said,*
>
> *"Oh! But I don't have any dark glasses!'"*
>
> *Dorothy said, "Oh, that's alright, you can take mine.'"*
>
> *Everyone laughed about the incident for years and they never saw the dark glasses again, but Dorothy didn't mind because Judy and Jackie had such a good time."*

Interestingly, Dorothy said that Judy had very bad vision problems, and refused to wear glasses. Because of this, when the girls went out to the movies, even though they didn't like to sit so close, they sat in the front row so Judy could see. Dorothy also noted that when Judy was out and friends waved at her, often she didn't respond simply because she couldn't

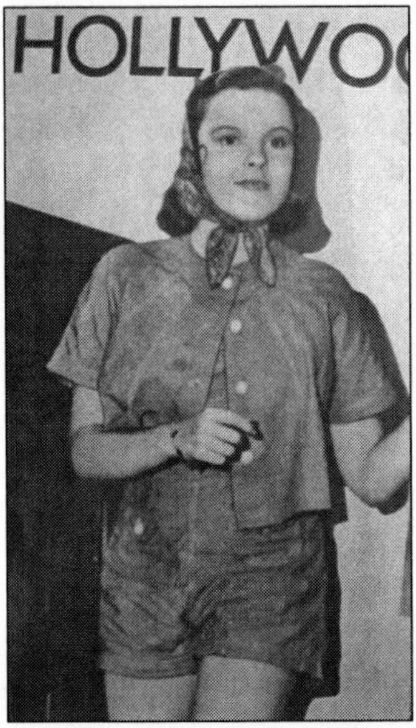

see them. Some people, not realizing this, interpreted her actions as "snooty."

Although Judy later got a car, Dorothy claimed that with her bad eyesight, she didn't drive. If she did, she must have done it in daylight, when she could see better or wear prescription sun glasses.

The year 1937 would be an extremely busy one for Judy. Already MGM had cast her in the film, *The Broadway Melody of 1938*. The film starred Sophie Tucker as her mother, with Eleanor Powell and Robert Taylor. Judy would also have a short dance number with Buddy Ebsen, a Broadway eccentric dancer who had come to Hollywood and made a success. Meanwhile, Judy was making numerous radio appearances.

While preparing for her upcoming film, Roger Edens made a new arrangement for Judy of a song made famous by Al Jolsen, *You Made Me Love You*. Instead of keeping the song up-tempo—the way Jolsen had sung it—Edens wrote a new opening, where Judy expressed her love and admiration for Clark Gable. Roger Eden's new arrangement of the song was brilliant and perfectly suited to Judy, who sang it with amazing artistry.

According to some accounts, Ida Koverman, who adored Judy, attended one of the rehearsals for this song and suggested she sing for Clark Gable's birthday on February 1st, which was just a few weeks away. It would be a great stunt to promote both Gable's new film and Garland's forthcoming one.

By August, *Broadway Melody of 1938* was out for previews, and there were rave reviews across the board. In August, Judy was given a role in *Thoroughbreds Don't Cry*. It was her first picture with her friend, Mickey Rooney, and the two made a great pair.

This was a turning point for the girl that previously MGM had no idea what to do with. By now, it was slowly but surely becoming clear that Judy Garland had a great future. Few could realize now how quickly her life was going to change.

Chapter 41

No Place Like Home

As happy as Judy was—for she was a happy girl—she often missed her father. When she attended her first film premiere, she cried, realizing he was not in the audience to see it. He had always made sure to attend her performances, hugging her and telling her how wonderful she was. Roger Edens was wonderful, but in the 1950s Judy said, "Although I had professional coaches training me for my film appearances, I longed to talk to my father about my work."[89]

Meanwhile, Judy was surrounded by a loving family, though mostly, they were a house full of women: Ethel, Jimmy, Grandma Eva and Aunt Norma, who often visited when she was performing in the area. Now that the family had a pool, they enjoyed spending their weekends in California style, swimming and relaxing in the sun.

Since childhood, Judy had been extremely sensitive to various pollens. In Lancaster, she even had asthma attacks as a result of them, though the family was not always aware of what triggered these attacks.

The backyard of the home on McCadden Place was made especially lovely by a large Acacia tree, which hung over the pool with its fuzzy pink blossoms. One day, Judy, Jimmy, and Dorothy were relaxing by the pool having a wonderful time. Aunt Norma was visiting as well, and the family stayed out by the pool most of the day. That night, Judy was to appear for a benefit at the Shrine Auditorium, but by evening when it was time for her to leave, she suddenly realized she could not make a single sound! Her throat closed up, and a doctor was called, but the appearance had to be cancelled. She was allergic to the Acacia tree. Sadly, the next day, the beautiful tree was chopped down.

Norma Milne had recently married John Gamble and was living in Oakland, California where she kept busy working with a local vaudeville group known as "The Beef Trust." The act, billed as a "fat girls" group (not considered offensive at the time), consisted of four or more large women whose weight totaled about 1500 pounds. In their act, the women sang and danced, as well as cavorted around for laughs.

An advertisement for "The Beef Trust" girls in 1939, read: *Giggling—Rollicking—Hilarious Kewpie Dolls Beef Trust Gay 90s Review.*[90] That particular show also starred Charlie McCarthy and Edgar Bergen. The group traveled with scenery and costumes loaded in a truck and generally worked with well-known vaudeville and burlesque names. Although there wasn't much vaudeville by the 1930s, Norma and the ladies were still getting gigs in California. At this time, Norma weighed close to 400 pounds and was affectionately known to family and friends as "Enormous Norma."

The Beef Trust girls had one gig down in Long Beach that everyone later recalled. The four women were dancing the hula on a makeshift stage when the entire stage began to shake and groan. The manager was frantic, fearing that the women might actually go through the floor. Later, while interviewing a man who had known Norma, he asked, "Say didn't one of those girls go through the floor down in Long Beach?"

Like everyone else, Norma enjoyed the weekend afternoons around the pool. One day, she was particularly excited because someone had given her a new rubber bathing suit. That day, when she came out of the house dressed in her new suit, she declared proudly, "Look at me!" Then, she walked to the side of the pool, and jumped in, sending four feet of wave of water over the side of the pool, and getting everyone wet.

When Norma hit the water, her suit split in two! There she was in the pool with nothing on. The woman all ran franticly, and got towels to cover her up, but as she came out of the pool, she was fuming. "I'm going to sue those sons of bitches," she said in a furry, while everyone laughed so hysterically, they couldn't stop.

~

A visit with the Gumm Family around 1937 or 1938: left to right back row, Judy, Uncle Bob, Ethel, Suzie; front row, Jimmy, Aunt Belle, thought to be Jimmy's boyfriend, Cousin Richard.
(Courtesy David Richardson)

With success clearly on the horizon, following *Thoroughbreds Don't Cry*, Judy was immediately scheduled for a new film, *Everybody Sing* starring singer Allen Jones, and the great Fanny Brice. From here on, as soon as she finished one film, Judy began another. This busy schedule was fun and exciting in 1937 and '38, but it would continue for the next ten years, until finally her health began to break down.

In late October of 1937, a news reporter for *The Evening Telegram* in Superior, Wisconsin called the Gumm home to see if she could arrange an interview with Judy and her mother. The woman, Ruthalice Selznick was quite surprised to learn that Ethel Garland had married Judy's father twenty-two years earlier in her hometown. Ethel invited Miss Selznick to the set the following Saturday, and after passing through a series of MGM publicity men, Ruthalice landed on the set for *Everybody Sing*.

Since she and Ethel were from the same hometown, the article was filled with references to local people and places that they both knew. While Ethel's fingers "flew over her knitting," she chatted happily about her past, and the day she married her husband.

Meanwhile, Judy, who was "lounging" in Allen Jones' trailer/dressing room, was constantly running in and out with comments and requests for her mother. Judy was described as "in makeup," and a "bright green ensemble" with matching socks, apparently one of her costumes in the film.

When the photographer for the paper attempted to take a photo, Ethel ran out of the picture saying, "You don't want me in this." Miss Selznick insisted that they did, and Ethel went to comb her hair. She described as wearing navy blue silk with white polka dots and a wine red coat. Judy, who by now had changed to navy as well, was soon called off the set to change once more into peach satin pajamas and pink mules for her next scene.

Meanwhile, Mrs. Gumm and Miss Selznick continued to talk about the past. At one point, Ethel said, "There's one girl I used to play for that I've often wondered about. Her name was Maude Ayers ... Maude had a perfectly beautiful voice..."

"Mother!" Judy called excitedly. Ethel excused herself and went to see what Judy wanted. On returning, she explained to the reporter that they were building their own home, and Judy was constantly getting ideas for the new house. "Every time Judy sees something on the set that she thinks we should have, I've got to rush right away to see it. She has very definite ideas about what she wants."

Mrs. Gumm told the reporter that she found her daughter rather amazing. "I often wonder when she gets her lines. She never looks at them," she said, to which Judy replied, "I remember them when I get up there." Miss Selznick added in her article that Judy could learn a song in fifteen minutes. Because of that ability, Ethel added, "she doesn't have to work so hard."

The article stated that Judy was only allowed to work four hours a day. Of course, she usually didn't work four hours in a row. She filmed a bit, and then attended school, and after a while, returned to film another scene. Mrs. Gumm noted that although Judy would be finished with school in a year (actually, she was only finishing junior high), she would have "a welfare worker on the set" until she was eighteen. When the writer asked about Ethel's presence on the set, she said, "Oh, I'm just her mother! The state law requires it. And that's just as well. A welfare worker backed by state law can say 'no' and mean it when a few more shots may be needed after the allowed eight hours have passed." Apparently, Mrs. Gumm had already seen something about how the movie business worked.

Another interesting story about Judy was revealed in the article. With all the money she was making, the family had opportunities to help members of their family in ways previously not possible. Grandma Eva, who was living with the Gumms, had not been back to see her family for years. As a birthday gift that year, Judy decided to give her Grandma a trip to visit all of her children, grandchildren and relatives she had been longing to see. The trip took her to Minnesota, Michigan and Mississippi. "Judy insisted on making all the arrangements herself," her mother said, "even to the sleeper accommodations. She had yards and yards of tickets when she came home." Mrs. Gumm added, "I thought it was so sweet. Her grandmother got back just two weeks ago. She saw relatives she hadn't seen in 30 years. She had a marvelous time."[91]

With all the talk of family, one event had taken place that September that no one mentioned. Ethel's father, John Milne, who had been living at the Railroad Men's house, a retirement home in Highland Park, Illinois, for the past six years, had passed away on September 7th. Only one or two of his sons went to his funeral.

Around this same time; Laura Gilmore passed away. Although the Gumms and the Gilmores had remained in touch, just how close they were during this period is unknown. Frank's passing had been an adjustment, and Ethel was busy now with Judy. Just as the Gumm girls had mourned their father, the Gilmores children, mourned the loss of their mother. Bill Gilmore's granddaughter recounted that Bill was very "broken up" over Laura's passing, and it was a very difficult time for them. Meanwhile, Ethel had other things on her mind.

~

In 1937, Jimmy began dating a young guitarist at MGM. He was six feet tall, blond, handsome and an excellent musician. Born Robert James Sherwood in 1914, like the Gumm girls, "Bobby" had been born in heart of America. Before being hired by MGM, he played guitar in Bob Crosby's band. According to Dorothy Walsh, Jimmy and Bobby had met earlier in Lancaster. Bobby apparently had some friends who lived in town, and he came out fairly often to visit them.

Of course, Ethel hated the fact that Jimmy was following in her sister, Suzie's footsteps. There was another thing Ethel did not like about

Bobby—he was married. Ethel wanted to protect her girls from heartache, and she just could not get over their bad taste in men. When Jimmy brought Bobby Sherwood over to the house, Ethel was not pleasant to him.[92] Despite that, Bobby continued to call on Jimmy, and even invited Judy to come along with them on their dates. Later, Jimmy was surprised to learn that her fifteen year-old sister had a serious crush on her beau.

Bobby Sherwood was a brilliant jazz musician, but in the heart of the depression he was lucky to have his MGM job. Many other fine musicians were struggling to survive. In the 1930s, Bobby's friends were jealous when they learned that he was making $8–$10 an hour at the studio.

Before long, Jimmy was pregnant, but Bobby, who was known for being something of a playboy, seemed in no hurry to marry her. In fact, neither of them seemed in a hurry. Meanwhile, Jimmy was deeply in love. Nothing seemed to matter to her but being with Bobby. As Jimmy's pregnancy began to show, Ethel was absolutely scandalized that her daughter showed no shame about her condition. Jimmy even tagged along with Bobby to his gigs, getting up on stage to sing.[93] Despite Ethel's feelings, noted Dorothy Walsh, "no one could tell Jimmy anything."

With Judy Garland's star on the rise, it seems likely that MGM finally stepped in. It would certainly not do for the sister of their budding young star and one of their own musicians to have an illegitimate child. By the time Jimmy was about seven months pregnant, the couple went to Vegas. After Bobby worked there long enough to get his residency, he got a divorce, and married Jimmy. From there, they traveled to Laporte, Indiana where their daughter was born away from the prying eyes of the movie industry and fans.

~

With *Everybody Sing* completed, Judy went to work right away on *Listen Darling*. The film did not take long to complete, and Judy was scheduled for a long publicity tour which began February 10th in New York City.

In January of 1938, accompanied by her mother, Judy embarked on a long publicity tour to promote her new film, *Everybody Sing*. Mother and daughter took the Super chief from Los Angeles to New York. Roger Edens, who helped Judy pick out a new wardrobe for the trip, had also been assigned by MGM to travel along back east as her accompanist.[94]

In true star style, the studio supplied them with their own compartment. It was an exciting journey for Judy. In a sense, this trip was the beginning of stardom for her. Unlike the trips she had taken in her childhood, everything now was planned.

The tour began in Miami Beach, Florida on February 4th with the world premiere of *Everybody Sing*. From there, she and her mother traveled to New York City where on the 10th, where Judy appeared on the huge Loew's State Theatre stage. Several days later, she had a radio appearance.

During this time, it was announced that Judy had been chosen to play Dorothy in *The Wizard of Oz*. This was a great surprise to the public, since it had long been assumed that Shirley Temple would get the role. It was also a great honor for the young star. Meanwhile, mother, daughter and Roger Edens traveled to Columbus, Ohio, followed by Chicago, Pittsburgh and Detroit.

Besides the excitement of all these events, fifteen year-old Judy and her mother had something very important planned when they finished their official tour. Ethel had received permission for them to take a one day trip to their old hometown, Grand Rapids. It was something Judy told her mother she wanted to do, and MGM granted the request. At last they would take the trip they had planned four years earlier. Although they were returning in triumph, for both mother and daughter, the visit to their old hometown must have evoked many emotions now that Frank was gone.

There were three things Judy had told her mother she wanted to do on this trip: see her childhood home, meet the doctor who brought her into the world, and visit her best friend. According to the Superior paper, although Judy was only four years old when she left Grand Rapids, she and her friend, "Marty Shook," were still writing to one another. In *The Superior Telegram*, Mrs. Gumm revealed that Marty was the daughter of a woman who lived behind their house, and for a time, had worked as their maid. The Shooks were actually the descendants of the people who in 1892 built the Gumm house.

There was a big celebration for the Gumms' (now Garlands) arrival. They disembarked the Hiawatha train in Aitkin, where they were met by "a cavalcade of cars." From there, they were driven 52 miles to Grand Rapids.

Later that day, mother and daughter went to the little, white house they had once called home. A few months after Frank died, Ethel had sold the house to the Raymond J. Beckfelt and Galen L. Finnegan for $2,000.[95]

As with most people who return to the home of their childhood, the house seemed much smaller to Judy than she remembered. Still, being in the rooms she had once lived with her father and where she remembered happiness must have brought her some peace. If only she could close her eyes and see him there. How could she not look for those places where the memories were dear. There was the stair landing where she and Janey and Jimmy used to rehearse, and the spot where her daddy had held her in his arms and sang to her at night.

Later, Judy visited with her old friend, Marty Shook. It must have felt a bit awkward because so much time had passed. Now, they had little time to spend together. Perhaps, during this trip Judy realized how much she had changed. Even though part of her still longed for the world she had lost, she was becoming a real celebrity. The people of Grand Rapids wanted to talk to her and have her sign autographs. Though Judy probably would have liked to make this trip as a private citizen, her life was now being swept by a tide beyond her control.

That night, Judy appeared on the stage of the Rialto, the theatre next door to her father's old theatre. She was introduced and spoke, but per her MGM contract, she was not allowed to sing—which must have been a disappointment to those in Grand Rapids, and possibly to her, as well, but her contract had to be obeyed.

That night, Ethel and Judy stayed at the Riverside Hotel in the apartment of Ethel's old friends, Mr. and Mrs. George O'Brien. After Judy went to bed, Ethel and her hosts may have had some time to talk about the old days.

With this trip, Judy was saying goodbye to the past. She was about to be launched on a journey of professional triumph and fame from which there could be no return. Yet the memories of the past would never be far from her mind.

The time in Grand Rapids flew by quickly, and early the next morning, Ethel and Judy had to catch the train again. Waving goodbye to all their old friends, they boarded the train back to Minneapolis, where they caught a faster train to Los Angeles. The next day, April 4th, they were back in L.A. Judy had a radio appearance on April 7th. Around this same time, she was due on the MGM lot to start her pre-production work for her next film, *Love Finds Andy Hardy*. But the thing Judy was most excited about was the arrival of her sister's new baby.

~

The Sherwood baby was born in the "sleepy little town" of LaPorte, Indiana on the 24th of May, 1938, a Saturday. They named her Judith Gayle Sherwood (the Gayle being for Bobby's mother). It would not be long, however, before Bobby and Jimmy started calling her Judaline.

A month or so after her birth, the Jimmy and Bobby returned to Los Angeles. Judy was thrilled with her little niece. Judaline was fair with blond hair and chubby cheeks. She took after her father in that way, rather than the dark eyes and hair of the Gumm family, though clearly, she did have some of the Gumm features.

Meanwhile, according to stories placed in the news papers, Judy was in a car accident the very day Judaline was born. Supposedly, she had not wanted to worry her mother and walked to a phone with three broken ribs and a sprained back. In the process, it was said that her broken ribs puncture a lung. According to the article, Judy was in the same hospital where her niece was born. Since Judaline was born in Indiana, the entire story remains somewhat questionable, though for the next seventeen days, she did not work. In any case, it seems the studio publicity machine was at work, hoping to distract from the fact that Judaline's birth had almost been illegitimate.

When Judaline was three or four months old, the Sherwoods found a cheap but beautiful two-story home by Beverly Glen in Bel Air. Because they had very little money, they decided to share the house with Dorothy's brother, Bob and his new wife, Helen Bambury.

Still, with the depression on, the couples were so poor they didn't have much money for food or heat. The house had a big fireplace, so one day when a telephone pole got knocked down, they dragged it into the house, put one end in the fireplace, and started a fire. In the beginning, the pole was so long, they had to leave the front door open. The Sherwoods and the Walshes kept a big bucket of water next to the fireplace so they

Dorothy Walsh with Jody and Judaline around 1939. (Courtesy JoDee Hunt)

could put out the fire when they left the house. Otherwise, they watched it. As it burned, they pushed the log further into the fireplace.

Dorothy, who was now married, and lived nearby, had just given birth to a little girl of her own named Jody. She came to visit Jimmy and the baby at least several times a week. One day, when she came into the house, Jimmy had the place so hot, Dorothy was worried she was going to roast little Judaline, and begged her to turn the heat down for the sake of the baby!

As time passed, Judaline and Jody spent so much time together, they were like two sisters, and the best of friends. Since Dorothy had lost her mother, Ethel became like a grandmother to little Jody. At this point in time, Dorothy and Jody started calling Ethel, "Nonna," for grandmother. Whenever Ethel went clothes shopping for Judaline, she always bought two little dresses, one for each girl.

While Jimmy was at home taking care of Judaline, Bobby was called in to work at the studio every few days. Helen Walsh was bored at home, so one day Bobby invited her to go along with him to the studio. When Helen continued to go to the studio with Bobby, Jimmy began to suspect there was something going on. After all, Bobby was handsome and a womanizer and Helen was a very beautiful girl.

A short time later, Jimmy and Bobby moved to an apartment. Meanwhile, Bob and Helen's marriage was over. Destroyed by the knowledge that his young and beautiful wife had cheated on him, Bob Walsh eventually joined the Army in November of 1942. He became a Technical Sergeant in the 36 Infantry, 91st Division, and was stationed in Florence Italy, but he never returned. Bob was killed on September 14th, 1944. He was honored with a Purple Heart and a Silver Star.

After Bobby and Jimmy moved out of the big house, Jimmy became aware that Bobby had had more than one dalliance with another woman. She realized she had to divorce him. Just as her mother had predicted, he

Suzie Gumm with Mr. Walsh, Dorothy and Jody. (Courtesy JoeDee Hunt)

could only break her heart. By 1942, Jimmy had moved back with her mother. Eventually, she was hired as a script girl at MGM.

Now that Dorothy had a baby, she did not get out to visit Ethel and Judy as often as before. She only lived a few blocks from Jimmy, but it was quite a ways further once Judy moved into the Stone Canyon house. Sometimes, when she was in the area, on her way home she drove by the Garland house. She could always tell when Grandma Eva was at home alone at night because she had every light in the house turned out. The old lady still believed in being frugal.

Meanwhile, Suzie Gumm had moved back in with Ethel and Judy. Just as Ethel had predicted, there were problems with the marriage and broken hearted Suzie was getting a divorce.

That June, Judy had a huge birthday party with all the friends she had met over the last years, including the Rabwins. As a gift, Ethel gave her a red roadster.*

~

With everything else that was going on, Ethel did not forget Frank's family. For James Gumm's birthday (Allie and Minnie's son), Ethel sent him a note and a check. She would continue to keep in touch with

* The fact that Judy supposedly had a car accident in May, but was given a new car ten days later does seem rather odd.

Frank's brothers and some of the other relatives she met while they were married. While the complaints about Ethel, her coldness, and bossiness have become infamous, few, if any reported on her thoughtfulness or generosity, something that Judy herself may have learned from her mother. During these years, Ethel tried to do some of the things she thought Frank would do if he were there.

That June, Judy was busy at the studio with *Listen, Darling*. By October, she would be recording the songs for *The Wizard of Oz*.

At home, Judy lived in a house full of women. There was Grandma Eva, who kept rather quiet these days. She enjoyed cooking for them, and playing her old-fashioned melodies. But Judy had her head filled with other music.

Soon, the MGM executives began to tell her what she could eat and what she couldn't. It certainly wasn't the kind of thing Grandma Eva or Mother cooked.

Around this same time, the studio also gave her some little yellow pills that were supposed to take her hunger away. No one thought much of them at the time. They seemed to be something like a vitamin that would fix what ails you. Jimmy later said that her mother would never have given them to Judy if she had really known they were harmful or addictive.

The pills were Benzedrine discovered by a chemist looking for something that would treat allergies and asthma. Hollywood discovered that these pills also took away hunger and allowed the user to go for hours without feeling tired.

When Judy took the pills, she got so wound up she felt her thoughts were coming faster than she could speak. In addition, she couldn't sleep at night. Finally, at Ethel's suggestion, she stopped taking them.[96]

Dorothy Walsh later recalled that the MGM people were always coming over to the house, "snooping around." Whether these were actors or others is not clear, but Dorothy didn't like them very much and found them not all that friendly. With the excitement of becoming a star and earning a great deal of money, Judy did not realize that slowly but surely, her life was being taken over, and would not longer be her own.

Meanwhile, whenever Ethel wasn't busy with Judy, it seemed she was always running off to be with Bill Gilmore, the man no one in the family

Judy's 1937 MGM photo and writing sent to James Gumm for his birthday by Ethel that year. (Courtesy James Gumm)

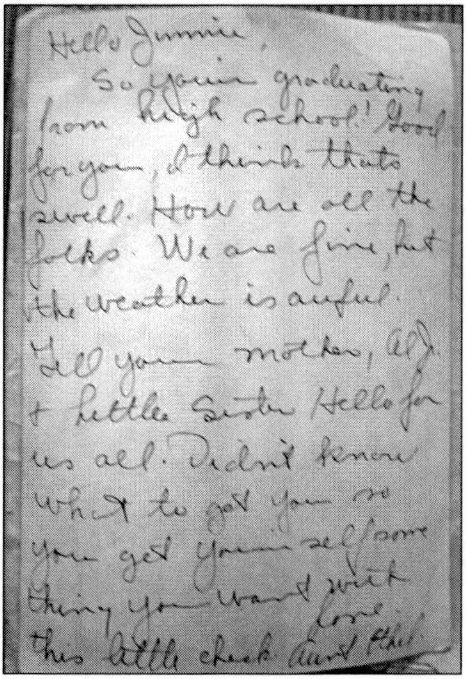

Hello Jimmie
So your'e graduating from high school! Good for you, I think thats swell. How are all the folks. We are fine, but the weather is awful. Tell your mother, Al Jr. & little Sister Hello for us all. Didn't know what to get you so you get yourself some thing you want with this little check.
Love
Aunt Ethel

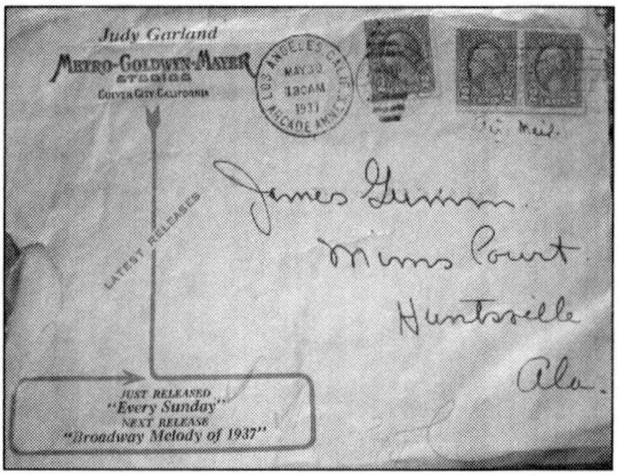

really seemed to like. Although Jimmy thought Judy was way too busy with her own life during this time to notice anything else, Judy later said she simply could not understand why her mother had to go with that man. It was a cause for deep resentment.

To everyone else, it was clear that Judy was first in Ethel's life. She took an active interest in what she was doing, what her needs were, and what was going on at the studio. She wasn't about to turn her daughter over to their studio's control. When the MGM executives began to demand that Judy loose weight, Ethel said she believed that young girls should eat well and have a little weight. When it was time for them to be thinner, they would become thinner naturally.

Dorothy Walsh said that Ethel loved to make a pie that she called "kiss pie." It consisted almost completely of whipped cream, and was very rich. In fact, it was so rich, nobody liked to eat. Judy and Ethel were the only ones. Meanwhile, when Ethel thought she had gained a few pounds, she'd go back on her orange juice fasts.

Along with protecting her daughter at the studio, Ethel was also very protective about any news stories that appeared in the papers about Judy. If there was something she didn't like, she'd call the papers and tell them. It was Dorothy's opinion that early in Judy's career, Ethel rubbed some of the columnists in the wrong way. As a result, later, when they wrote about Ethel, she did not always appear in a favorable light.

Chapter 42
The Wonderful Wizard of Oz

ORIGINALLY, THE STUDIO WANTED SHIRLEY TEMPLE FOR THE ROLE, BUT others knew better. Judy Garland *was* Dorothy, the little girl from Kansas, who went on a wonder-filled trip to Oz. It didn't work out with Temple, and Garland got the job. No doubt, songwriters Arlen and Harburg were happy; Judy could really sing.

The Wonderful Wizard of Oz by L. Frank Baum had captured the imagination of young and old alike since its first publication in 1903. The book was so popular, that Baum had written a total of sixteen sequels. The first book had already been portrayed both on stage and on film, but in 1938, MGM was planning the grandest version of all—a musical in Technicolor.

E.Y. Harburg later told the story of how he wrote the lyrics for the film's most famous song. He was driving though Hollywood, in the rain when suddenly a rainbow appeared. He had been struggling with the idea—a song for Dorothy in Kansas where everything was gray. The songs for the land of the Munchkins and Oz were easy, but Kansas? Then, he saw the rainbow. In the colorless land of Kansas, as Baum had described it, what would be the most wonderful thing a little girl could see? A Rainbow! Right there, *Over the Rainbow* was born.

After the song was recorded and filmed, the songwriters must have known they had seen artistry at its best. But the big men at MGM said the film was too long. Get rid of the song! Luckily, they didn't.

With all the problems they had: Buddy Ebsen poisoned by the silver paint of the Tinman, and being replaced by Jack Haley, Margaret

Hamilton being seriously burned as she descended in a plume of fire—the making *The Wizard of Oz* was an incredible experience for everyone.

The filming took much longer than they had planned and involved three directors—King Vidor, George Cukor, who was taken off to direct *Gone with the Wind*, and Victor Fleming, who received the credit. Others involved would be Mervyn LeRoy, Richard Thorpe, and Norman Taurog.

It had taken some time as well to gather over 100 little people from all parts of the United States to play the Munchkins. They too were awestruck by the beautiful sets, and the lovely young girl playing Dorothy. Even though later, Judy told tall tales for the entertainment of late night talk show audiences about the Munchkins' wild escapades, there was no hint of this on the set.

The beginning of the film was fun for Judy. She was told to take the little dog playing Toto home with her for a while, so that they could bond. Judy loved dogs, and the little terrier was soon following her around like he was her own puppy.

As the filming progressed, word spread on the MGM lot that something quite remarkable was taking place on stage—Judy as Dorothy also began to get a great deal of attention. She was so transformed in the role, people thought of her as Dorothy.

During the filming, L. Frank Baum's widow came to visit several times. Her granddaughter, Florence Baum, the daughter of L. Frank's second son, Robert, came more often. As a Baum descendant, she was allowed to visit the set as often as she wanted. Florence, who was only fifteen years old at the time, was enchanted by the set and by Judy as well. The two girls became friends. As Florence later described it, she was Judy's "hopeless slave," who was happy to do anything she asked.

~

During this time, Mr. Mayer decided that his new star really needed to loose weight. He put her on a strict diet consisting of his recipe for Jewish Chicken soup and cottage cheese. No matter what Judy ordered, following Mr. Mayer's strict orders, the staff served her chicken soup. Although Louis B. Mayer believed that his Jewish Chicken Soup remedy contained every vitamin needed by the body, it is doubtful that Judy's bowl contained much more than chicken broth. After Judy ate her soup, and skipped down the yellow brick road a few times, she was starving.

Judy worked hard making this film, and the long hours, under the hot lights made her extra hungry. When Florence was on the set, Judy asked her to go to the commissary at lunchtime and bring her some mashed potatoes with gravy. Since Florence could order anything she wanted in the commissary without question, she'd order a double helping of mashed potatoes with gravy and sneak it back to Judy.[97] The potatoes must have helped to take the edge off during her long hours of filming.

While Judy was filming *The Wizard of Oz*, there were many changes at home. Their grand, new Stone Canyon house was completed. They had hired Jackie Cooker's mother, who had previously worked as an interior decorator interior, to design in the inside of the house. Although the Stone Canyon house looked quite modest from the front, it was actually quite large. There was a grand living room where Judy could entertain her friend and a special suite for her consisting of three rooms. She also had her own private entrance, something that made her quite grown-up at seventeen.

The Wizard of Oz filmed from October of 1938 to March of 1939. After finishing *The Wizard of Oz*, almost immediately, Judy went to work on her next film, *Babes in Arms*. From her portrayal of the classic Dorothy Gayle in pigtails, Judy was now playing a modern character, her own age. Once again, she and Mickey Rooney were working together.

Although Judy Garland would make many more films, and record scores of songs that were loved by her audiences, she would never make a film that meant more to the public at large than *The Wizard of Oz*. Her part in that film ensured its success and it, likewise, ensured that she would never be forgotten.

After *The Wizard of Oz* had been edited, Ethel was given permission to bring little Judaline and Jody for a special private viewing. Although the two little girls were toddlers at the time, the film made such an impression on them that their memories of seeing it at this age were never forgotten.

~

In August of 1939, Judy and Mickey Rooney traveled across the country promoting *The Wizard of Oz* and *Babes in Arms*. From Bridgeport and New Haven, Connecticut, they went to Wisconsin and then New York. Everywhere they went, they caused absolute pandemonium, showing studio officials, just how popular they were. The pair appeared at the

Capitol Theater in New York, performing five shows a day. It must have seemed like glorified vaudeville to Judy, although apparently at one point she had been working so hard, with so little food, she passed out. Ethel, who was along on the trip, tried to protect Judy was insisting that she rest between each show. That October, at the premier of *Babes in Arms*, Judy and Mickey were given the honor of putting their hand and footprints in the courtyard of Grauman's Chinese Theatre.

On November 17th, Ethel's birthday, and the fourth anniversary of Frank's death, an unwelcome change took place in the Gumm/Garland household; Ethel Gumm traveled to Arizona with Bill Gilmore and the pair were married. Later, Jimmy would say that her mother had no intention of marrying him and had written a letter to tell him why she could not marry him, but he told her he never received it and not having the heart to tell him "no" after all these years, Ethel went ahead with the marriage.

That Christmas when the Gilmores came to the Stone Canyon house, they discovered the wealth of Judy's success in films—more than half of the huge living room in the Stone Canyon house was covered with Christmas presents.

Photos that year show the family, including Ethel and Bill Gilmore, along with Judy, Jimmy, Judaline and Mickey Rooney, all happily seated in front of the Christmas tree.

Chapter 43

1939–1941—Family Life

DOWN SOUTH IN TENNESSEE, AS FAMILY MEMBERS SAW JUDY GARLAND on the movie screen, listened to her on the radio and continued to read about her in the press, they were amazed and exciting that someone in the family, their own cousin Frank's daughter, had reached this level of success, and at an age so young.

Ruth Dunn remembers a day in Old Jefferson when two girls came up from Murfreesboro with a movie magazine. They were laughing excitedly as they showed one of the Wade cousins Judy's pictures.

Some of Judy's cousins, like young Claire Rion, Nannie Rion's granddaughter, felt sad when, on the advice of her grandmother, she had written to Judy but never got an answer. Others, like the Anna Lee Mertz, remained in touch with Ethel, and eventually came out to visit in California.

Uncle "Bobby"—as Judy loved to call him—had done very well with *Garland's Lomita Theater*. In fact, for a while his daughter-in-law, Geri Gumm, later said, "It seemed as if everything he touched turned to gold." Although Bob was making a lot of money at Garland's Lomita Theater, the area they lived in, Torrance, was rather rough. Bob wanted Richard to grow up in a nicer area, so he went out and found a theatre in a small town called Brea.

Once the family moved to Brea, Bob nearly went broke. Brea was a small community, and rather narrow minded. People didn't want to spend money in their own town. Instead, they'd drive to Fullerton, where there were bigger stores and theaters, and spend their money there.

Judy and her beloved "Uncle Bobby" about 1940, one of the last times he came to visit. Note the back of the Stone Canyon house behind.
(Courtesy James Gumm)

When Uncle Bob and the family visited the "Garlands," he mentioned that the theater wasn't doing too well. Judy said she would come out and sing at the theater, and bring some business in the way the Gumm sisters had long ago for their father. Although it was mentioned (maybe by Ethel) that it was against the rules of her MGM contract, Judy said, "I don't care." So, Judy went out to Brea and sang at her Uncle Bobby's theatre, which apparently helped the business.

Sometime after Bob moved to Brea, Uncle Will brought one of Allie's sons out to California for a visit. During their visit, they had loads of fun with Belle and Richard, and took lots of photos. At one point, Uncle Will even played golf with Bob Hope. Meanwhile, Judy, who was kept very busy at the studio, didn't have much time for visiting.

Although Ethel was married to Bill Gilmore, they each kept their own homes. During the week, Ethel devoted herself to Judy's needs, and on the weekend, went to be with Bill. Always social, she did enjoy the times when she was able to have parties and spend time with family and friends gathered around.

When Uncle John Milne came out to visit, both Ethel and Judy tried to get him a job at the studio. His voice was truly beautiful, but his height,

The trip to California – above, Uncle Will W. Gumm, James Gumm and Cousin Richard in front of the Brea Theater and below, the Bob Gumm's home.
(Courtesy Bill Gibb)

The back yard of the Stone Canyon house, left to right, Uncle Bob, Suzie, Judy, Cousin Richard, Sergei, Aunt Belle and Ethel. Circa 1939. On the back of the photo Bob Gumm wrote, "The sourpuss on me is because I was trying to tell the fellow how to work the camera." (Courtesy David Richardson)

which was about 5′4″ or less, was a stumbling block for the executives. They wanted a tall singer.

Periodically, Ethel gathered the dresses Judy wasn't going to wear again, and sent to Jack's family in Duluth. By now, Jack and Margaret had fourteen children; there were six boys and eight girls. Most of Judy's dresses were way too fancy for the life the Milne girls lived, so their parents traded them for the things they needed, including food.

Every year, Ethel ordered Jack and Margaret a large turkey with all the "fixings." One year, the turkey was so large; they had to take it to a nearby hotel to have it baked because it wouldn't fit in their oven!

Sometime around 1940, Robert Gumm wasn't feeling well. He'd had a cough, and seemed to have lost some weight. He, Belle and Richard visited Ethel and the girls in the spring, and the family took a nice photo that included Judy's St. Bernard, Sergei. Someone had give Judy the dog as a gift. That day, everyone laughed as Bobby tried to figure out how to work his new camera.

A few months later, Uncle Bobby was taken to Cedars of Lebanon Hospital, the very same hospital where his brother died. He was diagnosed with lung cancer, and died not long after in 1941. Judy insisted on paying all his medical bills. Meanwhile, the seeming curse of the Gumm family had repeated itself; Judy's cousin, eighteen year-old Richard, had lost his dad.

Belle almost went crazy with grief after Bob died. In time, her life went on. She had a trailer in Palm Springs and spent a good deal of time there. She also loved to travel, visiting with friends around the country. Belle, who never married again, lived on until 1965.

~

In the summer of 1940, William Gilmore planned a big family reunion. It would include Bill Gilmore's mother, his seven brothers, their wives and children. His father had been killed in a train wreck when he and his brothers were children. Of course, the Stone Canyon house would be perfect for this event and Ethel agreed to host it.

Jack Gilmore remembers that day. He was eight years old, and after a day of fun, he was put down for a nap upstairs in Judy's four poster bed.

Billy Gilmore, the son of William Gilmore's brother, Frank, was six when he attended the family reunion. He remembers the sound of Judy's

The Gilmore Family Reunion, June 1940. Front Row: *Jack (son of Tim)*, *Billy Joe (son of Frank)*. Second Row Seated: *Nellie Gilmore (mother of Bill, etc)*, *Jimmy and Judaline*, *Mamie (Jim's wife) and Ethel*. Standing: *Jack (Bill's son)*, *Judy*, *Ella*, *Evelyn (Tim's wife)*, *Mary (Frank's wife)*, *George*, *Ruth (Bill's daughter) and Harry*. Back Row: *Jimmy (Jim's son)*, *Frank*, *Bill*, *Hugh*, *Jim*, *Bill, Jr. (Bill's son) and Tim*.
(Courtesy Jack Gilmore)

laughter, ringing through the house. Everyone said it was contagious. He was excited about the large pool in the backyard, and the free "soda pop" machine.

Judy and Jimmy were there to welcome the Gilmores. Of course, they had been friends with Bill, Jr., Ruth and Jackie, so everyone got along and enjoyed the day. That night, when the entire family went out to see a performance of *Swan Lake*, Billy Gilmore, who was only six, was put to bed in Judy's four poster.

~

As time went on, Dorothy Walsh seldom saw Judy when she visited the house. MGM kept her so busy, and when she did come home, Judy spent most of her time upstairs in her room.

In later years, Dorothy felt sad that Ethel had been so misunderstood. She thought the MGM press had spoken badly about her from the beginning. Ethel fought back at MGM, unafraid of what they thought. She would also call reporters about the things they wrote, saying, "That is unkind. Stop it." She told off Louella Parsons a "number of times" said Dorothy. Of course, Louella retaliated.

Ethel fought for Judy at MGM, and she rarely left her daughter alone there. She would sit on the sidelines knitting because she really couldn't read a book there and pay attention—that was her other favorite thing to do. Judy's career was what they had been working for.

Eventually, Ethel was forbidden to be on the studio lot. Between the pills and overwork, Ethel felt that MGM had practically killed Judy. Ethel had been advised by friends when Judy was young that she should get her own contract and pay from MGM, but Ethel had refused to do that. She always believed that Judy would take care of her. Why wouldn't she? She did everything she could to take care of her.

During the 1930s and even the early 1940s, Judy and Ethel went everywhere together. Even after Judy was married, that was true. And if Ethel couldn't go along, one of Judy's sisters would go with her.

Ethel's marriage to Bill Gilmore would not last long. As Bill's children saw the marriage, it was doomed from the start—there were children on either side, each grieving their lost parent; there was Bill, the brash Irishman who put up with no nonsense, and there was Judy, who was used to having her way, and who was now becoming a huge star. Then, there was Ethel, who was totally preoccupied with Judy. She couldn't be the wife Bill Gilmore wanted. In a choice between Bill and a life of her own, or her daughter, Judy won. Ethel's life had centered around Judy for so long, she couldn't let go. Meanwhile, it seems that Bill Gilmore was not the man she wanted after all.

Chapter 44

Family Reunion

In 1938, Nannie Rion wrote to her ex-daughter-in-law that she would like to have Judy and the cousins her age, Claire, Mildred and Patsy come to Murfreesboro and spend time together. She thought it would do the girls some good. Maybe she was remembering the fun she had with her sisters and cousins when she was a girl, but neither she nor any of the people back home could imagine what being a star of Judy Garland's magnitude meant.

While Judy might have late nights to herself, or weekends, she was not free to go off for a get together with cousins, or visit Grand Rapids when the town folks invited her. But by now, Judy likely didn't care about doing such things. MGM was her world and her family. Her sense of herself as a major motion picture star had changed everything. Judy Garland was a major moneymaker for MGM Studios; she was living the dream of every young girl and woman in America. What more could she want or need? For the time being, the needs of a real girl named Frances Gumm were forgotten.

Whatever criticisms there were of Ethel, this life was what Judy had wanted. And like every artist, she understood that in order to achieve her art, there must be sacrifices along the way. If Ethel had not pushed Judy when she wanted to stay home and play with her friends, she might not have achieved this dream in the way it was happening now.

~

One day, when Judy was in her dressing room, nursing the broken heart Artie Shaw had left her, there was a knock at the door. Opening the door, Judy saw Tony Martin's handsome musical director, David Rose, standing there with a big piece of chocolate cake. Right away, Judy felt better.[98]

Judy and David Rose soon became good friends, and before long they were going out on double dates with Tony Martin and his date, Lana Turner.

The beginning of 1941, David and Judy worked on a radio show together called *Love's Sweet Song*. It was based on a story Judy had written. Judy played her first straight dramatic role on this program.

On June 2nd of 1941, David Rose and Judy Garland sent out engagement party invitations. Sunday, June 15th, there was a joint birthday-engagement party at the Stone Canyon home for 600 guests. At this party, Judy dressed beautifully in a chiffon gown. For the first time, she felt grown-up, and she looked her most beautiful.

Although the marriage was set for September, in July, Judy grew impatient. The evening of July 27th, David and Judy, flew to Las Vegas with Ethel and Bill Gilmore. They were married at 1 AM on July 28th. Almost immediately after the wedding, Judy sent Arthur Freed a telegram informing him of the wedding, and saying she'd be back soon.

This was the first time Ethel had attended the wedding of one of her children. According to some fan magazines, she encouraged David and Judy to take a honeymoon, but Judy was aware that she had probably already upset the studio officials, and was delaying her new film. The following day, July 29th, she showed up on the *Babes on Broadway* set.

Judy was ecstatic at the beginning of her marriage, but having spent most of her life at the studio while her mother managed everything else, she had no idea how to manage a house, let along a marriage. Perhaps she thought David would be like a father, and take care of everything for her. Meanwhile, besides music, David had his own interests—electric trains that were big enough for him to ride in.

Judy wanted someone to love and take care of her, and it seems David wanted the same thing. The marriage would not last long. Ultimately, both of them were too busy with their careers. Neither wanted to work on the marriage, and perhaps they both realized that they were simply not suited to one another.

Early in 1942, Judy and David Rose moved into the ill-fated home that had once belonged to star Jean Harlow and her husband, Paul Bern.

The house had a dark side for it was here that Bern, also an employee of MGM, had killed himself. It is not known whether Judy and David knew about this when they moved in. The beautiful house and grounds were the main attraction for both of them. The layout of the grounds would allow David to set up his train collection.

~

In the midst of everything else, the war in Europe was heating up. On December 7th, 1941, the Japanese bombed Pearl Harbor. Four days later, Congress approved war with Japan. That same day, Hitler and Mussolini declared war on the United States. The draft bill had already been enacted in 1940. Now, young men from all over the country were joining the army, navy and air force.

Beginning in 1941, Judy had performed at various war related benefits. It was soon clear to her what she wanted to do. She asked for permission to go to the army bases and entertain the soldiers. Permission was granted.

On January 21st, 1942, Judy, David Rose, and Ethel boarded a train and set off on a month long tour to entertain the soldiers who would soon be embarking for Europe and Japan. Judy Garland was possibly the first person to volunteer to entertain these young men who were about to lay their lives on the line. According to the schedule, she was to perform four shows a day, singing twelve songs in each show.[99]

Judy was deeply touched by her time with the troups. These were young men, and they were going to war, maybe never to return. They were down to earth and interested in her as a person, and she would later say in an interview with Walter Winchell, "I wanted to know about them."

For a while now, Judy had been performing almost exclusively on film. She was on the radio fairly often; performances which usually took place before a fairly small audience. Once in a while, she appeared at a benefit. Whether Winchell's interview can be believed or not, Judy says that during her first performance before the troops, her knees shook and her voice trembled.

> *"It seems silly now, as I look back on it. Every performer dreams of stopping a show, but believe me, no show was ever stopped with the thunderous applause and appreciative response that greets an entertainer playing to a group of soldiers."*[100]

The trip was an exciting one for Judy. It reminded her of the times she and her parents had performed in theaters, and she realized how much she missed performing live (even though she had from time to time for MGM). The show she was doing was not by herself, and in Winchell's column, Judy mentions that some of the same people she met in vaudeville were there. "It was like old home week." Judy says that among the performers on this tour, was her favorite comedian from her childhood, Willie Shore, the "Abba-Dabba Man."

Another fun part of the trip was that Judy actually got to eat. She says they ate in the mess hall with the boys and the meals were mainly steak, fried potatoes and fried chicken. No more chicken soup for her. "I gained eight pounds," she said. According to Winchell's article, Judy was so enamored by her trip, she wanted to go to the front.

The article may have been in part advertisement for her upcoming film. Judy would go to the front in *For Me and My Gal.*

That January, Nannie Rion's son, Ed, saw a notice in the newspaper that Judy Garland was coming to town to entertain the troops at Fort Knox. The army base, near Elizabethtown, was not fifty miles away from where Ed Rion and his family were living. In the last years, Ed had been working as an arbitrator for the AFL. He was married to Virginia Carter, and they had two little girls, Joy and Wanda.

The day before the concert, Ed found out that Judy and her new husband, David Rose, along with her mother, Ethel, were staying at the Brown Hotel. He called up Ethel, and she invited him and the family to come and visit. She also told him that she'd arrange admittance to the concert for them.

Early in the afternoon, on January 24th, dressed in their very best dresses, coats and hats, Joy and Wanda Rion climbed into their Dad's automobile and rode to the Brown Hotel.

For seven-year-old Joy, it was an amazing day. She had always been told that movie star and singer, Judy Garland, was her cousin. The family had all seen *The Wizard of Oz* and other films Judy was in. But when Joy told her friends at school that Judy Garland was her cousin, no one believed her. Now, she, Joy Rion, was actually going to meet Judy!

The Rions rode up in the elevator and knocked on a door. It was opened by a rather short, heavy woman, who was very gracious to them. That was Ethel, Judy's mother. Coming inside, there was Judy. "She looked so beautiful," recalled Joy. While she and her sister sat quietly on the sofa, the adults proceeded to converse as families do about how they had been. They also talked about memories of the old times. Joy was struck by the fact that Ethel called her father, "Edwin." Everyone she knew called him "Ed." She also heard them talk about "Frank," which she knew was Judy's father, her dad's first cousin. The things they said didn't seem to mean anything, because she had never met "Frank." What did impress her was the fact that when they spoke about Judy's father, it was in hushed tones. Maybe that was because he had died.

Before it was time to leave, Joy told Judy about how her friends at school didn't believe that she was their cousin. Then, she brought out her

Joy and Wanda Rion around the time they met their cousin, Judy Garland. (Courtesy Joy Rion Nelson)

Judy Garland singing for the WWII troups.

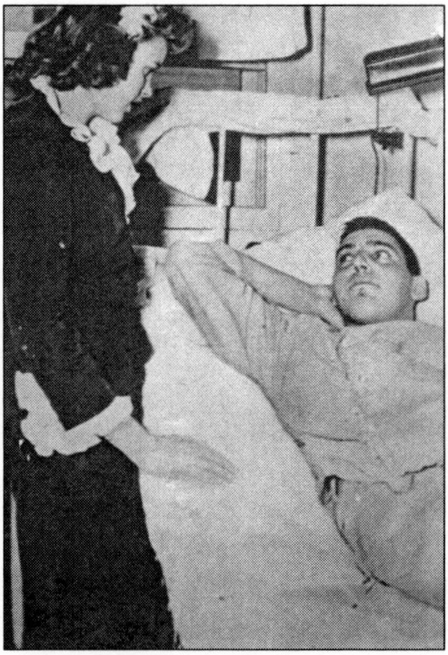

Judy visiting a wounded soldier.

precious autograph book, and asked Judy to sign it, which she did, "To Joy and Wanda, with love and kisses from their cousin Judy Garland." That would prove to anyone who doubted that they were cousins.

The visit was only about a half an hour long, and then they had to leave. Judy Garland was a very busy person. Before they left, Ethel handed Ed Rion a pass to get them into the concert at Fort Knox that evening.

Later, the four Rions went through "security" to the area where Judy Garland was to perform. They sat in the midst of a sea of service men who cheered for the girl who was their cousin. With that slight giggle that made her the girl next door, Judy breathed deeply and opened her mouth letting out the voice that went straight through, like an arrow, into the heart. It was a voice that brought both smiles and tears. Little Joy would carry into adulthood, the memory of her cousin singing "Blues in the Night."

For this moment in time, the past and the present had reached a full circle. Judy had traveled to an area not far from where fifth great grandfather began his journey as a pioneer. She was part of a history she could scarcely know. Judy would return to Hollywood, to triumphs and sorrows, broken marriages and beloved children, a journey no less difficult than the one begun by her ancestors long ago. All Joy could remember of that day was that Judy was so beautiful, Joy could scarcely believe it.

In the weeks that followed, Judy grew tired. After she performed at Fort Custer in Michigan, Jefferson Barracks outside St. Louis, Missouri, Camp Robinson in Little Rock, Arkansas and Camp Wolters in Mineral Wells, Texas, she had to cut the trip short and return home. She had strep throat. A short time later, David Rose went into the service.

Chapter 45

Afterward—Real People

Over the years, despite what the world saw outwardly, Judy Garland still had connections to her roots in Tennessee and Minnesota.

After Bettie Gum Fox's sudden death of an apparent heart attack in 1944, Anna Lee and Paul Mertz returned to Murfreesboro with their family, and moved into an elegant home near Lytle and Highland streets with Anna Lee's father. The home was the childhood residence of Jean Faircloth, who married the American war hero, General Douglas MacArthur, around this same time. Mrs. MacArthur would become one of Murfreesboro's most touted celebrities. The Faircloth home was an elegant mansion, which contained about twenty rooms, and six fireplaces. Eventually, it was torn down for a parking lot.

Like Judy, Anna Lee loved to write. She was considered quite a character in town. She had two Siamese cats, smoked non-stop and drank whiskey. "She had a gruff voice, and the kindest heart," said Mrs. Polly Ridley, who worked with her. "She was the funniest person I ever knew, and she was proud of her relation of Judy Garland."

Anna Lee's daughter, Barbara enjoyed tap dancing, but like her mother, smoked constantly and kept a bottle of bourbon in her lingerie drawer. Along with the affinity for the arts, both Anna Lee and Barbara were interested in public service. Still, the tendency toward addiction runs deep in the Gumm family. By the time Barbara was 50, she recognized the fact that she had a problem and began attending AA. Sadly, she died of lung cancer before her time.[101]

Around 1943, Anna Lee got the wild idea that she and her daughter should drive out to Hollywood and visit Judy. Whether they were just up for a lark or Anna Lee hoped Judy might find a job in show business for her gorgeous daughter is not known.

Barbara Mertz Goenne, 1950s. (Courtesy Cecil Elrod)

Arriving at MGM, the two women were escorted onto the set of *Meet Me in St. Louis*. Vincente Minnelli took them back to see Judy in her dressing room. As the two women came in to see Judy, they couldn't help noticing that she had a framed photo of Frank Gumm on her dressing room table.

Anna Lee, Barbara and Judy chatted for a while, and took a photo. While everything seemed pleasant enough, Anna Lee later told her nephew, Henry, that they didn't feel all that welcome and had decided not to contact Judy again. Of course, they had come to visit her rather innocently, and neither of them fully comprehended all that was going on with her.

Around this same time, or shortly thereafter, Henry Lee Fox, who had joined the Navy, was out in California on leave and decided to contact the family. Henry had never met Judy, but after his father, Jack died, he went to live with Anna Lee in Chicago and learned more about the family's relationship.

After Henry contacted Mrs. Gumm, he was taken under the wing of Suzie's new husband, orchestra leader Jack Cathcart. Jack met Henry, and took him around town, giving him "the royal treatment." Henry was also introduced to Vincente Minnelli, who, in turn, took him to see Judy. "She was very lovely then," he recalled.

Henry met Ethel later during the visit, but felt she was rather reserved. Perhaps that was because she and Judy were not getting along so well at the time. Henry recalled that Ethel's style of living was rather middle class, and in no way as fancy as Judy's.[102]

In the future, whenever Henry Fox met Judy, she was always very warm to him. When *A Star Is Born* came out, Sid Luft arranged for Henry and his wife to come to the premiere.

To show just how connected Judy Garland was to her father's hometown, in 1962, she accepted a request to be a call-on guest of the WGNS radio in Murfreesboro.

The radio studio had been built in 1941 above a shop on the town square, which was a great boon to the area. At the time it was built, it was a big deal to get a radio frequency. Tommy and Jimmy Dorsey came and stayed in a house on East Main Street so they could broadcast on the station. The studio had a grand piano, and the music broadcast was all live performance. Among the other performers who broadcast from there were Pat Boone, Elvis Presley, and Mother Maybell Carter.

At the time, Anna Lee's sister, Martha was married to Jack Todd, the Mayor of Murfreesboro. Martha didn't have to work, but she went to work for the Welfare Office and was happy every day to be able to help people who needed it. The Todds, Jack Todd in particular, had done a great deal for the town as well, and Mr. Todd was friends with Mr. Elrod, who ran the station.

This was right after Judy's first triumphant concert at Carnegie Hall, and everyone was thrilled that she had agreed to be on the live hookup. That evening, everyone waited breathlessly for Judy to come over the airwaves via telephone. Then, the first thing Judy said was, "How is Martha doing?"[3]

~

In the mid-1940s, the Gumm family was living under one roof once again, in a house on Ogden Drive. Along with Grandma Eva and Ethel, there were Jimmy, Judaline, Suzy and her new husband, Jack Cathcart. Then, Judy, who was now separated from David Rose, and had lived on her own for a while, said she was lonely, and asked if she could come home. It was a full house!

Meanwhile, all three girls were working at MGM. Suzie, who was considered to be a fine dancer, got a job in that capacity, while Jimmy worked as a script girl. The sisters usually tried to get together for lunch several times a week. A fan magazine of the period reported that one day, to the surprise of the packed MGM Commissary, the three sisters broke out into one of their old "Gumm Sisters" routines.[4] Later, while Judy was making *Meet Me in St. Louis*, Jimmy was hired to sing Lucille Bremer's part with

Judy for the title song.[5] Together, Judy and Jimmy created an authentic sisterly harmony.

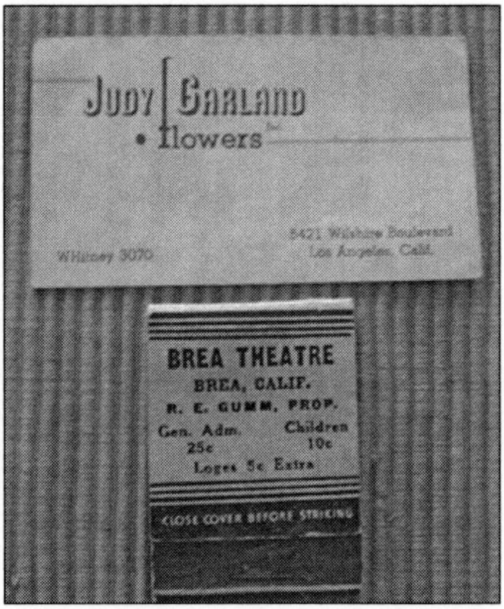

Business card for Ethel's flower shop and Robert Gumm's theatre matches. (Courtesy James Gumm)

Although Judy was still the same fun-loving, talented girl she had always been, her continual work schedule, Hollywood lifestyle and the pills which she was now taking on a regular basis made her nervous and on edge. When Mary Astor, who first worked with Judy in 1937, asked her what had happened to her, Judy told her that she was taking some pills and she couldn't sleep.[6]

There were days when Judy was sick of Hollywood, and wanted to just be herself, not the Hollywood star. During this time, Dorothy Walsh heard Judy complain when she came home from the studio that she was sick of being called "precious" and "lamby pie."

In the mid to late 1940s, whether because of drugs or fatigue, some of the time, Judy no longer seemed to enjoy her work, her co-stars or her friends. She would come home and complain about the people she worked with. Sometimes, she'd see a friend drive up to the house, and say, "oh, no. I don't want to see them." She was so tired, she just didn't want to be bothered. She wanted to be Judy, the real person, the person her family and friends knew before fame.

Later, when Judy dated Sid Luft, he seemed to be the total opposite of the men she had known previously. She said he was rough with her, and, according to Dorothy, they fought like cats and dogs. Some of her friends and family appealed to her not to go with Sid, but as Judy had stated earlier, she "was so sick of being called 'precious,'" and treated that way, it almost seemed as if she liked this change. Dorothy would never forget one year when Judy gave Sid an Eskimo cap for his birthday. She told him, "I want to keep your head warm."

Dorothy didn't see a lot of Judy during these years. Judy was just too busy to see anyone, and often when she came home, she'd go up to her room to rest.

~

During WWII, one of Jack Milne's sons, seventeen year-old, Jim, had joined the Navy. While stationed in Long Beach, he went to visit his Aunt Ethel and Grandma Eva periodically. While he was there, he often saw Judy as well.

One day, while aboard ship, Jim Milne was bragging about Judy being his first cousin. Of course, no one believed him. His shipmates decided that they would make a pot totaling $600 (= about $7,000) on a bet that Jim could not get Judy Garland to come down to the ship "to say hello."

Jim went and made a call to the house. He was going to win that pot. About an hour later, Judy and Jimmy showed up at the ship, waving and shouting to be let onboard. The two sisters were let on the ship, and the commanding officer came out to shake hands with Judy. Meanwhile, Jim was called in, and the guys had to pay up because he had won the wager.[7]

~

Ethel Gumm Gilmore loved her little granddaughter, Judaline, and Judaline, in turn, adored her grandmother. Although people were curious about Judy's niece, and whether she had the same kind of talent as her aunt, Judaline seemed blissfully ignorant of this. Of course, she could sing because that's what people in the Gumm family did, but her main interest was in animals.

Once asked if she would like to be a film, Judaline only interest was in whether she would be able to ride a pony; if not, she wasn't interested. Sometimes Jimmy brought Judaline to visit her Aunt Judy on the set. Judy loved her niece and was eager to show her off, but if anyone mentioned the idea of Judaline going into show business, she would flip.[8] Clearly, her attitude and view of the career she was in, and of MGM had changed.

Judy and Vincente were married at Ethel's home. Originally, they wanted to be married at the Little Church Around the Corner in New York City, a sort of tradition for theatrical people. Since L.B. Mayer

Ethel loved to entertain. Going around the table to the right, Ethel, one of her brothers and his wife, Uncle Bob Gumm, Ethel's sister, Cevila, Cousin Richard, Ethel's friend, Grandma Eva, and James Gumm. Late 1930s or early 1940.

Will Gumm playing golf with Bob Hope, 1940s (Both photos courtesy Bill Gibb)

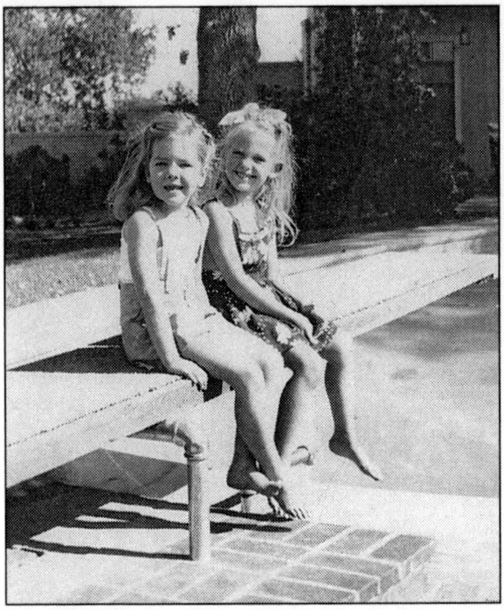

Jody and Judaline (right), the best of friends. (Courtesy JoDee Hunt)

wanted to be present at the wedding and he couldn't get to New York, they settled for Ethel's home.[9] Her dress was pale gray, almost silver.

Ethel didn't like Vincente, Dorothy Walsh later intimated, adding, "She didn't want Judaline near him." When Judy found she was pregnant, she told them, "I don't know what I'll do with a baby." Although Judy loved children and motherhood seemed to come easily to her, she had become so used to working day and night; it was difficult for her to picture another life.

In 1949, when Judy was let go from MGM, Jimmy was fired as well. Without a job, Jimmy decided the she would create her own nightclub act. She hired Johnny Thompson as her rehearsal pianist.

Jimmy appeared in Vegas for a while. She even had her own chorus boys; at least one of her boys was a dancer from MGM, but according to him no one was very interested in Judy Garland's sister. In addition, according to her future son-in-law, Dennis Havens, Jimmy wasn't that good. Her voice was much rougher than Judy's and she often went off pitch. Meanwhile, Jimmy and Johnny Thompson decided to get married.

Johnny was a brilliant arranger. He was a Julliard graduate, and had arranged a good percentage of the great Big Band music for Benny Goodman, Harry James, Tommy Dorsey and others. He had no trouble finding work.

After Jimmy and Johnny were married in Tijuana, Mexico on September 11th, 1949, they moved to New York with Judaline. Johnny went to work for Tommy Dorsey. They traveled all over, including down to Havana, Cuba. Judaline grew up surrounded by great music and the musicians were her playmates.

Jimmy, like her mother, worked at writing songs. Eventually, she created a musical review which was performed at the Playboy Club in NYC in the 1960s.

After many years of traveling, Johnny Thompson finally decided that he wanted to go back to Texas and settle down. His parents had a large plot of land in Pleasant, Texas, and Johnny decided to build a house for him and Jimmy right next door. In that way, he could look after his parents, who were now elderly. Meanwhile, the family settled in another house for a while, and Johnny went to work for the Post Office. In his spare time, he still wrote arrangements for various people. Jimmy's granddaughters remember that there were piles of scores in the house.

By now, Judaline was ten or eleven. She became friendly with the girl next door, Jonne McGugan, and her mother, Zella. Judaline still had a great passion for animals. She wrote a play, and put shows (with some of the passion that Mickey and Judy had in their old movies) in order to raise money for "poor animals," who needed help. At one time, she collected pennies to build a pound for lost dogs. She just loved all kinds of animals.[10]

The McGugans thought that Mr. and Mrs. Thompson were a wonderful relaxed couple. They seemed to have lots of fun and enjoyed laughing.

Back in Hollywood, Ethel had been living alone with Grandma Eva in the big house at 750 S. Ogden Drive. Of course, Johnny and Jimmy were in New York with Judaline. Suzie and Jack Cathcart had moved to Las Vegas where Jack was managing the talent for the Sands Hotel. Ethel spent a good deal of her time over at Judy's house and with Liza.

Over the years, Judy and Ethel had fought from time to time as mothers and daughters do, but at this point, Judy was in terrible shape. For a time, she had gone to a sanitarium to try to recover her health. The years of work and pills and unhealthy diets had taken their toll. She was diagnosed with malnutrition and it was advised that she take a long rest.

When Judy returned to MGM, she had gained some weight and once again the cycle returned. Judy was under the care of an eminent doctor, but was so nervous she was making several calls a day to him. Judy was in a dangerous state, and those around her were aware that the slightest thing might be the straw that broke the camel's back with her. During this time, Judy and Ethel had a terrible fight. It concluded when Judy told her mother that she never wanted to see her again. Not only that, she would not allow Ethel to see Liza either.

Though the sequence of events during this time is unclear, in October of 1949, Grandma Eva had a stroke and was rushed to the San Laurel Hospital. Three days later, on October 17th, she passed away. She was buried on October 20, next to her beloved son-in-law, Frank Gumm.

At this point, realizing that Judy was in a bad state and was not going to change her mind, Ethel, encouraged by Jimmy, sold her California house, and a good portion of her belongings. The balance, including Judy's French Provencal bedroom set with the four poster bed and other furniture from the Stone Canyon house, were shipped to Texas. Perhaps she wanted to give some of it to Judaline. Eventually some of this furniture was bought by the McGugans.

For a time, Ethel seemed happy in Pleasant. She got an apartment and was able to find a job managing a small local movie theater. Ethel loved being with her granddaughter, Judaline, and often invited Jonne over as well.

Zella McGugan thought Ethel was the loveliest women she had ever met. She was always kind and generous; the family could never say enough nice things about her. Johnny Thompson, who was described by his son-in-law as being sometimes nice and sometimes not, rolled his eyes when the subject of Ethel came up. Though he would never say anything in front of Jimmy about his mother-in-law, he hinted that she was not always easy to get along with, possibly, because she was "bossy" with him, just as she had always been. In Jimmy's presence, he would only admit, "she was one of a kind."[11]

Eventually, although Ethel had seemed quite settled and happy with her life in Texas, she returned to California. The time period for this is unclear. Some reports say she returned after hearing that Judy had tried to kill herself. For years now, she had been aware that Judy was in deep trouble, yet Judy, who was addicted to pills which obviously were destroying her mentally and physically, was also a huge star, who until she became too ill to work, denied that she needed help. In her mind, she had to keep going no matter what.

Jimmy had tired to dissuade her mother from leaving. She and Johnny were happy to be out of "the Hollywood rat race," but Ethel had made up her mind. She must see if there was something she could do to help her youngest daughter. It was a sad move.

Ethel Gumm suffered greatly over the separation between her and Judy. She could not understand why Judy had cut her out of her life. She wanted the chance to talk to her, but Judy refused. Sid Luft later recounted that when they were in San Francisco, he saw a small, older woman outside the theatre. She approached him, and introduced herself as Ethel Gumm. Then, she begged him to let her see her daughter. She was desperate.

Sid went back and asked Judy, but she refused to see her. When this author asked Sid if he had spoken to Judy about her mother and her feelings toward her, he told me he had not. Although he was her husband, and probably closer to her than anyone else, he said he felt it was none of his business.

As time went on, Ethel suffered so greatly over the fact that Judy would not see her, she became distraught. By now, she was working as a clerk at the Douglas Aircraft factory. Her salary was barely enough to support her. At one point, in anger, thinking perhaps it might get Judy to call her; she allowed her story to be told in the press.

While visiting with one her oldest friends, Peg DeVine, Ethel began to cry uncontrollably. Peg thought she was not well. Ethel had diabetes and high blood pressure, but although Peg tried to calm her, Ethel could not stop crying. She kept asking what she had done to cause Judy to hate her so.

Early on January 5, 1953, on her way to work Ethel dropped dead of a massive heart attack. She was getting out of her car when it happened. Hours later she was found face down in the parking lot.

The last time Dorothy Walsh saw Judy was at Ethel's funeral. Dorothy didn't think Judy was so broken up over her mother's death, though appearances can be deceiving. Dorothy would say later, "The girls picked little spats with each other as girls in families do, but these were blown out of proportion." She believed that the way the press picked up the slightest thing about the family, and blew it up, made it worse. "The Gumms, with all their highs and lows, were a normal family," she said.

~

Jimmy, like many of the Gumms, was an alcoholic, a family friend later revealed. While Judaline adored her grandmother, she was not comfortable with her mother; she even seemed afraid of her. In order to get out of the house, Judaline decided to marry a young boy from school. For reasons of his own, the young man was also eager to be married. Judaline soon found out that he was homosexual.

A short time after her marriage, Judaline left her husband and traveled out to California, where she contacted Dorothy Morrison. She had no money, and told Dorothy she needed help. Dorothy, not knowing the situation, felt she didn't want to give her money, but said she could come over to the house. Instead, Judaline went to Las Vegas to stay with her father's sister, "Aunt Toots." In Las Vegas, she reconnected with her father, Bobby Sherwood, and eventually, met her husband, Dennis Havens. Dennis was a fellow musician friend of Judaline's cousin, Carl Saunders, who is now considered one of the best trumpeters in the business. Dennis wryly commented later, that Ethel would have had a fit seeing the continued series of marriages between Gumm descendants and musicians.

Judaline and Dennis were married on March 27th, 1961, and remained in Las Vegas where they had two daughters, Alondra and Stephanie. During their marriage, Judaline formed an amateur theatrical group, and in 1978, Sid Luft donated some of Judy's things for the theater group's fundraising benefit. Whenever Judaline's cousins, Liza Minnelli and Lorna Luft came to town, they would get together. However, there was an unwritten rule in the family ("to put it mildly," Dennis said), that their relation to Judy Garland and her children was not to be mentioned or used in any way.

In her mid-40s, Judaline died tragically of Gillain-Barr Syndrome. The talent of the Gumms, Sherwoods and Havens continues now with Jimmy's great granddaughter, a singer songwriter, Audra Mae.

For many years, Suzie Gumm had lived in a beautiful two-story apartment in Las Vegas with her husband, Jack Cathcart. Jack managed the talent for the Sands Hotel. Suzie loved children, but for some reason, she never had any. When Jack became interested in another woman, the couple divorced. From there, Suzie's life disintegrated.

She began to date a Las Vegas singer. The family felt he was on the shady side, and believed he was physically abusive toward Suzie. There were also rumors that he was involved with the mob. In December of

1963, Suzie overdosed on pills and was taken to the hospital. She seemed to be better for a time, but on May 27th of 1964, Suzie was found dead. Officially, the death—which may have been due to an overdose—was listed as: "Asphyxiation due to Aspiration of gastric contents due to convulsive seizure."

Although the press reported Suzie's death as a suicide, and subsequent books on the Judy Garland have continued to do so, none of the family believed that Suzie killed herself. They thought she had been murdered, or at the very least, hurt in a way that led to her death. Meanwhile, shortly after Suzie died, the man she had been dating disappeared.

Surprisingly, throughout her life, Ethel remained in touch with her husband's brothers and their families. Judy also would see these relatives during the times she was on tour. In 1962, while performing in Birmingham, Will Gumm's wife, Frances Gumm, came to visit her. Uncle Will had passed away in 1955.

Uncle Bob's daughter, Mildred, also came to visit Judy backstage after one of her triumphant concerts in Washington State, though Mildred's daughter recalled, "Mother went back and met Judy, but she was very shy."

Geri Gumm also remembered how she and her husband, Judy's cousin Richard, went to visit with Judy in Philadelphia. She said that Richard had beautiful brown eyes, like Judy, and loved to laugh. "He would roll on the floor with laughter when he watched Jackie Gleason." And she added, "He would have been so angry at anyone saying anything about Frank Gumm!" Judy was very nice when they met her, but it was apparent she was "on something" and they did not see her again.

In later years, while Judy was appearing in Minneapolis, she hired a car to take her and her son, Joe Luft, to Grand Rapids. Unbeknownst to the local citizens, they rode through the town, looking at the old familiar sites.[12]) Yes, Grand Rapids was dear to her, and she spoke of it as the one place where she had been truly happy.

~

Judy Garland and her sisters remained in touch for many years after their mothers' death, but periodically, they would fight, particularly about Ethel. When they did, Judy's son, who could not stand altercations, would try to tell them to "stop it."

In the 1940s, Ethel Gumm Gilmore visited her Gumm-in-laws in Alabama. These photos were found among Minnie Gumm's personal effects. Top, l. to r. Minnie, Ethel and Frances Gumm. Below, Ethel, Bob and Frances. Minnie's son, James, died in the war in 1944. He received a Bronze Star. Alle Gumm, Jr. would die in 1957. Minnie lived until 1980, Frances until 1973. (Courtesy Bill Gibb)

There were things that Ethel had said and done during the past years that Judy could not forgive. While no one truly knows what was said between mother and daughter, there were two things that almost certainly occurred. Desperate over her daughter's condition, Ethel suggested that she needed to be committed to a sanitarium. Then, one day in an effort to explain her past actions, and in the heat of the moment, Ethel told Judy that her father was homosexual.

To say that someone was homosexual in the 1940s was like accusing them of a crime. To Judy, this was a slap in the face, an attempt to denigrate the father she almost worshipped. She was incensed. How could Ethel say this about her beloved father? The insult was more than she could take.

It seems the complete truth about Frank Gumm cannot be known. His own family and Ethel's family would both forever defend him and swear to the fact that Frank and Ethel were devoted to one another. Yet, in almost every town Frank Gumm lived rumors would arise about his interest in men. As his life went on, these rumors, and the resulting problems, intensified.

Throughout her life, Judy continued to remember her father as the kindest, most handsome and wonderful person. If nothing else, the memory of his love sustained her. It was easy then for her to be angry with her mother. She needed someone to blame for the sorrow and the hardship. And, in part, like any mother, Ethel could be blamed. She had tried her best, but she made mistakes.

Judy's life was full with professional triumphs, her concerts and her children, and there were also the illnesses and addictions. But through it all, the question of her mother's words and actions remained with her. Shortly before her death, Judy asked the one person who might know something—the person who had known her parents before she was born—Dr. Marc Rabwin. It took courage to ask that question, but finally she did, "Was my father homosexual?" Rabwin told her "no."

A few years later, when speaking to author Barry Kehoe, Rabwin told him, "I didn't tell her. I figured what difference would it have made for her to know."

In fact, it might have made a great deal of difference to Judy. Knowing the truth might have explained so many things to her, beginning with the reason for many of her mother's actions. For once, she might have understood that many times her mother was simply trying to protect her, rather than take her away from the father she loved.

As a woman, Judy might also have understood the deep pain and confusion her mother suffered. Judy had married a homosexual man as well, Mark Herron, and had spent long nights bemoaning the fact that he was not home, loving her. For a time, she was blind to the reason, feeling insufficient. Maybe this situation caused her to her wonder about her mother as well.

Ethel Gumm made the mistake of thinking that fame and stardom would ensure happiness. No one could have imagined where it would take her daughter. Like her pioneer ancestors, Judy Garland had journeyed to the Promised Land, a land of beauty, only to find that there were more dangers than she could have dreamed.

Judy Garland, born Frances Ethel Gumm, was a descendant of pioneers, people of strength, generosity and incredible compassion. They were also people who told the story of their journey in song. Without knowing it, she carried on their heritage.

Benjamin Marable Baugh's son, Owen Baugh with his wife, Jesse Runnels. Both Owen and his wife lived to be nearly 100.
(Courtesy John Fox)

Mildred Finlayson, daughter of Susie Gumm, and her little sister, Suzanne. Susie died of a heart attack when Suzanne was about 14.

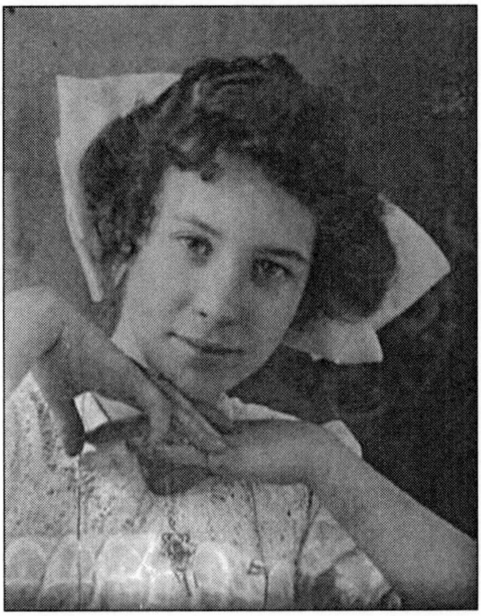

Zehra Baugh, who bears a resemblance to Judy, was born in 1899- and died at the age of 27 from a rare condition. She left behind three children.

The author with Mary Fox, the granddaughter of Willis Baugh and the great granddaughter of Miranday Miller, also known as "Mammy Ran."

Endnotes
Book 3—Those Gumm Girls

1. Newsweek, April 10, 1967, Letter to the Editor by Ruth Gunderson
2. Itasca County Deed Record, No. 87, April 19, 1919
3. *Get Happy*, Gerald Clark, p. 10
4. *Judy Garland*, David Shipman, p. 9
5. *Judy*, Gerold Frank, Harper & Row Publishers, 1975, p. 3
6. *Young Judy*, p. 25
7. *Judy*, Gerald Frank, p. 3–5; all accounts of Rabin taken from this book
8. Nannie Gum Rion letter to Aileen Rion, about 1937, Claire Rion.
9. Although Gerold Frank's book "*Judy*" states that only Frank went to see Rabwin, in their interview with Dr. Rabwin, Barry Kehoe and David Dahl were told that both Frank and Ethel came to see him.
10. *Judy* by Gerald Frank, p. 7
11. Eleanor Downing, interview with author, 1990s.
12. Told to the author by Eleanor Downing
13. Judy, Gerald Frank, p. 16
14. Robert Milne talk at the Judy Garland Birthplace, June 2004
15. Transcribed from Judy Garland's taped interview with Gerold Frank
16. Judy Garland's recorded interview on her early life in Grand Rapids.
17. Grand Rapids newspaper of September 22nd, 1923
18. Judy Garland's taped interview with Gerold Frank. Later printed in McCalls magazine.
19. Mark Hartman

20. Curry Wolfe, Family Group Record for John "Jack" Mason Marable Baugh, #33

21. Story told to me by John Fox as told to him by Alice Pruitt in the 1970s.

22. City directories state that in 1923, Alle's family lived at 207 and Will at 307 No. Greene

23. Author's Interview with Bernie Morris, 1997

24. Talk give by Robert Milne at the Judy Garland Festival, June 2001

25. *The Deer River News*, Deer River, MN July 15, 1925; July 18, 1925

26. *Judy*, Gerald Frank, Harper & Row, Publishers, 1929, p. 15

27. Clipping from *The Itasca County Independent* as shown in Rita Piro's book, *Judy Garland, The Golden Years*, p. 23

28. Memories of Wilma Hendricks Caspar as told to the author in 1995-96.

29. Ibid

30. Interview with Wilma Hendricks Caspar, 1996. Wilma never wanted to say anything bad about Mrs. Gumm, but that these were the facts as she remembered them.

31. Jimmy Gumm interview, 1972?

32. Sheet Music of "Nobody Knows the Trouble I've Seen" by

33. Taped interview with.Judy Garland

34. Judy Garland taped iterview with Gerald Frank.

35. Personal interview and "Letter from Home" Vol 2, No. 1, Spring 1996, published by the Judy Garland Birthplace

36.

37. Judy Garland News Grand Rapids

38. Ethel later said—as noted in Rita Piro's book, "Judy Garland, The Golden Years"

39. *Judy Garland, The Day-by-Day Chronicle of a Legend* by Scott Schecter, Cooper Square Press, 2002, p. 7

40. Jimmy Gumm quote by Christopher Finch, Rainbow, p.

41. Judy Garland taped interview

42. *Judy Garland:* David Shipman, Hyperion, NY 1992

43. *Get Happy*, p. 23

44. Ibid p. 4

45. Young Judy, p. 57

46. *Get Happy*, p. 24

47. Ronald Carter told me that in 1952, there was a fire in the French Café Bar next door to the theatre and it nearly destroyed the theatre. Following this,

an arcade was built, and finally it was all razed for a parking lot at Lancaster and Milling Streets.

48. Taken from Scott Schector book, p. 9
49. *Rainbow*, Christopher Finch p. 36
50. Letter from Will Lundy, July 10, 2007
51. Schector, p. 9
52. http://en.wikipedia.org/wiki/Mickey_Rooney
53. *Young Judy*, p.90; *Judy*, (Frank) p. 27, *Rainbow*, p. 37
54. It appears that Frank Gumm always used the term "bought" when speaking of his theatres, which in actuality he never owned the theatre, other than the shared ownership of the New Grand. In most castes, he simply managed them.
55. All information from Glen Settle comes from personal interviews with the author which took place over a period of years.
56. Schector, p. 10
57. *Judy* by Gerald Frank
58. *Rainbow*, p. 37–38
59. Schector p. 10
60. Schector, p. 11
61. *Young Judy*, p. 99
62. Notes from Jack Milne's son, Robert Milne
63. An observation by Glen Settle
64. Interviews with Dorothy Walsh Morrison, 2004–2007
65. *Rainbow*, p. 40
66. *Young Judy*, p. 117
67. *Get Happy*, Gerold Clarke, p. 39
68. *Rainbow*, p. 40
69. Letter from Will Lundy, July 7, 2007
70. Taken from Dorothy Walsh Morrison's interview with Laureli Lunn, 1977. *This story may be of any earlier dance group idea in Lancaster ... the old memories were somewhat confused.
71. Interviews & meeting with Glen Settle, 2003–2009
72. *Young Judy*, p. 130
73. *Get Happy*, Gerald Clarke, p. 41
74. Ibid, p. 41
75. *Rainbow*, p. 43
76. *Judy* by Gerold Frank, p. 45
77. Quote from Jimmy Gumm in *Rainbow*, p. 48
78. *The Nashville Tennessean Magazine*, March 27, 1955

79. *Rainbow*, p. 48—Jimmy thinks it as the next day
80. *Day In the Life . . .* , Scott Schector, p. 31
81. Judy, Gerold Frank, p. 56-59
82. *Judy*, Gerold Frank, p. 58-59
83. Laureli Lunn, Dorothy Walsh Morrison's granddaughter's paper from 1977
84. *Young Judy* by Gerald Frank, Harper & Row, Publishers, 1975, p. 64
85. Dorothy Walsh Morrison, interview with the author, 2004
86. *Lomita Progress*, Thursday, November 21, 1935, front page
87. Misplaced note—to be found.
88. *The Evening Telegraph, Superior*, WI, Monday, Nov 8, 1937, p. 1 C2
89. *The Nashville Tennessean Magazine*, March 27, 1955, p. 20
90. *The Oakland*, February 15, 1939
91. Ibid, p.
92. *Judy* by Gerald Frank, Harper & Row Publishers, 1975, p. 88
93. This story came from Dorothy Walsh Morrison, however, Bobby Sherwood's son-in-law, Dennis Havens, later said he doubted Bobby would have allowed Jimmy to sing with his band. He didn't think Jimmy was a very good singer.
94. *Judy*, Gerold Frank, p. 112
95. Itasca County, Minnestoa Deed Record "115" April 10, 1936
96. *Judy*, Gerold Frank, p. 99
97. *The Baum Bugle*, Augtumn 1999, "Oz in Hollywood," Florence Baum Hurst, p. 16
98. *Rainbow*, Christopher Finch, p. 113
99. *Judy Garland: A Day in the Life . . .* , Schector p. 81
100. "Walter Winchell on Broadway," *The New York Times*, 8/11/1942
101. Leeann Harry
102. Henry Lee Fox interview w/author
103. Cecil Elrod
104. Reference misplaced—TBF
105. Interview with the President of Judy's First Fan Club, Albert Poland
106. *Judy*, Gerold Frank, p. 204
107. Bob Milne papers dated 2004—A talk for the Judy Garland Festival
108. *Judy*, Gerold Frank, p. 219
109. Ibid, p. 213 and Dorothy Walsh Morrison
110. Jonne McGugan interview
111. Interview with Dennis Havens, 2011
112. As told to the author by Joseph Luft.

Appendix A

Will of Mary Ann Baugh

State of Tennessee,
Rutherford County

Know all men that I, Mary A. Baugh of the State and County aforesaid do hereby make and publish this my last will and testament and I hereby revoke all former wills by me at any time heretofore made.

Item 1 I direct that my debts and funeral expenses be paid by my Executors hereinafter named as soon after my death as practicable out of my personal estate, and if that be not sufficient to pay them, I charge them upon the real estate devised in the 3rd item hereof.

Item 2 I give, devise and bequeath to my daughter Clemmie Gum, wife of W.T. Gum, the real estate described in this item of my will for and during the term of her natural life, to her sole and separate use, free from the debts, liabilities and control of her present or any future husband with remainder to her children, their heirs and assigns forever.

Said real estate is described as follows to wit: Beginning on the West side of the West wall of the brick tenement house on in the 6th Ward of Murfreesboro, Tenn. At the brick pavement in front of said brick tenement, and running thence South to the garden fence, thence East with said fence to the end thereof, thence South with said fence to Vine Street, thence East with Vine Street to Maney's Avenue; thence with Main Street West to the beginning.

Upon said lot are situated said brick tenement house, the store house in which R.N. Ransom Agent is now doing business and a frame tenement house which fronts Vine Street.

Item 3 All the balance rest and residue of my estate of every description, real and personal I give, devise and bequeath to my children named in Item 5 hereof to them, their heirs and assigns, share and share alike, without any limitation, except as to the share of my daughter Clemmie Gum which will be disposed of in Item 4 hereof.

Item 4 The share of my said daughter, Clemmie Gum arising upon the proceeds of the property devised in the 3rd item hereof I give and limit to her and her children exactly as the property devised in the 2nd Item hereof is given and limited to her and them, and I direct my said Executors to use her share thereof in building her a dwelling house on the lot devised in the 2nd Item hereof or in purchasing another lot and erecting thereon a dwelling for her. She will determine the question whether the dwelling shall be erected on the lot bequeathed herein Item 2 hereof or on a lot to be purchased. If a lot is purchased the title thereto shall be taken to her and her children as the property in Item 2nd is devised.

Item 5 My children to whom the property in Item 3 hereof is devised are the following to wit, Eliza Pruitt, Elizabeth White, Mollie Howland, John M. Baugh, Joseph L. Baugh and Clemmie Gum.

Item 6 I hereby nominate and appoint my sons Joseph L. Baugh and John M. Baugh Executors of this my last will and testament and having confidence in their honesty and integrity I exempt them from giving security in their bonds as such.

And I hereby authorize, empower and direct them to make sale of all the real estate disposed of in Item 3 hereby by public or private sale upon such time as they deem best, not to exceed however two years. The proceeds arising from said sale and from any personal property I may die possessed of will be paid by my Executors to my children as directed in Item 3, 4 and 5 hereof.

I refer to my deeds and other title papers for a description of my property real and personal.

Mary M. Baugh

January 25, 1892

Witnesses, H.E. Palmer

A.R. Richardson

Bibliography

A History of Rutherford County, Carlton C. Sims, Editor; Rutherford County Historical Society, 1947

Annals of Rutherford County, John C. Spence, Vol 1 & II, Rutherford County Historical Society, 1991

Captain Tom Ryman: His Life and Legacy, Charmaine B. Gossett, Providence House, 2001

Cemeteries and Graveyards of Rutherford County, TN, compiled Susan G. Daniel, RC Historical Society, TN, 2005

Falling Leaves, Elisabeth O. Howse, 1970

Falling Stars, Elizabeth O. Howse, 1972

Flowers for Grace, Elisabeth O. Howse, 1971

Get Happy, The Life of Judy Garland, Geralde Clarke, Dell Publishing, 2000

Grand Rapids Companion 1891–1991, Grand Rapids Centennial Committee, 1991

History of the University of the South at Sewanee Tennessee, George Rainsford Fairbanks, 1905

Hollywood's Child: Dancing Through Oz, Caren Marsh-Doll, Joshua Tree Publishing, 2003

Judy Garland, David Shipman, Hyperion, NY 1992

Judy Garland: The Day-by-Day Chronicle of a Legend, Scott Schecter, Cooper Square Press, NY 2002

Judy Garland: The Golden Years, Rita E. Piro, Great FEATS Press, 2001

Judy: The Films and Career of Judy Garland, Joe Morella and Edward Epstein, Citadel Press, 1969

Judy Garland: World's Greatest Entertainer, John Fricke, MJF Books, NY, 1992

Lancaster Celebrates a Century 1884 – 1984, City of Lancaster, 1983

Lanterns on the Levee, Recollections of a Planter's Son, William Alexander Percy, Louisiana State University Press, 1941, 1968, 1973

Memories of a Munchkin, Meinhardt Raabe, Backstage Books, 2005

Pillar and Ground, First Baptist Church 1843–1993, Homer & Mabel Pittard, First Baptist Church, 1993

Rainbow, The Stormy Life of Judy Garland, Christopher Finch, Grosset & Dunlap, NY, 1975

Rutherford County, Mabel Pittard, Memphis State University Press, 1984

Tennesseans and Their History, Paul H Bergeron, Stephen V. Ash, Jeanette Keith, The University of Tennessee Press, Knoxville, TN 1999

The Wizard of Oz, John Fricke, Jay Scarfone, William Stillman, Warner Books, 1989

Young Judy, David Dahl & Barry Kehoe, Mason/Charter, 1976

Index

C

D

G

H

L

M

N

O

P

T

V

W

CPSIA information can be obtained at www.ICGtesting.com
263811BV00001B/5/P